Reasoning

A Practical Guide

ROBERT C. PINTO
University of Windsor

J. ANTHONY BLAIR
University of Windsor

Prentice Hall, Englewood Cliffs, New Jersey 07632

Library of Congress Cataloging-in-Publication Data

BLAIR, JOHN ANTHONY.
    Reasoning : a practical handbook / JOHN ANTHONY BLAIR, ROBERT C. PINTO.
    p.   cm.
    Includes bibliographical references and index.
    ISBN 0-13-767245-4
    1. Reasoning I. Pinto, Robert C. II. Title.
BC177.B515   1993
160—dc20   92-35573

Acquisitions editor: *Ted Bolen*
Editorial/production supervision and interior design: *Edie Riker*
Cover Design: *Carol Ceraldi*
Cover photo: Dibenkorn, Richard; *Ocean Park 115.* 1979. Oil on canvas, 8'4" x 6'9".
    Collection, The Museum of Modern Art, New York. Mrs. Charles G. Stachelberg Fund.
Prepress buyer: *Herb Klein*
Manufacturing buyer: *Patrice Fraccio*

Credits and copyright acknowledgments appear at the back of the book
on pages 289–290 which constitutes an extension of the copyright page.

©1993 by Prentice-Hall, Inc.
A Simon & Schuster Company
Englewood Cliffs, New Jersey 07632

Printed in the United States of America

10 9 8 7 6 5 4 3 2 1

ISBN   0-13-767245-4

Prentice-Hall International (UK) Limited, *London*
Prentice-Hall of Australia Pty. Limited, *Sydney*
Prentice-Hall Canada Inc., *Toronto*
Prentice-Hall Hispanoamericana, S.A., *Mexico*
Prentice-Hall of India Private Limited, *New Delhi*
Prentice-Hall of Japan, Inc., *Tokyo*
Simon & Schuster Asia Pte. Ltd., *Singapore*
Editora Prentice-Hall do Brasil, Ltda., *Rio de Janeiro*

Contents

PART II   INFERENCES

Appendices

Preface

We wrote this guide to help students reason better about what to believe and what to do. The book takes the viewpoint of someone trying to decide whether to agree with something that's being said, or whether to draw some conclusion. It offers ways to go about answering the questions, "What should I believe (or do) in this situation?"

The theme of the guide is the part of reasoning called "inferring"—drawing conclusions from what has been observed or written or said. A good inference has two parts: it starts from information that's worth believing (or from assumptions it's reasonable to make), and it arrives at a conclusion that is justified by the information or the assumptions with which it started. Parts I and II are devoted to these two elements of inference: deciding what information should be believed (or what assumptions should be made), and deciding how well the information or assumptions support conclusions inferred from them.

Part I is about how to determine the belief-worthiness of claims that have been put forward as true. Chapter 1 introduces basic concepts needed to be clear about the nature of claims. Chapter 2 deals with the credibility of sources—a topic that is crucial, since most reasoning is based on information supplied by other people. Chapter 3 discusses the information supplied by the mass communications media (and especially the news media), among the most pervasive sources of all.

Part II is about deriving conclusions from the information at our disposal or from what we already believe. Chapter 4 explains the nature and structure of inference. Chapter 5 introduces some of the logical relations between propositions relevant to the assessment of inferences. And Chapter 6 gives a general method for evaluating inference strength.

In our opinion it is essential to understand the general features of inference dealt with in Parts I and II. But we also agree that reasoning has specialized features idiosyncratic to particular contexts. Thus, in Part III we devote chapters to reasoning that employs special tools, follows specialized patterns, or is used for special purposes. Chapter 7 takes up inferences in and from opinion polls. Chapters 8 and 9 deal with causal reasoning and its particular application to scientific studies. Chapter 10 focuses on reasoning to well-grounded evaluations. And Chapter 11 offers advice about the reasoning involved in making decisions about what to do.

The appendices contain extra material for instructors who have special preferences or needs—material readily integrated into the course at different points. For a modicum of formal logic, Appendix A is a skeleton introduction to propositional logic; for attention to language, Appendix B identifies several sources of confusion and misunderstanding in language; and Appendix C tackles the problem of coping with unfamiliar terminology. Last, we supply a method of diagramming inferences or arguments in Appendix D.

For students, there are model answers to selected exercises in Appendix E. They show how we recommend doing the exercises at the end of each chapter. For quick reference, there's a glossary of the specialized or technical terms introduced throughout the book.

Experienced instructors will have preferred topics, as well as their own spins on standard material. Our approach follows established conceptualizations and methods, except where we think the tradition could stand revision. But we think the book has some distinctive features.

> Assessing the credibility of sources of information needs a lot more attention than it usually gets. Most of the information we base our reasoning on comes from the reports and testimony of others. Our treatment of credibility in Chapter 2 and our approach to the media in Chapter 3 address this need in depth.
>
> Our method of evaluating inferences in Chapter 6 has the virtue of being applicable to any sort of inference—deductive, inductive, conductive, or any other kind. We have adapted it from Stephen Thomas and others.
>
> In Chapters 7 and 9 we help students to become critical consumers of reports of opinion polls and scientific studies. The emphasis on the assessment of reports of studies, in particular, is a distinctive feature of this book.
>
> In focusing exclusively on reasoning about what is true or probable, most texts overlook two of the most usual types of reasoning—reasoning about what is good or worthwhile (for example, as consumers) and reasoning about what to do. We address such reasoning in Chapters 10 and 11. The methods we introduce are straightforward, and readily become part of students' reasoning repertoires.

The approach followed here works well as a one-semester course in critical thinking. It also works as an introduction to more advanced courses in informal logic or in argumentation. It introduces many of the principles of reasoning used in more advanced courses in other disciplines.

The material in the book is open to a variety of orderings. We use it in our course in the order given. Starting with claims and moving next to inferences has worked well for us. It's equally possible to use Part II first and Part I second. Instructors strapped for time, or who want to use this text along with another, could omit Chapter 3 and Chapter 5 from the first two parts without confusing students. In Part III four more-or-less independent subjects are covered. The exception is that Chapter 8 (on causal reasoning) gives background needed for Chapter 9 (on studies); but otherwise the instructor can pick and choose chapters from Part III without causing mixups for students.

Appendix A on elementary formal logic could be used together with Chapter 5 on logical relations. Appendices B and C, which concern problems with language and with unfamiliar terminology, could be taught at the beginning of the course, or fitted in among the chapters of Part III.

As any experienced instructor knows, it's one thing to learn the concepts connected with reasoning and quite another to apply them with facility in interpreting texts and in reasoning well. The aim of this book is primarily practical—to improve students' reasoning ability. Each chapter has been written to provide the theory, and examples of its application, needed to perform particular reasoning activities. Hence, the exercises at the end of each chapter are essential. For the most part they contain actual examples of reasoning, taken from media students are likely to be familiar with. There are more than enough examples to use with each chapter.

We call this book a "guide" for very specific reasons. The classic "textbook" provides an exposition of the scholarly literature in a field, albeit organized and simplified with students in mind. The textbook *reports* material that is found in journal articles and monographs, primarily what is accepted by consensus, but occasionally also controversial material (with due notification of its status). With the classic textbook, there is general agreement in the field about what the student should learn at each level and in each branch of the field.

Critical thinking instruction and informal logic, the fields to which this book belongs, have not yet amassed a large enough body of theoretical literature to support a classic textbook in the sense just explained. Untypically, many developments in these fields have first appeared in books writen for use as texts for teaching. Although there are some areas of consensus about theory in such books and in the growing journal literature, the conditions which would qualify these teaching texts as "textbooks" in the classic sense are not yet present. Also, there is no consensus about what should be taught in an introductory course. It was these consideration that led us to put the word "guide" in the title.

But a guide is also a manual that has a practical purpose. And such is precisely the orientation of this book. It contains the material that seems to us most essential for a course designed to enhance the practical skills required to reason well about everyday matters and to cope with the world as we live in it.

The book is not about arguments (understood as rational persuasion) nor about logic (narrowly conceived as the study of deductive implication), though it touches on both. Nor do we claim to cover every conceivable area which might be treated in a critical thinking course. However, there is plenty of material here for a 13- to 15-week course with a clear focus on reasoning—in particular, on drawing conclusions about what to believe or do.

We have benefitted from helpful suggestions and comments from the many students, colleagues, and graduate assistants who have used or read earlier versions of this guide or discussed the issues treated in it with us. Among our colleagues (at Windsor and elsewhere) and graduate assistants, we wish especially to thank Ralph Johnson, Kate Parr, Martin Morf, Ann Wilbur MacKenzie, Tjark Kruiger, Perry Weddle, Hans Hansen, Francisca Snoeck Henkemans, Alan Kidd, Charles W.B. Jones and John McKay. We are also grateful to Prentice Hall's readers for numerous constructive suggestions. At Prentice Hall, Edie Riker has been unfailingly helpful, and our editor, Ted Bolen, has been strongly supportive from start to finish.

For their constant encouragement and support, as well as for practical assistance in all sorts of ways, we thank our families—Brone, Laura, and Rob Pinto, and June and Jay Blair.

Robert C. Pinto
J. Anthony Blair
Department of Philosophy
University of Windosr

1

Introduction

1.1 REASONING

What is reasoning? The best way to show you is to give some examples. Here is one.

When you need to know what time it is, you normally look at your watch, find a clock, or ask somebody else who knows or can check. But sometimes there's no way to look and see, and no one to ask; then you're thrown back on your wits. Perhaps you can tell the hour from the angle of shadows cast by the sun. If your neighbor's TV can be heard through the wall, and you know when different programs come on, maybe you can tell the time by identifying the program on now. Perhaps the pitch of the traffic noise outside tells you it's rush hour. However you do it, in cases like these, when you need to figure out the time from such indirect clues, you do so through *reasoning*.

Here is another example. There's usually no mystery about how you get home from work or school. You walk, cycle, or drive along a certain familiar route; or you take the bus, tram, or rapid transit train that you normally take. There is nothing to *think* about; you just follow your usual pattern. But if your bicycle is stolen, a street is blocked off, your car won't start, your driver doesn't show up, or there is a transit strike, you will have to *figure out* how to get home in these new circumstances. You'll consider alternatives—such as finding another ride, hitch-hiking, walking, getting somebody to come and pick you up, or borrowing a bicycle. No doubt you'll immediately rule out some of the alternatives as being impractical (it's too far or too cold to walk) and then decide which of those remaining seems best. However you do it, you arrive at a decision about how to get home through *reasoning*.

In both examples you have *questions*—"What time is it?" and "How am I to get home?"—and the answers to these questions are not given. There is nobody around to tell you what the answer is, and there is no ready way to look it up or to find it through simple perceptual examination. You have to rely on clues, on evidence, on information from memory, on indirect signs and on assumptions, and then draw a *conclusion* from these. Reasoning is the business of drawing conclusions under such circumstances.

These examples typify two different types of reasoning. In the first one, the question concerned the facts about the time. What was important was that the answer you came up with be *true* (or as probable or plausible as can be, or is needed, under the circumstances). In the second, the question was about what to do. What was important there was that the course of action you decided on be a *good* one (or good enough, or the best one available, under the circumstances). These examples typify two different types of reasoning.

Reasoning, the business of drawing conclusions, is sometimes a matter of trying to find out the truth about something. In such cases, it's called *inquiry* or *investigation* (what people call "problem solving" is often a special case of inquiry). At other times, the goal or point of reasoning is not to find out the truth, but instead to decide what to do. In those cases it's called *deliberation* (or decision making). These two aren't the only types of reasoning activity, but they're among the most common and most important, and in this book we concentrate on them.

You don't need to learn how to reason; you already know how. You would not be reading material like this if you couldn't reason: you wouldn't have reached this point in your education if you weren't able to figure things out through reasoning. But most people's reasoning could be *better* than it is. If they made changes in the ways they go about reasoning, their reasoning would be more likely to achieve the results they want. In the case of inquiry, that result is truth (or some approximation of it). In the case of deliberation, people want to make good decisions—to choose actions that are suitable and sensible. Improving one's reasoning is a matter of learning ways to conduct it that make it more likely the resultant beliefs will be true and the decisions good ones.

This book aims to help you to improve your reasoning. How can it do that? You are already competent at reasoning about most of the straightforward situations you encounter in everyday life. That's because (1) you have had lots of practice at reasoning about such things and (2) you get feedback about the results of your thinking very quickly. If you come up with the wrong answer about what time it is, or decide on an impractical or inefficient way of getting home, you immediately discover that you've made a mistake. And you have already learned through practice and experience to minimize such mistakes or to avoid them altogether.

Rather, if you are like most people, your reasoning is likely to need improvement in areas where (1) the issues tend to get complicated and (2) either you don't get a lot of practice or you don't get immediate feedback. For example, if you are in your late teens or early twenties, you probably find yourself making decisions about your career or how to make a living. Many of those decisions require sorting through a complicated variety of factors: what your talents are, what your interests are, what salary levels are and will be for jobs of various kinds, how much job security there is in various occupations, what sort of training or education you will have to acquire to pursue various careers, what the current demand is for workers in various occupational and geographic areas, what the competition is for jobs of various kinds, what the demand and competition will be like a few years from now, and so on. In such cases, it is easy to lose your way because of the complexity and sheer quantity of the data. For one thing, it is easy to overlook crucial factors, or to overrate some and underrate others. For another, with so much data to manage, it is easy to misinterpret or misconstrue some of it. Moreover, you won't know for years whether your conclusions or decisions were good ones; immediate feedback, in light of which you could correct your habits or practices, is not available.

There is no foolproof way of reasoning about complicated or unfamiliar matters. But there are three sorts of things people can do to help improve their reasoning.

1. A person can acquire certain *habits of mind*, in particular
    a. habits of *monitoring and assessing their reasoning*
    b. habits of *sensible or judicious skepticism*
       Our reasoning often goes astray because we are too quick to reach a conclusion about complicated matters or too gullible (or too skeptical!) about what we read, hear, or are told. Hence among the things we often need to do is to stop and think about whether we *should* draw the conclusion we are tempted to draw and whether we should accept the data and the assumptions on which we are about to base that conclusion. Learning to do this when it's appropriate is probably the single most important thing you can do to improve your reasoning.
2. A person can learn how to use some *organizing concepts*: premiss, inference, conclusion, evidence, assumption, proposition, assertion, and others. Since a big problem in reasoning well about complicated matters is getting lost in a swarm of data, possessing such organizing concepts and knowing how to use them can prove invaluable. Moreover, these concepts are the ones people have to use when they monitor and assess their own reasoning.
3. Finally, a person can learn to ask certain *guiding questions* about their own reasoning. The following three general questions strike us as central.
    a. *What exactly is the conclusion I am drawing and what exactly are the grounds (the assumptions and data) on which it is based?* We often draw conclusions without being clear about what exactly we are concluding. (If you don't believe us, try stating in a single, clear sentence any judgment you make

on the basis of watching a news broadcast; or try to express the theme of a TV show or a movie in a single informative sentence.) You need to be clear about the inferences you make.

b. *Are the grounds (the data and the assumptions) I am relying on acceptable, that is, worthy of being believed?* The data you are using are likely to be thoroughly trustworthy if they come from a highly reliable source. But if their source is only somewhat reliable, the data need to be used with caution. And if their source is untrustworthy, it may simply be a mistake to base any conclusion on those data. Also, your assumptions may be beyond any reasonable doubt, or they may be reasonable but still open to question, or they may be quite unreasonable. You need to know how solid are the grounds of your reasoning.

c. *How strongly do the grounds support the conclusion I am drawing?* Even thoroughly trustworthy data can support conclusions in varying degrees. Sometimes data conclusively establish a conclusion; sometimes they render a conclusion probable but do not establish it conclusively; sometimes the data available do no more than make it reasonable to suspect the conclusion is true; and sometimes the data provide no real support for the conclusion at all. You need to be clear about how much support your grounds provide for your conclusions.

In the material that follows, we will be explaining the rationale or theory behind the points we make, because we are convinced no reader can adequately understand what we say without understanding why we say it. So the book contains some theory, which you should master. However, our main objective is to help you to improve your reasoning, and that cannot occur without actually engaging in reasoning. As with any skill, improvement comes only with practice. Therefore, successfully completing the exercises is what really counts and is the true test of both understanding and improved reasoning skills.

1.2 ORGANIZATION OF THE BOOK

Part I is about claims. Most of the information on which we base our reasoning comes from claims or assertions made by sources other than ourselves. Section 1.3 of this chapter is concerned with claims or assertions and how to identify them. Chapter 2 presents guidelines for assessing the credibility of assertions made by other people. Chapter 3 discusses some of the pitfalls in using the media—the origin of many of the claims to which we are exposed in daily life—as a source of information.

Part II is concerned with inference, which we take to be the heart of reasoning. Chapter 4 introduces the notion and structure of inference. Chapter 5 presents some of the logical relations which are relevant to inference. And Chapter 6 provides some strategies and techniques for evaluating inferences.

Part III presents five more specific topics with which it is especially useful to be familiar. It presents background information and guidelines that seem to us to be necessary for reasoning well about specific kinds of material. The topics dealt with are interpreting public opinion polls (Chapter 7), reasoning about causes (Chapter 8), using studies conducted by other people (Chapter 9), evaluating or judging the worth of things for a variety of practical purposes (Chapter 10), and deliberating about what to do (Chapter 11).

The appendices contain additional material that you might find interesting or useful. Appendix A sets out in a preliminary way some of the concepts of formal logic and relates most directly to the material in Chapter 5. Appendices B and C address language, the mastery of which seems essential for most reasoning. Appendix B explains some of the primary sources of confusion in language, and Appendix C offers advice about dealing with unfamiliar language. Appendix D outlines a technique for diagramming the structure of complicated reasoning.

Appendix E contains model answers for some of the exercise questions found at the end of each chapter. Those questions for which there is a model answer in Appendix E are marked with a double asterisk (**).

1.3 CLAIMS

In most cases, your reasoning will be based on information you obtain from other people. The quality of that reasoning will be affected by the quality of the information on which it is based. Part I of this book deals with some of the problems you encounter in obtaining and assessing such information.

One set of problems consists in understanding just what information you are being presented with. That is the subject of the rest of this section. A second set of problems concerns deciding whether to believe the information supplied to you by others; that is the subject of Chapter 2 (Credibility). A third set of problems arises because of the ways in which the mass media structure and color the information they present; that is the subject of Chapter 3 (Information and the Media).

Information can be communicated in a variety of ways: through words, through gestures and facial expressions, through pictures, through maps and diagrams, and so on. In this chapter, we concentrate on information communicated through written or spoken language.

Statements or Assertions

The most direct way to convey information through language is to make *statements*—to utter sentences in which you describe the way things are. Two other words that pick out basically the same thing as the word "statement" are the words *claim* and *assertion*.

In this book, we use the word "statement" for a special kind of utterance that's different from a question, a command or a request.[1] For one thing, statements have a special grammatical form. Look at the following four **sentences** to see what we mean:

Statement: Harvey left the room.
Question: Did Harvey leave the room?
Command: Harvey, get out of the room!
Request: Harvey, please leave the room.

Statements are made using declarative sentences.

For another thing, statements, questions, commands, and requests do different jobs. Look again at the four examples just given. They all center on the idea of Harvey leaving the room.

- The *statement* presents the idea as true—as correctly depicting the way things are.
- The *question* doesn't present the idea as true and doesn't present it as false; rather, it's an attempt to find out *whether* it is true.[2]
- The *command* and the *request* both assume that the idea isn't true *yet* (that Harvey didn't yet leave the room). Rather they are attempts to get Harvey to behave in a way that would make it true that he left the room.

Statements purport to describe the way things are. Commands and requests are attempts to change the way things are. And questions are attempts to find out how things are.

We'll call the idea that Harvey left the room a **proposition**.[3] When you state or claim that Harvey left the room, you *assert* the proposition that he did. When you claim he didn't leave the room, you *deny* the proposition that he did. When you ask whether Harvey left the room, you are trying to find out whether the proposition that he left the room is true.[4]

Asserting and Implying

Sometimes people communicate the fact that a proposition is true (or false) directly, just by asserting (or denying) it. At other times, they communicate the same information indirectly, by *implying* a proposition is true (or false) without *explicitly* asserting or denying it.

You explicitly **assert** a proposition when you put it forward as true *by uttering or writing words which express it*.[5] What you assert is, roughly, what the words you write or speak say or mean. So if you say, "Dana spends tons of money on Pat Boone records," you've *asserted* the proposition that Dana spends lots of money on records made by (1960s pop singer) Pat Boone. But you may well be *implying* a proposition you haven't asserted, for example, the proposition that Dana has terrible taste in music.

When you **imply** a proposition (for example, that Dana has bad taste in music), you do it by asserting some other proposition (for example, that Dana went broke buying Pat Boone records). How is it that by asserting one proposition, you can imply that some other, different proposition is true? You can do it, because you can count on your reader or listener to draw conclusions that go beyond what you've explicitly said.

Usually, you expect your audience to accept the propositions you assert.[6] And frequently you expect your audience to put two and two together—to put what you've said together with other things they know or believe and to draw certain conclusions. If you think Pat Boone records are awful and you're pretty sure your audience agrees with you, then you can expect them to draw the conclusion that Dana has poor taste in music from the fact that Dana's so keen on Pat Boone. (But at a meeting of the Pat Boone fan club, someone who said that Dana spends thousands on Pat's records would not be implying that Dana has questionable taste in music.)

When speakers and writers communicate, we expect them to be candid, forthright, and relevant—to refrain from asserting things they don't believe, to disclose pertinent information, and to make points that have a bearing on the issue at hand. Those expectations give rise to further kinds of conclusions and implications. For example, in a discussion about whom to hire as the bookkeeper for her company, Ada says, "Mario is an extremely conscientious worker, but Sarah has taken a course in accounting." Ada would be implying something she hasn't explicitly asserted, namely, that Mario has never had an accounting course. Why that implication? Well, Mario and Sarah are being compared, and what's relevant are the *differences* between them; mention of Sarah's accounting course wouldn't be relevant unless it were a feature she had and Mario lacked.

Indirect Communication: Innuendo and Irony

Among the ways an author can imply propositions without asserting them explicitly or directly, two more should be mentioned.

One of these is by **innuendo**. Innuendo occurs when a speaker or writer hints at a proposition (usually an unfavorable judgment) rather than stating it explicitly, especially when aspersions are cast on the character or reputation of another person. People who make innuendos rely on their audience to draw the intended conclusion from what they say, usually by a combination of the literal meaning of what they say with the circumstances in which it is said.

Consider this example. A merchant is trying to find who is responsible for employee pilfering and asks one clerk whether another has been stealing. The clerk replies, "I don't have any direct, firsthand knowledge she has been stealing." The clerk's innuendo, clearly, is that she has some indirect evidence that the clerk in question is stealing. The normal negative reply would be something like, "Not as far as I know." By adding "direct, firsthand," the speaker implies that this is not a situation where a normal negative reply would be sufficient and, in so doing, implies that she has grounds for doubting the clerk's innocence.

You ought to be cautious, by the way, when you encounter innuendo. Frequently speakers resort to innuendo rather than outright accusation because they don't have the evidence to back up the negative judgments that they imply.

Another form of indirect communication is **irony**. Irony is the figure of speech in which the author's intended meaning is the opposite of what is expressed by the words used. By tone of voice or by the obvious contradiction between the literal meaning and what the audience expects to hear, the author makes it clear that what he or she says is not to be taken at face value. **Sarcasm** is a common form of irony in which irony is used to belittle someone or something. For example, you might say sarcastically of another student you hold in contempt, "He gave another brilliant answer in class this morning!" What you are implying is quite the opposite of the normal meaning of the words you use.

Attribution: Quoting Statements and Ascribing Beliefs

Another way that propositional information can be conveyed is through **attribution,** that is, through quotation and its cousin, the ascription of belief.

Quotation occurs when a speaker or writer reports to a listener or reader what someone else has said. **Direct quotation** reports the exact words a person used; in writing, there are quotation marks around the directly quoted words. **Indirect quotation** or **paraphrase** conveys the ideas someone else has asserted without repeating the exact words that were used; in writing, there are no quotation marks around statements that are indirectly quoted. Instead they are introduced by clauses such as, "He said that . . .," "She stated that . . .," "He wrote that . . .," "According to her, ..."[7]

Something similar to quotation occurs in the *ascription of belief*. This is what happens when someone reports what another person thinks, supposes, concludes, believes, and so on. If we tell you Plato *wrote* that not all pleasures are good, we quote Plato indirectly. But if we tell you Plato *thought* that not all pleasures are good, we ascribe a belief to Plato.

In both quotation and ascription of belief, one says that a certain proposition has been asserted or is believed by someone, without vouching for the truth of that proposition oneself. (If you tell someone Plato said that some pleasures are bad, you don't vouch for the truth of the proposition that some pleasures are bad, although you *do* vouch for the truth of the proposition that Plato *said* such a thing.)

Quotation and its cousins are important vehicles for conveying information, since we are often inclined to accept the authority of the person being quoted and hence to accept the propositions which they are quoted as having asserted or believed. Examine most newspaper stories, for example, and you will find that much of the information they convey is in the form of direct or indirect quotations from the sources on which the story is based.

Careful Reading and Listening

When others attempt to convey information to you through assertion, implication, or quotation, you are faced with the problem of deciding whether to accept what is asserted, implied, or quoted. In large measure, such decisions should be guided by the considerations that are dealt with in Chapter 2 (Credibility) and Chapter 3 (Information and the Media). But before you can apply those considerations, you need to be sure you understand what exactly has been said or written and that you are not reading into it implications which are not there and not drawing conclusions which it isn't reasonable to draw.

Recall Ada's comment about Mario in the preceding section. If we assumed Ada's remarks were candid, forthright, and relevant, it was reasonable to conclude from her assertions that Mario hadn't taken a course in accounting. But suppose someone took the fact that she described Mario as "an extremely conscientious worker" to mean she was implying he was plodding and unimaginative. That would, in our opinion, be an unwarranted conclusion and a sign of careless reading—for a person can certainly be conscientious without being dull and unimaginative.

In Chapter 6 we will describe in detail the criteria for deciding when a conclusion is warranted or reasonable to make. But we hope you already begin to appreciate the dangers of drawing unwarranted conclusions from what you read. Consider the following two examples.

A few years ago there was a disastrous crash at an air show at a U.S. Air Force base in Ramstein, Germany. Three of the jets of an Italian air force stunt team crashed, one into the crowd of spectators, killing more than 45 people. One newspaper account carried the headline, "Ramstein crash due to pilot error." The only part of the report that referred to the cause of the crash read as follows:

> The pilots of the three jets were killed, and the Italian air force official who co-ordinated the team's stunts said one of the jets caused the crash by flying into an intersecting manoeuver at the wrong altitude and speed.

Does this paragraph say that the crash was caused by pilot error? Not at all. First, the report itself does not make any straightforward assertions about the cause of the crash; it merely quotes an Italian air force official. And we don't know for sure whether the official's explanation was correct. (Perhaps there was a question whether the stunt was dangerously designed, and the official was trying to shift blame from the real cause.) Most important, however, the proposition that the official was reported to have asserted is that the crash was caused by one of the jets flying incorrectly into a manoeuvre. That is different from the proposition that the pilot of that jet made an error. The plane responsible for the crash might have had a mechanical problem that caused its controls to lock, sending it into the manoeuver at the wrong altitude and speed in spite of the pilot's best efforts to control it. The headline writer's conclusion was not based on a careful reading of the report of the crash; he read into the report something that wasn't actually there.

Here is another example. It is common for advertisements to say such things as, "List price, $50.00; Lo-boy's price, $35.00." Should you conclude that Lo-boy's price is a bargain and that if you buy at Lo-boy's you'll save money? No doubt that is what Lo-boy is implying—what the advertiser wants us to conclude. And, of course, the proposition asserted in the ad implies that Lo-boy's price is 30% less than the *list* price. Many products, however, are routinely sold well below the manufacturer's list (or "recommended") selling price. Perhaps all Lo-boy's competitors sell this product for $35.00 too; perhaps most of them sell it for $30.00, and Lo-boy's price is in fact higher than that of other stores. So it would be a mistake to conclude without further information that you'll save money if you buy at Lo-boy's. Be wary of reading into what is said propositions that are not asserted and not implied by what is asserted, especially when reading advertisements.

Expectations, desires, and unwarranted assumptions all give a boost to careless concluding from what others say and write. Given a firm expectation about what someone will say, we often hear it in words that say nothing of the sort or even that deny it. When we dearly want something to be true, the faintest suggestion that it might be can send us away with the solid conviction that it is. And if we take certain things for granted, then we often shoehorn what we hear or read into an interpretation that fits those assumptions, blithely ignoring the absence of propositions or implications that justify such conclusions.

1.4 SUMMARY

Reasoning is drawing conclusions from evidence, grounds, or assumptions. Two central purposes of reasoning are determining what is true or worthy of belief (inquiry) and deciding what to do (deliberation). Three things you can do to improve your reasoning are (1) acquire the habits of self-reflection and judicious skepticism, (2) master concepts and vocabulary that help in organizing your thinking, and (3) learn to ask certain guiding questions: What is my conclusion? What grounds are there for that conclusion? How reasonable is it for me to accept those grounds? How well do those grounds support that conclusion? This book is designed to help you improve your reasoning in these ways; it focuses on assessing claims, assessing inferences in general, and assessing claims and inferences in reasoning about a set of widely encountered particular topics.

Although some understanding of theory is needed, reasoning well is a skilled activity, so practice is equally important, and this book contains many exercises and model answers to guide you in doing them.

In reasoning, the conclusions are frequently based on information supplied by other people. That information is often communicated in the form of statements or assertions in which an idea or proposition is presented as true or as depicting the way things are. Asserting a proposition needs to be distinguished from implying it and also from quoting it. Special forms of indirect communication are innuendo and irony (sarcasm). In reading and listening carefully, so as to interpret accurately what was asserted, we need to attend to these distinctions.

1.5 EXERCISES

Exercise 1

In this group, 1–3, each item is followed by a set of propositions. On the basis of the passages, decide whether each proposition below it is
(a) asserted in the passage (that is, by the author(s) of the passage)
(b) quoted, directly or indirectly, in the passage
(c) implied by the author of the passage
(d) implied by someone quoted in the passage
(e) none of the above
In each case, explain your answer.

1. *Background.* The shooting down of Korean Air Lines flight 007 by the Soviet Union was a major news story in 1983. The following short piece appeared in the *Chicago Tribune* on June 9, 1991

Soviets found KAL recorders, report says

SEOUL (Reuter)—Soviet divers recovered two flight recorders from a South Korean jumbo jet 50 days after it was downed by Soviet fighters in 1983, South Korea's semi-official Yonhap news agency said Saturday.

It said the divers found the recorders after the attack, which killed all 269 people aboard, and handed them over to the military.

The Soviet Union has maintained that the Boeing 747 was on a spying mission for the U.S. and has never acknowledged finding the plane's fuselage or recorders.

Yonhap said its report is based on an interview with the head of the diving team who now is living in the Soviet Far Eastern island of Sakhalin.

Korean Air Lines flight 007 from New York to Seoul via Alaska plunged into the sea off Sakhalin when it was shot down after straying into Soviet air space.

The U.S. and South Korea have denied the spying charges, as well as Soviet contentions that U.S. air traffic controllers knew the plane was flying into Soviet airspace.

(a) Soviet divers recovered two flight recorders from the South Korean jumbo jet 50 days after it was downed.

(b) Soviet divers uncovered evidence that KAL flight 007 was on a spy mission.

(c) KAL flight 007 strayed into Soviet airspace.

(d) The Soviet Union has only recently announced that it found the flight recorders shortly after the plane went down.

2. The following Associated Press report appeared in August 1988.

Blast kills 7 on Belfast army bus

BELFAST (AP)—A landmine explosion destroyed a military bus carrying British soldiers to their barracks Friday night. Police said at least seven troopers were killed but the final toll was expected to be higher.

A spokesman at the British Army's headquarters at Lisburn near Belfast said 11 soldiers were wounded.

He said the military bus, which bore no markings, was taking 38 soldiers to their barracks at Omagh, 80 km west of Belfast, following their leaves in England. The vehicle detonated the mine on the road between Omagh and Ballygawley in County Tyrone.

Paddy Bogan, president of Northern Ireland's centrist Alliance party, who lives near the scene of the blast, described the attack as "a terrible slaughter."

Bogan, who went to the scene with other local people, said: "The bus was a mess of mangled metal. It was a miracle anyone got out of it alive. The faces of the injured were terribly cut and bleeding."

No group immediately claimed responsibility for the attack. But suspicion inevitably fell on the Irish Republican Army.

Earlier Friday, an IRA bomb injured three police officers and another damaged Northern Ireland's newest luxury hotel, police said.

Also Friday, funerals were held for a British soldier the Irish Republican Army killed in Belgium last week and a Protestant grocer shot to death Wednesday in his Belfast store.

(a) Twenty soldiers on the bus were not wounded by the landmine explosion.

(b) The landmine was set off by remote control.

(c) Probably the IRA was responsible for setting the landmine.

(d) The faces of the injured were cut and bleeding.

(e) The bus looked like a regular civilian bus.

(f) Of the 11 soldiers who were wounded, some were not expected to live.

3. The ad for "Vigorexx" that follows is our invention, but it has features copied from a number of actual advertisements. (Advertisers refused us copyright permission to reproduce actual ads.)

**ANNOUNCING *VIGOREXX*
A MEDICALLY SAFE TREATMENT FOR THINNING HAIR**

It can help your hair feel thicker, fuller, and healthier looking for as long as possible.

Penetrates the scalp to energize and revitalize follicles from which hair grows.

Studies show that 70% of men tested reported that their hair felt and looked thicker after 60 days (study available on request).

No prescription necessary. No testosterone.

No physician's supervision. No morning and evening applications.

The longer you use it, the longer you will feel the benefits continue.

Important: VIGOREXX treatment does not prevent baldness or restore lost hair. But it can help provide fuller, thicker, healthier feeling and looking hair for as long as your hair naturally remains.

(a) Vigorexx prevents hair from falling out.
(b) Vigorexx will cure baldness.
(c) Vigorexx increases the rate at which hair grows from hair follicles.
(d) Vigorexx will cause your hair to be fuller and thicker.

Exercise 2

Each passage in this group, 4–6, is followed by questions relating to it. Read the assigned passages and answer the questions following each one.

1. The following article appeared in a national newspaper.

**Experts Claim . . .
BEING MESSY IS A SURE SIGN OF HAPPINESS**

If you're untidy, don't feel guilty—it's a sign that you're a happy, well-balanced person, say experts.

Untidy people have their lives well-organized in their heads—and do not feel the need to constantly rearrange things, says Dr. Hedi Daoud, a psychiatrist who has spent 15 years studying the effect of too much neatness on families. "People who are very strictly organized, where everything has its place and nothing can be moved, are people who are, in fact, fighting against totally chaotic tendencies within themselves," added Dr. Daoud. "They're not sure of themselves and don't have confidence in their own convictions."

Dr. Beryl West, a Middle Tennessee State University psychology professor, said that overly tidy people make rigid rules to give themselves a feeling of control over life—and they expect others to be tidy like them because it makes them feel more secure.

—Cliff Barr

(a) Does the content of the article warrant the headline? Justify your answer.

2. Here is a news report from *The Windsor Star*, August 22, 1988, when Canada Post and the Public Service Alliance were still negotiating and prior to the strike that began two days later.

Postal strike 'won't happen'

OTTAWA (CP)—If both sides work hard, the postal dispute will be resolved before Tuesday's midnight strike deadline, federal mediator Mac Carson said Sunday.

"I'm still optimistic. But it's going to take some work and accommodation on both sides," Carson said.

"There's no question in my mind the deadline can be met," said the veteran mediator.

Weekend talks between Canada Post and the union representing 5,800 technical and administrative workers pushed into Sunday night and were to resume today.

"They've been going on an as-needed basis all weekend," corporation spokesman Dave Newman said late Sunday.

Canada Post and the Public Service Alliance of Canada, the union representing the workers, have agreed not to release details of the talks held at a downtown hotel.

The central issues for the union are job security and salaries.

(a) Does the content of the article warrant the headline? Justify your answer.

3. The following report appeared in a national newspaper.

Harvard Professor Reveals . . .
Our Health Has Never Been Better, But We're Worried Sick About It

Even though Americans are physically healthier today, we're feeling worse mentally, says a Harvard expert—we're more inclined to believe there's something wrong with us than ever before.

"The major indexes that we use to measure our health status—mortality rates, life expectancy, infant mortality rates—have improved dramatically," said Dr. Arthur J. Barsky, associate professor of psychiatry at Harvard Medical School.

But a recent Harris poll showed the proportion of Americans who are satisfied with their health and physical condition has fallen from 61 percent in the 1970s to 55 percent in the 1980s, he added.

"The healthier we've become, the healthier we think we should feel. So much attention is being paid to health and the body that people are beginning to notice all kinds of minor discomforts that were dismissed in the past.

"Psychologically, it's been shown that if you focus on your body—if you spend a lot of time thinking about it—you'll pick up all sorts of sensations you didn't notice before.

"We're experiencing discomfort and anxiety over disorders that 30 years ago we might not have even noticed. This increased self-scrutiny is causing us to feel worse."

The reason for this problem has been the tremendous surge of health issues on TV and in newspapers, magazines and books—and a mistaken belief that if we're healthy we shouldn't have any aches and pains, according to Dr. Barsky.

"We need a dose of realism," said Dr. Barsky, author of "Worried Sick: Our Troubled Quest for Wellness."

"Good health, even during our youth, is not necessarily a pain-free state.

"We should stop imagining the worst every time we're beset by a variance from what we perceive to be the norm. Not all pains are indicative of an underlying disease."

Philip Smith

(a) Does the content of the article warrant the headline? Justify your answer.

NOTES

1. Statements, questions, requests, and commands are all speech acts. In addition to these four, there are numerous other kinds of speech act which we won't go into here, for example, promises, prayers, exclamations, wishes, and greetings.

2. Sometimes people use a sentence that has the grammatical form of a question to make a statement rather than to ask a genuine question. That's called a **rhetorical question**. For example, in the middle of a sermon a preacher says, "Do you want to burn in hell for all eternity?" He or she doesn't really expect an answer and isn't really trying to find out what the congregation wants. Rather, the preacher is reminding members of the congregation that they don't want to burn in hell.

3. This is the word that is used in logic. Why call such things "propositions"? Well, think of them as things that have been, or at least could be, *proposed* for acceptance or belief.

4. A *proposition* may be defined as anything which has the following two characteristics: (1) it can be expressed by a declarative sentence, and (2) it is either true or false. You can think about a proposition (that is, about what is expressed by a declarative sentence) without being sure whether it's true or false—but it must in fact be one or the other. Moreover, you can think about propositions that nobody has ever in fact asserted.

   The word 'assertion' has two distinct but related senses. In the first sense, an assertion is the *act* of claiming some proposition to be true. In the second sense, a proposition that has been claimed to be true is called an assertion.

   It's important to learn these concepts by seeing how they are used and using them correctly yourself; memorizing their definitions isn't necessary.

5. And do so "in your own name," as it were. When you *quote* someone else, you use words which express a proposition without asserting that proposition. For example, suppose you utter "Yeltsin says that communism was a mistake." You use words which express the proposition that communism was a mistake, but *you* don't assert that proposition. You merely report that Yeltsin asserted it. See page 8.

6. An exception to this is irony. See page 8.

7. Sometimes you have to glean from the context that the words used are intended as a paraphrase of what someone other than the writer has said. Newspaper reports frequently start out explicitly quoting some expert or source in the first few paragraphs and then continue paraphrasing the source without including a "He said" or "She said" in every sentence or paragraph. Sometimes it's clear that paraphrase is intended; sometimes it's not.

2

Credibility

2.1 INTRODUCTION

Only a relatively small amount of the information we rely on in our reasoning and deliberation is obtained from our own direct observation or investigation. Most of it is acquired from other people, directly or indirectly, in a vast pooling of information. Just start to go through a typical day, and you will see what we mean. You wake up and *turn on the radio to get the right time.* You shower and dress. You bought the clothes you are wearing at stores *recommended to you* by family, friends, or *something you have read.* You eat breakfast. Is the cereal you are eating really made from corn? *The box says* it is. Is that 2% milk? *The carton is marked "2%."* You bought the food at a store *you found out about* from someone else. You *listen to the radio to catch the news, sports, and weather.* What time does your bus come by? *According to the schedule,* 8:20 A.M. Clearly, just in the first hour of your day you have relied on others for all sorts of information. That information consists in *propositions that we have accepted on the authority or say-so of others.*

This chapter is about assessing the information and opinions we are invited to accept on the say-so of others; it is about deciding when such information and opinion *ought* to be accepted or believed. Another way of saying that something deserves to be believed is to say that it is *credible.* So deciding whether a proposition someone asserts should be accepted on his or her say-so is deciding whether that proposition is credible. And as we will see, to decide whether such a proposition is credible you usually have to decide whether the person who puts it forward is credible or believable.

Since so much of what we believe and the basis of so much of our reasoning is accepted on the authority or say-so of others, the study of credibility is crucial to the study of reasoning. In fact, even when we rely on our own observations or the results of our own investigation, the question of their credibility can arise. It would help if there were general principles or guidelines to distinguish credible information, opinions, and people from those that are not credible. We believe there are some, and will present them to you in this chapter.

2.2 THE CREDIBILITY OF SOURCES

Credibility of Testimony and Credibility of Sources

We will often call information supplied by others **testimony**, borrowing and extending the term used in courts of law. Testimony varies in **credibility** or the degree to which it deserves to be taken seriously or believed. Some such information is highly credible, for example, entries found in a first-rate dictionary. Some testimony is barely credible, for example, the things some computer salespeople tell you about what a particular machine will do. Some testimony is just not credible at all, for example, the astrologer's birthday predictions for your life over the next year.

In deciding whether to accept a piece of testimony on someone's authority or say-so (in judging the credibility of the testimony), two factors need to be taken into account:

1. the *credibility of the source* (e.g., the person or organization or institution) that puts forward the information or opinion as true
2. the *plausibility*, given other things you know, of the proposition asserted or put forward as true

Whether *the propositions* that someone asserts are credible depends in part on how believable or credible *that person* is. But the source's credibility alone does not make the testimony believable; the credibility of the testimony also depends on how well that proposition fits in with other things we know, on how plausible it is.

For example, if a pilot flying a commercial jet for a major airline reports a UFO of classic description half a mile to the south of the aircraft, you are faced with a report of something implausible made by a presumably credible source. The great implausibility of this report should make you hesitate about accepting it without further investigation or corroboration just on the say-so of the source; the presumed credibility of the source should make you hesitate about simply dismissing the testimony out of hand.[1]

On the other hand, if you go to your doctor with a fever and red spots on your chest, and after a careful examination *she* says you have measles, her diagnosis is highly credible. First, she is presumably credible when it comes to such judgments under such circumstances, and, second, the *diagnosis* is plausible, assuming you know about the common symptoms of measles.

When assessing the credibility of a report or piece of information, then, take both the credibility of its source and the plausibility of the information itself into consideration. In general, the less plausible a proposition, the greater must be the credibility of the source if its testimony is to render that proposition credible.

The remainder of this chapter is restricted to a discussion of just the first of these two factors—the credibility of sources.

Limitations of a Source's Credibility

1. *A source's credibility is relative to subject-matter.* A person can be a credible source of information on one subject-matter but totally noncredible, or not particularly credible, about another. We have a friend, Harvey, who lived in Acapulco for 12 years and is a credible source of information about Mexico and its customs, but he is next to useless as a source of information about Bulgaria, and what he says about the history of England is sheer fiction. The person who teaches the course in particle physics at your university is (we hope) a credible source of information about the behavior of subatomic particles, but may not be a credible source of information about the biochemistry of one-celled organisms or the history and customs of Mexico. So questions about the credibility of sources must concern their credibility as sources of specific *kinds* of information.

2. *The kind of experience or training required to be a credible source varies.* To be a credible source of *some* kinds of information, one needs highly specialized training and/or expertise. If your physics professor is a credible source of information about particle physics, it is just because of such specialized training or expertise. But for certain other kinds of information, no such specialized training or expertise is required to be a credible source. Harvey knows a lot about Mexico, because while living there for many years, he learned the language and indulged his avid curiosity about the country, not because of specialized training or expertise in Mexican studies. Someone who has lived in a neighborhood all her life will be a credible source of information about the names and locations of neighborhood streets.

3. *The credibility of sources comes in degrees.* One source can have greater credibility than another. We can recognize four main categories of degree of credibility.

a. *Authoritative (or definitive)*. It is reasonable to accept its testimony as decisive, even in the face of some conflicting evidence. Expert testimony is often, though not always, authoritative.

b. *Credible but not authoritative*. It is reasonable to accept its testimony if there is no conflicting information, but that testimony may be called into question by conflicting information. Much eyewitness testimony is of this sort.

c. *Worthy of consideration, but not persuasive just by itself*. It is reasonable to accept its testimony *if* there is corroborating evidence. Some eyewitness testimony is of this sort: we are willing to accept it only if there is corroboration from other witnesses.

d. *Not worth considering*. The source's testimony is quite worthless; we should pay no attention to it at all.

These are rough and ready categories. The boundaries between them are *not* sharply defined, and there can be variation in degree of credibility within each category. One expert can be more authoritative than another, one eyewitness can be more credible than another, and so on. Also remember that someone who is an authoritative source about one subject-matter might not be worth considering on another.

The Three Dimensions of the Credibility of a Source

A variety of factors affect the credibility of the information coming from any particular source. As well, which considerations are pertinent varies considerably according to the type of information in question. Nevertheless, these factors and considerations can all be ranked under three general headings, which might be called the *three dimensions of any source's credibility*. They are:

1. Opportunity—being *in a position to find out* the truth about the issue at hand (for example, because you were located where you could witness things for yourself, or because you've looked the matter up, or because you've conducted an investigation of the matter or done calculations to get the answer, and so on)

2. Ability—having the *skill or competence* needed to find out the truth, given the opportunity you've had (for example, because your eyesight and hearing are good, or because you have the background knowledge needed to understand and interpret the data, or because you've mastered certain techniques of investigation or calculation, and so on)

3. Dependability—being (a) *responsible* (observing or investigating in a careful and unbiased fashion) and (b) *trustworthy* (reporting findings accurately and honestly)

Let us illustrate each of these dimensions.

Opportunity

When we rely on others for information, we want something better than their guesses, prejudices, or groundless hunches. We want information or opinions that they have acquired in reputable and rational ways. (Why? Because information and opinion so acquired are more likely to be true or to be sensible.) Accordingly, there are questions to be asked about the source's opportunity to ascertain the truth of the propositions in question—about where the source was or what it did. Here are a few examples. Was the source present when the riot about which she is reporting occurred? Was she there the whole time? Was she close to it or some distance away? And so on. Or again, if our source is an American describing Japanese customs, has he lived in Japan? For how long? Has he traveled widely in that country, or seen only a part of it? Has he studied Japanese culture or history in any formal way, and if so how extensively? Or, again, has the psychologist testifying about the competence of the defendant to stand trial actually interviewed the defendant, or has she merely read other people's reports about the defendant's behavior? If she has interviewed him, how many and how extensive were the interviews and under what conditions did they take place?

Ability

Does our source have the ability, competence, or expertise to take advantage of the opportunities that were available to determine the truth of the matter? Does our witness to the riot have good eyesight and hearing? Does she have the sort of background knowledge about mob behavior that would enable her to look for the right things, or is she likely to have overlooked very significant events? Does our friend who lived in Japan actually speak and understand the Japanese language? Is the psychologist who is testifying about the defendant a practicing clinical psychologist? How extensive is the experience and knowledge she brings to the examination of the defendant?

Dependability

Someone with an excellent opportunity to determine the truth, and with the ability or competence to exploit that opportunity, may still fail to be a credible source of testimony because we have reason to think his or her testimony is undependable, either about the particular matter in question, or in general. A source's dependability will depend on a number of factors, such as his or her trustworthiness, record for care and precision and for accuracy of reporting, and absence of bias. Was our psychiatrist careful and methodical in arriving at her judgment, or did she do a sloppy job of applying her skills? Is she appropriately qualifying her opinions and conclusions, or is she passing on what is only a reasonable hypothesis as if it were a certain truth? Can we be confident that she based her conclusion solely on the evidence, or was she unduly influenced by a bias for (or against) the defendant? Might she simply be lying or attempting to deceive us because she has something to gain if she can get us to believe her?

Opportunity and ability have to be considered in conjunction with each other. *Which* abilities (skills and competencies) are needed depends on what kind of opportunity the source has had. If the source's opportunity to find out the height of the Eiffel Tower was by calculating it on the basis of measurements she took with a transit and tapemeasure, the source needs the skills of a surveyor. If the source's opportunity consists in having looked it up in a reference book, she needs the ability to read the language in which the reference book was written and the ability to choose an authoritative reference book.

Occasionally, opportunity and ability will seem to coalesce—for example, where a source is credible on a certain topic basically because of her education. Your history professor is usually a highly credible source of information about elementary historical fact in her area of specialization because her doctoral studies provided her with the opportunity to read many accounts of those facts and also with the ability to discriminate between accurate and inaccurate accounts. (Of course, even here dependability might be questioned if you had some reason to suspect bias or dishonesty.) Usually, however, opportunity and ability, though interrelated, remain distinct.

When it comes to assessing dependability, it is usually reasonable to presume that the source is dependable unless you have some special reason for believing he or she is not. Assume that a source is honest and unbiased unless you're aware of specific bias that person has or some specific motive that might lead the source to lie about the matter at hand. Assume that source's investigation was careful and that his reports are accurate unless you have a specific reason to doubt them.

2.3 EVALUATING THE CREDIBILITY OF SOURCES

We rely on other people for information because, for the moment at least, they are in a better position to determine it than we are. For example, when your roommate, looking in the cupboard, informs you that you are out of coffee, or when the full-service gas station attendant checks your car's oil level for you and tells you it is low. In these cases, you could in principle find out for yourself, though it might be inefficient or inconvenient for you to do so. Quite often, though, it is simply impossible for us to find out for ourselves. If you're in Chicago and you want to know the temperature today in Perth, Australia, you have to rely on someone else to tell you. If you don't know the correct spelling of a word, you have to check a dictionary or ask someone.

General Principles

By and large, it is legitimate to accept a proposition based on someone else's say-so provided that the person has had the opportunity to determine the truth of the proposition, has the competence to determine its truth, and is a dependable source about that proposition. From this general rule we can derive a list of questions to ask about claims put forward on the say-so of nonexpert sources of information. Question 1 concerns opportunity, questions 2a and 2b concern ability, and question 3 concerns dependability.

   1. Did the person have an opportunity to discover or learn the truth of the matter? If so, how good was the opportunity?

Example: A fellow camper says there is a bear near the campground. What leads her to say so? Did she see it? But it was dusk, and she didn't have her contact lenses in. Might it have been a raccoon? (See the section that follows on observation reports.) Another example: Your roommate tells you that dolphins, though mammals, have gills that enable them to breathe under water. How much does he know about such things? Has he taken courses in zoology? If so, at what level—high school, university? Has he read extensively about such matters? If so, what sorts of books, science or fiction?

   2a. Does the source have the competence or background knowledge to judge or report about this matter accurately?

Example: You are a lawyer and your client says the car that rear-ended him was a Mazda. But does he know a Mazda from a Toyota? Example: It would save time to make do with your desk-mate's summary instead of reading one of the articles assigned for the course, but does he know enough to get it right? If you can't be sure and the article might be on the exam, you had better read it yourself—or get a summary from someone who's pulling straight A's in the course.

   2b. Does the information or belief being expressed call for specialized knowledge or training (expertise)? If so, does the source have such expertise?

Example: The university calendar is ambiguous about a course requirement, and a friend claims that you don't need a particular course to graduate. Your friend might be right, but the Admissions office will know for sure. Example: One of your housemates says you should use turpentine to thin latex paint. If she's wrong, all your work in repainting could be wasted, so you had better look it up in your home-decorating handbook or call the paint store—sources with the expertise to know the answer.

3. Are there excepting conditions in this case, which would call the person's dependability into question (for example pressure, bias, interest, haste)?

Example: A friend reports that your girlfriend was having a very, very intimate conversation with a strange male in the pub last night. How close a friend is your "friend"? Might he be up to mischief—trying to create ill-will between you and your girlfriend for some ulterior purpose? Example: Your brother tells you that the veterinarian said your cat might die of its injuries after being hit by a car last night. But he was badly upset from having witnessed the accident himself and is tired after driving the cat to the animal hospital. He might well have misunderstood the information; you had best check with the veterinarian yourself.

Special Problems

Reportage

To buttress their contentions people will often quote others who take the same view. They may quote directly (attempting to report the author's or speaker's exact words) or indirectly (paraphrasing: attempting to state the gist of what they said or wrote). Such a use of quotation is often referred to as **citation**. People will also report other's assertions just to convey information. This might entail direct or indirect quotation, or it might consist of summarizing—perhaps the results and conclusions of a study or investigation that others have made, or the plot of a TV episode or of a movie. Such cases of reportage require us to judge whether the person doing the reporting is quoting, paraphrasing, or summarizing accurately and fairly. A newspaper report of a press conference, a textbook account of the contents of a famous scientific treatise, a friend's account of a conversation are all cases in point.

People who are quoting a conversation or who are summarizing the results of a study are likely to quote or summarize inaccurately if they don't *understand* what they are reporting. This is true even if they are attempting direct quotation. For one reason, what we "hear" and "read"—which words we recognize and what we recognize them as—are affected by what we expect to hear and by what makes sense to us. If someone does not understand what he is hearing, he may well mishear it. For another reason, in quoting directly it is necessary to select appropriate "chunks" of text. If someone doesn't understand what he is hearing or reading, he may well quote things out of context in a way that is highly misleading.

Inaccurate reporting can cause serious damage. If a person who has little or no understanding of medical science and medical research attempts to cite the results of a recent medical study, his report of those results may well be inaccurate in ways that matter considerably. He may omit crucial qualifications in the study's conclusion because he doesn't appreciate that they are crucial. Or, more crudely, he may confuse one technical term with another (for example, substitute 'thyroid' for 'thorax' because the words sound the same to him and the former is more familiar). For these reasons, it is advisable to be especially cautious about reports of scientific, technical, and medical matters found in the popular press.[2]

Find out where the person who gives a citation obtained the information. If Lee tells you that studies have shown that pornography causes sexual assaults, has she actually examined those studies herself? Has she read about their results? If so, where? (And if she read a secondary source, where did it get *its* information?) If the information has passed through a series of citations, the chances of its being inaccurate increase as the number of such relays increases.

For example, you might have heard the sayings "Consistency is the hobgoblin of small minds" and "A little knowledge is a dangerous thing." But what Emerson, who originated the first line, actually said is "A *foolish* consistency is the hobgoblin of little minds [adored by little statesmen and philosophers and divines]."[3] Alexander Pope, who is the original source of the second aphorism, actually said, "A little *learning* is a dangerous thing; [/Drink deep, or taste not the Pierian spring;/ There shallow draughts intoxicate the brain,/ And drinking largely sobers it again]."[4] The differences are important. The people who pass along these misquotations have never read or looked up the original Emerson or Pope, have forgotten what they read, or mistakenly think learning and knowledge are the same or that consistency amounts to foolish consistency.

In sum, questions of competence and opportunity arise even for reportage.

Eyewitness Testimony and Observation Reports

We introduce the term **observation reports** to refer to the statements made by people describing events or objects that they have witnessed (or are witnessing) firsthand.

Observers sometimes make mistakes. They can mistake what they observe, or they can misdescribe what they observe, or both. Presented with observation reports, we therefore have to make up our minds whether to accept them. In making such decisions, we can be guided by what we know about five sorts of factors which affect the value of such reports.[5]

1. *Situation of the observer.* Was the person who is making the report close by to what she is reporting on? If the report is based on visual observation, did she have a good look, or did she just glimpse something of out the corner of her eye. How *long* did she look? Was she paying attention to the matter on which she is now reporting, or was her attention on something else? Was she upset or under stress while she was making the observation (for example, during a car accident or a robbery)? In short, how good an *opportunity* did she have to determine perceptually what

happened and how well disposed was her *state of mind* for making accurate observations?

2. *Perceptual acuity.* Some people have better eyesight than others, some have better hearing, some can discriminate tastes better, some can distinguish shades of color better, and so on. Accordingly, one of the things to know is whether a reporter has average, above-average, or below-average **perceptual acuity** in the sense modality on which the report is based. Does he need glasses or a hearing aid? If he does, was he using them at the time?

3. *Environing conditions.* We can see better in bright midday light than in the waning light of dusk, hear what is said better when there is no background noise, discriminate colors better in sunlight than in artificial light, read tiny print better if we are using a magnifying glass. All of us have a great deal of commonsense knowledge concerning what sorts of environing conditions affect the reliability of perceptual reports. In light of that background knowledge, we can find out pertinent facts about the conditions that actually obtained for the observation being reported.

4. *Instruments.* In many cases, the observations performed involve the use of equipment or instruments. Observers depend on eyeglasses, hearing aids, microscopes, binoculars, telescopes, telephones, or P.A. systems. The credibility of their observation reports can be affected by the presence or absence of such instruments, and by their quality and state of repair. If the reporter was not wearing his glasses, or the telephone lines were very noisy, then the accuracy of what he says he saw, or the precision of his report of a telephone conversation, is compromised.

5. *Training/knowledge of the observer.* Observations do not just happen. People making observations need to look in the right place, from the right angle, and to recognize what they see. If they do not know what to look for, or how to look for it, or are unable to recognize it when they see it, their observation reports are unlikely to be true. The observer must also be in possession of an adequate descriptive vocabulary, which is also frequently a function of training and knowledge. In some cases the vocabulary is technical—as would be needed for a description of the positions of the various movable parts of an airplane's wings and tail when it was landing. In some cases all that is needed is training in making a description precise, something fostered in a high school or college writing class. In general, then, what are required are the knowledge and training necessary *to make* and *to describe* the observation.

Consider something quite simple—an observation report of the precise color or hue of a room's walls. Most people have a small vocabulary for talking about different shades of red and are not able to make many fine-grained distinctions of shade. But a painter, an artist, or an interior decorator can give us much more reliable information about such things than can the average person.

Consider next a report based on the application of some simple test, such as reading a mercury thermometer. We typically rely on the reporter to have ascertained (1) that a non-defective thermometer was used, (2) that the instrument was shaken down and then inserted in an appropriate place, for an appropriate amount of time, (3) that the thermometer was read before it was shaken down again or affected by something very hot, and (4) that he saw how far the mercury column actually extended. Each of these tasks requires skill and background knowledge: we don't trust a four-year-old to take his own temperature. If a person lacks that skill and background knowledge, his report of the patient's temperature will not be credible.

Or again, consider someone reporting what she has heard another person say. How familiar is the reporter with the language the speaker used? If it was English, is the reporter fluent in English? If it was a dialect of English, or slang, is the reporter familiar with that dialect or with that slang? If the speaker was using technical terminology, is the speaker conversant with it? If the answer to any of these questions is "No," then the report's credibility is reduced.

In general, then, it is necessary to know (1) whether special knowledge or training is essential for making reliable observations on a given matter and if so, (2) whether the person making the report has it.

2.4 EXPERTS AND EXPERTISE

In certain situations, obtaining the information we want requires specialized knowledge or skill (as when your ophthalmologist says you don't need a new eyeglass prescription yet or physicists tell us that the earth's ozone layer is thinning). Not many of us could find such things out for ourselves, for any of several reasons. We may not have the training or experience needed to know what observations to make, what equipment is needed to make it, how to make the observation, or how to interpret the observed data. We might even be incapable of acquiring that knowledge or skill. For example, some of us are simply incapable of mastering the advanced mathematics needed to understand a physics experiment or to interpret its findings. Or someone might be tone deaf or color-blind. Another consideration is that there is far too much scientific and technical knowledge for any one person ever to learn it all. It would even be impossible for any one person to acquire the expertise needed to find out everything one needs to know in a lifetime. In fact, if expertise is needed to acquire some particular bit of information, the only time *you* can find it out for yourself is when you happen to be an expert on precisely that matter and it is practically possible for you to make the requisite observations.

We shall use the term **expertise** to refer to such *extensive, specialized knowledge or skill*, and we shall use the word **expert** to refer to *a person who has such expertise*. People can be experts in areas of knowledge, such as microbiology or medieval history, or in matters of skill, art, or craft, such as roofing installation, watercolor painting, or origami.

We seek out experts or people with expertise when we need to rely on their knowledge and skill, and we do so because we expect them to give us correct answers to our questions and good advice about what to do. But being an expert does not mean always being right, though experts are more likely to be right about matters within their areas of expertise than are others, simply because of their training and experience.

That last qualification—"within their areas of expertise"—is important. As is the case with credibility in general, expertise is always relative to a particular field of knowledge, type of skill, or kind of art or craft. Rare is the person who is an expert in more than one thing. Moreover, in today's highly specialized world, most experts are limited in their authority to narrow, very particular corners of their fields. An orthopedic surgeon's special expertise might be limited to hip replacements, and such a doctor might know less than other orthopedic surgeons about shoulder or ankle problems, less than a well-trained midwife about obstetrical problems, and no more than an informed layperson about psychiatric problems. A physicist's particular expertise might be restricted to a specialization *within*, say, particle physics—itself just one specialized area within physics, among several others.

Recognizing Experts and Expertise

When should we consider someone an expert in an area? On what basis can we tell whether someone has expertise of a certain kind? Among the bases on which we can judge someone to have specialized knowledge or skill, two are especially prominent: the person's credentials (both institutionalized and informal) and the person's track record.

By **credentials** we mean public tokens of the recognition of a person's expertise *by other experts*—by those who are in a position to distinguish genuine from bogus expertise. Such tokens consist in degrees, licenses, awards, positions of authority, and so on; to count as genuine credentials, those tokens must be conferred by other experts in the same subject area. Credentials can be either formal (institutionalized) or informal.

Formal Credentials

When the credibility of people claiming expertise is socially important, societies tend to set up institutionalized procedures for assessing and certifying expertise. This is the case in our society with, to list a few examples, engineers, architects, accountants, lawyers, physicians, aircraft pilots, captains of large vessels, social workers, and psychiatrists. People in such roles must have, in addition to the knowledge and skills themselves, also appropriately certified credentials, in the sense just defined. Such credentials are highly formalized, as when a lawyer is "admitted to the bar" of a state, a scholar is awarded a Ph.D. degree or a qualified skilled tradesperson receives his or her "papers."

Informal Credentials

In many other cases, expertise is acknowledged by credentials which are not institutionalized, but informal, as when someone wins prizes for her roses in flower shows year after year, a tennis player is ranked in the top ten in the world, or a college basketball player is picked in the first round of the professional draft. Such recognition counts as a credential because it is conferred by other experts in the subject area.

Track Record

When we judge others to be experts because of their credentials, we are relying on the judgments of experts about who is an expert. Sometimes we ourselves can see that a person has expertise simply by examining his or her **track record**— his or her record of successes and failures. So a coach who produces a string of winning teams or athletes, or a lawyer who usually wins her cases in court, or an engineer who has a great many patents to his name will be judged to have expertise.

Comparing track records of two experts can be useful in deciding who has the greater degree of expertise and (potentially) the greater credibility. Other things being equal, a scientist with a lengthy record of significant publications in serious scientific journals would be judged to have greater expertise than one with just a few publications.

Evaluating the Credibility of Expert Reports

Most of us are rarely in a position to challenge, second-guess, or check up on the claims experts make within their areas of special competence. One would have to be an expert oneself in order even to understand how to go about doing so. We rely on experts, and reasonably so, just because they are and we are not in a position to know when there is sufficient direct evidence or other grounds for believing claims that lie within their competence. The conditions under which it is reasonable to question experts, therefore, have more to do with factors that raise doubts about whether the judgment belongs to experts than with direct challenges to expert testimony. Here is a partial list of questions based on such conditions.

1. Does the proposition supposedly warranted by expert testimony belong to an area where expertise is required or can exist?

There are some sorts of beliefs that are not matters of knowledge or skill that require, or are decidable solely on the basis of, highly technical or specialized expertise. Whether you should major in music or geology is a matter only you can decide, for example. Similarly, on such questions as whom one should vote for, whether there is a God, or whether freedom is more important than security—among thousands of others—it is inappropriate to call upon experts.

That is not to say that deciding these matters does not depend in part on information for which it makes sense to turn to experts. The point is that no expert has the authority to make the final decision or judgment about such matters, because such decisions or judgments do not turn exclusively on specialized knowledge or experience.

We are, nevertheless, often invited to accept the so-called authority of experts on precisely such questions. Much advertising invokes background appeals to experts in matters belonging to personal good judgment.

2. Does the person appealed to as a credible expert need credentials? What are those credentials and does the alleged expert have them? Is that person an expert in the particular area to which the proposition in question belongs?

Sometimes experts are appealed to on matters not strictly within their particular competence—with or without their authorization. For example, Dr. Linus Pauling, a Nobel laureate in chemistry, is often referred to as an expert on the benefits of vitamin C, about the benefits of which he has forcefully expressed his opinion. And sometimes the issue on which the expert is appealed to is outside *any* expert's specialized authority. Think of actors endorsing political candidates, or doctors advising about the morality of abortion. Sometimes celebrities who have no discernible expertise whatever are used in commercial or political endorsements, and in those cases, their say-so is no reason whatever to accept the claims they are endorsing.

3. Has the expert actually conducted an investigation of the matter on which he or she is making a pronouncement? And if so, how thorough an investigation?

This is a question that you should raise whenever an expert offers an opinion about some particular person, thing, or event, for example, the economist who is commenting on the causes of last week's decline in the stock market, the psychiatrist who is quoted as saying that the prime minister of England is really borderline schizophrenic, the eminent chemist who says that alar is not a threat to humans when sprayed on apples in small amounts. Are they reporting the results of investigations they have conducted or closely inspected, or are they giving an off-the-cuff opinion, with little greater credibility than anyone else's?

4. Do different more or less equally authoritative experts disagree about whether the proposition in question is true or probable?

If experts Gomez, Johnson, and Smith tell us that a proposition, P, is true, and experts Garcia, Jackson, and Smoot tell us that P is not true, and if the two groups are roughly equally authoritative, then we nonexperts cannot decide for or against P on the basis of what the experts say. We find ourselves in this situation when some fisheries experts say the cod stocks in the North Atlantic fishery are depleted and others say they are not; when some atomic energy scientists and engineers tell us that a nuclear power plant is safe and others tell us it is dangerous; when some forestry experts say Canada is running out of commercial lumber and pulpwood forests and others contend that the supply is plentiful. The best we can do is try to find out if the people appealed to really are equally authoritative or if some are more trustworthy than others on the proposition we want to know about (see the next question).

5. Are there specific reasons to suspect that the expert appealed to might not be candid or might unintentionally mislead?

If a particular expert has a financial interest in your accepting the proposition in question (perhaps is being paid to do a commercial, or works for a company manufacturing the product), or is staking his or her reputation on being right, or is riding a hobby horse, or can be shown to have prejudged the matter, then that expert's judgment can be questioned or challenged.

2.5 SUMMARY

A proposition is credible just in case it is worthy of belief or acceptance. Most of our beliefs come from other people, and the assertions of these sources are credible to the extent that the sources are credible and their assertions are plausible, given everything we know. A proposition is credible *to* a person, relative to what he or she is justified in accepting. The credibility of a source is always a matter of degree. Whether a source has to be an expert to be credible depends on the subject.

Whether someone is a credible source of a given proposition depends on three things: the opportunity he or she had to know it, the ability he or she has to understand or interpret it, and whether there is any reason to consider him or her undependable with respect to it.

The testimony of a nonexpert source is to be evaluated by judging whether (1) the person has had the opportunity to make a judgment, (2a) the person has the requisite competence or background knowledge, (2b) the matter can be known to a nonexpert, and (3) there is no reason not to trust the person on this occasion. When dealing with reportage, we want to know that the source understands the material well enough to report it accurately and that the original source was credible. When dealing with someone's eyewitness testimony or observation reports, we want to check on the situation and attitude of the observer in relation to what was observed, the observer's perceptual acuity, his instruments, whether he needed training, and what the conditions of the observation were.

Expertise is extensive specialized knowledge and skill. We can identify experts by their credentials, which indicate an authority bestowed on them by other experts and by their track record. We assess the credibility of an expert's testimony by seeing whether (1) expertise is required, (2) this person has the requisite credentials, (3) the expert had an opportunity to investigate the matter, (4) the matter is not controversial among experts, and (5) there is no special reason to question this person's dependability on the matter in question.

2.6 EXERCISES

Exercise 1

For each of the following passages, we have identified one or more propositions which you are invited to accept on the say-so of a source quoted in the passage. For each proposition listed below the passage, answer the following questions:
  (a) What or who is the source of the claim? Is the source presented as an expert?
  (b) If the source *not* presented as an expert, is it a credible source for this proposition? Defend your answer.
  (c) If the source is presented as an expert, then:
    (i) What are the source's credentials?
    (ii) What is the source's specific area of expertise?
    (iii) Does the proposition fall within the source's area of expertise? Explain your answer.
    (iv) As far as you can tell, has the source actually conducted an investigation of the matter on which he or she is making a pronouncement? If so, how thorough was the investigation? Explain your answer.
    (v) Is there any reason to challenge the appeal to this expert or to any expert on this question? Explain your answer.

  1. *Background.* The following Canadian Press story appeared in Sept. 1989 under the headline "Ads target smokers only, court told."

Ads Target Smokers Only, Court Told

MONTREAL (CP)—A senior tobacco company official, testifying at a court challenge to the federal ban on cigarette advertising said Tuesday his company's multi-million-dollar advertising budget targets only smokers, not at enticing non-smokers to take up the habit.

Advertising is so expensive that the three major tobacco companies in Canada find it hard enough to "maintain brand loyalty" or to win a single percentage point of market share away from a competitor, Peter Hoult of North Carolina-based RJR Tobacco Ltd. told Quebec Superior Court.

"GETTING PEOPLE to smoke is a much

Continued

more fundamental change of behavior, compared with changing brands, and we just don't have the funds," said Hoult formerly president of RJR-Macdonald Inc. of Toronto.

HOULT, WHO was trained as a psychologist, gave a fascinating glimpse into the advertising strategies of the tobacco industry, which tries to build up brand loyalty around particular lifestyles.

The Canadian industry spent $40 million on advertising and marketing in 1989, said Michel Descoteaux, spokesman for industry leader Imperial Tobacco Ltd.

Surveys by sophisticated private agencies tell the tobacco companies who smokes which brand—by age, gender, income and even region. Smokers are described in terms like "small-town traditionalist" or "status seekers."

For example, MacDonald knows that its Export brand is strong in Eastern Canada and with blue-collar men, while Vantage appeals to white-collar urbanites, Hoult told Mr. Justice Jess-Jude Chabot.

But Hoult, in a clipped English accent, affirmed that "ads to non-smokers don't work, any more than ads can get people to stop smoking."

And the tobacco industry does not aim advertising at people under 18, he added.

CIGARETTE smoking has been on a steady decline in Canada since it reached a peak of 66 billion cigarettes sold in 1981, said Imperial's Descoteaux. In 1988 the figure dropped by 30 per cent to 51 billion. He said sales are expected to drop by eight per cent this year due to another tobacco tax increase in the last federal budget.

The case, which began Monday, is expected to last several months.

Claim: Cigarette advertising is not aimed at enticing nonsmokers to take up the habit of smoking.

2. *Background:* The following is an excerpt from an advertisement for PowerBar in *Runner's World,* April 1991, p. 7.

... "I'm not a masters runner, I'm a runner" says New Zealander Campbell from his home in Pittsburgh PA. "I want to win races. That means being first across the finish line, not just first over age 40."

At the Boston Marathon in April, he broke another masters world record with a time of 2 hours, 11 minutes, 4 seconds, placing fourth overall.

John began eating PowerBars three years ago. "I often felt I needed something in my stomach before a long run, but every runner worries about getting an upset stomach. Two PowerBars and a couple of cups of water, about two and a half hours before a hard run or a race really fuels me up." ...

The emergence of a masters running circuit with substantial sponsorships and prize money motivated him to begin competing again in his late 30's. His contract with PowerBars enables him to devote full time to training.

"It's nice to promote a product you use and believe in" he says. "Now, when people at races ask me what my secret is to beating the young guys, I hand them a PowerBar."

The rest of his secret is training: 130 to 145 miles per week, even when he's racing.

"I love racing, I love being competitive" he says. "My body's geared for racing frequently." ...

Claim: Eating PowerBars will improve your performance as a runner.

**3. The following is excepted from the August 1989 issue of the Canadian magazine *Chatelaine*.

The benefits of solitude
It can boost your health & your relationships

By *Eleanor Jungkind*

Some people fill up their schedule because they thrive on being busy, and others have little choice—demands at home and/or outside the home leave them with little time for themselves. But in many of these cases, making time for yourself can be beneficial and necessary for your physical and mental well-being, according to mental health experts.

Dr. Judith Milstein Katz, a Toronto psychologist, says that spending time alone can improve your health by reducing stress and tension. You can let down your guard, do what you want and not worry about how others will react. Solitude can also enhance your creativity and problem-solving efforts because you have more time to think.

You personal relationships can benefit too.

When spouses have time for special interests and hobbies they enjoy on their own, they are less likely to be critical and irritable with each other and generally are more willing to cooperate when they are together, says Dr. Katz.

To get the most out of your solitude, it's important to focus on something other than your current concerns and to relax. For example, try to avoid spending all your time stewing about the argument you had with your boss or spouse.

For many women, one of the biggest obstacles to making time for solitude is convincing themselves that it's worthwhile, according to Dr. Katz. She says that women ought not to feel guilty about taking the time for their own needs and interests.

Claim: Women ought not to feel guilty about taking the time for their own needs and interests.

4. The following article is from a national newspaper.

Psychologist Reveals . . .
Why Gals Go for Baby-Faced Stars Like Michael J. Fox & Tom Cruise

Why do women find baby-faced stars like Michael J. Fox and Tom Cruise so irresistible—even though they don't have the perfect masculine features of heart-throbs like Ted Danson and Michael Douglas?

It's because women judge attractiveness on more than one level, says a psychologist who has studied the subject for years.

"On one level, women look for a dominant and mature look in men," declared Dr. Michael Cunningham, assistant professor of psychology at the University of Louisville. "It satisfies their need to be protected and taken care of."

But women don't want men who are TOO rugged-looking, he said. "Women tend to be uncomfortable with guys who look too strong
Continued

or appear too dominant. By and large, women don't like muscle men. They want a guy who is friendly and easy to get along with."

Women also need to nurture—and that's why they like baby-faced males.

"So considering all of women's needs, there is a series of ideal male faces that are all extremely attractive to females. They range from the relatively more baby-faced to the relatively more mature. The ideal male face is some combination of the two.

"Fox's face radiates a boyish vulnerability as well as a friendly, cooperative nature.

"Ted Danson is also in this ideal range although he leans more toward the mature side.

"Along with a strong chin, high cheekbones and bushy eyebrows—all traits of the mature look—Danson also has big eyes and a wide smile that give him a little of that baby-faced, innocent look.

"Michael Douglas is about one step closer to the baby-faced end of the ideal range than Danson. He can look vulnerable in his eyes and open with his smile but he's also got that strong chin and a high forehead.

"Tom Cruise's face is still maturing, but he's currently closer to the range of a Michael J. Fox than a Ted Danson or a Michael Douglas. He

brings out women's need to mother, to cuddle and nurture.

"And take a look at the sneer on Sean Penn's face.

"Fortunately for him, his attractiveness to women stems from his baby face which transforms that sneer into more of a babyish pout that brings out the mother in women, too.

"Sylvester Stallone is an older version of Sean Penn. He may have this nail-tough image, but women see past the obvious to discover a certain vulnerability beneath his shell of rugged, exaggerated manhood.

"Burt Reynolds' baby face is nonthreatening—even though he tends to portray a macho type.

"He, too has a boyish charm that is accentuated by a lift in his eyebrow when he laughs or smiles or looks puzzled.

"Clint Eastwood is at the extremely rugged mature end of this ideal range of male facial attractiveness. He has small squinty eyes, big cheekbones and a big chin.

"But he still has a touch, however small, of the boy in his face."

—Jim Mittlager

Claim: A dominant and mature look in men satisfies women's need to be protected and taken care of.

Exercise 2

The following passages contain one or more propositions which you are invited to accept on the say-so of a source or sources quoted in the passage.

(a) Decide which claims or propositions we are invited to accept on the basis of someone's testimony. If there are just one or two, write them out. If there is a large number, characterize them in a general way.

(b) How credible is each source? Defend your judgment in light of opportunity, ability, and dependability of the source.

1. *Background:* This Canadian Press story appeared in November 1983.

Caught with a prostitute, politician quits

EDMONTON (CP)—Alberta Premier Lougheed said today he has accepted the resignation of Solicitor General Oraham Harle, who was found with a prostitute in his car by police.

Lougheed said Harle submitted his resignation Tuesday. Attorney General Neil Crawford will assume Harle's responsibilities.

Harle said Tuesday he was simply conducting a one-man investigation of prostitution when police found him with the prostitute in his car a week ago in a seedy area of the city.

IN AN INTERVIEW, he said he has talked to prostitutes since becoming Alberta's solicitor general in 1979, all in an effort to resolve the issue of prostitution control.

"You don't get first-hand information by going through several people, do you?

So far, he said, his only finding in the investigation is that prostitution "doesn't appear to be a problem right at the moment."

Before his resignation, Harle had said he would continue the work.

Harle said he had insomnia the night police found him and the prostitute in his government-issue executive Chrysler.

HE SAID HE invited the girl into his car because "she was on the street obviously looking to me like she was looking for a ride."

Harle said he had no clue she was a prostitute until they started talking.

He said he devotes "miniscule" time to his investigation and hasn't done similar work on other crimes.

2. The next excerpt is from a page headlined "Calling the Doctor," consisting of advice about medical care for children. It appeared in *Newsweek*, Special Issue, Summer 1991.

RECOMMENDED IMMUNIZATION TIMES

The following are immunization times recommended by the American Academy of Pediatrics:
   DTP: 2 months, 4 months, 6 months, 15-18 months, 4-6 years
   Polio: 2 months, 4 months, 15-18 months, 4-6 years
   Measles: 15 months, 11-12 years
   Mumps: 15 months, 11-12 years
   Rubella: 15 months, 11-12 years
   Haemophilus: 2 months, 4 months. The schedule for additional shots varies.
   Tetanus-diphtheria: 14-16 years

3. This is excerpted from a story entitled "Timing Is Everything" that appeared in July 1991.

TIMING IS EVERYTHING

By Trish Hall
New York Times

People are always talking about how busy they are, how starved they feel for time.

But do they really have less of it today? John Robinson, a University of Maryland professor of psychology who has been studying the way Americans spend their waking moments for 25 years, asserts that the perception does not match the reality. His findings show a steady increase in free time.

"I'm the guy with the odd data," says Robinson, who became interested in the use of time when he was a graduate student at the University of Michigan and now directs the Americans' Use of Time Project at the University of Maryland's Survey Research Center in College Park.

He agrees with the widely held notion that people feel more harried. Surveys by poll takers like Louis Harris and Associates, for instance, say they have found that people feel the work week has been increasing and leisure time has been decreasing.

But Robinson, a man of diverse interests and multiple projects who seems perfectly confident that his numbers tell the real story, holds that people remember the past inaccurately.

"The perception of a time crunch appears to have gone up in the period of time where free time has increased," says Robinson, who, in those 25 years, has studied thousands of diaries that men and women around the country have kept on how they spend their time.

Since 1965, he says, men have gained seven hours of free time in a week, to 41 hours from 34 per week.

Women, he reports, have gained six hours of free time, to 40 from 34, in a week. Robinson defines free time as any time when people don't have commitments to work, family, chores, or personal needs like sleeping, eating and grooming.

Robinson is considered one of the few experts on spending time who is able to make comparisons over decades.

"Very few people actually study how we use time," says Geoffrey Godbey of the leisure studies department at Pennsylvania State University.

He characterizes Robinson's work as "first-rate," an evaluation echoed by colleagues in the field.

**4. The story that follows appeared in May 1988.

Noriega linked to killing of Panamanian priest

By Larry Rohter
New York Times Service

WASHINGTON—Panamanian strongman Manuel Antonio Noriega participated in the killing of a priest in 1971, a fact known almost immediately to the United States because of intelligence monitoring of Panamanian military communications, a former U.S. Government official says.

Rev. Hector Gallegos had been deeply in-

volved in organizing peasants in the countryside, which offended the country's military leadership, then headed by General Omar Torrijos Herrera.

At the time, General Noriega was chief of Panama's military intelligence. Now head of the Panamanian Defence Forces, he is the country's *de facto* ruler and is engaged in a bitter struggle to remain in power.

Panamanian opponents of the regime have always maintained that Father Gallegos was killed when he was thrown from a helicopter by soldiers, but have never been able to provide conclusive proof.

In an interview in Washington on Tuesday, a former U.S. Government official who asked not to be identified said Gen. Noriega was on board the helicopter when Father Gallegos was killed and, in fact, supervised the operation.

The death of Father Gallegos has been cited frequently by International human-rights groups as an example of the disrespect of Panama's military rulers for human rights.

Gen. Noriega's involvement in the killing became known almost immediately to Washington because it was intercepting telephone and other communications among Panamanian military leaders, the official said.

The administration of president Richard Nixon did not seek to punish either Gen. Noriega or Gen. Torrijos because of the larger interests at stake in Panama, the official said. At the time of the killing, the army still had its headquarters in the Canal Zone.

Among the installations run by the U.S. military in Panama, current and former U.S. officials say, are several that intercept electronic communications.

---

5. *Background:* Billy Martin was a well-known baseball player and manager. On Christmas Day 1989, he was killed in an accident in upstate New York. His friend, William Reedy, was charged in connection with the accident, in which a vehicle occupied by Martin and Reedy crashed into a tree on Martin's property. The following story appeared in the *Detroit Free Press* on April 12, 1990 under the title "Billy Wasn't Driver, Martin's Widow Says: Reedy lied about lying to police, she claims."

"Billy Wasn't Driver," Martin's Widow Says!
"Reedy Lied About Lying to Police, She Claims"

By Frank Bruni
Free Press Staff Writer

In an angry retort, Billy Martin's widow said Wednesday that Detroit bar owner William Reedy lied when he told the Free Press that Martin—not he—was driving in the Christmas Day accident that killed the former baseball manager.

"It's a lie," Jilluann Martin said in a telephone interview from her upstate New York farmhouse. "I'm not going to put up with that . . . I won't put up with trying to put the blame on Billy."

Police identified Reedy as the driver in the crash near Binghamton in upstate New York. He is charged with driving while intoxicated and is scheduled to appear for a pretrial hearing in May in Broome County.

Reedy told the Free Press on Tuesday that just after the accident, he lied to police and told them he was the driver in order to protect Martin, whom he thought was alive and just "knocked out."

Jilluann Martin laughed when told of Reedy's statement.

Then, in a harsh tone, she denounced Reedy's comments.

"I wish the Reedy's the very best," she said. "It was an accident, a terrible accident that will change all of our lives forever. But I won't put up with trying to put the blame on Billy. I just can't believe he (Reedy) would say something like that. That's a terrible thing to say."

Broome County Sheriff Anthony Rufflo said Wednesday, "We're certain that he (Reedy) was the driver of the vehicle."

Continued

Reedy refused Wednesday to comment further on the case.

A DWI conviction in New York calls for a fine of $350 to $500, up to a year in jail and revocation of a driver's license for at least six months.

Elizabeth Boyd, spokeswoman for the Michigan Secretary of State's office, said penalties imposed in other states on Michigan drivers can be imposed in Michigan, too.

6. The following is excerpted from *Chatelaine* August, 1989.

Do you really need surgery?

Often, there are less risky alternatives—medication, say, or a change of diet. Sidney Katz guides you toward making an intelligent choice.

If your doctor tells you that you need an "elective" or nonemergency operation, designed to improve the quality of your life rather than save it, think twice. Take the time to explore the need as well as the risks and potential benefits. It often comes as a surprise to the layperson that doctors sometimes have conflicting opinions about whether surgery is necessary, and that views may vary from hospital to hospital and from region to region. As a result, some surgery is performed without good reason.

In *Second Opinion*, the recently published appraisal of Canada's health care system by Michael Rachlis, M.D., and Carol Kushner, the authors note that the hysterectomy rate among Canadian women is twice that of Britain and Continental Europe, and that, per capita, 10 times as many gallbladder operations are per-formed in Canada as in Denmark, although there's no evidence that the need for either procedure is any more prevalent in this country. Last year, a study published in the Journal of the American Medical Association concluded that nearly half of all coronary artery bypass operations were done for questionable or inappropriate reasons.

Although operating rooms have never been safer, the hard truth is that, in the words of Toronto physician and author Kenneth Walker, "There is no such thing as minor surgery." He was referring to the potential dangers posed by anesthesia, infection, allergic reactions and, occasionally, misadventure, even in the simplest nonemergency procedure. As a woman, you are at greater risk of having needless surgery than a man because you visit doctors more frequently. And because your reproductive organs are so often the subject of health complaints, they are likely to be the site of surgery.

7. This Associated Press story appeared in September 1990.

Khrushchev's remarks 'absurd,' say sons of executed Rosenbergs

By Michelle Locke
Associated Press

SPRINGFIELD, Mass.—The sons of Julius and Ethel Rosenberg said Monday their parents didn't help the Soviet Union develop an atomic bomb, and dismissed Nikita Khrushchev's memoirs thanking the couple as "wholly absurd."

Robert and Michael Meeropol, who have

worked for years to clear their parents' names, said they weren't shaken by the remarks by the ousted Soviet leader, contained in tapes he made during seven years of house arrest before his death in 1971.

"I'll tell you what the big shock was, the first shock when I was 7 years old listening to 'The Lone Ranger' when the FBI arrested my father," said 47-year-old Michael Meeropol, a professor at a small private college in Springfield. "After that, you know, shocks don't happen to us. We expect them."

Khrushchev says in the memoirs that he heard from both Soviet leader Josef Stalin and Vyacheslav Molotov, then minister of foreign affairs, that the Rosenbergs "provided very significant help in accelerating the production of our atom bomb."

"My reaction . . . is that it's wholly absurd," said 43-year-old Robert Meeropol, a Springfield lawyer.

The Rosenbergs, who maintained their innocence, were executed June 19, 1953, for conspiracy to commit espionage. Their sons, who took their adoptive parents' last name, have used the Freedom of Information Act to force the release of classified documents in the case.

They said their reseach of their parents' trial and execution turned up affidavits by scientists who said none of the evidence brought by the government amounted to substantially useful information about the atomic bomb.

The brothers said Khrushchev may have misunderstood Stalin or Stalin may have been lying to create the impression of having a huge network of spies.

8. This is excerpted from a story that appeared in *Time*, June 17, 1991, p. 34.

Crawling Out Of the Slump

By John Greenwald

Not for months has Alan Greenspan been so downright bullish about the U.S. economy. Speaking last week in Osaka, the normally dour Federal Reserve chairman said he saw "clearly encouraging" signs that the recession is ending and mounting evidence of a stronger than expected recovery." . . .

Says Allen Sinai, chief economist for the Boston Co. Economic Advisers: "A strong hint that the recession has just about ended or may have already ended, showed up in the May jobs report," But he added that the economy "is crawling out of the recession, not bursting out of the gate."

Many forecasters predict that the economy will grow less than 3% in the 12 months that follow the recession, in contrast, to a vigorous 6% average for previous postwar turnarounds. The consumer won't feel any sense of recovery until December or early next year, says Susan Sterne, president of Economic Analysis Associates, in Stowe, Vermont, Concurs, Wall Street economist Lawrence Kudlow, "This recovery just isn't going to have much torque."

In fact, the economy seems to be headed for a return to the same type of feeble expansion that saw GNP rise just 2.5% in 1989 and about 1% in the first half of 1990, before the downturn took hold. "The recession is just one part of the big picture of sluggish growth since 1989," says Sinai. "It should be seen in that light."

9. This story appeared in *The New York Times* on September 10, 1989.

Mugging Suspect Dies in Custody in the Bronx, and Witnesses Say Officers Beat Him

By Howard W. French
Special in The New York Times

NEW YORK, Sept. 9—An unarmed mugging suspect died in police custody in the Bronx early today shortly after violently resisting arrest, the police said.

Witnesses to the incident, however, said the victim, a 25-year-old black man, died after being beaten for as long as 30 minutes by two police officers at East 163d Street and Southern Boulevard in the Hunts Point section.

The man was identified as Henry Hughes of 120-34 Elgar Place in the Kingsbridge Heights section.

WITNESSES AND POLICE DISAGREE

The witnesses said the officers, a white man and white woman, shouted racial insults at the handcuffed victim while they beat and kicked him in the head and groin.

The witnesses said the beatings stopped when other police officers began arriving shortly after 6 A.M.

The police said the arrested man died after waging a "fierce, fierce struggle" with the arresting officers as they tried to subdue him.

A police spokesman, Detective James Coleman, said that while officers were assisting the victim of a purse snatching at the Hunts Point subway station, they heard a scream from the intersection of East 163d Street and Southern Boulevard and saw a man fleeing.

While being chased, the fleeing man "crashed into a Plexiglas door" at 1018 East 163d Street, Detective Coleman said. "He struggled so much they had to link two pairs of handcuffs together to arrest him," the detective added.

A unit of the Emergency Medical Service arrived minutes later and declared the arrested man dead at the scene, the police said.

This afternoon, the door of the building where the arrest took place was badly shattered and blood stains lay on the ground nearby.

Detective Coleman said that the victim was identified by the screaming woman as the person who had attacked her, but the victim of the first robbery had not seen her assailant's face.

"He was lying on the ground and they kept hitting him," said Maria Jiminez, a fifth-floor resident of 1018 East 163d Street who said she watched the incident from her window. "It lasted at least 20 to 25 minutes. He kept saying, 'Help me, help me,' but the police, forget it, they kept hitting him.

'I WAS SO SCARED'

"I felt I should call the police, but this was the police. I wanted to help, but I didn't want to go outside. I was so scared," Mrs. Jiminez said.

The Associated Press reported that Victor Vega, a Bronx resident, said he witnessed the incident and said that at one point during the beating the male officer warned witnesses at gunpoint to stay away, saying "We know what we are doing."

"After a while the guy stopped screaming." The Associated Press quoted Mr. Vega as saying. "They told the guy to stand up, but he was already dead."

Juan Mendez, an employee at the La Giralda Bakery, at 1035 East 163d Street, on the block where the incident took place said: "This morning after we came in, customers said they had seen the police kill a man in handcuffs."

HOMICIDE INVESTIGATION URGED

The lawyer, C. Vernon Mason, who was engaged by Mr. Vega to represent him during an investigation of the matter, said today the incident should be investigated as homicide by the office of the Bronx District Attorney.

"It should not be pursued as an ordinary affair," Mr. Mason said. Referring to the police, he added: "They will come up with a drug story or some other story, say that the man had fallen."

At a news conference this afternoon at the 41st Precinct, Assistant Chief John Holmes, commander of patrol for the Bronx, said of the incident, "At this point we are examining all of the statements."

Asked if he believed Mr. Hughes had died

as a result of a beating, Chief Holmes said, "I don't believe there were any beatings."

Chief Homes said an autopsy was being performed "immediately."

Names of the arresting officers were being withheld by the police, pending further investigation.

Another witness, leaving the police station after an interview there, told reporters that the police involved in the arrest "were covering their badges with their hands."

"They were beating him with night sticks, two officers and a lady cop," the witness, Steven Perez of the Bronx, said.

10. The following story appeared in *The Globe and Mail* on April 26, 1988.

MDs oppose withdrawal of risky acne drug

By Andre Picard
The Globe and Mail

Canadian dermatologists are "unanimously opposed" to a ban of an anti-acne drug blamed for causing birth defects and may have the clout to block any federal Government attempt to do so.

"Accutane is the closest thing to a sure cure for acne that has ever been invented. It would be a shame to lose it as a treatment," F. William Danby, secretary-treasurer of the Canadian Dermatology Association, said in an interview yesterday.

Accutane is the trade name for the drug isotretinoin, which is marketed by Hoffmann-La Roche Ltd. in Canada.

About 100,000 Canadians undergo Accutane treatments each year, and sales total close to $4-million annually.

A recommendation on withdrawing the drug from the market will be made before week's end by the expert advisory committee on dermatology.

Five members of the eight-person committee, which reports to the federal health protection branch are dermatologists and "unanu-

mous in their opposition to a ban," Dr. Danby said.

In a confidential memorandum obtained by The New York Times, the U.S. Food and Drug Administration estimated that 1,300 babies were born with severe defects from 1982 to 1986 because of the drug.

In addition, it said that 5,000 to 7,000 abortions were performed on U.S. women because of exposure to Accutane and 700 to 1,000 miscarriages were directly linked to use of the drug.

Only 61 cases of birth defects were reported in the United States, but the federal agency estimated that the balance went unreported.

In Canada, the federal Government received four reports involving Accutane from January, 1983, when it became available, to early 1987. Two women gave birth to babies with severe defects, and defects were found in aborted fetuses of patients.

Yesterday, the advisory committee on dermatology held a preliminary meeting and will make a final recommendation to the Government on Friday.

Continued

"There is a range of options ranging from an outright ban to doing nothing at all. They are all being considered," Richard Graham, acting director of the bureau of human prescription drugs, said in an interview.

Dr. Graham said dermatologists "didn't exactly suggest a ban, but I can assure you the committee won't come up with do-nothing recommendations."

The committee will likely be influenced by a meeting of the FDA today in Rockville, Md., where a ban will be considered.

Carolyn Glynn, a spokesman for Hoffmann-La Roche, Inc. in Nutley, N.J., said the company will attack the FDA study as "statistically flawed" and "meaningless."

But she said the company will change its packaging and step up its education campaign in both the United States and Canada.

The Canadian Dermatology Association, for its part, is calling for better enforcement of current prescribing procedures.

"The bottom line is that the drug should be prescribed only by dermatologists. Unfortunately, that isn't practical in every community in Canada," Dr. Danby said.

He stopped short of criticizing general practitioners, but he said "dermatologists follow a very strict procedure."

An information sheet distributed by doctors says "there is absolutely no doubt that Accutane causes major deforming birth defects" and the "medication is absolutely forbidden for patients who are pregnant, or could get pregnant."

Dr. Danby said female patients must take birth control pills for the duration of the anti-acne treatment and agree to undergo an abortion if they become pregnant.

NOTES

1. In a real-life case of this sort, it turned that the pilot in question had made four other such reports and that radar failed to reveal any object in the area where the sighting was claimed. The additional information about the pilot throws his credibility into question, and the additional information from the radar makes his report even more implausible. Once this additional information was unearthed, many judged the pilot's report to be simply not credible. See *The Skeptical Inquirer*, Vol. 11 (1987) pp. 322–326.

2. "Science reporters" are becoming more common, fortunately, and usually have the background to report in fairly accurate, informative, and helpful ways. But much of the straight "news" reporting of scientific and medical matters still shows little evidence of such specialized reporting expertise.

3. *Essays*, First Series, "Self Reliance." See John Bartlett, *Bartlett's Familiar Quotations*, 14th ed., edited Emily Morison Beck (Boston: Little, Brown, 1968), p. 606.

4. *An Essay on Criticism*, Part II, pp. 401–403.

5. We are leaving aside here two other factors which ought to be attended to in real-life situations: the honesty of the reporter and the reliability of the reporter's memory and/or records. Human memory is notoriously unreliable; caution is advisable when there are no careful notes contemporaneous with the observation. And as for honesty, when a lot hangs on a particular description's being accepted, human moral uprightness can be fallible: even scientific heavyweights have been discovered fudging their results to bear out their cherished theories.

Information
and the Media

In this chapter we discuss the **news media** as sources of information. Directly or indirectly, we obtain much of the information we use in our daily reasoning from the media. We should assess its credibility as we would any other, but media information raises questions over and above the ones dealt with in the previous chapter. For besides supplying us with information, the media communicate to us a sense of the *significance* of the information conveyed and they *shape our attitudes* toward it. Some events come across as important, others as trivial; some events are portrayed as welcome, others as unfortunate; some people come across as sensible or attractive, others as silly or sinister. Thus the media communicate more than the "facts," they communicate an impression of the value and significance of those facts.

Section 3.1 puts media in their historical, economic, and political context. In Section 3.2 we note how the media's mode of presentation affects the information conveyed. In Section 3.3 we suggest ways to assess the contents of media reports.

3.1 BACKGROUND

Apart from the observations each of us makes personally, the source of all our information is other people. But our personal communications with others are limited by time and space. Historically, access to information was greatly expanded by books, especially beginning with the invention of printing in the midfifteenth century.[1] The twentieth century witnessed a revolutionary transformation in access to information as a result of the development of mass media. Newspapers and mass circulation magazines were the first, and they continue to be an important element. Think of the thousands of newspapers and hundreds of specialty magazines now available and in worldwide circulation. Radio was the next development, followed by film. Then television emerged, and was extended by the video camera and worldwide satellite transmission. Private communication has been dramatically enhanced too by national and international computer networks, but we will deal only with mass public information communication in this chapter.

These media of mass communication have transformed the information available to us in several ways. One is the speed of transmission. Today, with live television, we can literally watch events while they unfold, albeit always through the selected vantagepoint of the camera and of the network of people who locate and direct it. Television, radio, and newspaper news reports inform us of events only hours, or in some cases just minutes, after they have occurred. Another transformation is the reach of information gathering. The idea that parts of the earth are inaccessible is no longer valid. At least some sorts of information are available instantaneously from anywhere on the planet. In a village, news travels fast, and there is no seclusion, which is why Marshall McLuhan dubbed the world created by the modern **mass communications media** the "global village."

A third transformation is the quantity of information available and a fourth is the information-receiving literacy of the world's population. Both are also functions of mass education, which in turn is both a cause and an effect of economic mass production and mass consumption.

Connections between mass media and our economic system of industrial capitalism are worth noting. (1) Dissemination of certain kinds of information is essential to liberal democracy—the political system which protects and fosters capitalism. (Capitalism is the economic system in which individuals and groups own and exploit for private profit the production, distribution, and exchange of goods and services in the society as a whole.) Hence mass media are recognized as essential to liberal democracies. Freedom of the press is enshrined in the American Constitution (the First Amendment) for example. (2) At the same time that they provide for the transmission of information, the privately owned mass media are sources of substantial profits for their owners. They are also essential means of mass market advertising for producers of goods and services, and so for the profits of those owners as well. Mass media are thus undoubtedly necessary in several ways to the growth and maintenance of our contemporary consumption-oriented economy.

The twofold function of mass media—economic and political—helps shape their nature. The population genuinely needs and wants information of many sorts; the media supply it and at the same time influence the population to want it and to want to consume the economy's goods and services. The political function of the mass media is in turn twofold. In addition to supplying the information necessary to sustain democratic citizenship, the mass media explicitly and self-consciously play the role of defenders of the politico-economic system. No sinister government pressure is involved. The various organs of mass communication are themselves mostly privately owned, and the owners have an interest in maintaining the system. In addition, the mass of people in the society, including the journalists who run the news media, believe in the system, want to maintain it, and welcome the deliberate use of the media to reinforce acceptance of the basic values of the society. Thus the Western media, while "free" in important respects (in spite of occasional government pressures and attempts by interest groups to manipulate them), tend not to be independent or objective when it comes to the ideology of industrial capitalism and the consumer society.

We mention these economic and political roles of the media because they influence what information reaches us—and what does not—and the form in which it reaches us. In trying to obtain accurate and complete information, it is necessary to take into account how the medium affects the message. We get into some of the specifics shortly.

In what follows we focus on ways the mass media shape and color the information they transmit. Our aim is to provide an account that can be used to help you to screen or monitor information conveyed via the mass media, so that you may receive and record it with the appropriate qualifications. Our comments cover two topics: (1) how the mode of presentation itself can affect the information transmitted and (2) the content of the information conveyed.

3.2 MODE OF PRESENTATION

Symbolism

One way the media affect the information they transmit is by the manipulating symbols, or **symbolism**. What we mean is best explained concretely.

> **Example 1:** When the newspaper puts one news report across the top of the front page, under a 2-inch headline, and gives it 40 column inches of type (carrying over to an inside page) accompanied by pictures, and puts another story at the bottom of the inside back page of the third section and gives it a ¼-inch headline and 2 column inches of type, the symbolic message is that the events reported in the first story are acutely important, and those in the second story have the most minor importance.
> **Example 2:** When Sam Donaldson, standing in front of the White House in Washington, reports on the president's activities (ABC, "World News Tonight"), that backdrop lends the authority of what it symbolizes—the office of the president of the United States—to Donaldson's report. The symbolic message is that his report is as authoritative and credible as the venerable institution in the background.

What has happened is that the forms of the media—space in the first case and filmed image in the second—work as symbols which, because of their independent meanings for us, color the information transmitted. The way symbolism functions in each medium to affect the information it conveys is a topic worthy of in-depth study—beyond our competence as well as the space available to pursue it here. We mention it because (1) we think it is an influential factor in mass media, not to be overlooked and (2) we think you can watch for examples of it, or study the phenomenon in the depth it deserves.

> **Experiment:** Examine the front page of today's paper, watch the local TV news and watch the national TV news. Find at least one example of symbolic effects of the following: (1) photos in newspapers; (2) juxtaposition of reports in newspaper, radio or TV news; (3) appearance of TV journalists (clothing, hair, age, sex, race); (4) the phenomenon of the "anchorperson" on TV news; (5) voice quality of radio news readers, and (6) the order of radio or TV news lineup.

News Reports as "Stories"

Journalists refer to news reports as "stories." It's not that they are fictions, but they are of necessity crafted by the reporter, who has to organize and present a coherent account out of a plethora of details connected with the events being reported. An honest and conscientious reporter is constrained by the actual events being covered. But which details are selected for mention, how they are described, and the way the presentation is organized are, *unavoidably*, choices made by the reporter (alone or together with an editor or producer). Of all the hundreds of details available about even the most mundane event, the reporter must decide which are "relevant." Is the race of someone arrested for a crime relevant? What about the person's religion, age, occupation, family status, health, education, physical description, place of residence, sexual orientation, political affiliation, employment record, clothing worn when arrested, . . . ? The answer of course is that "it all depends," for relevance is always relative to a point of view or purpose. So even the most mundane news report must presuppose an orientation—assumptions about what is important and significant in general.

The receiver of news media information can consider whether the selection, description, and organization of the news report are likely to misrepresent the events reported, or whether they include or exclude information that is relevant from the receiver's point of view. We will say more about selection shortly, but first a few points about description and organization.

Descriptions

Here are the lead paragraphs from two front-page stories in Toronto *The Globe and Mail*, July 10, 1989, followed by our comments about each.

Example 1: As the Palestinian uprising against Israeli rule in the occupied territories entered its 20th month yesterday, the government issued an urgent plea for calm among Israelis in the face of attacks.

Comment: (1) An "uprising" is usually a single organized revolt. Were the stone-throwing, shootings, and bombings against Israeli targets coordinated? Was there a single mastermind behind them? (2) "Rule in the occupied territories" carries a more benign association than, say, "military dictatorship in the illegally occupied Palestinian homeland." (3) The phrase, "plea for calm among Israelis in the face of attacks" suggests a reasonable stance in the face of unwarranted provocation: one is "attacked" by an aggressor. Should Israel be considered the aggressor, not the Palestinians of the West Bank?

We don't raise these questions to suggest that a pro-Palestinian word choice would be preferable or even that a more neutral one is possible (though it might be). Our point is rather to show that the choice of words in the paragraph represents one point of view, and a contested point of view at that. The reader who does not notice how the word choice conveys a point of view, and who treats the report as conveying neutral information, has misread—and been taken in by—the description. By the way, we doubt that the Israeli point of view in the preceding description was intentional, but whether it was or not is immaterial to the reader who fails to notice it.

Example 2: Moving swiftly to rescue an Argentina he described as ruined, President Carlos Menem prepared yesterday to impose sweeping measures designed to bring order to the country's chaotic economy.

Comment: (1) Describing President Menem's measures as a "rescue" and reporting his description of Argentina as "ruined" gives a dramatic interpretation to the Menem's action. It conjures up a commando attack to save kidnapped hostages, or other heroic actions. (2) Saying the measures are "designed to bring order to the country's chaos" also conjures up the dramatic Promethean myth of a god saving the human race from destruction. The two phrases, *via* such associations, attribute a lot of power to Menem and, incidentally set us up to regard any failure of his economic reforms as a failure of major significance.

An alternative possible rendering would be to regard President Menem as taking some steps among many that are possible, hoping to improve Argentina's economic performance in a difficult situation not likely to be amenable to dramatic transformations. Which of the two gives a more accurate picture? That cannot be decided without a lot more information. Our point is only that language selection portrays the events in a certain light and that responsible information collection requires noticing and taking account of how it does so in this and other cases.

These examples come from the newspaper. But television and radio news reports also use language and so must choose descriptions to use. The news broadcast listener can, by paying close attention, note how words or expressions convey one among alternative possible interpretations of the events reported.

Quotations and Visuals

A form of selection that gives a particular cast or interpretation to print, radio, and TV news reports is the choice of quotations taken from interviews, and in the case of television news, the choice of visual material—visuals—used.

Politicians and others who want media attention have learned to try to give their interviews in 15- or 30-second **clips** which cannot intelligibly be cut up and are self-contained replies to the questions. They do this to avoid having what they say edited—thereby trying to control the message sent. In spite of their efforts, most quotations can be, and are, edited to even shorter segments. The listener or watcher can only speculate about what else the person interviewed said, such as added qualifications or remarks that put the quoted segments in quite a different context, and whether these might have changed the meaning or been otherwise significant.

In the case of television, we have not just the interviews to consider, but all the visual material as well. "Live" visuals are almost always taped and edited (untaped interviews from the floor of a national political convention during continuous coverage would be an exception). Other visual images, such as file footage, and exterior and interior backgrounds, are carefully selected, to try to convey accurately the "story" they are reporting. Ordinarily the selections are made by the news producers; however, political campaign organizers select the sites and timing for press access to their candidates ("photo opportunities") in an effort to control the impressions conveyed to the viewer by the symbolism of the context.

The importance of visuals in information broadcasting is enormous. Like it or not, one gets a powerful impression from the visual image. Think of how forceful, competent, and likable General Schwartzkopf was on TV press briefings during the Persian Gulf war in January 1991. His "image" lent the U.S.-led coalition's military actions both credibility and legitimacy.

Images that symbolize for us powerful forces in the culture and in our psyches will bring that power to the information they are connected with on the TV screen. Science and technology, for instance, have immense, almost sacred, authority in our world views. We see science as giving us power over the terrifying unknown which is nature, and we see technology as giving us the means of exercising that control in specific concrete ways. So when news footage shows a laboratory, or a rocket, or a robot, the images evoke the feelings associated with what they symbolize. (Advertisers take advantage of this fact by dressing up actors in lab coats or having them wear stethoscopes in commercials.) Other symbols: the setting or the rising sun, children at play, pets, old people, the flag, nature, the sea—the list goes on and on.

The imagery of visuals isn't necessarily false or misleading, but it can be.

The hard thing to do is to block or counter the effects of the images that risk distorting the information we receive. We have no formula to offer, magic or otherwise; what we suggest is self-awareness and self-examination. "I find I'm really being convinced by this person; why?" "I'm feeling hostile toward that person and find myself tending to discredit what she says; why?" "I'm feeling really good (or bad) about these events; why?" Sometimes you will discover that the sorts of considerations that should justify your attitudes are nowhere in evidence, which suggests that some other aspects of the media presentations may be playing a role in influencing them.

Experiment: Watch one of the national television news programs, paying particular attention to the visuals accompanying each story. Try to think of other camera angles, or subject matter, that could have been used. Think about how you might have been responding, unconsciously, to those visuals had you not been deliberately noticing them.

Perhaps the main inference to draw from the fact that news reports are (necessarily) stories is that it is always possible to tell a different story using the same people and events and casting them in a different light. Having imagined other possibilities, one is then in a position to wonder whether there is one in particular that is more plausible, more consistent with everything else that is known, than the others. The choice is absent if you assume that the only possible version is the one conveyed by the particular presentation of one media report.

Experiment: Attend a meeting of City Council and immediately write a report of it. Then watch the television news report later that night, and read the newspaper's report next day. Note how the three reports are different.

Headlines

The title of any newspaper story set in larger type at the top of the columns containing the report is called the **headline**. Its function is normally twofold: to inform the reader about the report's contents and to interest the reader in the story. As a rule, a headline is not written by the reporter who prepares the story. The editor or headline writer who composes the headline—usually shortly before the newspaper goes to press—has only a few minutes to scan the story to get an idea of its contents and then compose a headline that will fit a preassigned space and type size. As a result, sometimes headlines are inaccurate, and sometimes they are misleading.

A headline also predisposes us to interpret what we read in terms of the slant or angle it gives to the story. It is hard to avoid coming away from a story with the impression of the events reported that is conveyed by the headline, even when a careful independent reading shows it to be a false or misleading.

Experiment: Look through today's paper for headlines that give a misleading angle to the story. Give your reasons for claiming the angle is misleading. Try writing a headline to replace the misleading one. Make it accurate and catchy, and the same number of letters; and give yourself five minutes to do it after reading the story (good luck!).

Lead

The opening couple of paragraphs of a news story are called the **lead** (pronounced "leed"). In the traditional news story, the lead is a short paragraph (two sentences, for example) that attempts to sum up the most important facts or ideas in the story in an attention-getting way, and it usually communicates the angle or slant of the story. Like the headline, it predisposes us to interpret the rest of what we read in terms of that angle or slant. Unlike the headline, the lead is usually written by the reporter or copywriter who has put the story together, so that it seldom turns out to be simply false in light of the rest of the story. However, the lead needs to be an attention-grabber, and typically it reflects the value system and perspective of the news gatherers. A critical reader will scrutinize the lead and decide whether the slant it takes is a misleading one.

3.3 CONTENT OF THE INFORMATION

Any news report provides an interpretation of the events reported. How accurate is that interpretation likely to be? Providing an accurate picture, it should be clear, cannot be just a matter of being "true to the facts," for as we have seen it is possible for quite different stories to be equally consistent with the same set of bare facts.

News reports occasionally do get the "bare facts" wrong. A report says "over 30" people died in a train derailment when it turns out that 21 people were killed. But two points apply here. First, even this invented example is unfair. Usually the news story will say, "early reports state than over 30 people were killed"—which is accurate and which also informs the reader that (1) this is an estimate and (2) it is not based on access to complete information. Second, getting details such as numbers or spellings of names right is usually not a significant factor in getting "the story" right. Not that such inaccuracy should be tolerated. But our understanding of an event is usually not altered by changes in minor details. What is more important is learning why the event occurred, and whether its occurrence is indicative of larger economic, social, and political developments. The adequacy of the picture conveyed by a news report is much more likely to be jeopardized by factors other than incorrect facts.

Incompleteness

We think the most important cause of news inadequacy is what is *left out*. There are two importantly distinct kinds of omission responsible for inadequate or misleading news stories. One, **topical incompleteness**, is the omission of details the reader needs to acquire an adequate understanding of the reported events. The other, **systematic incompleteness**, is the omission of whole classes of information that are needed to acquire an adequate understanding of our world.

Topical Incompleteness

Missing balance. A report lacks **balance** when, although it concerns a *dispute* between two or more parties, it doesn't present the views of all parties to the dispute. Case 1a: The news reports the announcement of a new government policy, but no report of the minority side's views. Case 1b: The company's comments on a strike are reported, but no reaction from the union is provided (or vice versa). These are cases where understanding the significance of the events requires hearing the opinions of all the interested parties, but some are left out.

Why they are left out doesn't matter. The effect is the same whether the reporter was lazy or biased, or the union refused to return the reporter's calls, or the paper had to go to press before a minority spokesperson could be contacted. Sometimes lack of balance is due to poor reporting; sometimes the report is unbalanced due to no fault of the reporter or the news organization.

Limited sources. News reports frequently rely on one or two **sources** for their facts, often sources whose competence and/or impartiality is unclear or dubious. In the rush to meet deadlines and to fill air time or news columns, reporters and editors take extensive advantage of press conferences, interviews with politicians or administrators, statements by special interest spokespersons, reports issued by government agencies or by research groups, and (especially at the local news level) police reports and "news releases" (publicity material generated and delivered to the media by private and public interest groups). Even where there is no particular dispute at issue, this reliance on a limited diet of sources can result in an unbalanced or incomplete picture that represents only the world-view or values of the source(s) used.

Missing background. Case 2: A long newspaper report in 1990 tells the story of the killing of 39 people in a jungle village at a remote location in the Philippines. According to the report, the New People's Army guerrillas were responsible, and the victims were mostly unarmed women and children. There appears to have been some sort of feud between that particular group of guerrillas and those particular villagers. The reader's problem is that without both extensive background knowledge of the Philippine guerrilla war that has been going on for years, and extensive knowledge of the characteristics of the people and of recent events in this area, there is just no hope of gaining anything like an adequate understanding of this event. In this case, understanding the event requires extensive background knowledge that even a long newspaper report cannot provide. One is left with a chunk of more or less useless information—and possibly the illusion of being more "informed."

Missing Connections. Case 3: A story about a Commonwealth commission report on the effect of economic sanctions on South Africa informed readers that the report claimed sanctions had already cost South Africa billions of dollars and also that effective new sanctions would create more jobs for black workers there. The story went on to give some background about sanctions, the commission and its report. So far so good. But someone who had not been following the debate about whether economic sanctions were a good way of pressuring South Africa to end apartheid would not have appreciated the special significance of the second claim made in the story—that new sanctions would create more jobs for black workers in South Africa. Happily, in this case the news story provided an explanation. One of the key arguments used by the opponents of sanctions, the story explained, was that they are most damaging to the black population—the very population they are intended to help. So, if the Commonwealth commission report was correct, that objection to sanctions was undermined. Most of us will appreciate the significance of the commission's claim only if the connection between that claim and the arguments against sanctions is explained.

All too often news stories contain only reports of events, or politician's assertions, without setting them in their social and political contexts. The press has recognized this defect, yet has had the legitimate worry that "explanations" must consist of interpretations which will reflect a point of view, often a controversial one. One solution has been to introduce columns labelled "Analysis," which are designed to make needed connections while serving notice that the explanations may be colored by the author's point of view. That's a help, but for the majority of news reports the reader is left to supply his or her own analysis of the connections which give the events reported their significance— or else the analysis is built into the way the story is reported, but without being labeled as such.

Systematic Incompleteness

Some media critics[2] argue persuasively that besides omitting information needed to make sense of news reports and so to assess how credible they are, the mass media in any society systematically block out information that is incompatible with the fundamental values and operating assumptions of the society. What occurs, say these critics, is sometimes deliberate censorship, but more often unconscious self-censorship, of information that would tend to undercut the established order of power and authority in the society.

If this claim is true, it is much more difficult for us citizens to be aware when such information is left out of news reports than it is for us to recognize topical incompleteness. Presumably most of us share the very values and assumptions at issue. And even if we did not, how would we know when to suspect the omission of information incompatible with them?

That question does have an answer of sorts. We would expect the suppression of this deeply discordant information particularly when there are strains on the system. For example, if a country is at war, or sees itself locked in an ideological struggle with an adversary, one would expect it to be particularly intolerant of conflicting information. A concrete example is the failure of the U.S. news media to report—many years after it was known to knowledgeable observers—that President Ortega of Nicaragua was not running a Soviet beachhead in Central America or that President Noriega of Panama was a cruel violator of civil rights, active in the cocaine trade. During the actual fighting, opposition to the 1991 Persian Gulf war was scarcely mentioned, though it had been reported before the U.S.-led forces went on the attack, and criticisms of the military strategy have been reported since the Iraqi capitulation.

So two rules of thumb are (1) suspect the objectivity of media reports that are hostile to ideological foes or friendly to ideological allies, especially in times of active hostilities, and (2) in such circumstances, expect that there are legitimate critical points of view which are not being reported.

A third rule, while not practical in the short run could be useful over the long term. It is (3) get acquainted with the fundamental assumptions and values of your society, and with the standard objections to them. From the perspective of such understanding it should be easier to know where to suspect or look for systematic self-serving omissions.

Experiments: (1) Explain why most newspapers have a "Business" section but not "Labor" section, or why Europe, the Middle East, and the Pacific Rim countries are reported in most U.S. newspapers, but South America, Africa, and India and the Far East (with the exception of Japan and the Philippines) are rarely in the news. (And why are Japan and the Philippines exceptions?) (2) Some have claimed that news reports about China were generally sympathetic or favorable before and during the student "democracy" occupation of Tiananmen Square and have been universally unsympathetic or hostile since the student demonstration was suppressed. Identify the ideological values that might lie behind such a shift.

Fragmentation

The accuracy of the picture of the world we obtain from news reports is subject to another major systematic limitation. News coverage is almost universally a collection of short, unrelated snippets of information. The information in a half-hour (actually, 20-minute) television news broadcast, where most people obtain their "news," would fit on a couple of pages of most newspapers. Most newspapers are 40–60% advertising and contain only a few dozen news reports. Radio news is no better. Admittedly a single day's coverage should not be the measure, but even if we constructed our knowledge of the world from a steady diet of the mass news media, it would have huge gaps and in many areas little substance—yet that is where most people do get most of their information about the world beyond their immediate personal acquaintance.

As we know from our own lives, daily events are meaningful only in a context—in relation to a history, a complex meaning system and a dense institutional and cultural framework. (To give just one example, in a fascinating study, *The Rituals of Dinner*, Margaret Visser needs over 400 pages to explain "the origins, evolution, eccentricities and meaning of table manners"—why we eat with knives, forks, and spoons—or chopsticks—for example.[3]) Yet it is largely on the basis of the picture of our society's history, institutions, and culture which we get from media reports that we must make sense of our lives. Thus we face the uphill struggle of having to piece together the context-thin fragments of information supplied by the news media into a picture of the world in order to have the background we need to make sense of our own experience.

It seems clear that the news media cannot rectify their own deficiencies in this respect without totally changing the way they operate, which is unlikely to happen. In order to be responsible custodians of our own belief systems, we must take independent action. We need to expose ourselves continuously to a variety of information sources, including news magazines (available on television and radio as well as in print), current affairs journals, and readings in anthropology, political science, sociology, and history. Only against such a deep, rich background can we make full use of the news media's snippets of information.

Bias

Some people think the news media are biased, even unavoidably so, and they see this as a fatal detraction from media credibility. According to one version of this view, since everyone is biased, the media can be no exception, so their bias must taint all their reports.

But what is **bias**? In fact there are at least the following two notions of bias in circulation, and they tend to get confused. In one sense, being biased is having a point of view or a perspective. Every one of us is necessarily biased in that sense. Each of us sees the world from a personal, social, and historical vantage point, different in varying degrees from that of everyone else. So far as its effect on news reports go, the relevant question is whether a reporter's bias in this sense precludes an accurate or informative news report. In most cases, we suggest, it does not. Events occur, statements are made, and the personal perspective of a reporter does not prevent him or her from describing or reporting these accurately.

When it comes to interpreting the significance of events, and to judging them, then of course the analyst's personal perspective will come into play. But at that point the analyst presents the evidence or reasons supporting his or her interpretation, and we may then judge their adequacy for ourselves. When reportage and analysis are mixed together—as they so often are, especially on television news—then it behooves us as viewers to learn the personal points of view of the various reporters, anchorpersons, and networks and to filter their reports through that understanding.

Bias in this first sense—having a perspective—is unavoidable, but it can be compensated for by the critical news consumer. There's a second sense of bias in use, however. In its terms someone is biased, or has a bias, when they have a special interest in an issue such as something personal to gain—perhaps a grievance to settle or a benefit to secure—*which may be expected to cause them deliberately to be misleadingly selective in representing their point of view*. In this sense, for example, Democrats and Republicans tend to be biased about political issues, or developers tend to be biased about the benefits of office towers and housing developments. The point is not that people who are biased in this second sense will lie (though they might), but rather that they will tend to play up their own point of view and downplay any that disagree, because they have a lot to gain from having their point of view win out.

Are the news media biased in this second sense? Perhaps occasionally, but we know of no evidence which shows they are systematically, or even usually, guilty of deliberately misrepresenting the events they report in order to benefit some person or group.[4]

So while we agree that the press is (unavoidably) biased in the sense that reporters, editors, newspapers, and networks have points of view which can shape their selection and analysis of events covered, we don't agree that this causes them to distort or falsify their reports. We don't agree that the press is systematically biased in the sense that its practice is to use news reports deliberately to benefit one or another special interest group—such as advertisers or a political party.

> **Experiment:** Design a test for the Pinto-Blair theses just stated. What kinds of evidence would refute their claims about bias in the news media? What evidence would tend to confirm their theses? Study the media for signs of such evidence.

3.4 TELEVISION NEWS

Everything we have said so far applies to television news no less than to newspapers or radio news broadcasts. However, TV's visual dimension and extremely restricted time limitation add some distinctive features. There is a big literature on TV news which you really should dip into;[5] we can't begin to do justice to the subject. We'll settle for a few salient points.

Many of our own students believe that TV news is unique in that only there can we the viewers actually judge for ourselves the events reported because we can see them occurring with our own eyes, without having to trust the interpretations or deal with the biased language of reporters.

This faith in TV news overlooks two things. First, at any given moment the eye of the television camera picks out and focuses on one aspect of one event, and almost always physical action. Unlike our eyes, it does not constantly scan the whole scene. But like our eyes what it sees is restricted to where it is located; even two or three cameras in different locations cannot record everything. So the first point is that the eye of the camera is highly selective—and it usually selects action, or in general what is considered visually interesting. What we see is what it sees, but only what people making decisions point it at, and only from its vantage point. The television camera takes us out across the world, but it brings us, visually, only the world as seen through its tiny, journalistically aimed beam.

Second, each television news story is a carefully crafted dramatic narrative episode—and that is especially true for national network news. In a memorandum to his staff at NBC "Evening News", Reuven Frank once wrote:

> . . . every news story should have structure and conflict, problem and denouement, rising action and falling action, a beginning, a middle and an end.[6]

Such a policy, which is practiced by all the networks, has the result, as Edward Jay Epstein has pointed out, that in TV news reports events will not be conveyed in the order in which they occurred, with all the details intact, in a disorganized way.[7] Instead, a **story line** is prepared for each report, and the video material is edited to fit that story line. Moreover, there naturally develop a set of formulas for story lines, and these are learned by reporters who then seek out material for events they are covering that can be used within one or another of these formulas.[8]

In short, each television news story is a dramatic construct. Its brief amount of video material (usually snippets of less than a minute and rarely more than 2 or 3 minutes long) will be selected both from all the actual material shot and from all the possible material that could have been shot but wasn't. And that video material itself will be presented in a structured way—according to a predetermined story line that will give it its meaning for us.

In the best of circumstances, such a TV news story will give us a plausible and defensible interpretation of the events reported. Video and reports from different sources will give us a well-filled-in and balanced understanding of an event. But the idea that we can judge those events for ourselves because we can "see for ourselves what is happening" is obviously based on a lack of understanding of how TV news stories are put together.

3.5 A MEDIA CHECKLIST

To establish a measure of independence from the media's outlook, and to evaluate the information the media provide, one has to become a viewer, listener, or reader who actively engages the news while watching, listening to, or reading it. Here is a checklist with some of the main questions an active, critical media consumer will ask and try to answer.

FOR ALL NEWS MEDIA

Headline   Is the headline's or summary's angle justified by the events reported in the story?

Lead   Are there more important aspects of the story than the one(s) featured in the reporter's opening paragraphs or the anchor's introduction?

Language   Would alternative descriptions or word choice cast the events reported in a different light?

Balance   Are the views of different parties to a dispute reported equally and adequately?

Sources   Does the story rely heavily on one or two sources? If so, do those sources have an interest in how the story is presented? Do they represent a restricted point of view? In general, do the sources seem credible (see Chapter 2)?

Background   Is enough background supplied to permit you to understand the events and their significance?

Assumption   What assumptions about what is important underlie the decision to report these events. What assumptions underlie the way that the events are reported? Is there any reason to question those assumptions?

Bias   Is there evidence in the way the story is written that the reporter is promoting a partisan viewpoint on a controversial issue as if it were the objective truth?

ESPECIALLY FOR TELEVISION NEWS AND TV NEWS MAGAZINES

Visuals   Does the film used have an impact that is justified by the message of the voice-over or the "talking head"? Is either justified?

Drama   What is the story line—the "plot outline" conveyed by the packaging of the report? What is the "predicament" and how is it "resolved"? Is there a hero or a villain? Is there a "moral" to the story? Is this story presented as an episode in a larger drama? Is either the dramatic structure or the larger dramatic context controversial or questionable?

3.6 CONCLUSION

Few college-age people read the news columns of the newspaper regularly; relatively few listen to radio news broadcasts or watch television news regularly. Yet most of their information about current events in the world around them in fact comes from the news media—if not directly through their own observation, then indirectly through the even less reliable reports of other people. It is our view that the news media can be used as sources of information about current events, provided that how they function and their attendant limitations are understood and kept in mind.

But even more important than being aware of the how the media function, and what their limitations are, is developing alternate and supplemental sources of information. Only exposure to such other sources will enable us to develop a solid perspective on the information provided in the media. Among such additional sources of information are

- Weekly news magazines, both print and electronic (which sometimes treat stories in slightly more depth)
- Newspapers and periodicals representing more specialized points of view, for example, of the labor movement, of political parties other than the two major parties, of special interest groups (consumer magazines, *The Wall Street Journal*), of aboriginal peoples, of regional interests, trade periodicals and so on
- Scholarly and serious journals (such as *Public Affairs*)
- History books and scholarly monographs
- College courses and textbooks

Of course, such alternate sources of information have their own strengths and weaknesses, and you need to learn something of what those strengths and weaknesses are to use them intelligently. But they provide an essential counter-balance to what is found in the popular news media.

3.7 SUMMARY

In this chapter we have discussed the mass media as sources of information about our world. The speed of their transmission, the quantity and reach of their information, and their influence are unprecedented, not surprisingly, since they are products of and contributors to modern industrial capitalist social, economic, and political societies.

The way the mass news media present information and the limitations on the content they present impose major restrictions on the value of that infor-mation as grounds for inferences about the meaning of what is happening in the world. In addition to explicit news presentation, the media convey inter-pretations symbolically. Also, the media unavoidably cast news in the form of stories, and by their descriptions, quotes, visuals, and headlines these stories unavoidably give a particular angle or interpretation to the events reported. With respect to the content of information, accuracy of factual detail is not usually a major problem. Potentially more misleading is the incompleteness of news reports. You will regularly encounter topical incompleteness of balance, sources, background, and connections. In addition to such topical incompleteness, there will be a systematic omission of world views or values incompatible with the dominating outlook of the society. The fragmentation of the news—its lack of context—interferes with our need to form a coherent picture of our world and to find a coherent picture of our own lives within it. Bias in the sense of a perspective will be omnipresent, but bias as deliberately self-serving distortion is not a common practice. The selectivity of camera shots and the dramatic narrative structuring of TV news belie the impression that television is the exception where the viewer can simply "see for himself or herself" what occurs.

No ready solutions to the limits of information conveyed by mass media suggest themselves. Reading, watching, or listening to the news in an active, questioning way will serve to give us some measure of an independent vantage point. Combine that with a regular exposure to a variety of media, including in-depth analyses, and a grasp of the history and values of one's society, and you can end up with a more or less coherent and meaningful understanding of current events and how they affect us.

3.8 SOME REFERENCES

If you want to read further about the media, here are just a few of the many worthwhile books on the subject.

DAVID L. ALTHEIDE and ROBERT P. SNOW, *Media Logic*. Beverly Hills, CA: Sage, 1979.
NOAM CHOMSKY and EDWARD S. HERMAN, *Manufacturing Consent*. New York: Pantheon Books, 1988.
EDWIN DIAMOND, *Good News, Bad News*. Cambridge, MA: MIT Press, 1978.
EDWARD JAY EPSTEIN, *News from Nowhere: Television and the News*. New York: Random House, 1973.
HERBERT JAY GANS, *Deciding What's News: A Study of CBS Evening News, NBC Nightly News, Newsweek and Time*. New York: Vintage, 1979.
MARSHALL MCLUHAN, *Understanding Media*. New York: McGraw-Hill, 1964.
NEIL POSTMAN, *Amusing Ourselves to Death: Public Discourse in the Age of Show Business*. New York: Penguin Books, 1985.

3.9 EXERCISES

Exercise 1

Write out an alternative word or short description for each term in the following list.

terrorist	rebels
skyrocket	refugee
massive	mishap
freedom fighter	prolife
chaotic	prochoice
warring parties	bloodbath

Exercise 2

The following is a selection of articles taken from newspapers in the United States and Canada. Write a brief critique of the article from the viewpoint of an active, critical media consumer. Use the concepts presented in Chapter 3. Try to emphasize major faults and shortcomings. Be sure to close with a summary in which you state an overall judgment of the article.

**1. The Canadian Press story reproduced here was printed in the spring 1988. Bowmanville is situated between Toronto and Kingston, Ontario, just off the freeway running between the two cities. It is 35 miles from downtown Toronto, and about 120 miles from Kingston.

Triplets' birth has mom flying

TORONTO (CP)—The mother of premature triplets was turned away from a city hospital and forced to fly to Kingston to give birth to her daughter and two sons.

Penney Sisnert, 26, of Bowmanville was in labor on New Year's Day when her doctor at Toronto East General Hospital said he didn't have enough equipment and staff to deliver the triplets.

It was ironic for Sisnert, who likely wouldn't have been pregnant at all if it hadn't been for the hospital's embryo-implant program which involves removing an egg for fertilization outside the womb.

If things weren't bad enough, there wasn't enough room in the government Learjet for Sisnert's husband to join her on the 20-minute trip to Kingston.

Wayne Sisnert, 33, a foreman at a container factory, had to make the 255-km trip by car.

By 9 p.m. Saturday, doctors in Kingston had delivered the triplets—six weeks premature.

"I'm scared of flying," Sisnert, 26, said from her bed at Kingston General Hospital on Sunday. "So on top of the fact that I was going into labor, I was going to fly and my husband wasn't going to be there. I was in a real nice state."

Dr. Robert Hall, who took over her care while her regular doctor was on vacation, phoned hospitals across Toronto and in Ottawa, London and Kingston before finding one where Sisnert could be admitted.

"It's just disgusting as far as I'm concerned— nobody should be put through this," said Wayne.

Ken Keyes, parliamentary assistant to Health Minister Elinor Caplan, said Sunday that the ministry will look into the incident today and decide whether to take any action.

The babies, Chelsea, Jonathan and William, weigh from 680 grams to 1,219 grams, and each needs to breathe oxygen through a respirator for part of the day.

Doctors at Kingston General Hospital want them to stay there for up to 10 weeks, said Penney.

"So now I have worry about finding accommodation when I'm released. Wayne has to find accommodation and my family that comes to help me all have to find some place to stay," she said.

2. This story appeared in the *Detroit Free Press* on July 19, 1991.

Bush says he'll work to settle Cyprus issues

By Charles Green
Free Press Washington Staff

Athens, Greece—Kicking off a four-day visit to Greece and Turkey, President George Bush pledged on Thursday he would try to help the two countries end their long and bitter feud over Cyprus by year's end but admitted he had "no magic wand" to resolve the dispute.

Underscoring the intensity of feelings on the issue, 2,000 protesters massed in a city square while Bush was having dinner at the presidential palace, and smaller groups set fires and fought with police.

The bands of demonstrators, protesting Bush's visit and demanding U.S. action expelling Turkey from Cyprus, were repelled by police wielding clubs and firing tear gas.

In Washington, the State Department said it had indications that terrorists might try to target U.S. interests in Greece and Turkey during Bush's visit and it advised Americans traveling in the two countries to take extra precautions.

Bush, the first U.S. president to visit Greece since Dwight Eisenhower in 1959, is backing a United Nations attempt to arrange a peace conference on Cyprus, the Mediterranean island that has been partitioned between Greek and Turkish Cypriots since 1974.

"None of us should accept the status quo in Cyprus," Bush said in an address to the Greek Parliament. "And today I pledge that the United States will do whatever it can to help Greece, Turkey and the Cypriots settle the Cyprus problem, and do so this year."

Turkey invaded Cyprus in 1974 after the military junta then ruling Greece engineered a coup on the Mediterranean island. Since then, the island has been divided between Turkish Cypriots in the north and Greek Cypriots in the south. A UN peacekeeping force patrols a buffer zone of barbed wire, sandbags and mine fields.

At a news conference, Bush said he had no Cyprus plan of his own, but would try to use U.S. influence in the region to persuade the parties to sit down at a UN-sponsored conference.

"I don't want to suggest that the United States can wave a wand, a magic wand, and solve a problem that has plagued this part of the world for a long time," said Bush, "but we're going to try."

The Associated Press contributed to this report.

3. The following Associated Press story appeared in January 1991.

LOVEBIRDS ROCK JAILHOUSE

Steamy prison romances put coed programs on hold

Associated Press

BISMARCK, N.D.—Coeducational programs have been suspended at North Dakota State Penitentiary, where prison romances have gotten out of control, the security chief said.

"I assumed that we could create an atmosphere similar to society. Apparently, I was wrong," Security Chief Steve Scott said Wednesday.

In some ways, they did.

A 19-year-old prisoner, Karen Nowacki, is pregnant as a result of a kitchen tryst with Danny Bushaw, a 25-year-old prisoner, Scott said.

Scott said he found out about the pregnancy about two weeks ago, when Bushaw came to his office and asked whether he could give Nowacki

Continued

an engagement ring. He told Scott it was "the right thing to do."

"I asked him point blank, 'Is she pregnant?' and he hemmed and hawed and said, 'Yes, she might be pregnant,'" Scott said.

A blood test confirmed it.

Scott said men and women no longer will mingle at work assignments or during recreation time, religious activities and educational classes.

He said segregated but equal access to prison facilities is being set up, despite complaints from prisoners.

Coed activities began in 1987 as a result of pressure from the American Civil Liberties Union, which contended the prison—which houses 30 female inmates among 549 prisoners—was not providing equal programs for men and women, Scott said.

Last October, coed activities were suspended for two months. Scott said after they were reinstated in December, prisoners became obsessed with "sexual inappropriateness."

Prison sex, he said, "is very irresponsible," and prison romances don't succeed.

"Prison is not a place where you make major life-altering decisions like marriage, divorce, having children."

4. The following Associated Press story appeared in January 1985.

'Nearly wild' kids found in filthy bus

ST. JOSEPH, Mich. (AP)—An excrement-strewn bus where police found three shoeless, nearly savage children dressed in dirty rags was inspected last summer by welfare officials and cleared for limited migrant housing, authorities said.

The children, ages eight months, three and four years, were removed from the bus, examined and put in state custody after they were discovered locked inside the rusted-out vehicle with several dogs, state trooper Larry Krieger said.

THE CHILDREN'S parents, Donald and Eva Monk, were arraigned Monday on three counts of child abuse and neglect. Monk posted $1,000 bail and was released, but his wife remained in custody early today.

Social services workers told police the family was living in the bus last summer but that their living conditions apparently had worsened considerably since.

When the children were found Sunday in this southwestern area of Michigan, they were "dressed in dirty rags," state police Sgt. Larry Semas said. "They are nearly feral (wild) chil-dren with practically no communication skills and no knowledge of eating utensils."

THEIR PARENTS were away pruning fruit trees when the children were found, police said.

Semas said the bus was "full of human and animal fecal material generated (by the family) and their two dogs."

Wes Bowerman, a spokesman for the state Department of Social Services, said the bus, parked 500 metres (1,600 feet) off a road near abandoned shacks in the community of Berries Springs, had running water and that its windows were intact when it was inspected last summer.

There also was a toilet outside and the department declared the vehicle suitable for summertime migrant housing, Bowerman said.

"THE children were clean at the time, well dressed," Bowerman said.

But when people on a sleigh ride spotted a child's face in one of the bus windows Sunday, the bus windows were broken. It had electricity and a space heater, but the family had been using a can for a toilet, state police Sgt. James Uebler said.

Bowerman said Monk told the department he and his family had planned to drive the bus to Florida for the winter. In September, Bowerman said, workers confirmed with Monk that he was making preparations to leave before cold weather came.

KRIEGER said Monk told him he originally was from Florida and his wife was from Kentucky. Monk gave conflicting statements about his age, saying that he was 64 years old, born on Jan. 17, 1930.

Krieger said Monk appeared to be in his 30s, and his wife said she was 32.

Monk told Krieger he and his family lived in the bus because they did not want to accept welfare. Monk, who called himself a "self-taught reader," said he had lived in Berries County off and on for about 10 years, and worked in fruit orchards, Krieger said.

Preliminary examinations for the Monks have been set for Feb. 7. Each charge carries a maximum penalty of four years in prison and a $3,000 fine.

5. This story appeared in Toronto's *The Globe and Mail* on May 25, 1988.

Advice on treatment stirs cancer debate

By Lawrence Surtees
The Globe and Mail

NEW ORLEANS—Cancer specialists are debating a controversial recommendation from the U.S. National Cancer Institute that all breast cancer patients should have chemotherapy or hormone treatment after surgery, even if there is no evidence that the cancer has spread.

The NCI made its recommendation last week on the basis of three still unpublished studies.

The Institute also took the unusual step of alerting 13,000 cancer specialists about the findings and its own policy change through an electronic data base and a letter, rather than waiting several months for the data to be published in the New England Journal of Medicine.

The clinical alert reverses the policy of the cancer institute, part of the U.S. National Institutes of Health.

The NCI, based in Bethesda, Md., previously had said that there was no reason to administer drug therapy to women who had surgery for breast cancer if the cancer had not spread to the lymph nodes.

The institute changed its advice to doctors because of many studies throughout the world that show that at least 30 per cent of women with early-stage breast cancer who are treated with surgery or radiation alone develop other tumors later.

That finding led to trials to compare the rate of recurrence in women treated with surgery alone with that in women who underwent surgery plus chemotherapy.

"These studies indicate that women with early-stage breast cancer and their physicians should consider adjuvant (combined) chemotherapy, hormonal therapy or both following the primary treatment," Dr. Vincent DeVita, director of the NCI, said in the bulletin issued to doctors late last week.

But many cancer specialists say this may not be the best advice for all women.

Side effects of the powerful chemotherapy "cocktails" vary, but can include kidney failure, pain and severe discomfort, and depression of the immune system leading to dangerous infections.

The use of such therapy to prevent recurrence must be determined on an individual basis and should not be regarded yet as standard treatment for all women with breast cancer, Dr. B.J. Kennedy, president of the American Society of Clinical Oncology, said in an interview. More than 3,500 cancer specialists are attending the society's annual meeting here.

Dr. Kennedy argues that women who are unlikely to have a recurrence should not have to

Continued

suffer the side effects of unnecessary additional treatment.

More than 145,000 women in North America get breast cancer each year. One-third of these cancers are classed as estrogen-dependent, and can be treated with hormones or radiation after surgery.

Breast cancer is the most common cancer in Canadian women, accounting for 25 per cent of all cancers and 20 per cent of cancer deaths in Canada last year. The National Cancer Institute of Canada estimates there were 11,200 new cases of breast cancer in 1987 and 4,400 deaths from it last year.

Treatment varies and depends on whether the cancer has spread to other parts of the body or invaded the lymph system.

If the cancer is confined to the breast and is at an early stage, the recommended treatment until now has been a lumpectomy—surgical removal of the tumor itself. At later stages, the entire breast may be removed and the patient treated with hormones or chemotherapy.

However, only half of all patients with cancer confined to the breast are cured by surgery alone, the NCI says.

Two of the U.S. studies were directed by Dr. Bernard Fisher of the University of Pittsburgh as part of a large trial program at more than 150 medical centres in Canada and the United States. The third was run by the Eastern Cooperative Oncology Group and the Southwest Oncology Group, two hospital consortia.

It has taken the NCI and U.S. researchers three years to reach the conclusions a major European study reported in 1985. Two other European studies, one in Scotland and one in Italy, were published last year.

The studies all found that recurrences are fewer in women who have combined treatment than in those who have only surgery.

But they differed widely in the drugs used and the number of women found to benefit.

The Milan study reported that 91 per cent of women treated with surgery plus chemotherapy remained free of cancer for five years, compared with 47 per cent of women who had surgery alone.

A study published in the British medical journal Lancet in 1985 found only a slight increase in remissions: 83 per cent over three years for women treated with both methods, compared with 76 per cent in the group with just surgery.

Some critics also believe the follow-up periods in most of the studies, including the three U.S. studies of 3,500 women, are too short to reach proper conclusions.

Dr. William McGuire, chief of oncology and a breast cancer expert at the University of Texas Health Science Centre in San Antonio, said Dr. DeVito and the NCI have gone too far in issuing the new advice.

"I don't think we should meddle with many of these women and give them more debilitating treatment when we can't reliably determine which patients are most at risk of a recurrence and which patients will benefit," Dr. McGuire told reporters at a briefing on breast cancer advances yesterday.

But he also believes the data released by the NCI last week are too weak to support Dr. DeVito's dramatic advice.

"In one group of patients, only 5 per cent of patients received any extra benefit from the extra therapy and in another group with a different drug, only 9 per cent responded," Dr. McGuire said.

Among the three U.S. studies cited by Dr. DeVita, the best results were found among patients who were treated the most aggressively with three different drugs, in addition to surgery. About 16 per cent of the women in this group had a second tumor, compared with 33 per cent who did not have additional therapy and had a recurrence.

6. This story appeared in the *Detroit Free Press* on June 20, 1991.

Illicit drug sales top $40 billion

Spending on cocaine alone was $18 billion, study says

By Paul Anderson
Free Press Washington Staff

WASHINGTON—Americans spent more than $40 billion last year on illegal drugs, more than they spent on tobacco products and nearly what they spent on alcoholic beverages, according to a new estimate released Wednesday by drug czar Bob Martinez.

That includes about $18 billion on cocaine, $12 billion on heroin, $9 billion on marijuana and $2 billion on other drugs.

The total nearly matches the $46 billion the federal government spent on all criminal-justice programs last year.

"That's a hell of a lot of money," Martinez said, although he admitted the estimates—compiled by his staff and a consultant—are rough calculations based on earlier surveys of the number of drug users in the country, drug seizures and other factors.

The figures prove "this is no time to turn tail" in the war on drugs, Martinez said, despite surveys showing that casual drug use is declining and drug seizures are up.

The report estimates that drug purchases have declined over the last three years, from $51.6 billion in 1988 to $49.8 billion in 1989 to $40.4 billion in 1990.

But Rep. Charles Rangel, D-N.Y., chairman of the House select committee on narcotics, repeated his own estimate that Americans spend over $100 billion each year on drugs, saying Martinez's study misses the homeless and others.

Martinez told a conference of law-enforcement and drug-counseling leaders that he wants to emphasize more treatment and education—including targeting the use of alcohol and tobacco by children and teenagers as "substance abuse."

Martinez, the former governor of Florida who took over the Office of National Drug Control Policy three months ago, also vowed to step up U.S. pressure on foreign countries where drugs are produced.

He singled out Colombia, warning that "the American people are waiting to see" how the government there treats drug lord Pablo Escobar, whose surrender was reported Wednesday.

"Pablo Escobar is a symbol of all that is wrong with narco-trafficking . . . He heads up a major cartel with octopus tentacles worldwide," Martinez said.

Martinez and his aides admitted the estimates of American drug purchases are rough. Bruce Carnes, his planning and budget director, who oversaw the study, said it is based on "estimates of estimates."

Reaction to the report was mixed.

Rangel called the report "irrelevant and insignificant. It adds nothing to the policy discussions and debate over how we should slay the drug dragon."

However, those who advocate easing drug laws noted that this study drops earlier efforts to calculate the social costs of drug abuse, such as lost productivity on the job.

"It looks like this is the first report from the drug czar's office not based on hysteria and hype," said Arnold Trebach, president of the Drug Policy Foundation.

7. Here is a report (August 25, 1988) of a survey conducted in the spring of 1988 at the University of Windsor.

Image of pipe-puffing prof has substance at university

The stereotype of the pipe-smoking university professor was reinforced in a recent survey on smoking habits at the University of Windsor.

The survey found faculty members were five times more likely to smoke pipes or cigars than other members of the university staff.

About 6.7 per cent of teachers surveyed admitted to puffing pipes or smoking cigars, compared with 1.2 per cent of the staff, said university safety manager Keith Nelligan.

The survey was commissioned by the university's central safety committee which is preparing a smoking policy for recommendation to university administrators.

Nelligan said the committee will likely call for a partial ban because, of the 1,850 faculty, staff and students surveyed, a majority favored the creation of designated smoking areas, although 77.3 per cent of the respondents were non-smokers and ex-smokers.

The survey found 67 per cent wanted smoking limited to designated areas, 24 per cent wanted a total ban and 6.2 per cent wanted no controls.

Nelligan noted smoking appears to be on a decline. Younger respondents were less likely to be smokers, and if the apparent trend continues, there will be no smokers on campus by the year 2010.

Slightly more than 16.3 per cent of those surveyed said they smoked cigarettes; pipe and cigar smokers accounted for 2.3 per cent.

The committee will submit its recommendation to the university's president, Ron Ianni, and its board of governors.

8. This report appeared in *USA Today* on June 26, 1991.

Gay 'witch hunt' charged

Air Force conducts inquiry before discharge

By Debbie Howlett
USA Today

WASHINGTON—Air Force Capt. Greg Greeley says he was liberated by leading a parade Sunday down the streets of the capital during the city's annual Gay Pride Day festival.

But he won't feel truly free until today. "Then, I will feel like the last chains are gone."

Greeley was honorably discharged at 12:01 a.m. today, after creating a stir by leading the parade featuring shirtless women on motorcycles and men in high heels and tiaras.

"This is our day," he was quoted as saying. "We can come out in the daylight and not be in some dim bar."

But the Air Force reacted by halting Greeley's discharge for a day and beginning what he calls a "witch hunt."

National activists seized Greeley's case—and a leaked Army memo—to again object to a Pentagon policy that says "homosexuality is incompatible with military service."

The memo, a document in another gay rights case, calls the policy "a civil rights issue of discrimination" and recommends lifting the ban. An Army spokeswoman says the document was drafted 18 months ago but hasn't been approved.

"They're running out of excuses for keeping gay people out," says Robert Bray of the National Gay and Lesbian Task Force.

The Pentagon maintains there are no gays in the military. "If they are found out to be homosexual they are discharged, so technically they're aren't any," says Maj. Doug Hart, a spokesman.

Since 1980, the military has discharged more than 20,000 members, citing homosexuality, according to estimates.

During the final three months of 1990, the last quarter for which figures are available, 360 service members were discharged over homosexuality. Women are three times as likely as men to be dismissed for homosexuality, records show.

But the Air Force says it was following department procedures in Greeley's case.

"The Air Force took routine, precautionary measures of questioning him to ensure there was no breach of national security," says Maj. Kathi Blevins, a spokeswoman at Bolling Air Force Base.

"There are several reasons a person might be questioned for security purposes. Homosexuality happens to be one," Blevins says. Others: rape, theft, child molesting, wife swapping.

Greeley, 27, who attended Massachusetts Institute Technology on an Air Force scholarship, was a computer systems analyst at the Pentagon with a "high" security clearance.

He told investigators he was never blackmailed or compromised, and thinks the inquiry was meant to force him to disclose the names of gays in the military.

"I'm outraged that on the pretext I'm a security risk they would start a witch hunt. I refused to give them names."

Greeley says he'll go to work for a private, Washington-area computer firm.

And, he says, "I'll continue my involvement with the (gay) community."

Exercise 3

This exercise calls for some cooperation among students in the class. Divide into groups so that each group has among its members at least two people who have access to a television set hooked up to a VCR and some blank tapes.

(a) On a given day, tape the national evening news broadcasts of the major networks—CBS, ABC, NBC, and CNN.

(b) List the lineup of stories and the amount of time given to each story.

(c) Sometimes coverage of an event will consist of a package of several reports. Analyze these both individually and as a group.

(d) Compare the coverage of stories carried on more than one network with respect to (i) ranking (placement in the lineup, length, reporter, video, other), (ii) story line (angle and emphasis), and (iii) other. What hypotheses might explain their multiple network coverage?

(e) Examine the stories carried on only one network with respect to ranking and story line. What hypotheses might explain their multiple network coverage?

(f) For each story covered by more than one network, and in the light of comparisons made in (d), discuss the credibility of the information communicated in the reports.

(g) Were there any common denominators among the events reported or among the angles taken on those events? What events might have been covered that day but were not? What message about what is important or significant does national TV news project, based on the (unrepresentative) sample of this one day?

(h) With regard to the international news only, would someone from England, Australia, Nigeria, India, or Brazil likely share the U.S. editors' judgments about what should be covered and the way it was covered in tonight's network news broadcasts? If not, what follows?

Exercise 4

The idea of this project is to compare newspaper stories. Buy at least two daily newspapers for any given date. If you have two newspapers in your city, buy those two plus one out-of-town newspaper. If you have just one local newspaper, buy it plus one out-of-town paper. If you have no daily newspaper in your community, buy two newspapers circulated in your area.

(a) What stories are covered on the front page? What national and international events are reported that day elsewhere in the papers?

(b) Rank the national and international stories, respectively, in terms of the importance accorded them (placement, headline size, total number of column inches), group them by subject-matter (if that's possible), and identify the angle taken in the lead paragraphs of events covered in more than one newspaper.

(c) Itemize the similarities and differences among the newspapers you've examined in terms of topics covered, importance, subject-matter, and the angles of the leads.

(d) For each story covered by more than one paper, and in the light of comparisons made in (c), discuss the credibility of the information communicated in the reports.

Exercise 5

Half the class do Exercise 3 and half the class do Exercise 4, for a given day. (Compare the evening's network news broadcasts either with a newspaper published the same evening or one published the following morning.) Discuss the similarities and differences between television and newspaper news on the basis of this sample.

NOTES

1. We are speaking here of printing in Europe and European civilization. Printing had been invented independently earlier in China and Korea. (See *Columbia Encyclopedia*, 3rd ed. Columbia University Press, New York, 1963, Printing, p. 1723.)
2. Such as John McMurtry, "The Unspeakable: Understanding the System of Fallacy in the Media," *Informal Logic*, vol. 10, no. 3, 1988, and Noam Chomsky and Edward S. Herman, *Manufacturing Consent* (New York: Pantheon Books, 1988).
3. Margaret Visser, *The Rituals of Dinner*, (Toronto: HarperCollins, 1991).
4. The systematic incompleteness charged by such media critics as McMurtry and Chomsky would not be bias in this second sense, since they are not claiming that particular sources have a special interest in particular stories, nor are they alleging conscious or deliberate misrepresentation of the events reported.
5. See the references, Section 3.8.
6. Quoted in Edward Jay Epstein, *News from Nowhere, Television and the News* (New York: Random House, 1973), p. 153.
7. Ibid.
8. Ibid., pp. 53–54.

4

Inference

4.1 What Inferring Is

Reasoning and Inferring

By **inferring** we mean the act of drawing a conclusion (that is, arriving at a belief or other attitude) on the basis of information or opinions already in our possession. Inferring plays a central role in our reasoning.

We turn to reasoning when the answers to our questions are not directly available from memory or observation. But when we reason, we still have to base our conclusions on facts or beliefs that *are* presently available.

Take the example of Pat, who had just applied for a summer job, and then wondered whether his friend Cheryl would be applying for it too. Then he remembered that Cheryl had told him earlier that she was going to Europe for the summer. He concluded that Cheryl wouldn't be competing with him for the job.

Pat was able to draw the conclusion about what Cheryl would do partly because of his recollection of what she had told him about her plans. But that isn't all he needed for his inference. He could reasonably draw the conclusion he did only if, in addition, he assumed that Cheryl was telling the truth, that she had not changed her plans, and that she wouldn't apply for that job if she planned to go to Europe for the summer. What makes it reasonable to assume such things in most cases is one's knowledge of how humans—or at least people like Cheryl—generally behave. Pat's conclusion, then, was based on his beliefs about a number of different, though related, matters.

Consider a slightly different case. Jan's compact disk player has broken, and she wants to know whether it is still under warranty. She recollects clearly that it has a two-year warranty from the date of purchase, which was around two years ago, but she can't remember exactly when she bought it. She goes through the bottom draw of her desk and finds the bill of sale, which has the purchase date on it: two years ago and two weeks earlier than today's date. Jan is thus able to conclude that the warranty expired two weeks ago.

In both cases, Pat and Jan find answers to their question by drawing conclusions from other information. In the first case, the information Pat needed was already in his possession; he had only to consult his memory. In the second case, the information Jan needed had to be ferreted out another way.

It ought to be apparent from these examples that inferring is a central phenomenon in reasoning. It is the mental operation we perform to arrive at answers we are looking for.

A note about terminology. The act of inferring is also described as drawing or making "an inference." The noun 'inference' in that case denotes the mental process or operation of inferring. "He didn't divulge the secret to me; I made the inference from other information," is an example. But 'inference' is also used to refer to the result or product of such an operation, namely, the conclusion that is inferred. Thus someone might say, "Your inference is correct" when they mean "The conclusion you inferred from those facts was the correct conclusion to draw." In the first use, 'inference' denotes the mental process; in the second, it denotes the product of that process. Both uses are common. You will usually be able to tell from the context which one is intended.

Inferences and Propositions, Premisses, and Conclusions

The two examples just discussed typify the following three general features of inferring.

1. In these examples, Pat and Jan made up their minds about something they were in doubt about or had a question about. They came to have a belief, or a belief-like attitude (see p. 72), which they did not have before.
2. Both came to have this attitude toward a proposition. In the first example it was the proposition that Cheryl wouldn't be competing with Pat for the summer job he had applied for. In the second example, Jan came to believe the proposition that her compact disk player is no longer under warranty. In every inference there is a proposition toward which someone adopts an attitude, and that proposition constitutes the **conclusion** of the inference.
3. The conclusions were drawn based on things Pat and Jan knew, believed, or accepted. In the first example, Pat arrived at his conclusion from facts

about what Cheryl said, combined with assumptions about how people who say such things will behave. In the second example, Jan drew her conclusion from facts about the length of the compact disk player warranty and the date of its purchase. Thus in every inference there is, in addition to the conclusion, a **ground** or *basis* from which the conclusion is inferred.

The facts and assumptions that provided a basis or ground for Pat's and Jan's inferences did so just in so far as, and to the extent that, Pat and Jan believed or accepted them. Thus the basis for anyone's inference can be construed as consisting of one or more propositions which that person happens to believe or accept. In logic, it has been traditional to call the propositions which form the ground or basis of an inference the **premisses**—either of the inference or of the person drawing it.

When we call a proposition a conclusion or a premiss, we are referring to the role the proposition plays in an inference. One and the same proposition can be a premiss in one inference (playing the role of support) and a conclusion in another (being itself supported). One and the same proposition can be a conclusion in someone's reasoning today, and one of their premisses for another conclusion tomorrow.

Here is an example. Imagine that Ian's company in Chicago is sending him on a trip to Ecuador in February and he knows nothing at all about that country. It occurs to Ian, although he knows no Spanish, that "Ecuador" sounds like "equator," and he concludes that Ecuador is probably located at the equator. He reasons further that since countries near the equator are warm year-round (or so he believes), then probably Ecuador will be warm in February; so he should pack warm-weather clothes for his trip, even though it's freezing in Chicago. Ian's reasoning contains the following series of inferences.

First inference
Premiss: 1. "Ecuador" sounds like "equator."
Conclusion: 2. Ecuador is located at the equator.
Second inference
Premisses: 2. Ecuador is located at the equator.
                3. Countries on the equator are warm year-round.
Conclusion: 4. Ecuador will be warm in February.
Third inference
Premisses: 4. Ecuador will be warm in February.
                5. I should pack clothes appropriate to the climate I'll encounter in Ecuador.
Conclusion: 6. I should pack warm-weather clothes for my trip.

Writing out Ian's inferences in this way makes it clear how the conclusion of one inference can serve as a premiss of another, and so how inferences can be linked together in chains, connected by those common propositions. In Ian's reasoning, propositions 2 and 4 play this dual, and linking, role.

Beliefs and Belief-Like Attitudes

Believing a proposition is taking a certain attitude toward it—the attitude that it is true. We are not always so confident about propositions. Our attitude may be belief-like, but qualified. In fact there is a range of possible **belief-like attitudes** we can and do take toward propositions, from complete uncertainty at one end to total conviction at the other. Something of this variety can be conveyed by the following list of attitudes one might take toward a proposition:

- *Having no opinion about whether it is true* (You have no belief about the proposition whatsoever.)
- *Thinking it's possible that it is true*, without having any idea about how likely it is (You don't rule it out of consideration, but you're no more inclined to accept it than its opposite.)
- *Suspecting it's true* (You're not ready to make up your mind whether it's true, but you think it bears further investigation.)
- *Being inclined to believe* it is true without being very confident that it is (You'd rather not bet on whether it's true, but if you were forced to bet you'd bet it's true rather than false.)
- *Being quite confident* it is true, without being 100% sure (You're ready to act on the assumption that it's true, but you know there's a genuine chance it could turn out to be false.)
- *Being completely convinced* that it's true; unqualified belief (You don't think there's any real chance it could turn out to be false.)

These attitudes all belong to the same spectrum of attitudes in the respect that they are incompatible with one another—only one of them can be held or taken at a given time toward a given proposition. If you unqualifiedly believe a proposition, then your attitude toward it cannot be one of (merely) being inclined to believe it is true or of having no opinion as to its truth.

These belief-like attitudes are relevant to the study and practice of reasoning in the following way. Reasoning takes place when we have a question which we cannot immediately answer in a satisfactory way because we do not know what to believe about a matter that concerns us. We try to make up our mind about what our attitude should be toward the various propositions connected with the matter by drawing inferences from what we do believe. The upshot of our inferring *may* be that we come to be confident of the truth of one or more of those propositions. But it may instead be only that we come to take an attitude that falls short of belief. One measure of good inferring is that it culminates in an attitude toward a proposition that is *appropriate* in light of the evidence used. We return to this point at the end of this chapter and develop it more fully in Chapter 6.

The Bases of Inference: Beliefs, Assumptions, and Evidence

The bases of the inferences we actually make—the propositions that serve as their grounds—tend to be mixed. Some propositions we know for certain to be true, others we believe on reasonable grounds to be probably true, still others we happen to believe despite the fact that it is unreasonable for us to do so. As we will see shortly, a key factor in the correctness of any inference is the reasonableness or acceptability of its premises.

The grounds of inferences can be classified not only according to their reasonableness, but also with regard to the general role they play in our reasoning. Some of the premisses of a particular inference will consist of "foreground" information concerning the particulars of the issue at hand, while other premisses of the same inference will consist of "background" information of a general sort used to interpret the foreground information. This distinction was illustrated in Pat's inference about Cheryl: the foreground information consisted of Pat's knowledge of what Cheryl said about her plans, and the background information consisted in his beliefs about human behavior (or at least about Cheryl's behavior) that led him to assume that if Cheryl said she was going to Europe for the summer, then she would not apply for a summer job at home. Similarly, in Ian's second inference, his knowledge that equatorial countries are warm year-round was background information he used to link the premiss that Ecuador is located on the equator to his conclusion.

One term used for some kinds of inference grounds is borrowed from the language of law: **evidence**. A recent dictionary defines the legal concept of evidence as follows:

> something that furnishes proof: testimony, *specifically*: something legally submitted to a tribunal to ascertain the truth of a matter.[1]

A tribunal, judge or jury is presented with a body of information called evidence. They are expected to draw conclusions about what occurred and usually, in light of those inferences, about guilt or liability. To reach their conclusions, they must draw on what they know from common sense (for example, that a person cannot be in two places at the same time or that the prospect of obtaining large amounts of money with little effort can tempt people to break the law), and they must usually make other assumptions of various sorts about the case at hand (for example, that a witness is credible). Hence the basis of their inferences consists both of the evidence presented in court and also of the background knowledge, and assumptions, that they bring to bear on the case.

Another term used for some kinds of inference grounds is the term **as-sumption**. We tend to call a ground an assumption when either

1. We don't think that ground is something that is known (or known for sure) to be true
2. The ground is not explicit in the reasoning (an unconscious assumption that influences the conclusions we draw) or is not made explicit in the verbal expression of the reasoning (unexpressed or unstated premisses in an argument, for example)

You can no doubt identify assumptions Ian was making in order to draw the conclusions he did. For instance, in the first inference he seems to have assumed that if "ecuador" means "equator" in Spanish, then the country was called Ecuador because of its latitude. In his third inference he seemed to have assumed that it is sensible to pack clothes that suit the climate of the country you're traveling to. Both these are assumptions of the second kind—nonexplicit grounds of Ian's reasoning.

In the remainder of this book, we will frequently use the words 'evidence,' 'background knowledge,' and 'assumptions' in referring to the bases or premisses of inferences. When we do so, the context will make it clear that we have premisses in mind. We use these terms because they are more natural, and often more informative, than the logician's technical term 'premiss.' However, it is often not obvious to which of the categories a particular premiss belongs. When that happens, it is pointless to quibble over whether one of these terms is more suitable than the others.

4.2 SOME ADDITIONAL NOTES ABOUT INFERENCE

The preceding section contained a sketch of the key elements of the concept of inference. This section fills in some of the details.

Inferring, Giving Reasons, and Offering Arguments

Inferring is a mental activity which can be carried on without any overt verbal expression.[2] But we can give linguistic expression to inferences in a couple of noteworthy ways: (1) giving reasons for our beliefs and (2) offering arguments in order to persuade someone else of something.

Reasons

Sometimes we are asked why we believe what we do, that is, we are asked to explain how we arrived at a belief. "What makes you think your instructor doesn't read students' essays carefully before he grades them?" someone might ask after you have made such an accusation. In answering, you give your **reasons** for your belief: "Well, he never puts any comments on essays; and when I tried to talk to him about my essay after he had graded it he didn't seem to have any idea what I had written."

In giving our reasons for a belief, we cite the evidence on which we based our belief; that is to say, we cite the propositions from which we inferred that particular conclusion, or in yet other words, we state the premisses in relation to which that belief is our conclusion. (We here assume a case in which we did have reasons or evidence for our belief; of course, it is also true that each of us holds many beliefs without having, or at least without being able to produce, any evidence for them.)

Arguments Used to Persuade

Sometimes we try to persuade others to accept a proposition by making and offering **arguments**—formulating and presenting reasons that we believe or hope they will find convincing. "Republicans won't support social welfare programs for the poor because they're the party of big corporations," charges a Democrat. In doing so, she is urging her listeners or readers to follow her in concluding that Republicans won't support social welfare programs for the poor from the premiss that the Republican party is the party of big corporations. This kind of argument is characterized by the key property of being an invitation to draw an inference. Arguments in this sense, like inferences, have premisses and conclusions: to offer an argument to persuade is to offer premisses from which you hope your audience will draw the conclusion you want to persuade it to accept.

Inference Chains

We have already seen, in the example of Ian's reasoning about Ecuador, how we string inferences together, like links in a chain, using the conclusion from one inference as a premiss for another one. **Inference chains** can be extremely long and intricate, and it helps in keeping straight what leads to what if you can label different parts of the reasoning.

Main Premisses, Main Conclusions, and Premiss Support

We will use another example to introduce these terms.

> (a) It makes sense to take challenging courses at university because (b) they prepare you better for later life than do easy ones. For instance, (c) from a challenging course you can acquire much more new knowledge than from an easy course, and (d) that's added preparation for later life.

In this text, we call (a) the **main conclusion** of the reasoning, since all the other propositions are used to support (a), directly or indirectly. (a) is inferred directly from (b): the proposition that it makes sense to take challenging courses at university is supported directly by the contention that challenging courses prepare you better for later life than do easy ones. We shall term such premises as (b), the ones that directly support the main conclusion, the **main premisses** of the inference.

As you will have recognized, there is a second inference in the text—the inference from the pair of statements (c) and (d) to (b). That challenging courses prepare you better for life than do easy ones is inferred from the propositions that you can acquire more new knowledge from them and that such knowledge helps prepare you for later life. Premisses which support other premises in the context of such a chain of reasoning we shall call **premiss support**. The idea behind the label is that such grounds constitute support for premisses. They also are indirect support for the main conclusion, by supporting premisses which, in turn, support the main conclusion.

We might represent the structure of the reasoning as follows:

$$\{(c),(d)\} \rightarrow (b) \rightarrow (a)$$

and think of it as containing a *series* of two inference steps to reach the conclusion. What comes at the end is the main conclusion; what is contained in the link that leads directly to the main conclusion are the main premisses. And whatever leads to the main premisses is called premiss support.

Independent or Parallel Inferences to the Same Conclusion

Sometimes when people reason to a conclusion, they use what might be thought of as two or more **independent** or **parallel inferences** to arrive at one and the same conclusion. Imagine, for example, someone who reasons as follows:

> Morelli is the best-qualified woman who has applied for the job, and since we are trying to correct the male-weighted gender imbalance in our staff, we should try to hire her for that reason. But besides that, she is the only candidate who has actually had extensive job experience with mainframe computers, and we can't afford to hire someone without hands-on experience of that sort. So for this reason as well we should offer the job to her.

In this case, the reasoner recognizes one set of reasons for hiring Morelli— the company's policy of redressing gender imbalance plus Morelli's ranking among the female applicants. Then quite independently of that, Morelli's experience with mainframes is also taken as a reason for hiring her.

Notice that the main conclusion is

C   The job should be offered to Morelli

and that four distinct main premisses function in support of that main conclusion:

P1   Morelli is the best-qualified woman who has applied.
P2   We are trying to correct the male-weighted gender imbalance in our staff.
P3   Morelli is the only candidate who has had extensive job experience with mainframe computers.
P4   We can't afford to hire someone lacking experience with mainframe computers.

But those four premisses fall into two distinct groups, and as a result we can think of the reasoning as containing two inferences which are quite independent of each other, both leading to the same conclusion. P1 and P2 are the premisses of the first of those inferences, and P3 and P4 the premiss of the other. We might represent the structure here as follows

P1, P2 → C
P3, P4 → C

and think of the reasoning as containing two *parallel* ways of reaching the same conclusion.

What makes for *groups* of premisses which are *independent* of each other? The fact that premisses work in combination to support the conclusion constitutes them as a set or group, and the fact that the premisses of each group are able to provide their support without any help from premisses in any other group make them independent of each other.

Reasoning can exhibit quite complicated structures when it contains *both* parallel inferences *and* chain reasoning (or premiss support). We will not attempt to deal with such complicated structures in this chapter. Appendix E (Diagramming the Structure of Reasoning) describes one way of representing such inferences in a diagram.

Drawing Inferences from Suppositions

There are times when it is useful to draw inferences from propositions which we neither believe nor disbelieve. If you are trying to decide whether to go to the trouble of finding out whether a proposition is true, seeing what follows from it can help you decide. Imagine a classmate tells you she's heard rumors that a mutual friend, Lillian, is quitting school and leaving town. "Do you think she is?" she asks. Well, if Lillian's significant other is the guy you're doing a major class project with, you can draw conclusions about what might happen on the supposition that the rumor is true and you should probably take the trouble to find out whether it's true.

Another occasion for drawing inferences from suppositions can be when you are investigating the truth of a proposition and you want to test the truth of the proposition indirectly. So you see what conclusions would follow if it were true, or false: you *suppose* it to be true and draw inferences from that supposition. These can indicate ways to rule out the proposition. Suppose you have reason to wonder if a rat is getting into your apartment. If there is a rat, you reason, it must be coming in through the bathroom window that won't close completely, since there is no other way it could get in. And if it's coming in through the bathroom window, it will leave tracks in powder scattered on the window sill. Using this reasoning you have devised a way of checking whether there is a rat; if you put powder on the floor and find no tracks, you can conclude that there is no rat.

In such cases, the reasoning (or one phase of the reasoning) takes as a premiss the **supposition** that a proposition is true and draws conclusions from that supposition, without any commitment to it's actual truth. Such reasoning is sometimes called suppositional reasoning, sometimes called "hypothetical" reasoning, since it involves starting from the hypothesis that a proposition is true.

Role Indicator Terms

We have available to us a variety of terms to indicate the organization of our reasoning when we are trying to communicate it clearly to others. It helps us make ourselves understood to make use of these **role indicator terms**. Conversely, when we are trying to understand the reasoning being expressed in the written or spoken texts of others, the presence of these terms serves as clues to the intended structure of their reasoning. What these role indicator terms do is indicate the role an asserted proposition is intended to play in the surrounding discursive context.

For example, if someone writes, "I shall list my points in descending order: first, . . . ; second, . . . ; and third, . . . ," the words "first," "second," and "third" are not part of the propositions asserted, but indicate their order of importance in the author's mind. Or again, if someone says, "Bush was out of town when the theft occurred, so he isn't the thief," the word "so" is not part of either proposition asserted, but is rather a signal that the proposition following it (that Bush is not the thief) is intended to be a conclusion drawn from the proposition preceding it (that Bush was out of town when the theft occurred). Table 4.1 lists common types and examples of role indicator words.

Table 4.1   Role Indicator Words

Type	Some Typical Instances	Example	Propositions Asserted in Example
Indicating order	furthermore, moreover, in addition, besides, first, second, third	*First of all*, you ignored my request; *second*, you didn't even tell me what you were going to do.	(1) You ignored my request. (2) You didn't even tell me what you were going to do.
Indicating contrast between assertions	however, although, nevertheless, on the other hand, yet	My professor has trouble communicating; *however*, she is very fair when she grades.	(1) My professor has trouble communicating. (2) She is very fair when she grades.
Conjunctions and adverbs indicating dependence of one assertion on another in the reasoning of the speaker	hence, therefore, so, thus, consequently, accordingly, since,[1] because[2]	She is a citizen; *therefore* she has the right to vote.	(1) She is a citizen. (2) She has the right to vote.
Modifications of main verb indicating dependence of one assertion on another	must, must be, must have (when used after "so" or "therefore")	He has a Ph.D., so he *must be* able to read and write.	(1) He has a Ph.D. (2) He is able to read and write.

[1]"Since" is not a role indicator word when it expresses *time*, as it does in "Since he first entered politics, Reagan believed that the world was threatened by an evil empire."

[2]"Because" is not a role indicator word when it expresses *causal dependence*, as it does in "Smith contracted lung cancer because he is a heavy smoker."

4.3 Evaluating or Appraising Inferences

The inferences we and others draw are sometimes good, sometimes bad. What characteristics does a good inference have, and what makes for a bad inference?

It's tempting to think that an inference is a good one if it leads to a true conclusion and a bad one if it's conclusion is false. But that is a mistake, for two reasons.

1. Sometimes people reason very badly yet just by luck hit on conclusions which happen to be true.

Imagine someone who reasoned as follows: "There are 6 players on a baseball team and 10 players on a football team, so we'll need at least 20 people if we are going to field both a baseball team and a football team simultaneously." Here both premises are wrong and, moreover, they don't lead to the conclusion. This is a terrible inference, but one whose conclusion happens, by sheer luck, to be true.

2. Occasionally, people reason in excellent ways, but end up with conclusions that are not true.

Suppose that Cheryl had told Pat that she was going to Europe for the summer, that Pat received a letter in her handwriting postmarked July 4 from Paris, and furthermore that Bernice told Pat she had run into Cheryl in August in Amsterdam. Suppose that Pat concluded on this evidence that Cheryl was in Europe for the summer. Pat's inference was a good one—even if in fact Cheryl was in Knoxville the whole time, and she and Bernice had participated in an elaborate ruse to deceive Pat.[3]

If it's not by having true conclusions, or true premisses, or both, then on what basis then are good inferences distinguished from bad ones? We suggest the following conditions:

An inference is a good one for a person to make just in case:

(1) It is reasonable for that person to accept each of its premisses, and
(2) the premisses taken together are suitably linked or related to the conclusion

provided that also

(3) The person has no additional relevant information which undermines the support which the premisses give to the conclusion (see Chapter 6, page 122).

Otherwise, it is not a good inference.

Accordingly, when we stop and think about our reasoning, and ask whether the inferences we are tempted to draw or see others drawing are good ones, there are two main questions that need to be asked about each inference:

1. *Are the premisses acceptable?* We need to ask of *each* premiss—of each piece of evidence and of each assumption—whether it is reasonable to accept it. If there are specific reasons to question a premiss or assumption, sometimes this will lead us to ask what evidence there is to support it; more frequently, a challenge will lead us to ask whether the information we are using as a premiss comes from a credible source. (See Section 6.1 in Chapter 6.)
2. *Are the premisses taken together suitably linked to the conclusion?* For example, are they sufficient to make us confident that the conclusion is true? This question is not asked of each premiss taken singly; rather, it is asked of the premisses *as a group*. (See Sections 6.2 and following in Chapter 6.)

We have already examined, in Chapter 2, the ways to decide whether an assertion comes from a credible source. In Chapter 5 we introduce "logical relations" between propositions, which are helpful in understanding the link between premisses and conclusion in a special subset of cases, but Chapter 6 is where we take up the general question of determining when the premises of an inference as a group are suitably linked to their conclusion.

Assertion Qualifiers

Our language supplies a range of expressions which enable us to communicate the precise belief attitude we hold toward any given proposition; these are called **assertion qualifiers**. If you strongly believe that a proposition is true, and want to convey that fact, you introduce your assertion with some such phrase as, "It is certain that . . . ," "I am convinced that . . . ," or "There is no doubt at all that . . .". If you are highly unsure about a proposition's truth, but don't discount it completely, you could qualify your assertion to indicate your attitude by using some such phrase as, "There is a slight possibility that . . . ," "Conceivably . . . ," or "It might be the case that . . .". A list of all the possible assertion qualifying expressions in the English language would be enormous. Anyway, the point is not to memorize such a list. For your own part, you should qualify your own claims appropriately. And when listening to or reading what others say, you need to notice whether and how they qualify what they claim. You can thereby express precisely your own belief attitudes and ascertain the precise belief attitudes of others toward what they claim. Table 4.2 lists some representative assertion qualifiers.

Some Examples

When the pollster reports, "Quayle will definitely win the election," the pollster is asserting strong commitment to the proposition, "Quayle will win the election." When the columnist writes, "Navratilova just might be the best female tennis

Table 4.2   Assertion Qualifiers

Type	Some Typical Instances	Example	Propositions Put Forward
Adverbial phrases	certainly, probably, perhaps, in all probability, conceivably, maybe	Television is *probably* the most effective of the mass media.	Television is the most effective of the mass media.
Phrases preceding "that" clauses	it's certain that, it's likely that, it's possible that, it must be the case that	*It is possible that* cable television will replace network television as we know it.	Cable television will replace network television as we know it.
Parenthetical phrases	as far as I know, I believe, I suspect, I know, I'm sure you'll all agree	More people watched television today, *I'm sure*, than read a book.	More people watched television today than read a book.
Modifications of main verb	might be, must be, could be	The Rolling Stones could be more popular than the president of the United States.	The Rolling Stones are more popular than the president of the United States.

player of all time," the columnist makes a qualified assertion, indicating the belief attitude that the proposition, "Navratilova is the best female tennis player of all time," is probably true. When your roommate says of your hour-overdue date, "Maybe his car broke down," she is qualifying her assertion, revealing that she considers the proposition "Your date's car broke down" slightly possible.

Assertion qualifiers relate to inferences in the following ways. First, if a premiss of your inference is what someone else claims, then any qualifications they make should be carried forward to the conclusion you draw. If a classmate claims she thinks the test *might have been* postponed, then the most you have grounds to infer is that you *might* have extra time to study—not that you definitely will have extra time to study. Second, if your own evidence for an inference is far from certain, then it's essential that you qualify your belief attitude toward that evidence appropriately. Qualify your own beliefs as called for, and then, as when inferring from another's claims, carry those qualifications forward and attach them to the conclusion you draw.

Thus, when you ask the two questions listed earlier—(1) Are the premisses acceptable? and (2) Are they suitably linked to the conclusion?—any qualifications made or appropriate must be considered. Perhaps the premisses are not acceptable without qualification, but would be acceptable if qualified. Perhaps the premisses do not support the conclusion inferred from them in its unqualified form, but would support a qualified statement of that proposition.

4.4 SUMMARY

This chapter has presented the anatomy of inference in some detail. Inferring is coming to adopt an attitude toward a proposition because one thinks that other propositions, which one already accepts, support it to some degree. The proposition toward which one comes to adopt the attitude is called the conclusion of the inference; the propositions on which the conclusion is grounded are called the premisses. A person's grounds will consist of what they take to be evidence or data for the conclusion, plus assumptions they already hold.

Inferring is different from giving reasons for a belief, for the latter is stating the premisses from which one has already made the inference. Inferring is also different from arguing, which is inviting others to draw from a set of reasons an inference that one might or might not have drawn oneself.

Inferences can link up, so that one can infer a conclusion from a set of grounds, then use that conclusion as a premiss in drawing a further inference, and so on indefinitely. Not only can premisses work as a set to support a conclusion, but independent sets of premisses can support the same conclusion. A hypothetical or suppositional inference is "what if . . ." reasoning—considering what would follow *supposing* certain propositions were acceptable as premisses.

Inferences can be good or bad, depending *not* on whether the conclusion inferred is true, but rather on (1) whether it is reasonable to accept the grounds that the conclusion was drawn from (acceptable premisses) and (2) whether the premisses are suitably linked to the conclusion. Both grounds and conclusions drawn from them should be qualified if and when that is appropriate.

4.5 EXERCISES

The purpose of these exercises is to sharpen your sense of what inferences are by giving you practice in identifying premisses that potentially support conclusions.

Exercise 1

Mark the conclusion that may be inferred from each of the following sets of statements.

1. S1   Thanksgiving is always the fourth Thursday of November.
   S2   The fourth Thursday of November this year is November 23.

   Which of the following propositions may be correctly inferred from the preceding statements?

   C1   Thanksgiving is later this year than last.
   C2   Thanksgiving is on November 23 this year.
   C3   The third Thursday of November this year is November 17.

2. S1   Thanksgiving is always the third Thursday of November.
   S2   The fourth Thursday of November this year is November 23.

   Which of the following propositions may be correctly inferred from the preceding statements?

   C1   Thanksgiving is on November 23 this year.
   C2   Thanksgiving is on November 16 this year.
   C3   November 21 falls on a Monday this year.

3. S1   Psych 256—"Introduction to the Brain and Human Behavior"—has Psych 115 and Psych 116 or permission of the instructor as prerequisites.
   S2   No instructor in the Psychology Department has ever given permission to take Psych 256 to a student who has not taken Psych 115 and Psych 116.
   S3   You want to take Psych 256 next year.
   S4   There is still time to choose your courses for this year.

   Which of the following propositions may be correctly inferred from the preceding statements?

C1   Instructors in Psych 256 are unreasonably rigid and unyielding.
C2   It's not worth taking Psych 256.
C3   You should sign up for Psych 115 and 116 this year.

4. S1   One-half of the deck was treated with RainProof stain a year ago, and
        the rain runs off it without being absorbed into the wood.
   S2   The other half of the deck was not treated at all, and the rain soaks
        into the wood and it is beginning to rot.
   S3   There was no other difference between the two halves of the deck.
   S4   Nobody wants a rotted deck.

Which of the following propositions may be correctly inferred from the
preceding statements?

C1   Rain causes rot in exposed wood.
C2   It's better to treat your deck with RainProof than with any other brand
     of deck stain.
C3   It's better to treat your deck with RainProof than not to treat it at all.

Exercise 2

Each of the following examples consists of a conclusion and two premises that
would support the conclusion if one or more additional assumption(s) was or
were true. The third group contains propositions that are candidates for that
role. Identify the proposition(s) that need to be added to the stated premises
so that the whole set supports the conclusion. (Assume that all the given premises
and all the premiss candidates are true.)

1. *Conclusion*: My car needs a tune-up.
   (a) My car doesn't start easily.
   (b) My car stalls when I stop at red lights.
   Which of the following should be added to (a) and (b) to enhance the
   support which they give to the conclusion?
   (c) My car is ten years old.
   (d) My car didn't give me any trouble last year.
   (e) Stalling and not starting easily are signs a tune-up is needed.
   (f) I get a tune-up on a regular basis.

2. *Conclusion*: I locked my keys in the house.
   (a) I can't find my keys in my purse, in any of my pockets, or on my office
       desk.
   (b) The house is locked.
   Which of the following should be added to (a) and (b) to enhance the
   support which they give to the conclusion?
   (c) I haven't been home for two days.
   (d) My keys must be either in my purse or my coat pocket, on my office
       desk or on the table in side the front door at home.
   (e) There are three pockets in my coat.

3. *Conclusion*: Hartford has a larger population than Washington, D.C.

(a) According to the *World Almanac*, Washington, D.C., has a population of 200,000.

(b) Hartford has a larger population than Portland, Oregon.

Which of the following need(s) to be added to (a) and (b) to have a group of premisses which supports the conclusion?

(c) Portland's population is 6,000,000.

(d) Hartford has a greater number of industrial workers than Washington does.

4. *Conclusion*: The "surprise" test will be held this Thursday.

    (a) The Professor said the "surprise" test will be held this week.

    (b) The Professor said the Thirty Year's War will be on the test and we won't have finished covering it until the end of Tuesday's class.

Which of the following need(s) to be added to (a) and (b) to have a group of premisses which supports the conclusion?

(c) The class meets only Tuesdays and Thursdays.

(d) The Professor would not test on material not covered in class.

(e) The Professor is trustworthy.

Exercise 3

Here are some examples consisting of a conclusion and a set of statements offered in support of it. One of the latter contributes nothing to the support of the conclusion. Identify the unnecessary premiss.

1. *Conclusion*: That alarm clock may break again if it is dropped.

    S1   I dropped that alarm clock once already and it broke.

    S2   I had it fixed and it works now.

    S3   It is a cheap alarm clock.

    S4   The warranty on the clock has expired.

2. *Conclusion*: Affirmative action for women need not be unfair to men.

    S1   Affirmative action for women is unfair to men only if it results in fewer opportunities for men than they would get if the society had a totally fair distribution of opportunities between the sexes.

    S2   Men may be complaining needlessly.

    S3   Some affirmative action programs for women provide no more opportunities for women than would be available to them in a society with fair opportunities.

3. *Conclusion*: The percentage of people under age 25 who are well informed about the news is less today than it was 30 years ago.

    S1   The percentage of people under age 25 are regular newspaper readers is smaller today than it was 30 years ago.

    S2   The percentage of people under age 25 who watch TV news regularly is smaller today than it was 30 years ago.

S3   People under age 25 buy more records and tapes of rock music than they did 30 years ago.

S4   For the last 40 years, the main sources of news information have been newspapers and TV news broadcasts.

Exercise 4

In the passages that follow, someone reasons to a conclusion. Write out that conclusion, omitting assertion qualifiers and role indicators and rephrasing where necessary.

(In some cases we have supplied background information you need in order to understand or interpret the passage. You should perhaps know that headlines for letters to newspapers and magazines are composed by their own staff, not by the authors of the letters.)

**1.   *Background*: In late October–early November 1988 three young whales were trapped by the early winter ice in the Arctic Ocean off Barrow, Alaska, before they could migrate south. Their plight attracted worldwide publicity, including nightly television news coverage for over a week. A breathing hole was kept open for them, and after a delay, and at great expense, icebreakers were dispatched to clear a path through the ice to open water. Eventually a Soviet icebreaker freed two of them. The following example was inspired by letters that appeared in several newspapers at the time.

We spend hundreds of thousands of dollars in the humanitarian attempt to save the gray whales. But in the meantime, we let the homeless men, women, and children of this great country remain sleeping in the streets and begging for scraps of food. This does not make sense, and it shows dramatically that we have our priorities sadly wrong.

2.   *Background*: The following passage is adapted from a letter to a national magazine back in 1980. The letter was prompted by an earlier story about a court ruling, by a judge named Owens, which had allowed the University of Georgia to demand that a university tenure committee reveal how its members voted. A university tenure committee consists of permanent faculty who must decide between granting a probationary faculty member permanent employment and not renewing the probationary appointment.

The ruling ought to be overturned. It's not hard to see why, for it sounds like the beginning of a totalitarian state. Judge Owens is violating the concept of the secret ballot by demanding that faculty members reveal how they voted. Next the government will want to prohibit secret voting in unions, professional organizations, civic organizations, corporations, and finally in general elections.

3.   *Background*: The following is a possible response to the recommendation that modern Canadian history be taught in Grades 9 and 10 (the first two years in a Canadian high school).

Certain people have recommended that the organization of the teaching of Canadian history in high school should be changed. But they are just wrong to suggest that modern Canadian history should be taught in Grades 9 and 10.

They are wrong because it would be extremely difficult for Grade 9 and 10 students to understand much of Canada's recent history without a background knowledge of early Canadian native, French, and British-Canadian history.

4. *Background*: The following is typical of letters that have appeared in many newspapers in the last few years.

   Your editorials have consistently supported the pro-choice option. In addition, its news writers consistently use the unequal terms "pro-choice" and "anti-abortion"— instead of the pair "pro-abortion" and "pro-life" preferred by those opposed to abortion. Clearly, therefore, your coverage of the abortion controversy is biased through and through.

5. *Background*: The follow passage occurs in Plato's *Timaeus* (51 d); the translation is by R. C. Pinto.

   . . . we must concede that knowing and having an opinion that happens to be correct are quite distinct, for they have a distinct origin and are of a different nature: one is implanted in us by instruction (or education), the other by mere persuasion; one is always bound up with genuine reasons, the other doesn't have a genuine reason to back it up; one cannot be overturned by mere persuasion, the other can; and finally, everybody has some correct opinions, but real knowledge is a possession of the gods and of very few men.

6. *Background*: The following is a famous passage from John Stuart Mill, *Utilitarianism*, Chapter 4. By the "general happiness," Mill means the happiness of human beings in general or as a group ("the greatest happiness of the greatest number of people").

   The only proof capable of being given that an object is visible is that people actually see it. The only proof that a sound is audible is that people hear it: and so of the other sources of experience. In like manner, I apprehend, the sole evidence it is possible to produce that anything is desirable, is that people do actually desire it. . . . No reason can be given why the general happiness is desirable except that each person, so far as he believes it to be attainable, desires his own happiness. This however, being a fact, we have not only all the proof which the case admits of, but all which it is possible to require, that happiness is a good: that each person's happiness is good to that person, and the general happiness, therefore, a good to the aggregate of all persons.

Exercise 5

In the passages that follow, someone reasons to a conclusion. (a) Write out the conclusion in your own words. (b) Then make a numbered list of the premisses from which the conclusion is intended to follow.

Ignore the sentences that do *not* express either premisses or the conclusion. When you write out premisses and conclusion, omit assertion qualifiers and role indicators and rephrase where necessary.

1. *Background*: The following excerpt is from Neil Postman, *Amusing Ourselves to Death: Public Discourse in the Age of Show Business* (New York: Penguin Books, 1985), p. 126.

   The television commercial is the most peculiar and pervasive form of communication to issue forth from the electric plug. An American who has reached the age of forty will have seen well over one million television commercials in his or her lifetime, and has close to another million to go before the first Social Security check arrives. We may safely assume, therefore, that the television commercial has profoundly influenced American habits of thought.

**2. It is clear that modern prisons are an abysmal failure. First, they don't rehabilitate anyone. Second, they don't so much punish as provide free room and board. This fact was first pointed out to me many, many years ago. Finally, by bringing criminals together, prisons allow them to swap information and refine their crafts.

3. A lot of people say that foods high in fat are bad for you, but you shouldn't pay any attention to them. Just think about it. The things that most humans spontaneously or naturally desire must be good for us. And it's clear that almost everybody desires foods that are high in animal fat. So it just has to be the case that fatty foods are good for us.

Exercise 6

In each of the following passages someone reasons to a conclusion. Write the main conclusion out in your own words. When you do so, be sure you omit assertion qualifiers and role indicators. Then make a numbered list of the main premisses (those which are intended to directly support the main conclusion). In some of these examples you will find premiss support; if you do, put an asterisk after any main premiss for which there is premiss support.

**1. Self-worth depends on an ability to exert some control over oneself and one's surroundings, and this ability is nothing else than power. So no one without power can preserve his or her self-esteem, but clearly, a person without money is a person without power. Hence a person without money can have no self-esteem.

2. In August many of the major cities of Europe are virtually empty. That is the month that is traditional for summer holidays over there and the natives exit the cities and crowd the beaches and holiday resorts. So August is not an ideal month to visit Europe, if you want to visit bustling cities or stay in uncrowded resorts.

3. It is obvious that capital punishment is not a deterrent to murder. For example, several studies show that murderers don't think about the consequences of their crimes before they commit them. Capital punishment should not, therefore, be reinstated.

4. The practice of employing surrogate mothers is, I am convinced, immoral. First of all, it discriminates against the poor. Only wealthy childless couples can get children this way. For example, recently a couple paid about $20,000 for the services of a surrogate mother. Yet infertility is not a problem limited to the rich. Furthermore, the practice puts unfair pressures on low-income women. The prospect of the high fees pressures poor women to become "baby farms" for rich couples, and that is not fair.

5. This is an excerpt from David Hume, *An Enquiry Concerning Human Understanding*, Section x, part 1.

   Nothing is esteemed a miracle, if it ever happen in the common course of nature. It is no miracle that a man, seemingly in good health, should die on a sudden: because such a kind of death, though more unusual than any other, has yet been frequently observed to happen. But it is a miracle, that a dead man should come to life; because that has never been observed in any age or country. There must, therefore, be a uniform experience against every miraculous event, otherwise the event would not merit that appellation. And as a uniform experience amounts to a *proof*, there is here a direct and full proof, from the nature of the fact, against the existence of any miracle. . . .

NOTES

1. *Webster's Ninth New Collegiate Dictionary* (Springfield, MA: Merriam-Webster, 1987), p. 430.
2. Sometimes, of course, we "think out loud," and then we give our inferences verbal expression at the very time we make them. But often we keep our inferences to ourselves; we draw a conclusion without giving voice to the fact we have done so.
3. Notice that Pat's evidence is the sort of evidence on which we usually base our opinions about the whereabouts of people who are out of town. If you insist in faulting Pat's reasoning in this case, you would have to maintain that most such opinions about people's whereabouts are based on faulty inference.

5

Logical Relations

In Chapter 4 we saw how propositions can be related as premises and conclusions in inferences. In the present chapter we introduce other relations that can hold between (or among) propositions, relations that can hold *irrespective* of the roles they happen to play in inferences. Following a common usage, we will refer to this special class of relationships as **logical relations** among propositions. Logical relations focus on whether the truth of one proposition has implications for the truth of another.

As we shall see, logical relations aren't the same thing as relations of inferential support. But there is a connection between the two kinds of relation. For if certain logical relations hold between two propositions, that fact will have bearing on how those propositions can reasonably be used in inferences.

5.1 Compound Propositions

To understand logical relations you need to be familiar with some of the ways individual propositions can be joined to form combinations or **compound propositions**. Three in particular are essential: they are (1) disjunctions ("either/or" propositions), (2) conjunctions, and (3) conditionals ("if/then" propositions).

1. *Disjunctions.* A **disjunctive proposition** or **disjunction** is a compound proposition formed by joining two or more propositions by "or" or its equivalent

("either . . . or . . .," ". . . , or else . . .," "one of . . . , or . . ."). Each component
proposition is called a **disjunct**.

When your intent is to claim that *only* one—and *at most* one—of the
disjuncts is true (though you're not committed to which one), the disjunction
is called an *exclusive disjunction*; when your intent is only to claim that *at
least* one of the disjuncts is true, but leave open the possibility that both
are true (and again, you're not saying which), the disjunction is called an
inclusive disjunction.

In either case, in claiming that a disjunction is true, you do not claim that
each individual disjunct is true, only that the disjunction is true. For example,
suppose Mo, betting all her chips at a Las Vegas roulette table, said "I'll either
win big or I'll lose my shirt." Mo used or expressed the two disjuncts:

P1   Mo will win a lot of money

and

P2   Mo will lose a lot of money.

But she didn't claim that both P1 and P2 are true. In fact she expected
one to be true and one to be false, though she didn't know which when she
uttered the disjunction. This example illustrates that you can sincerely claim a
disjunction to be true without being committed to the truth of both disjuncts
and without any commitment as to which of the disjuncts is true.

2. *Conjunctions.* Contrast disjunctions with the kind of compound proposition called a **conjunctive proposition** or **conjunction**. You assert a conjunction
when you claim that both (or all) of two (or more) propositions are true. A
conjunction is typically formed by joining two or more propositions by "and" or
an equivalent (such as "but," "moreover," "in addition," "also," "too," "however,"
"furthermore," "while," "whereas," "yet," "although," or "as well"). The component propositions are called its **conjuncts**.

In claiming that a conjunction is true, you thereby also commit yourself to
each conjunct being true. For example, if you contend that Francine speaks
fluent French while Juan speaks only Spanish, you have thereby committed
yourself to the truth of both:

P3   Francine speaks fluent French

and

P4   Juan speaks only Spanish.

One cannot sincerely assert a conjunction without being committed to the
truth of each one of the conjuncts. Conjunctions are different from disjunctions

in this respect; when you assert an either/or proposition, you don't commit yourself to the truth of each component proposition.

Not so with *denying* a conjunction (that is, claiming that it is *not* true). Try it out with the assertion, "It's not true both that Francine speaks fluent French and that Juan speaks only Spanish." Someone making that claim does not claim that both P3 and P4 are false, just that at least one of them is. The person denying a conjunction might not know which conjunct is false.

3. *Conditionals.* Last, we draw your attention to a third kind of compound proposition, called a **conditional proposition**, or a **conditional**. Conditionals are typically claimed by joining two independent propositions with "if" and "then," or the equivalent (such as "if" alone, "provided that," "given that," "on condition that," "conditional on," or "on the assumption that"). The clause which states the condition—the one following "if" in the "if . . ., then . . ." version, is called the **antecedent**. The other clause, the one following "then" in the "if . . . then . . ." version—which states what is supposed to be true if the condition holds—is called the **consequent**.

In asserting a conditional (like a disjunction), you commit yourself to the whole thing being true, but you don't claim that its components are independently true. It wouldn't be inconsistent to assert a conditional but deny both the antecedent and the consequent as independently true propositions.

For example, suppose a crop specialist claims that if there is a severe frost in Cuba next May, the year's sugarcane crop on the island will be destroyed. The specialist is not contending that the antecedent, "There will be a severe frost in Cuba next May," is true, nor is he claiming that the consequent, "Next year's sugarcane crop in Cuba will be destroyed" is true. The specialist may have no idea about whether these propositions are true, or might believe they are both false. But knowing what he does about the effect of severe frost in May on a sugarcane crop, he believes the conditional is true.

Frequently, asserting a conditional has a point only because you don't know whether the antecedent is true. You believe the consequent will happen provided the antecedent does, so you want to find out if the antecedent is likely ("If that's the hot wire, I'll be electrocuted if I touch it") or you want to prevent it from happening ("If the dam breaks, then all the ranches in the valley will be wiped out").

As you will see, the logical relations discussed in the rest of this chapter rely on an understanding of these three types of compound proposition: disjunctions, conjunctions, and conditionals.

5.2 ENTAILMENT

Consider the relationship between the truth of the first, conjunctive proposition and the truth of the second, simple one:

(1) Jake is 35 and Sal is 28.
(2) Jake is older than Sal.

It is impossible that (1) be true and (2) be false; in other words, if (1) were true—if it correctly states Jake's and Sal's ages—then (2) would have to be true as well. If (1) is true, then it has to be true that Jake is older than Sal.

When a pair of propositions has the feature that it is *impossible* for the second one to be false *if* the first one is true, we will follow conventional terminology in logic and say that a relation of **entailment** holds between the first proposition and the second and that the first proposition entails the other.

Notice that although the first proposition entails the second in our example, the second proposition does not entail the first one. For (2) to entail (1), it would have to be impossible for (1) to be false if (2) is true. But that is not the case here. It is quite possible for Jake to be older than Sal (thus for (2) to be true), yet for (1) to be false, for instance, if Jake is not 35 but 34 or if Sal is not 28 but 29.

We can now explain how the relation of entailment relates to inferences. If one proposition entails another, that means if the first is true the second *must* also be true. From this fact it follows that any time the set of premisses from which one is drawing an inference **entails** the conclusion, then if you know for sure that the propositions expressed by the premisses are true, you can be certain that the conclusion is true.

Entailment and Support for a Conclusion

Although the relation of entailment can be used in judging an inference, the fact that one proposition *entails* another is not the same thing as that proposition's **supporting** the other in the sense of making it reasonable to infer the other.

To see that this is so, notice first that every proposition *entails* itself. (Proof: If proposition **p** is true, then **p** cannot be false—and that satisfies the definition of **p** entailing **p**.) But it would not make much sense to say that a proposition *supports* itself, in the sense of providing a good reason for inferring it. For example, imagine the following crazy-sounding inference:

(3) Albert is a better physicist than he is a dancer.

So, (4) Albert is a better physicist than he is a dancer.

There is something seriously wrong with treating (3) as a sound basis for inferring (4), even though (3) entails (4). As we saw in Chapter 4, to draw an inference is to adopt a belief (or other attitude) on the basis of *other* propositions one believes or accepts. But if a person already believed (3), then since (3) and (4) are identical, there is no "other" proposition to serve as the basis for an inference. (Inferences in which the premisses from which the conclusion is drawn include the conclusion itself are said to **beg the question**.)

These considerations show that one proposition can entail another without supporting it, and therefore that entailment and support are not the same thing. However, to show or discover that a proposition that is in doubt is entailed by other, different propositions that are beyond question is to find support for the proposition that was in doubt.

There are untold numbers of excellent inferences in which the premisses clearly do support the conclusion, even though they do not entail it. Consider as an example the following:

> All major U.S. news media have reported that the Amazon Basin is being deforested at an alarming rate.
> So, probably the Amazon Basin is being deforested at an alarming rate.

The premiss here provides *very* strong support for the conclusion. But the premiss does *not* entail the conclusion, since it is *possible* (even though highly unlikely) that all the major U.S. new media have been wrong on this matter. That is, it is *possible* that the premiss is true and the conclusion is false, so no entailment.

5.3 EQUIVALENCE

With some pairs of propositions, each member of the pair entails the other one. The first entails the second, and the second entails the first as well. For example, consider the following:

(1) Pierre is Toby's cousin.
(2) Toby is Pierre's cousin.

If (1) is true, then (2) must be true—it couldn't possibly be otherwise— and if (2) is true, then similarly (1) must be true. And if each entails the other, then either one can be inferred from the other. Logicians call the members of such pairs **logically equivalent**. In non-technical language, we say they "say the same thing."

Since logical equivalents entail each other's truth, this concept can be used as a test of whether a restatement of a proposition is committed to more than the original formulation. For example, consider the following propositions:

(3) Paris is the largest city in France.
(4) No other city in France is as large as Paris.
(5) No other city in France is larger than Paris.

Are (4) and (5) just equivalent ways of expressing (3)? The first two are logically equivalent, for if either (3) or (4) is true, then the other must be true too. (Check it out for yourself.) So the answer is "yes" for (4). But (5) is not logically equivalent to (3)—or to (4). For it is possible to imagine a situation in which (5) is true but (3) or (4) is false. For instance, suppose some other French city, say, Marseilles, were the same size as Paris. Such a situation could exist, even if it does not in fact exist right now. In that case (5) would be true, but (3) and (4) would be false. So (5) expresses a different proposition from (3) and (4).

· One application of the idea of logical equivalence to inferring is this: if a given conclusion may be correctly inferred from a set of premises, then that set of premises warrants any proposition that is logically equivalent to the first one, as well. Logical equivalence also applies to the restating of someone's position. If you are paraphrasing, and you don't want to distort or misrepresent the person's point of view, make sure your restatement is logically equivalent to the original.

5.4 INCOMPATIBILITY AND CONSISTENCY

Two propositions can be **logically incompatible** with each other. That happens when *it is impossible that they both are true*. For example,

(1) The Republicans will get a majority of the congressional seats in the next election.
(2) The Democrats will get a majority of the congressional seats in the next election.

are incompatible. It is impossible that both parties have a majority (that is, impossible that they both have more than 50% of the seats in Congress). In the preceding example one of the incompatible propositions will be true, but there can also be cases where both are false. Here is an example:

(3) John F. Kennedy was first elected to the Senate in 1956.
(4) John F. Kennedy was never elected to the Senate.

If either (3) or (4) happened to be true, the other would have to be false, so they are incompatible, but in fact both are false, since John F. Kennedy was first elected to the Senate in 1952.

The opposite of logical incompatibility is **logical consistency**. Two propositions are logically consistent *if it is possible that they are both true*. For example,

(5) Madonna will give up singing and acting and become a nun.
(6) Madonna will be best remembered in history as the person responsible for pioneering female clergy in the Roman Catholic church.

are consistent; that is to say, they are not incompatible. It is possible, in the sense that it is conceivable, for them both to be true (although, obviously, at this time it seems unlikely that either one is in fact true).

Groups of more than two propositions can be consistent or inconsistent. In general, a set of propositions is consistent if it is possible that all members of the set are true. A set is inconsistent if it is not possible that all members of the set are true.

Consistency of sets of propositions applies to inferences. An inference based on a false premiss is not reliable. So when an inference is drawn from more than one premiss, it is essential that the premisses be consistent. If they are not, it means that at least one of them is false. (Proof: If they are not consistent, they cannot all be true; if they cannot all be true, then at least one of them is false.)

5.5 CONTRADICTION

In ordinary English, to say that two propositions are contradictory or involve a **contradiction** is simply to say that they are incompatible—that they cannot both be true.

We have already noted (see the example about when John F. Kennedy was first elected to the Senate) that a pair of propositions can be incompatible and *both* false. The water in a beaker might be *neither* colorless nor brown, it might be green. In that event, the propositions

(1) The liquid in that beaker is colorless.
(2) The liquid in that beaker is brown.

are incompatible, and both are false. You could say that (1) and (2) are mutually exclusive, but they do not exhaust all the possibilities.

Sometimes, however, two propositions are mutually exclusive, and they *do* exhaust all the possibilities, so if either one of them is false, then the other one, being the only alternative, must be true, and vice versa. For example, there is no other possibility besides

(3) The liquid in the beaker is brown.
(4) The liquid in the beaker is not brown.

Or, again, we can know that one of the following must be true and the other must be false—even if we don't know which is which.

(5) Somebody in this room has a cold.
(6) Nobody in this room has a cold.

We will call any two propositions which are incompatible and *also* have this additional feature **exhaustive alternatives**.[1]

With a pair of exhaustive alternatives it is impossible that both members be false and it is also impossible that both members be true. The pair is such that *necessarily* one and only one member is true.

It is possible to generalize the notion of exhaustive alternatives to apply to any set of propositions having more than one member. Such a set is a set of exhaustive alternatives just in case (1) it is impossible that all the propositions in the set are false and (2) it is impossible that more than one of the propositions is true.

Here is an example of such a set: {the water is green; the water is blue; the water is neither green nor blue}.

5.6 SUMMARY

This chapter introduced you to terminology for describing compound propositions: disjunction, conjunction, condition. It also introduced you to the following logical relations.

ENTAILMENT

A entails B.   = If A is true, B *must* be true.

EQUIVALENCE

A and B are logically equivalent.   = If A is true, B *must* be true and if B is true A *must* be true.

INCOMPATIBILITY

A and B are incompatible.   = A and B cannot *both* be true.

CONSISTENCY

A and B are consistent.   = It is possible that A and B are both true.

EXHAUSTIVE ALTERNATIVES

A and B are exhaustive alternatives.   = A and B cannot both be true, and one of them must be true.

We also discussed the relation of support:

SUPPORT

A supports B.   = If you know that A is true, you have a reason to believe that B is true.

5.7 EXERCISES

Compound Propositions

Exercise 1

For each of the following, invent as many examples as your instructor requires. Invent sentences that could be used to assert:
- (a) a conditional proposition
- (b) a conjunctive proposition
- (c) a disjunctive proposition
- (d) a conditional proposition with a disjunctive proposition as the consequent
- (e) a conditional proposition with a conjunctive proposition as the antecedent
- (f) a disjunctive proposition with a conditional proposition as one of the disjuncts
- (g) a conjunctive proposition with a conditional proposition as one of the conjuncts
- (h) a conditional proposition with a disjunctive proposition as the antecedent and a conjunctive proposition as the consequent

Exercise 2

Assume that each of the following sentences is used to assert a proposition.
- (a) Indicate whether the proposition asserted is (i) a conjunction, (ii) a disjunction, (iii) a conditional, or (iv) noncompound (none of the preceding). Treat attributions (quotations and ascriptions of belief) as noncompound propositions.
- (b) If the proposition asserted is compound, then write out each conjunct or disjunct, or the antecedent and the consequent, and *label each correctly*.

**1. Either professional sports stars are vastly overpaid or I'm a monkey's uncle.

**2. The data stored in the computer's RAM (random access memory) will be lost if the power goes off.

**3. The incredible sense of awe I had when I visited Chartres Cathedral in France last summer was one I shall treasure for the rest of my life.

4. Students who hand in all assignments and attend all classes will get at least a "C" in introductory philosophy courses.

5. Either the Calgary Flames or the Los Angeles Kings will win the Stanley Cup this year.

6. Most psychologists of the last generation thought that if infants were not kept to a strict feeding schedule, either they would develop colic or they would display behavior problems when they were older.

7. The movie *Godfather III* was Coppola's last chance to save his reputation and either the critics will like it or Coppola will lose his standing in the movie industry.

8. Madonna says that in the next year either she will put out two more albums or she will make another movie.

9. If the cost of tuition rises again, then either there will have to be an increase in student aid or many students will be forced to leave college.

Exercise 3

In each of the following passages, several propositions are asserted. Make a *numbered list* of the propositions asserted.

Write out each proposition asserted (but only propositions that are asserted), omitting any assertion qualifiers or role indicator words, and rephrasing where necessary. If you find a sentence that is not used to make an assertion, ignore it. If you find any conjunctions, make each conjunct a separate item on the list; do *not* include the conjunction itself in the list. Remember that the component parts of disjunctions and conditionals (disjuncts, antecedents and consequents) are *not* asserted.

**1. *Background.* The following appeared on the first page of a philosophy test.

> If you are in Section 01, you have 60 minutes to complete the test, but if you are in Section 03, you have only 45 minutes to finish. Students in Section 02 will write next week, so if you are enrolled in Section 02, you should not be reading these instructions. Do not begin the test until told to do so or communicate with any other student during the test. Good luck!

2. *Background*: Imagine someone offering you the following cynical piece of advice.

> Don't be taken in by the promises politicians make during elections. If you believe such promises, you're bound to be disappointed. Politicians just want to get elected, and therefore they tell you what they think you want to hear. But watch what they do when the election is over. In all likelihood, either they conveniently forget about the promises they've made or they find excuses for not keeping them. Federal politicians are just as bad as local ones. If you want to avoid disappointment, ignore what any politician tells you.

3. *Background*: The following except is from the instructions at the beginning of a recent *Consumer Reports Buying Guide* Issue:

> To find the report on a specific type of product, look in the index to the *Buying Guide* on page 388. That's where you'll find the page number if this issue has a Ratings report or a discussion of that product. If you're not looking specifically for something but are generally interested in aproduct area, consult the contents in the front of the book. There we have listed all the Rated products in nine categories of consumer interest.

4. *Background*: Imagine someone offering you the following piece of advice.

> If you don't maintain decent grades during your undergraduate years at university, you won't get into graduate school. But what can a student do these days to keep his or her grades as high as possible? Some recommend taking easy courses, some recommend getting a tutor, and some even recommend cheating. Forget about cheating, and don't waste your time ormoney on a tutor. Either you will go broke or you'll get caught and get tossed out of school. If you want decent marks, just never take more than four courses in a semester.

5. *Background*: The following is adapted from a junk-mail letter received by one of the authors.

> Congratulations! You have been selected to compete for one of our fabulous grand prizes. There are four prizes worth more than a thousand dollars each, and everyone who enters will win a prize! We are sure every winner will be delighted with

his or her prize. Read the contest rules and mail in the enclosed entry form today. If you don't send in the form, you will lose your chance to win up to one hundred thousand dollars. Can you afford to pass up a chance like that? Act now. We promise you won't be disappointed. How did you become eligible for one of these great prizes? Either you entered one of our previous contests or a friend supplied us with your name. Either way, take advantage of this glorious opportunity.

Logical Relations

Exercise 4

Several pairs of sentences follow. For each pair, decide whether it is an example of (1) entailment, (2) consistent propositions neither of which entails the other, (3) equivalence or (4) incompatible or inconsistent propositions.

1. (a) Some Russians drink beer.
   (b) No beer drinkers are Russian.
2. (a) Every member of my family wants to move into a new house.
   (b) Nobody in my family wants to move into a new house.
3. (a) Some of the best movies ever made were in black and white.
   (b) Colorizing black and white movies is a crime against cinematic art.
4. (a) Animals can't survive the arctic winter.
   (b) Dogs can't survive the arctic winter.
5. (a) Some people who drive a Corvette make less than $20,000 a year.
   (b) Some people who make less than $20,000 a year drive a Corvette.
6. (a) Cats mate in the spring.
   (b) Cats mate in the fall.
7. (a) Clint Eastwood is my favorite director.
   (b) I like Clint Eastwood as a performer, but I can't stand him as a director.
8. (a) Snow White lived with exactly seven little old men.
   (b) The number of little old men Snow White lived with was more than six and less than eight.
9. (a) Miller Lite tastes great.
   (b) Miller Lite is less filling.
10. (a) The Rolling Stones were a better rock and roll band than the Beatles.
    (b) The Rolling Stones are the greatest rock and roll band of all time.
11. (a) The man who wrote *Moby Dick* lived in the United States.
    (b) The man who wrote *Moby Dick* lived in the northeastern part of the United States.

Exercise 5

What is the logical relationship (consistency, entailment, incompatibility, equivalence) between proposition (a) and each of the propositions that follow below it?

(i) If there is more than one, list them all. (ii) For entailments, indicate which statement entails which. (iii) In every case, explain *briefly* why you answer as you do.

**1. (a) In North America, pop singer Madonna is more popular than jazz singer Ella Fitzgerald.

(b) Ella Fitzgerald is not the most popular singer in North America.

(c) Ella Fitzgerald is not as popular as she used to be in North America.

(d) North Americans as a group prefer jazz singer Ella Fitzgerald to pop singer Madonna.

(e) In North America, jazz singer Ella Fitzgerald isn't as popular as pop singer Madonna.

(f) In North America, pop singer Madonna is more popular than Whitney Houston, and Whitney Houston is more popular than jazz singer Ella Fitzgerald.

2. (a) More people die from heart disease than from cancer.

(b) The mortality due to cancer is less than that resulting from heart disease.

(c) Cancer kills more people than does any other ailment.

(d) Heart disease can kill you.

(e) Heart disease is the leading health problem in North America.

(f) Heart disease kills more people than does any other ailment.

(g) Cancer is a serious health problem in North America.

3. (a) Country music is easy to come by in Europe and in Britain.

(b) In Europe and in Britain one has no difficulty in getting to hear country music.

(c) Some of the music played in Europe is country music.

(d) Country music is hard to come by in Europe and in Britain.

(e) The only places you hear a lot of country music in Europe are in England and in The Netherlands.

(f) Country music is not the most popular form of pop music in Europe and in Britain.

(g) In any major city in Europe or the United Kingdom there will be a country music radio station.

Exercise 6

A number of passages describing disputes and disagreements follow. For each passage (a) identify any inconsistent or incompatible assertions made by parties to the dispute and (b) determine for any pair of inconsistent statements whether they constitute exhaustive alternatives.

**1. Spike Lee is a black film director. Film critic Janet Maslin wrote that the musical numbers in Lee's movie *School Daze* are beyond the range of Lee's technical abilities. Lee attributed to Maslin the view that black people don't have the technical know-how to be filmmakers and vigorously defended the view that black people do have such know-how.

2. At the sales meeting, George argued that since in most families women make the final decisions about the purchase of appliances and since women are more likely to buy appliances in the winter, the main advertising campaign should occur during the late fall. Martha was not impressed with that argument and contended, instead, that the product line's greatest appeal was to middle-income males and that they tended to make purchases

in the spring. Martha was adamant that main advertising campaign should take place in February and March.

3. Larry maintains that trade unions interfere with the free market economy, encourage laziness, and impede technological progress. He claims that they should therefore be outlawed. Moe protests that without the protection of workers' welfare which trade unions provide, private corporations would exploit workers mercilessly. Moreover, he contends, unions are necessary to keep the wages of working men and women high enough to provide them with a decent standard of living. If workers seem lazy, he says, it's because their work is often demeaning and mindless, not because of trade unions. Unions should remain legal, he insists.

Exercise 7

Invent pairs of sentences in which each of the following logical relationships hold. Make up as many pairs of each as your instructor assigns.
   (a) Entailment
   (b) Equivalence
   (c) Incompatibility
   (d) Consistency
   (e) Exhaustive alternatives
   (f) Entailment, in which the proposition which entails the other one is a conditional proposition
   (g) Incompatibility, in which at least one of the incompatible propositions is a conjunctive statement
   (h) Consistency, in which both propositions are conditional

Exercise 8

Write out five statements about the town or city in which your college or university is located and which you believe are true. For each one, write out a second statement which *supports* it. For example,

   Statement: Detroit, Michigan, is not just an industrial city.

   Support: Although Detroit is home to many large auto parts and assembly plants, it also houses a major symphony and an important art museum, several universities and colleges, some great clubs and restaurants, and a beautiful riverfront shoreline and parks.

NOTE

1. The vocabulary we use here is not the traditional logician's vocabulary. Tradiationally, a pair of statements which are exhustive alternatives were called **contradictories**, and a pair of statements which are incompatible but *not* exhaustive alternatives were called **contraries**. The traditional logician's vocabulary runs counter to the current ordinary meaning of 'contradictory' and takes a while to get used to. Moveover, our vocabulary is easier to generalize from pairs (which are sets of two) to sets as such.

6

Evaluating Inferences

When we make inferences, as we've seen, we form an attitude toward some proposition (called the conclusion) on the basis of information or beliefs already in their possession (called the premisses). For example, you might become quite certain that women tend to live longer than men when your mother reminds you that most of the women in your family outlived their husbands.

When we draw an inference, it's because we trust or take for granted the beliefs or information which constitute our premisses and because we think that those premisses justify us in taking some given attitude toward our conclusion. Our inference will be a good one if our trust in the premisses is well placed *and* if those premisses do in fact justify the attitude we take toward the conclusion.

We already pointed out in Chapter 4 the two chief criteria that must be met if an inference is to be a good one:

1. The grounds of the inference (the evidence and assumptions—the premisses) must each be *acceptable*.
2. The grounds taken together must be *suitably linked* to the conclusion.

Either of these criteria can be satisfied without the other being satisfied, but that's not enough. To be good, an inference has to meet *both* criteria.

No matter how solid the premisses are, if they do not justify the attitude we take toward the conclusion, then the inference is faulty. For example, even if there is no doubt about the fact that most of the women in one family have outlived their husbands, that's not enough evidence to justify confidence (not just suspicion, but assurance) that women in general live longer then men, because that family might be untypical. So in a good inference the link between premises and conclusion will have to be suitable.

And no matter how strong a link there is between the premises and the conclusion, if the premises are unacceptable, the inference is defective. For example, "All married women outlive their husbands, so many women live longer than many men." Here the premiss is so tightly linked to the conclusion that *if* it is true, then (granting the assumption that many women marry) the conclusion must be true too. But the premiss itself is not believable, and the inference is therefore defective. So in a good inference the premises will be acceptable.

The acceptability of the grounds, and the suitability of the link between them and the conclusion, are thus the twin topics that must be addressed in deciding whether an inference is a good one.

6.1 Evaluating the Premisses or Grounds

Acceptability

The grounds of an inference are acceptable just in case it is *reasonable* to accept them. Four remarks about the nature of **acceptability** so understood are in order.

1. *Acceptability is not the same thing as truth.* Propositions supported by careful observation or accepted on the say-so of highly credible sources are reasonable to believe and are therefore acceptable as premisses in inferences, even though occasionally such propositions turn out to be false (for example, a trustworthy physician's prediction, based on a close examination of your sore throat and other symptoms, that your throat will be cured in a few days if you take the prescribed medication). Propositions accepted on the say-so of sources lacking in credibility are not reasonable to believe and are not acceptable as premisses, even in those cases where by sheer luck they happen to be right (for example, a palm reader's prediction that you will live to be over 80 years old).

2. *Acceptability is relative to a person's knowledge and so can vary from one person to another.* Some grounds will be acceptable in *your* inferences because it is reasonable for *you* to accept them, but not acceptable in *my* inferences because it is not reasonable for *me* to accept them. If you happen to know something that I have no reason to believe (for example, you know that I am going to be offered that job I want, but I have no good reason to believe that I will be), then this proposition will be an acceptable ground in your inferences (for example, you can infer that I will be able to afford a car) but not for mine (for example, as yet I have no basis for concluding that I will be able to afford a car). When you are evaluating your own inferences, what matters is whether a premiss is (or

should be) acceptable *to you*. When evaluating another's inferences, what's relevant is whether their premisses are (or should be) acceptable *to them*.

3. *Acceptability can vary from one time to another.* A proposition which is reasonable for me to accept today may not be reasonable for me to accept tomorrow, if additional information comes to light which casts doubt on it. If today your physician tells you that your blood sugar level is abnormally high, that proposition is one that it is reasonable for you to accept and to use as a premiss in your inferences. But if tomorrow her office calls to inform you that your test results were mixed up with someone else's and asks you to go to back to the lab, the proposition about your abnormally high blood sugar level will then no longer be acceptable. When you are evaluating inferences and judging acceptability, you will usually be interested in whether a premiss is acceptable to you at that time.

4. *Acceptability is a property that belongs to each premiss taken by itself.* In the case of most inferences, the grounds appealed to come from a variety of sources and/or previous inferences and so may have varying acceptability. For example, if it's important to know a day's weather you might check the thermometer, listen to a weather report on the radio, and look up the long-range forecast in last week's newspaper. But if the thermometer is broken, and the long-range forecast has limited reliability beyond a couple of days, the information you get from those sources is unacceptable, whereas the radio report is likely to be based on the Weather Bureau's latest forecasts, so its information is acceptable. When assessing the premisses of an inference for acceptability, therefore, it is necessary to assess each proposition separately.

Standards of Acceptability

On what are we to base our judgments about whether a premiss is acceptable? Here are two conditions either of which makes the grounds of an inference acceptable.

1. The ground was accepted on the say-so of a credible source, especially if it was arrived at through the correct use of a reliable procedure or method.
2. The ground is a conclusion from a previously drawn good inference.

Explanatory comments about each of these points are in order.

1. *Credible sources and reliable methods.* The source of a premiss can be yourself as well as someone else. Each of us is normally a credible source for such information as is immediately available to our senses and our short- and medium-term memory.

An example where you are the source? If you are rested, wide awake, sober, and you know how to use a tape measure, then the fact that you've just measured your room carefully and found it to be 10 feet 4 inches wide makes that proposition about its width reasonable for you to believe. An example where someone else is the source? If your physician, who has a good track record with your family and a solid reputation in the local medical community, tells you, after a thorough examination and after checking test results, that you are in good health, then it is reasonable for you to believe that you are in good health.

The credibility of sources is a function of the factors discussed in Chapter 2.

2. *Previously inferred premisses.* A premiss used in an inference can be the conclusion of a previous inference. If that previous inference was a good one, then it is reasonable to believe its conclusion, which thereby can serve in turn as an acceptable ground for further inferences.

For example, if at 8:00 A.M. on a June morning you look at your outdoor thermometer, which is not located in the sun or where indoor temperatures can affect it, and which has been accurate in the past, and you see a reading of 80 degrees Fahrenheit on it, you can infer that it's probably going to be a hot day. You may then use that conclusion as a premisses in drawing other inferences—such as that you should wear light clothing when you go out or that you should turn on the air conditioner.

When a previous inference renders a premiss acceptable, it is with the proviso that *no additional information has since come to light which would undermine that earlier inference or cast doubt on its conclusion.* So, for example, if your roommate mentions that he broke the thermometer, or if you hear a weather forecast predicting a cold front moving into the area by 9:00 A.M., then your conclusion that it's probably going to be a hot day is no longer something you should accept without qualification. It should no longer serve as a premiss in your further inferences.

When Should a Premiss's Acceptability Be Checked?

In many cases the acceptability of the propositions from which an inference is drawn is quite unproblematic. There are enormous numbers of propositions that normal people of our culture obviously know to be true, for example, that the color of the sky on a sunny day is blue, that Washington is the national capital of the United States, or that computers run on electricity. When things like this, which are common knowledge in our culture, turn up in inferences, there is usually no point in worrying about their acceptability.

Three sorts of circumstances in which it is wise to investigate premiss acceptability are the following:

1. When there is *some particular reason for doubting or questioning* the information used as a premiss (for example, you're aware that there is controversy about the truth of the premiss or the premiss doesn't seem to square with other things you know or believe)
2. When the premiss concerns *unfamiliar or obscure information or suppositions* (for example, if a friend has told you about banking practices in Sri Lanka, you would do well to wonder whether she is in a position to know about those practices before you based any conclusions on what she says)
3. When *a lot depends on whether your conclusion is correct* (for example, before you sell your car to invest in a stock market tip, you really should scrutinize the reliability of the tip carefully)

These comments complete the present chapter's discussion of the acceptability of the grounds of an inference. When you have occasion to judge acceptability you will normally find it helpful to utilize either (1) the techniques for assessing sources that are detailed in Chapter 2 and Chapter 3 or (2) the techniques for assessing premiss-conclusion link that are discussed in the remainder of this chapter.

6.2 EVALUATING THE LINK BETWEEN PREMISSES AND CONCLUSION

People are often accused of "jumping to conclusions." That accusation amounts to the charge that a person has drawn a conclusion from evidence that provides only very weak support for it. In this section, we will discuss some ways of deciding what amount of support exists for a conclusion.

Strength of Inference Link

The link between the premisses and conclusion of an inference can vary in strength. Accordingly, we will use the term **strength of inference link** to refer to the quality of relationship between premisses and conclusion. As we use that phrase, assessing the strength of an inference link is *independent* of assessing the acceptability of the premisses.

When someone evaluates an inference link, he or she is asking what attitude toward the conclusion would be justified by the grounds (including any additional assumptions which may be made), *if those grounds were completely acceptable or known to be true*. The stronger the attitude that would be justified if the premisses were known to be true, the stronger the link between the premisses and the conclusion. The following examples will illustrate.

Assuming that the premisses are known to be true, then

- If the premisses should make a person *absolutely certain* that the conclusion is true, the inference link has *maximum strength*.
- If the premisses should make one *confident* (though less than absolutely certain) that the conclusion is true, then the inference link could be described as *strong*.
- If, accepting the premisses, one should simply be *inclined to think* the conclusion true, then the inference link might be said to have *moderate* strength.
- If, given the premisses, a person should only *suspect* that the conclusion might be true, then the inference link could be described as only *weak*.
- If the acceptability of the premisses should *make no difference* at all to a person's attitude toward the conclusion, then the strength of the inference link is clearly *zero* or *nil*.

Between maximum and zero, degrees of inference strength fall on a continuum. As we use them here, the words "maximum," "strong," "moderate," "weak," and "zero" do not connote precise degrees of strength but, rather, indicate in a rough and ready way *ranges* on that continuum. Of two strong (or weak) arguments, one might well be stronger (or weaker) than the other. Moreover, there is no sharp or definable boundary between strong and moderate or between moderate and weak. So these are not technical labels you are obliged to use, but verdicts expressed in everyday language that roughly indicate the strength of the link in various circumstances. If you find other terms which convey your assessment of the degree of strength of the inference link more informatively or more naturally, use them.

Support Comes from All the Premisses in a Group Taken Together

The strength of the link between premisses and conclusion depends on how strongly premisses *as a group* support a conclusion. Hence, deciding on the strength of that link requires considering what degree of support *the premisses taken together* give to the conclusion.

For example, if Hans's grounds for concluding that he has met a Nobel prizewinner are that (a) he met the novelist Saul Bellow at a party and that (b) Saul Bellow has won the Nobel prize for literature, then Hans has the strongest possible grounds for his conclusion. But this conclusion is not at all supported by either premiss considered just by itself. If Hans knows only that Saul Bellow won the Nobel prize for literature, he has no reason to conclude that *he* has met a Nobel prizewinner. And if he knows only that he met Saul Bellow at a party, he has no support for the conclusion that he has met a Nobel prizewinner. But when the two premisses are both known to be true—when Hans knows both that he met Saul Bellow and that Bellow won a Nobel prize—then they are linked to the conclusion with maximum strength. This example illustrates how crucial it is to look at the set of all the premises in order to evaluate the strength of their connection with the conclusion.

We saw in Chapter 4 that a piece of reasoning can contain two independent or parallel groups of premises that support one and the same conclusion—two *independent* inferences leading to the same conclusion. In such cases, you should consider each independent group separately and try to judge how strongly its premises taken together are linked to the conclusion. For example, Hans might have an additional reason for thinking he's met a Nobel prizewinner, namely, that (c) he met many Stanford faculty members while visiting that university and (d) there are lots of Nobel prizewinners on the faculty of Stanford University. Although (c) and (d) together provide some support to the conclusion, that support is much weaker than the support provided by (a) and (b) taken together.

In the next two sections (6.3 and 6.4) we will discuss the evaluation of cases where one thinks a group of premises taken together do support a conclusion to some degree. In Section 6.5 we will discuss cases where the premises don't seem to support the conclusion at all.

6.3 THE VARIETIES OF INFERENTIAL STRENGTH

We now review some of the different degrees of strength of inference, and at the same time begin to demonstrate a strategy you can use for estimating such strength.[1] In Section 6.4 we will describe that strategy in more detail.

Entailment

The strongest sort of link occurs *when the premises taken together entail the conclusion*—when it is *impossible* for all the premises to be true and the conclusion to be false. Where you are absolutely certain your grounds and assumptions are true, and you can see that in no imaginable circumstances could they possibly be true yet the conclusion be false, you may be certain that your conclusion is true as well. The example of Hans's meeting with Saul Bellow was an instance of entailment. Here is another one:

E1   Someone believes that Prince Charles's IQ is 190 and also that anyone with an IQ greater than 150 is eligible to join Mensa,[2] and he infers from these beliefs that Prince Charles is eligible to join Mensa.

In this case the premises are

P1   Prince Charles has an IQ of 190.
P2   Anyone with an IQ greater than 150 is eligible to join Mensa.

and the conclusion is

C   Prince Charles is eligible to join Mensa.

Try to conceive of a situation in which both these premises are true and that conclusion false. Perhaps, you might say, the rules of British royalty forbid Prince Charles from joining such organizations as Mensa; but if that were so, then the second premiss—that *anyone* with an IQ greater than 150 is eligible to join Mensa—would be false. Well then, perhaps Prince Charles is ineligible because his IQ is less than 150; but if that were so, then the first premiss wouldn't be true. There just isn't any conceivable situation in which both these premises are true and the conclusion false. That's why these premises taken together **entail** this conclusion.

Notice that the premises in E1 entail their conclusion even if—as we suspect—Prince Charles's IQ is *not* 190.[3] The strength of an inference link can be maximal even when some or all of the premises are false or not reasonable to believe. If the inference in E1 is defective, as we suspect it is, that is because at least one of its grounds is unacceptable, not because there is anything wrong with the link between those grounds and the conclusion.

Contrast E1 with the following example:

E2   *Grounds*: Gary is an intravenous drug user. He has looked sick for the last few months and has been depressed and irritable.
       Conclusion: Gary has contracted AIDS.

Here it is quite easy to imagine a situation in which the grounds are true but the conclusion false. Although Gary, as an intravenous drug user, is at risk for AIDS, we can imagine that his sickly appearance, depression, and irritability are due to any number of things other than AIDS—to poor nutrition, for example. Because we can conceive of such a situation, we can see that it is *possible* for the grounds to be true and the conclusion false. In other words, we can see that in this case the premises do *not* entail the conclusion.

Testing for entailment by trying to conceive of situations in which the premises could be true and the conclusion false is useful and usually fruitful, but it is not foolproof. There is always a chance that our powers of imagination will fail us, and we will overlook a genuinely possible situation in which the premises are true and the conclusion false. Despite these shortcomings, we recommend you use this technique when you try to ascertain the presence of an entailment.

There are more reliable ways to prove entailment for certain ranges of cases: the methods of formal logic and of mathematical proof and calculation. However, these methods tend to be quite technical, and there are problems with applying them to natural language discourse, so we will not attempt to introduce you to them in this book. See Appendix A for some rudimentary techniques from formal logic for ascertaining entailment.

Less than Maximal Strength

Most of our inferences in everyday life fall short of entailment or maximum strength of inference. That is to say, *our premises taken together support our conclusion even though it is possible or conceivable that the premises are true but the conclusion false.*

In such cases, the strength of the inference link will depend on *how likely or how plausible* it is that the conclusion is false on the assumption that the premises are true. When a set of premises supplies very strong support for a conclusion, then if those premises are true, the conclusion will very probably be true. Another way to put this point is to say that in such a case it is highly unlikely that the premises will be true yet the conclusion be false. On the other hand, when the inference link between a set of premises and a conclusion is weak, then it is quite probable that the conclusion is false even if the premises are true.

Following this approach, if someone has discovered that a set of premises doesn't entail the conclusion inferred from it, that will be because they have imagined one or more possible situations in which the premises are true and the conclusion false. They can then ask how likely such possible situations are, and base their judgment about the strength of the inference on their estimate of that likelihood—the likelihood of the possible situations in which the premisses are true and the conclusion false.

For example, when we considered E2, we imagined the following possible situation in which the premises were true and the conclusion false:

> PS   Gary's sickly appearance, depression, and irritability are due to the poor nutrition of his diet.

The possibility is fairly likely, because intravenous drug users tend not to have healthy diets. The drugs suppress their appetites so they don't want to eat, and their life-style tends not to include concern about nutrition. Accordingly, we conclude that the support in E2 is very *weak*. Although the evidence might warrant *suspicion*, it certainly doesn't make it reasonable for anyone to be confident that the inferred conclusion—that Gary is suffering from AIDS—is true. Compare E2 with another inference about Gary:

> E3   *Grounds*: Gary tested positive for HIV last year. This year, according to his doctor, he shows most of the typical symptoms of AIDS. *Conclusion*: Gary has AIDS.

Here the premises do not *entail* the conclusion either, for medical tests are never 100% reliable, having the HIV virus is not the same thing as having AIDS and symptoms are occasionally misleading, so we can imagine:

PS   (a) Gary's HIV test was misanalyzed, and (b) his AIDS-like symptoms
     are due to a disease that has nothing to do with AIDS.

However, neither (a) nor (b) is very likely, and that both of them should
happen together is extremely unlikely. Accordingly, it seems quite unlikely that
the conclusion is false if the premisses are true. So the link between premisses
and conclusion in E3 seems to us to be fairly strong.

Strength of Inference Link Is Distinct from Premiss Acceptability

We have said that the suitability of the connection between premisses and conclusion, and the acceptability of the premisses, are separate and independent
aspects of any inference. The point bears repeating. An inferential link can be
strong even if the premisses are unacceptable or weak even if the premisses are
acceptable. That is why, in considering the foregoing examples, we concentrated
our attention on the connection between the premisses and conclusion and
ignored the issue of the acceptability of the premisses.

This point often puzzles people when they first encounter it, but it is of
central importance. When we evaluate the link between premisses and conclusion, we are asking what attitude toward the conclusion would be justified by
our data and assumptions *if they were* completely acceptable or known to be true.
We are making no judgment about *whether they are* in fact acceptable. The strength
of the connection between a set of premisses and a conclusion is independent
of the acceptability of the premisses.

It might help you to appreciate the independence of the premiss-conclusion
link from the acceptability of the premisses if you think of situations in which
we assess inference links even though we have no idea whether the premisses
we're using are true or false.

In one kind of case we have information from which we might draw an
inference, but we don't know if that information is reliable. Suppose a male
student is thinking of taking a course from a female professor who, according
to a friend, is a feminist. Should her being a feminist make any difference to
whether he takes the course? Notice that we can debate, and perhaps decide,
this question in total ignorance of whether the information about the professor
is true. If we decide that the professor's being a feminist makes no difference
either way, we have in effect made the judgment that the strength of the link
between the premiss "The professor is a feminist" and the conclusion "He should
take the course from her" or "He should not take the course from her" is nil.
And if that is our decision, we do not have to bother to find out whether the
premiss is true. So here is a case which illustrates the independence of the
premiss-conclusion link from the actual truth or falsehood of the premisses.

In another kind of case, we draw inferences where we do not have any information at all—where our premises are pure suppositions. Imagine, for example, that you are planning a trip next day in North Dakota in the winter. Since the road you must take always gets snowed in during blizzards, you know a forecast of a blizzard the next day would give you strong grounds for moving your trip ahead a day or postponing it until later. In other words, you judge that the link between "There will be a blizzard tomorrow" and "I should leave today or postpone my trip until later" is a strong one. Recognizing that, you realize you need to get a weather forecast. So here is a case where we assess the strength of the inference link first, and only afterward, and on the basis of that judgment, try to find out if the premises are true.

6.4 A STRATEGY FOR ESTIMATING STRENGTH OF INFERENCE

Four Steps of the Strategy

In E1, E2, and E3 we were able to form an opinion about the strength of the link between premises and conclusion as a result of trying to conceive of situations in which the premises would all be true and the conclusion false. What we did in those cases involved four steps, which we can summarize as follows:

STRATEGY FOR ESTIMATING STRENGTH OF INFERENCE

Step 1   *Try to conceive of possible situations in which the premises are all true but the conclusion is false.*

Step 2   *Decide whether there are such possible situations, and if so what they are.* If every candidate for an additional possibility that you can think of contradicts one or another of the premises, for instance, then you can provisionally conclude that there are no possible situations in which the premises are true and the conclusion false (and that therefore the premises seem to entail the conclusion). If you succeed in thinking of one or more possible alternatives, jot down a succinct description of each of those possibilities.

Step 3   *If you have thought of possible situations in which the premises are true and the conclusion false, estimate* how *likely or plausible each of those possible situations is.* Where do get your estimates? You have to rely on your common sense and whatever background knowledge is available to you.

Step 4   *Rate the strength of the inference link on the basis of your estimate of the likelihood or plausibility of the alternative situations.* The more likely that one of the alternative situations might occur, the weaker the inferential link; the less likely one of those situations might occur, the stronger the link (see Table 6.1). From a strict theoretical point of view, the likelihood that one or another of the alternatives might occur involves the sum of the likelihoods of all the alternatives. In practice, you can usually base your rating on the likelihood of the most likely alternative. If there's even one alternative that is fairly likely, then the inference link is weak. If all the alternatives are highly unlikely, then the inference link is strong (even if there are a number of such highly unlikely alternatives).

This is a strategy to fall back on when you lack more specific skills or knowledge—as everyone inevitably does in real-life situations under the practical necessity of drawing conclusions in a limited amount of time. The verdicts arrived at using it will not always be correct, because there might be likely or plausible situations you did not think of. Some people are better at imagining possibilities than others, imagination can fail under conditions of fatigue or pressure, and in many cases a familiarity with a specialized subject-matter is necessary in order to think up realistic possibilities. In addition, your estimates of the likelihood of those alternative situations will be more or less good, depending on how much you know about the subject-matter under consideration. Still, this strategy is better than no method at all, and most important, it will lead you to ask the right questions.

Table 6.1   Testing for Strength of Inference-Link

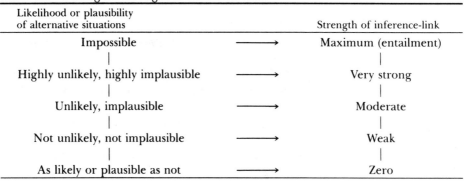

Likelihood or plausibility of alternative situations		Strength of inference-link
Impossible	$\longrightarrow$	Maximum (entailment)
Highly unlikely, highly implausible	$\longrightarrow$	Very strong
Unlikely, implausible	$\longrightarrow$	Moderate
Not unlikely, not implausible	$\longrightarrow$	Weak
As likely or plausible as not	$\longrightarrow$	Zero

Remember that this strategy is one to use when you think there is a positive connection between the premises taken together and the conclusion—where you think the premises do support the conclusion to *some* degree. In Section 6.5 we discuss what to do when you don't think the premises lend any support to the conclusion.

Some More Examples

Let us show you in more detail how the strategy works by considering some more examples. Our last series of examples (E2 and E3) involved inferences to an explanation. The next series (E4–E6) are concerned with a different kind of subject-matter, one that involves statistical considerations.

E4 *Grounds*: I had six students from my women's studies class over to study last night. When the subject of abortion came up, five of the six approved of abortion on demand.
Conclusion: Most college students disapprove of abortion on demand.

Step 1: Try to imagine or conceive of *a possible situation in which the premisses are true and the conclusion false*. It's easy to do so in this case. For it is quite possible that since all these students are from a women's studies class, they are not representative of college students as a whole. So it is possible that

PS1 Most college students who don't take women's studies courses favor abortion on demand.

Moreover, it is also quite possible that this sample of six is not typical even of students who take women's studies courses, let alone of college students as a whole. In that case, the following situation is possible:

PS2 Though a majority of college students—both those who take women's studies and those who don't—oppose abortion on demand, this group of six quite untypically contained five who favor it.

Step 2: PS1 and PS2 are both situations in which five of the six students from one particular class favored abortion on demand (that is, the premiss is true), but still most college students do not, so the conclusion is false. Since we can conceive of situations in which the premisses would be true and the conclusion false, these premisses do not entail their conclusion, and hence the inference link is not of maximum strength.

Step 3: Now we must estimate the likelihood or plausibility of PS1 and PS2. We might well suspect that students who take women's studies courses differ from those who don't in their attitude to abortion on demand. In light of that, we could judge it somewhat likely that women's studies students aren't representative of students generally when it comes views about abortion and, therefore, that PS1 is somewhat likely. Furthermore, a sample of six is almost certainly a very small sample of college students generally, so it's fairly likely that it won't be representative of the population of college students from which it's drawn, and this is especially so when it comes to a small sample all of whom were taken from the same class. So PS2 is fairly likely.

Step 4: Which of the possible situations we've imagined is the most likely? We speculated that PS1 is somewhat likely, but we'd need more information to be confident. PS2, however, seems fairly likely on the face of it. So PS2 is, for us at this time, the more likely of the two possible situations. Given the likelihood of PS2, how do we rate the strength of the inference in E4? Since we regard PS2 as fairly likely, we judge the link in E4 to be quite *weak*.

Now compare E4 with the following inference.

E5   *Grounds*: Samplings of attitudes of college students toward abortion over the past several years have shown a steady increase in the percentage who favor abortion on demand. And 20 years ago surveys showed that just over 25% of college students approved of it.
Conclusion: A majority of college students favor abortion on demand.

Step 1: The premisses contain claims about the trend in attitudes toward abortion on demand among college students. Moreover, they provide a base figure that is consistent with the possibility that approval is above 50% among college students today. Could other facts consistent with these grounds be inconsistent with the conclusion? Well, we do not know how large the increase has been, so we can imagine the following possible situation:

PS1   The percentage of college students who favor abortion on demand has increased steadily over the past 10 years, but only at the rate of 2% a year, so that today about 45% of them approve of it.

In this situation, the grounds would be true, but the conclusion that a majority of college students favor abortion on demand would be false. Thus when we get to **step 2**, we can say that the premisses don't entail the conclusion. Moving to **step 3**, we might suspect that the rate of increase in those approving abortion on demand was greater than 2% per year—given that there have been striking changes in social attitudes toward abortion over the last few years. Nevertheless, that figure remains a very real possibility: abortion is a highly charged issue on which people seem hesitant to change their views. In **step 4** we state our verdict: the strength of the inference from the grounds in E3 to its conclusion cannot be rated as strong; the grounds seem to us to provide *moderate* support for the conclusion.

Compare E5 with a somewhat different inference on the same topic:

E6   *Grounds*: In several surveys that included extensive probing of social and moral attitudes conducted between 1970 and 1990 by a highly reputable polling organization on representative samples of students, the percentage of college students favoring abortion on demand rose from just under 35% in 1970 to something over 65% in 1990. In these surveys, the margin of error was 4%; that is, the results are within four percentage points of the true figure 19 times out of 20.
Conclusion: Most college students favor abortion on demand.

Steps 1 and 2: We can say that the evidence in E5 does not entail the conclusion, for we can imagine the following possibilities:

PS1   The questions asked by the pollsters did not elicit honest answers.

PS2   The pollsters had bad luck and hit that 20th time when their results are off by more than four percentage points with each survey.

Step 3: Both these possibilities are *quite* unlikely. The polling organization was said to be highly reputable, so it be expected to know how to design and administer appropriate questions. And the likelihood of hitting one chance out of 20 even twice in a row is statistically small. **Step 4**: If these possibilities are the only basis for rejecting the inference, the link between the evidence and the conclusion in E6 is *fairly strong*. In other words, *if* the grounds were acceptable, they would pretty much establish the conclusion.

Still More Examples

Next we illustrate the strategy using examples of still another sort—inferences involving evaluations. If you are confident that you understand the strategy, you can skip to the next section. However, it will not hurt to read on, trying the strategy out yourself on these examples, then comparing your results with our analyses.

Consider, first, the following case:

E7   *Grounds*: The Nino gets more than 30 miles per gallon in city driving, is easy to park, and has excellent brakes.
Conclusion: The Nino is one of the best cars you can buy.

Steps 1 and 2: First, the conclusion is that the Nino is *better than* most other cars, but the data contain no evidence to suggest that the positive features mentioned are in any way unique to the Nino. So an important possibility that would render the premises true and the conclusion false is this:

PS1   Cars which get more that 30 miles per gallon in city driving, are easy to park, and have excellent brakes are common.

Second, the evidence concerns only a few of the many features that people are interested in when buying a car. Among the kinds of feature omitted: comfort, ride, handling, power, frequency of repair record, style, and safety. So the following possibility has to be considered:

PS2   The Nino is one of the worst autos when it comes to comfort, ride, handling, power, frequency of repair record, style, and safety.

Clearly the premises of E7 could be true and its conclusion false. The inferential link in this example is therefore less than maximal. Step 3: PS1 is fairly likely and PS2 is a possibility that can't be discounted. Step 4: Accordingly, the support in E7 is very *weak*.

Next consider a slightly different example:

E8   *Grounds*: In fuel economy the Nino exceeds every other car, *Car and Driver* magazine rated its handling as second only to the Mercedes, and its frequency of repair record is better than any other North American car. Although the comfort, ride, and power of larger cars is superior to the Nino's, it compares favorably with other midsized cars in these respects. And in these days of high gasoline prices, few of us can afford the luxury of large automobiles.
Conclusion: The Nino is one of the best buys on the car market today.

Step 1: (1) Though the Nino is claimed to be better than other cars in fuel consumption, handling, and frequency of repair, no indication is given of *how much* better it is in these respects; hence the following possibility:

PS1   The Nino's superiority to the average car is quite small and therefore of little or no significance.

(2) The crucial issue of *safety* is not addressed at all; hence the following possibility:

PS2   The Nino is unacceptable because it is substandard when it comes to safety features.

And (3) no information is given as to how the Nino compares with other than North American cars in frequency of repair; hence the following possibility:

PS3   A dozen different midsized "foreign" cars are almost as good as the Nino in the features where the Nino excels and markedly superior when it comes to frequency of repair record and safety.

Accordingly, the grounds here do not entail the conclusion (Step 2).
Step 3: Although perhaps none of these three possibilities is highly likely, the chance that one of them is so is not negligible. **Step 4**: We conclude that the strength of inference is *moderate* at best.

Yet another variant on the Nino example:

E9   *Grounds*: In rate of fuel consumption the Nino exceeds every other car; it gets 42 miles per gallon in city driving; the next best performer gets 38, and the average car gets 29. *Car and Driver* magazine rated the Nino's handling as second only to the Mercedes; it was one of only three cars whose handling was rated excellent by the magazine. Its

frequency-of-repair record is better than any other North American car and is exceeded by only one nondomestic car. Although the comfort, ride, and power of larger cars is superior to the Nino's, the Nino compares favorably to other midsized cars in these respects. The Nino's price is competitive with that of other cars in its class. And in these days of high gasoline prices, few of us can afford the luxuries of large automobiles. Finally, the Nino won the Ralph Nader award as the safest midsized car manufactured in the last 10 years.
Conclusion: The Nino is one of the best cars you can buy.

Step 1: One can imagine possibilities that would render the premisses true and the conclusion false. For example,

PS1   *Car and Driver* magazine botched its assessment of the handling of the Nino; in fact, the car is almost impossible to control at speeds over 40 mph.

PS2   The Nino received the Ralph Nader award as a result of a bribe and is in fact a death trap that is unsafe at any speed.

So (**Step 2**) the premisses do not entail the conclusion.

Step 3: But PS1 and PS2 are mere possibilities that are unlikely in the extreme. *Car and Driver* has a standard test it uses for scores of cars. And Ralph Nader is famous for his moral uprightness—a reputation his career depends on. **Step 4**: So the support in E9 is very *strong*.

6.5 ZERO SUPPORT

So far we have illustrated only inference links with strengths ranging from "maximum" to "very weak." Zero support is a special case. If you see no connection between the stated grounds and the conclusion of a proposed inference, or if the premisses seem to support the *opposite* of the conclusion, then you need to ask yourself whether there is in fact any positive link between the premisses and the conclusion.

But when the stated grounds seem to provide zero support for their conclusion, the question arises why anyone would be tempted to draw such an inference. Sometimes you will find that the reasoner made a simple mistake (for example, a calculation error or one of the errors in reasoning described in Section A.2 of Appendix A), which explains why they thought the conclusion followed from the premisses. At other times, it will be plausible to expect that the reasoner was making an **unstated assumption** that, when added to the stated premisses, increases the strength of inferential support. These two sorts of case are quite different, and we will discuss them separately.

Non Sequiturs

Consider the following variant on our earlier example, E1:

> E10   From the beliefs that Lady Diana's IQ is 190 and that anyone with
> an IQ greater than 150 is eligible to join Mensa, someone infers that
> Prince Charles is eligible to join Mensa.

There is something very wrong with this inference. You might be inclined
to say something like: "What does Lady Di's IQ have to do with whether Prince
Charles can get into Mensa? Whether he can join Mensa depends on what *his*
IQ is, and that's something he's born with and is not affected by whom he
marries." The inferential link in E10 isn't just weak, it's nonexistent. E10 is
an example of what is called a **non sequitur** (from the Latin for "it does not
follow").

As a matter of fact, it is difficult to imagine anyone drawing the inference
imagined in E10. But there are inferences that people actually make, and that
we ourselves might be tempted to make, which are non sequiturs. For example,
it is sometimes tempting to reason like this:

> E11   Very few women are doctors; therefore, very few doctors are women.

To see that the inference is a non sequitur, consider the following parallel
reasoning.

> E12   Very few members of the armed services are generals; therefore,
> very few generals are members of the armed services.

The reasoning in E12 is obviously defective, and it should call our attention
to the fact that knowing the percentage of A's which are B's tells us *next to nothing*
about the percentage of B's that are A's. So the premises in E11 and E12 give
no support at all to the conclusions inferred from them.

The mistake in E11 is a fairly common one; it is a defective pattern of
inference that people are prone to fall into—presumably because they are easily
confused when they deal with matters that fall within the area of class ratio
arithmetic.

Unstated Assumptions

Sometimes an inference is proposed in which the stated or explicit grounds do
not, strictly by themselves, provide any significant support to the conclusion. For
example,

> E13   Don't believe him: he's an atheist.

We're being invited to infer that the person should not be believed from the fact that he is an atheist. What does being an atheist have to do with believability? Not much—unless we assume that atheists are more likely to lie than are those who believe in God. In the case of an inference like E13, it is more likely that someone proposing it has some such assumption in mind than that he or she is guilty of a non sequitur. So in such cases it is reasonable to take them to be making the assumption that strengthens the inference.

To function as a reasoner's unstated assumption, a proposition must have the following characteristics:

(a) The proposition is something that the person making or proposing the inference actually believes or accepts.

(b) The person's acceptance of the proposition explains why he or she wants to infer the conclusion from the explicit premises.

In some cases (as in E13) it is pretty obvious what the reasoner's unstated assumption is. But it isn't always easy to be sure what (if any) is functioning as an unstated assumption because it can be difficult to know what's going on in the other person's mind.

If it seems likely that someone's unstated assumption figures in an inference whose stated grounds by themselves provide zero support for the conclusion, then proceed as follows:

STRATEGY FOR DEALING WITH INFERENCES THAT MAY DEPEND ON A REASONER'S UNSTATED ASSUMPTIONS

1. Formulate explicitly one or more assumptions that the person making the inference might have in mind. The assumptions you formulate should meet conditions (a) and (b).

2. For each such assumption you formulate, decide whether it is a reasonable one to make.

3. If the only assumptions you can come up with are quite unreasonable, then you may conclude that the stated premises provide zero support for the conclusion.

4. If you find an assumption that is plausible, then add it to the stated grounds and reevaluate the inference link using the strategy for assessing strength of inference.

6.6 SPECIAL FEATURES OF GROUNDS THAT SUPPORT BUT DO NOT ENTAIL THE CONCLUSION

We have so far illustrated the different degrees of support that evidence or grounds can provide for inferences drawn from them. We next introduce two particularly significant characteristics of inferences whose premises support but do not entail their conclusions.

The Effect of Subsequent or Additional Information on Support

When the evidence *entails* the conclusion, it means that no further evidence consistent with those grounds can conceivably overturn the conclusion. When the grounds do *not* entail the conclusion, but support it to a given degree, the addition of new evidence that points in a different direction from the conclusion is perfectly conceivable. With inferences of the second sort, we are never in a position to know with total certainty that no such contrary evidence exists. The stronger the support, the less likely such undermining evidence exists—in fact, that is part of what is meant by "strong" support. But the possibility that undermining evidence does exist cannot be ruled out.

Two lessons may be drawn from these facts about support:

1. It is unreasonable to refuse to revise one's opinions and conclusions in the light of additional information and evidence requiring such changes, if and when it arises.
2. Inferring a conclusion of any importance from just the evidence in hand is sometimes premature. It is necessary also to consider the likelihood that a search for additional relevant evidence will turn up information that would change the significance of the evidence in hand.

The Role of Background Knowledge in Judging Strength of Inference

To determine the strength of an inference link that is not an entailment, you almost always have to draw on some degree of background knowledge. Such knowledge is needed to recognize the difference between grounds (premises) that are relevant or have some bearing on the conclusion and information that has nothing to do with the conclusion—that would result in a *non sequitur* if an inference were drawn from it.

For example, if you are evaluating an inference about the relative virtues of computers, you need to know what sorts of features are desirable, what sorts are undesirable and what sorts are essential. You would not fault somebody for not factoring in the locations of the disk drives, but you should object if he ignored the number of disk drives or the processor speeds of the different brands and models.

Not only do we rely on background knowledge to decide what evidence is relevant; we also need it when we try to decide how likely it is that the conclusion might be false even though the premisses are true. That is, we need to draw on background knowledge to judge whether there are likely or plausible alternative situations consistent with the premisses that falsify the conclusion. "Could Gary have been an intravenous drug user, looked sick, and been irritable—yet *not* have had AIDS?" we asked about E2. And we also needed to know how likely was the possible situation in which those symptoms were due do something other than AIDS. Background knowledge is needed to be able to answer such questions.

When it comes to evaluating the strength of inferences, *there is no substitute for knowledge*. That is why it is impossible to have a concrete, mechanical method for appraising the strength of inferences: there is no way to identify all the possibly relevant background knowledge for every possible inference. The best we can do is suggest the kinds of question to ask. It is up to each person to ask the appropriate questions in any given situation and then use their knowledge, or find out the information to answer them.

Remember, the strategy described in this chapter for assessing strength of support—even when it is based on reasonable estimates of likelihood—is not foolproof. The method depends for its success on our powers of imagination and on our background knowledge, and both of these will be inadequate to the task in plenty of cases. However, using this method can point you in the direction of the information you need when evaluating inferences. The method's success will depend in part on how honest you are with yourself in recognizing when you don't know something and on how diligent you are in finding out what you need to know.

6.7 INFERENCE, ARGUMENT, AND EMOTION

The subjects we reason about, and which people make arguments about, typically involve our feelings, and sometimes powerful emotions. That is as it should be. Emotion is an essential part of human life; without it, nothing would matter to us, and we would lack any motive to engage in reasoning in the first place.

Contrary to popular belief, emotion—even strong emotion—need *not* be an enemy of reason or reasoning. It does happen, however, that powerful feelings sometimes lead us to reason badly—to make unwarranted inferences or to jump to conclusions when we have inadequate evidence. If we are angry, frightened, or anxious—if we want very much for a proposition to be true or for it to be false—we are tempted to accept information from sources lacking in credibility or to misjudge the strength of the link between premisses and conclusion. Therefore, at times like these, we ought especially to try to stop and think before we draw a conclusion. At such times it is especially useful to employ the methods described in this chapter for deciding which inferences are good ones and which are not.

Also, when others invite us to draw inferences by presenting us with arguments for conclusions they want us to accept, they sometimes try to confuse or manipulate our reasoning by using emotional or value-laden language in an objectionable way. Appendix B contains a discussion of the nature and uses of value-laden language.

6.8 SUMMARY

Evaluating inferences requires assessing (1) the acceptability of their premises or grounds and (2) the strength of the inference link the grounds provide for the conclusion.

In judging the acceptability of premises we look to (1) the credibility of the source from which the premiss comes or (2) the goodness of any previous inferences which led to that premiss.

In judging the quality of the link between premises and conclusion, we must realize that the strength of inference varies from maximum support (in the case of entailment) to zero support (in the case of outright irrelevance). There is a range of inference support between these two extremes, from very strong to very weak support.

As a rough and ready way to assess the strength of an inference link when there seems to be some positive degree of support, we introduced a strategy involving four steps: (1) Try to conceive of possible situations in which the premises are all true but the conclusion is false. (2) Decide whether there are such possible situations, and if so what they are. (3) If you have thought of possible situations in which the premises are true but the conclusion is false, estimate *how* likely or plausible each of those possible situations is. (4) Rate the strength of the inference link on the basis of your estimate of the likelihood or plausibility of the alternative situations. This strategy amounts to a check on the likelihood that there are other facts, consistent with the premises, that would rule out the conclusion. The greater the likelihood of such facts, the weaker is the support which the stated premises provide for the conclusion.

For cases where there appears to be zero support, try to find either an outright error in reasoning or calculation or else an unstated assumption that the reasoner might be making and that could connect the explicit premises to the conclusion. We outlined a four-step strategy for dealing with inferences that depend on unstated assumptions: (1) formulate the assumption explicitly; (2) decide whether it is a reasonable assumption to make; (3) if the only assumptions you can think of are unreasonable, conclude that the stated premises provide no support to the conclusion; and (4) if you find an assumption that is plausible, then add it to the stated grounds and reevaluate the inference link using the strategy for assessing strength of inference.

When support is less than total, there is always a possibility that additional information will alter the strength of an inference. When evaluating an inference, bring to bear background knowledge in assessing the likelihood of such additional information.

6.9 Exercises

Exercise 1

Consider the inferences in each of the following passages.

(a) Identify the conclusion and the premises from which it is inferred.

(b) If you think the conclusion is supported to some positive degree by the stated premises, use the strategy outlined in Section 6.4 to assess the strength of the inference link. In doing so, explicitly follow the four steps of the strategy.

(c) If you think that an unstated assumption is necessary to link the premises and the conclusion, then proceed according to the strategy for dealing with unstated premises on page 121.

**1. Obviously, North American voters have grown tired of politicians' rhetoric. In the last federal election, 25% of Canadians failed to vote for the country's highest office. In the United States only half of registered voters bothered to turn out to elect the arguably most powerful man on earth. (Scott Burnside, "Off the Wall" column in *The Windsor Star*, September 27, 1989, p. A13.)

2. From the fact that the victim's dog didn't bark when the intruder entered the house, we can deduce that the intruder was known to the victim, or at least to the dog.

3. Everyone knows what is morally right and wrong, yet many people act in ways that are morally wrong. Hence, sometimes people must actually want to perform morally wrong actions.

4. College students pay for their education through tuition, and later, through taxes, so college students should have more say in what they study and how it's taught.

5. Animals can suffer and feel pain, so we should not kill animals.

6. Since the Supreme Court recently ruled in favor of affirmative action in the hiring of women, women will get all the good jobs.

7. Everyone should learn self-hypnosis because it's one of the best ways to reduce stress.

8. The human mind will always be superior to the computer, because computers are only the tools of human minds.

9. War is inevitable, for humans are violent by nature.

10. Withholding information is just the same as lying. Lying is wrong, so withholding information is wrong too.

11. Most people who have studied nutrition prefer food with no preservatives added, so I imagine such foods are better for you.

12. Anyone who has the capacity to kill should avoid keeping guns around the house. Thus no one should keep guns around the house, since we all have the capacity to kill.

13. Capital punishment deters crime. It also ensures that a killer cannot strike again. If follows that capital punishment should be reinstated wherever it has been abolished.

14. Small size is both an advantage and a disadvantage in competing with other organisms for a food source. On the one hand, larger creatures can just brush the smaller aside; on the other hand, it takes less material to make a smaller organism. (Fred Hapgood, *Why Males Exist*, Mentor Books, New York, 1979.)

15. A study of 60 families 1, 5, and 10 years after a divorce reported in *Second Chances*, a book about the effects of divorce on children by Judith Wallerstein and Sandra Blakeslee (Thomas Allen & Son), found the following: Five years after divorce, more than one-third of the 131 children in the sample were doing significantly worse than before, for example, some were depressed or doing poorly in school or with friendships. Ten to 15 years afterward, many entered adulthood full of unresolved anger at their parents. They had low self-esteem and believed that they too would fail in an intimate relationship. More than one-third showed no ambition in their early career-building years. One in 3 men and 1 in 10 women ages 19 to 23 had committed legal offenses, such as theft. These data show why parents should endure a bad marriage out of consideration for the good of their children.

16. Cold baths immediately upon rising are inadvisable, for one is in one's lowest condition upon rising from a very warm bed, and the sudden shock of the cold water is undoubtedly harmful to the kidneys. (C. F. Upton, *The British Manual of Physical Training*, The Macmillan Company, Toronto, n.d., c. 1915, p. 18.)

17. Cold bathing when one is hot and perspiring is obviously dangerous, as it forcibly suppresses the natural working of the pores. (C. F. Upton, *The British Manual of Physical Training*, The Macmillan Company, Toronto, n.d., c. 1915, p. 18.)

18. The controlling metaphors in descriptions of cancer are ... drawn from the language of warfare: every physician and every attentive patient is familiar with, if perhaps inured to, this military terminology. Thus, cancer cells do not simply multiply; they are "invasive." ("Malignant tumors invade even when they grow very slowly," as one textbook puts it.) Cancer cells "colonize" from the original tumor to far sites in the body, first setting up tiny outposts ("micrometastases") whose presence is assumed, though they cannot be detected. Rarely are the body's "defenses" vigorous enough to obliterate a tumor that has established its own blood supply and consists of billions of destructive cells. However "radical" the surgical intervention, however many "scans" are taken of the body landscape, most remissions are temporary; the prospects are that "tumor invasion" will continue, or that rogue cells will eventually regroup and mount a new assault on the organism. (Susan Sontag, *Illness as Metaphor*, Farrar, Straus, Giroux, New York, 1978, pp. 64–65.)

19. There is an area in the Atlantic Ocean, popularly known as "The Bermuda Triangle," in which there have been a number of unexplained disappearances of ships and aircraft or of just the crews of some ships. Careful, thorough investigations have been unable to account for these disappearances. So, it could be that people, aircraft, and ships are being kidnapped

from the Bermuda Triangle by beings or forces from another world. (See Charles Berlitz, *The Bermuda Triangle*, Doubleday, Garden City, NY, 1974.)

20. It is wrong or prima facie wrong to *offer* bribes in business contexts. First, the bribery payment may be an attempt to gain an unfair advantage over one's competitors. Then, again, bribery offers often serve to corrupt the characters of those to whom they are made. Finally, bribery offers often cause the recipient to do things that have bad consequences, and the bad consequences of the action that the recipient is being paid to perform also count as bad consequences of the bribery offer itself. (Adapted from Thomas L. Carson, "Bribery and Extortion in International Business", in Wilfred Waluchow and Deborah Poff, eds., *Business Ethics in Canada*, Prentice Hall Canada, Scarborough, Ontario, 1987, pp. 310-322.)

21. A person without money can have no self-esteem. Yet surely women have as much right to self-esteem as men. It follows, then, that women should have as much money as men.

22. A more likely cause of overweight than sugar is fat in food. A teaspoon of sugar has 16 calories, whereas a teaspoon of fat has 39 calories. (Adapted from Sidney Katz, "Artificial Sweeteners, Do They Help You Lose Weight?" *Chatelaine*, October 1969, p 40.)

Exercise 2

In the following passages, there are inference chains; that is, a conclusion is drawn or inferred directly from a set of one or more main premises, and also one or more of those main premises is itself a conclusion inferred from yet other, subsidiary premises (called premiss support). For each passage (a) decide what is the main conclusion and what are the main premises (those from which it is directly inferred), (b) decide which main premises are themselves inferred from subsidiary premises—and which those are, (c) evaluate the strength of the inference link from the main premises to the main conclusion, and (d) evaluate the strength of the inference links from each set of subsidiary premises to the main premiss inferred from them.

**23. Either the butler committed the murder or the judge committed the murder. Since the butler was passionately in love with the victim, it was not he who committed the murder. So the judge must have committed the murder.

24. It's obvious that astrology is not a real science, since there aren't any universities that offer courses in it. I checked six different university calendars, and I didn't find even a single one that listed an astrology department.

25. *Background*: Several years ago, physical punishment, including the use of the strap, was banned in Ontario schools. One occasionally sees arguments like the following urging that this policy be reversed.

For years now the strap has been banned in Ontario's schools. Can anyone honestly say that youngsters are better mannered and more respectful of the rights of others than in the past? Obviously not. Are our streets safer since counseling has replaced many forms of swift punishment for antisocial behavior? They are not. Evidently the ban has not worked. It should be lifted and physical punishment reinstated in the public schools.

26. Either humans have free will or their actions are predetermined. If human actions are predetermined, they cannot be held responsible for them. If humans cannot be held responsible for their actions, moral praise and blame are out of place. The conclusion must be that either humans have free will or moral praise and blame are out of place.

27. If God were all-good and all-powerful, he would prevent undeserved suffering in the world. But God does not prevent undeserved suffering: millions of innocent children suffer starvation and disease through no fault of their own. So God is not all-good and all-powerful.

28. Since psychological as well as physiological factors play an important role in the feeling of comfort with the temperature and humidity in a room, opinion as well as "sensation" must be considered when deciding what room temperature and humidity are appropriate. This makes it difficult to state conclusively, in terms of hard facts, that certain interior conditions in a building are more comfortable than others. (Edward Mazria, *The Passive Solar Energy Book*, Rondale Press, Emmaus, PA, 1979, pp. 64–65.)

29. There is a close connection between the cleanliness of the skin and clean clothing. It is therefore important to change and wash underclothing at least once a week; dirt from the clothes reaches the skin, and dirt and perspiration from the skin soak into the clothing. (C. F. Upton, *The British Manual of Physical Training*, The Macmillan Company, Toronto, n.d., c. 1915, p. 90.)

30. He's been working on that paper for ages now, so it's probably a masterpiece. So he'll probably get an "A" on it.

31. Several studies show that murderers don't think about the consequences of their crimes before they commit them, so capital punishment can hardly be a deterrent to murder. Capital punishment should not, therefore, be reinstated.

32. There seems to be little chance that a conventional war between nuclear powers could stay limited. And this means that a conventional war between nuclear powers must not even be begun, since it threatens the same holocaust that the limited use of nuclear weapons threatens. (Jonathan Schell, *The Fate of the Earth* Alfred A. Knopf, New York, 1982.)

33. *Background*: In an article that appeared in *Popular Science* in the early 1980's, it was claimed that tanks of sodium sulphide (Na_2S) are completely safe for transport. The following is adapted from one reader's response to that claim.

As a chemist, I take issue with the statement in "Double-Duty Heat Pump" that tanks of sodium sulphide are completely safe for transport. Many chemicals that are "safe" in terms of pressure, temperature, and flammability become dangerous if they spill in a truck accident or train derailment. Spilled Na_2S in contact with water containing even a bit of acid could generate considerable hydrogen sulphide, a fairly poisonous and extremely bad-smelling gas (rotten eggs). And various nasty oxides of sulphur could be generated if the accident involved a fire.

34. Consumer products that threaten the health of large numbers of people should be made illegal, and birth control pills pose a threat to the health

of millions of women. It stands to reason, then, that they should be made illegal. Why do I say that birth control pills pose a health threat? Since birth control pills came into widespread use in North America in the 1960s, the number of North American women treated for gynecological disorders has increased dramatically. What more proof would anybody want?

NOTES

1. The assessment strategy we will recommend is similar to the method recommended by Stephen Thomas in *Practical Reasoning in Natural Language* (Englewood Cliffs, NJ: Prentice Hall, 1977).
2. Mensa is the name of a club in which people with high IQs fraternize and is open only to those with an IQ of 150 or higher.
3. We mean no disrespect for Prince Charles. We just infer that it is unlikely he has such a high IQ, on the ground that "[a]n IQ of 160 or better is obtained in only 3 cases out of 10,000." From Henry Gleitman, *Psychology* (New York: W.W. Norton, 1981), p. 591.

7

Opinion Polls

7.1 INTRODUCTION

One type of information we face with regularity is the public opinion survey or opinion poll. Reports of polls in newspapers, in magazines, and on television predict election or referendum outcomes and inform us about a variety of attitudes and beliefs—for example, what people think about political leaders, legalized abortion, or jobs for those people who have tested positive for HIV and what brands and what product characteristics people prefer. Since not all polls are reliable, or reliably reported, it is important to be able to read the results of polls or opinion surveys with a critical eye.

7.2 POLLING TERMINOLOGY

Polls are used to generate claims about members of a group based on a survey of the opinions of a portion or subset of that group. For example, "Most Americans are happy with their jobs"—a claim about all working Americans-might be based on interviews with 1,250 working Americans. The survey seeks to establish what percentage of the group possesses a given characteristic or property. Some terminology is useful here. The property of the whole group that is the subject of the survey (happiness with one's job) is called the **target property**. The group about which the generalization is made (in this case, Americans with jobs) is called the **population** (or the **target population**) of the poll. And the sub-group of the population that is actually surveyed is called the **sample**. Also, when pollsters speak of the percentage of the sample or the population which have the target property, they often do so by referring to the **relative frequency** of the target property in the sample or in the population.[1]

7.3 POLLING CRITERIA

What makes for a trustworthy poll is basically the same thing that makes for any trustworthy generalization.

1. The sample must be sufficiently representative of the population with re-spect to the target property. A poll which fails in this respect is said to suffer from a *sampling error*.
2. The information about the individuals that make up the sample must be accurate. A poll which fails in this respect is said to suffer from *measurement error*.

Representativeness

Roughly, a sample is representative of a population if it resembles the population. However, a sample can represent a population in one respect but not in another, for example, a sample of California voters can have a percentage of females that is similar to the percentage of female voters in California at large, but a very different percentage of alcoholics from the California population at large. So the representativeness of a sample always has to be relative to a specified property (or set of properties). To put it in a nutshell:

> A sample is representative of a population with respect to a given property if and only if the relative frequency of the property in the sample is equal to its relative frequency in the population, plus or minus some small amount of error.

If, for example, the target property of a survey is the federal voting pref-erences of eligible voters in the United States, the sample should be selected so that the percentages of voters favoring the Republicans and the Democrats in the sample will be pretty much the same as the actual percentages of voters who favor the respective parties in the country as a whole.

Some members of the population, but not all, will be selected to be included in a sample. How do pollsters go about selecting a sample which is representative of the target population with respect to the property they are interested in? There is no way to *guarantee* that the sample will be representative, but there are strategies that increase the likelihood that a sample will be representative.

One such strategy is to select members of the population randomly and thereby generate a **simple random sample**. In statistics and probability theory, randomness is a technical notion which definitely does *not* mean "haphazard" or "by chance." A method of sampling is **random** just in case *every member of the population has an equal probability of being selected by that method*. For example, putting the names of all the members of the population in a hat and then picking names blindfolded would generate a random sample; choosing the next 20 people you meet on the street would not. A major advantage of a simple random sample is that the likelihood that the sample is representative with respect to the target property can be easily computed and is readily calculated by anyone with the requisite knowledge of statistics.

However, for many problems, such as voting preferences, a simple random sample is not the most practical solution.

For one thing, choosing randomly from however many registered voters there are in over 250,000,000 Americans, and then interviewing subjects dispersed randomly throughout the country, are physically difficult and economically impractical. One solution to this problem is to use a technique called **cluster sampling**. The Gallup organization, for example, frequently uses such a technique in polls conducted during national elections: first, it chooses randomly a certain subset of electoral districts (for example, selecting 300 from a total of more than 200,000 electoral districts), then it chooses randomly a sample of individual voters from each of those 300 districts.

For another thing, it is often known that certain factors are connected with the target property. Suppose, for example, that a pollster is interested in the voting preferences of the American population at a certain time. It's known that traditionally there has been a higher concentration of Republican supporters than Democratic supporters among owners of businesses and a higher concentration of Democratic supporters among recent immigrants. As a result, if the proportions of business owners and recent immigrants in the sample differ from the percentages of those groups in the voting population as a whole, there is reason to fear that the sample will not be representative with respect to the target property of voting preference. But how to go about getting the sample to reflect appropriate percentages of these groups? If the pollster employs simple random sampling, chances are the sample won't have the appropriate percentages unless it is very large. A more efficient way of preceding is to *make sure* the sample contains appropriate percentages of business owners, recent immigrants, and so on, by deciding ahead of time to interview a certain number of people from each of these groups. If this is done simply by setting a quota for each such group, and the pollster doesn't use random methods to fill the quotas, the procedure is called **quota sampling**.[2] If the quota is filled by random sampling from the groups, the procedure is called **stratified random sampling**.[3] With stratified random sampling, it's possible to make do with a smaller sample, and that in fact is often done in polls for federal voting preferences.

This book is not the place for a discussion of how representative samples are constructed for such complicated distributions of properties in a population.

But from what little we have pointed out, you can see that sampling is a complex business requiring complex statistical and demographic knowledge. By the same token, it is a highly risky enterprise, fraught with opportunities for error. For example, if the traditional demographic voting preference patterns we mentioned in the last paragraph change—as well they might—pollsters will need to track those changes closely and adjust their quotas accordingly.

Margin of Error and Confidence Level

Suppose you survey 1,025 Americans over the age of 18, asking them whether they've smoked a cigarette in the last week, and 412 say they have. Exactly 40.195% will have answered yes to your question. But even if your sample is a very representative one and the people you asked are answering honestly, it isn't reasonable to suppose that *exactly* 40.195% of the population of Americans over the age of 18 have smoked a cigarette in the last week. The most you can reasonably hope for is that the percentage of the population that has the target property is somewhere *in the neighborhood* of 40.195%. (And in real life a competent pollster would never spell the figure out to three decimal places; she would talk of 40.2% in a case like this.) We spoke of *hoping* the sample is in the neighborhood, since it's impossible to be *completely* sure the percentage or relative frequency in the sample is even in the neighborhood of that in the population.

Statisticians have created a language for talking with more precision about what is to count as being in the neighborhood and about how confident a pollster should be that the figures are actually in that neighborhood. Instead of talking about whether the relative frequency of the sample is "close to" or "in the neighborhood of" the relative frequency of the population, they talk about whether the sample frequency falls with a given **margin of error**, which is expressed numerically as a ± percentage (for example, ± 3%). For instance, we might ask whether our sample frequency of 40.2% is within three percentage points of the relative frequency of recent smokers in the population—in other words, whether the percentage of recent smokers in the population is between 37.2 (40.2 minus 3) and 43.2 (40.2 plus 3). If so, then the sample frequency falls within a margin of error of ± 3%.

It turns out that for genuine random samples, a statistician can calculate the probability that the sample frequency falls within a given margin of error—a probability that depends largely on sample size.[4] That probability is called a **confidence level** (or "degree of confidence") and is expressed as a fraction (for example, 19 times out of 20) or a decimal number (for example, .95, which is equal to 19 divided by 20). A confidence level of 19 times out of 20 or .95 means there is 1 chance in 20 or a probability of .05 that the poll does not reflect the population, even over the range given by the margin of error.

The confidence level is *for* a margin of error. That is, a given confidence level states the probability that the poll will be accurate within the stated margin of error; conversely, a given margin of error is predicted only with the probability

Table 7.1   Appropriate sizes of simple random samples for specified margins of error, for three confidence levels.

These figures are for a population size of 1,000,000 when the true proportion of the target property in the population is 0.50.

| | Confidence Level | | |
Margin of Error	.90	.95	.98
± 1%	6,720	9,513	13,345
± 2%	1,690	2,395	3,370
± 3%	751	1,066	1,501
± 4%	423	600	845
± 5%	271	384	541

Source: From Chester H. McCall, Jr., *Sampling and Statistics: Handbook for Research* (Ames: Iowa State University Press, 1982), pp. 329–331.

of the stated confidence level. Some 95% of the time the sample will be within ± 3%, but 97% of the time it will be ± 4%, and so on. Other things being equal, the larger the sample and the more homogeneous the target population, the lower the margin of error and the greater the confidence level. See Table 7.1 for figures that typically apply when the population size is large. Be aware, however, that the margin of error is calculated on the assumption that the sample is randomly selected—that each member of the target population had an equal chance of being chosen. That assumption is seldom straightforwardly true.

Often the reported margin of error is idealized. For example, the margin of error reported may be for a truly random sample, when in fact the sample was not chosen by a strictly random method. Also, the reported margin of error only reflects the likelihood of sampling error; it makes no provision for the possibility of measurement error. One critic of survey research and its reporting, advises as follows:

> . . . read poll results very cautiously. As a general rule regarding commercial polls, I would say: Double the size of measurement error margins suggested by the pollster. If an error margin of 3 percentage points is suggested, make it 6; and if you don't see a spread of at least 12 percentage points between any two scores, regard them as the same. Given the wide variety of polling practices and topics, in the long run you will probably accept fewer falsehoods with such working rules. You will be less likely to make something out of nothing.[5]

Suppose that one week before the date of a municipal election in which Lowperson and Highperson are the candidates for mayor, a poll of 1,582 eligible voters is conducted in which Lowperson is said to have the support of 33%, and Highperson 37%, of decided voters. The polling organization says that "a sample of this size is estimated to be accurate within a margin of about plus or minus three percentage points, 19 of 20 times." This would mean that according to this poll the actual levels of support could be 36% for Lowperson (33% plus 3%) and 34% for Highperson (37% minus 3%). In other words, Lowperson might actually be ahead since the results are within the margin of error claimed for this poll. When comparative results projected lie within the margin of error, as is true in the example here, the comparison is *too close to call*. No reliable inference about which candidate has more support or will win can be made based on the data. Moreover, if we follow the advice quoted, then even if the results were 38% for High and 30% for Low, the reported 3% margin of error should be doubled, and the poll results would still be too close to call.

Frequently, pollsters will report percentages for subgroups in a sample without reporting a margin of error for the results concerning those subgroups. For example, you will read that 63% of 1,500 voters surveyed think the president is doing a good job, and that the approval rate is 69% among males but only 57% among females. If you are told that a "sample of this size" is considered accurate within three percentage point 19 times out of 20, that margin of error applies only to the results reported for the sample as a whole (in this example, the combined approval rating of 63%). But the sample size of the females and the sample size of the males in the survey is probably only about half of 1,500 (assuming a roughly 50-50 split in the sample, which is normal). Therefore the margin of error for any results concerning just the females or just the males, given the samples of only about 750, will be much greater than ± 3%.

Validity of the "Measuring Instrument"

In survey research, not only are people selected to be questioned or tested, but also some procedure to determine whether each person selected has the target property is carried out. If the target property is attitudes or beliefs, the procedure used will typically be to ask questions. If the target property is some medical condition, the procedure might well be some laboratory test administered by a competent medical technician. The procedure or test employed is called the **measuring instrument**.

A sample's measurement is **valid** when the measuring instrument gives just the information it is supposed to give. Imagine a test of basic reading literacy—defined as the ability to read and understand simple prose using common words—which consists in having the people in the sample answer questions about a passage of prose they had just read. If they are not allowed to reread the passage while answering the questions, the test would become one of memory as well as of literacy. If the questions were difficult to understand, the test would become one of analytical skills as well as of literacy. If the passage contained unusual or technical words and long, grammatically complex sentences, the test would be a test of advanced reading literacy, not basic reading literacy. These are some of the ways such a test could be invalid—ways in which it did not measure what it was supposed to measure.

Now think of a polling question asking about voting preferences. It might be worded in a way, or asked in a situation, that leads people to answer dishonestly or inaccurately. It has been found that poll respondents tend to try to please a person filling out a questionnaire in person, and so give the answers they think the interviewer wants. Any verbal or body language signals the interviewer inadvertently gives might skew the answers, and the questionnaire will not give an accurate reading. Or people may be unwilling to commit themselves publicly, and so be counted as "undecided," when they have in fact already made up their minds. The sample's "information" will be invalid in such cases.

Formulating and posing questions which are valid measuring instruments are said to be the most difficult parts of reliable public opinion sampling. Some reasons why include (1) people are often reluctant to reveal their true opinions because they fear the disapproval of the interviewer, (2) people often say what they think the interviewer wants or expects to hear rather than what they believe, and (3) people are often unaware of their own deep beliefs.

The questions should be neutral. That is, they should not be "leading" questions—questions that are phrased in a way that invites, pressures, or leads the respondent to a particular answer. A question like, "Mayor Bilcar is running for reelection. Are you in favor of her candidacy?" leads toward a "yes" answer because it alludes to Bilcar's experience and doesn't mention the other candidates. Compare the more neutral question: "Which of the candidates for mayor do you prefer: Bilcar, Mastronardi, or Smith?"

In sum, a critical assessment of any survey results requires attention to the factors that might have influenced either the sample's representativeness or the validity of the measurements. When the sample is not representative of the population with respect to the target property, there is said to be a *sampling error*; when the measuring instrument (for example, the group of survey questions used) lacks validity and gives incorrect results, there is said to be a *measurement error*.

7.4 SOME ADDITIONAL FACTS ABOUT POLLS AND POLLING

In this section we list some additional facts it is useful to know when you are assessing polls and their reports.

Sample Size

We have already seen that in a random sample, margin of error depends largely on sample size. A common misconception is that a sample should be some appropriate *proportion* of the size of the population. For example, it's thought that an appropriately sized sample of American citizens would have to be 10 times as big as such a sample of Canadian citizens (since there are approximately 10 times as many Americans as Canadians). That is totally incorrect. A genuinely random sample of 1,000 Americans is usually about as reliable as a genuinely

Table 7.2 Appropriate sizes of simple random samples at various population sizes for three specified margins of error.

These figures are for a confidence level of .95 when the true proportion of the target property in the population is 0.50

Population Size	Margin of Error		
	± 4%	± 3%	± 2%
100	86	91	96
1,000	375	516	706
10,000	566	964	1,936
25,000	586	1,023	2,191
100,000	597	1,056	2,345
1,000,000	600	1,066	2,395
2,000,000	600	1,067	2,398

Source: From Chester H. McCall, Jr., *Sampling and Statistics: Handbook for Research* (Ames: Iowa State University Press, 1982), pp. 330.

random sample of 1,000 Canadians. This surprising fact is explained by the laws of probability. Once one is dealing with population sizes over 25,000, the sample size required for a given degree of reliability increases by only small amounts with increases in population size.

Once the population sizes are much over 1 million, virtually no increase in sample size is required by an increase in population size. (See Table 7.2.) So for large populations, what matters is the absolute size of the sample, not its proportion of the population.

The appropriate size for a given population, and the minimum size for a reliable sample, are complex matters requiring an understanding of statistics and demographics beyond the scope of this book.

Self-selected Samples

Some sampling techniques—such as a phone-in or write-in poll—yield a **self-selected sample**. People in effect select themselves to become members of the sample by calling or mailing in their responses. Samples generated in this way are not random samples. Moreover, in such samples, only those with a strong interest are likely to respond, and their opinions or attitudes are unlikely to be representative of the population as a whole. When there's a magazine or newspaper, TV, or radio mail-in or phone-in poll where any reader, viewer, or listener who wants to can respond, the sample will almost certainly not be representative of the target population with respect to the target property.

The Timing of the Poll

In general, a poll taken during or right after events that can cause temporary reactions untypical of the long-term convictions of the respondents will tend to be an unreliable measure of such opinions or attitudes. People polled soon after a brutal murder that has been prominently in the news tend to register much more concern about crime and public safety than they do when polled at a time when there are no such crimes in the news. Polls taken just after each of the presidential nominating conventions, during which the party holding the convention and its candidate usually dominate the news, tend to show inflated support for the candidate just nominated.

Method of Contact (How the Polling is Done)

The actual surveying can be done through in-person interviews, through telephone interviews, or via a written questionnaire. Twenty or 30 years ago, many argued that in-person interviews yielded better results than the other two kinds. Today, the preference is for telephone interviews. Face-to-face interviews are more likely be adversely affected by unskilled interviewers whose manner or appearance may influence the respondents. Also, certain kinds of questions can elicit inaccurate answers in face-to-face situations (for example, questions about matters people consider to be private). However, using the telephone can easily result in an unrepresentative sample when a significant portion of the target population lacks phones.

The Polling Organization and the Sponsor

Reliable polling requires highly specialized skills in sample selection, question formulation, and interviewing techniques. There are reputable professional organizations that know what it takes to do a poll well. The identity and reputation of the polling organization are among the most crucial facts to know about any poll.

The groups that want information—such as companies, newspapers, or political parties—will almost always hire a professional polling company to conduct their polls. If a poll is done by a reputable polling organization, the fact that it was sponsored by an individual or group with an vested interest in the outcome is *not* a reason to doubt the accuracy or reliability of the results. The business of the polling organization depends on having a reputation for the reliability of its information, and it is not likely to compromise that reputation to please a client. However, the **sponsor** controls the release of the polling information, and it might make public only those figures which favor its point of view.

7.5 The Reporting of Polls

We, the members of the general public, get most of our information about public opinion surveys from the reports of such surveys which appear in newspapers and magazines, or on TV or radio. There are good reasons to regard these reports with great caution. We think it is safer to risk erring on the side of skepticism rather than gullibility when it comes to accepting the reports of polls.

Rarely is there an opportunity to appraise the poll's methodology and results firsthand—even if we are competent to do so. Moreover, not all reports of poll results include all the information that even nonspecialists need in order to decide how reliable a given poll is likely to be and how much credence should therefore be placed in its results. Furthermore, a poll may be *reported* in a misleading manner even though the pollsters have done a good job and the **sponsor** has released all of the poll results, accompanied by the information needed to make an intelligent layperson's assessment of the poll's significance. The way a poll is *reported*—the generalizations drawn from it and stated by the reporter (or by the headline writer)—can be misleading, even when there is no reason to doubt the accuracy of the basic data.

For these reasons it is useful to have a succinct list of questions to keep in mind when reading reports of opinion surveys. These "guidelines" are reminders that should enable you to spot inaccurate or unwarranted news reports, given the information provided, and to recognize when you haven't been given sufficient information to judge whether the poll's findings are reliable or whether the generalizations that the reporter has made based on those findings are warranted.

In using the guidelines, distinguish between

1. Problems with the poll itself which we can identify on the basis of the information that has been supplied
2. Problems with the reporting of the poll
   a. relating to information needed to judge its reliability
   b. relating to judgments or generalizations that seem unwarranted given the information supplied

7.6 HOW TO READ THE REPORT OF A POLL

A. Assess the Poll to the Extent that the Report Allows

1. *Orient yourself.*
   a. What is the "target property"—what's the poll asking about?
   b. What is the population—to what group is the information gathered in the poll supposed to apply?
   c. What is the sample—who were contained in it? how were they selected?
2. *Check the basic data.*
   Do the numbers add up?
   One poll in 1988 reported Bush with 45% support, Dukakis with 41%, Others with 1%, and 19% undecided. That adds up to 106%! Probably the

percentages for the candidates represented the percentages of *decided* voters, while the percentage of undecided was a percentage of *total* voters. So the reporting of the figures was sloppy. And if Bush had 45% support of the 81% of voters in the poll who were decided, then he in fact had about 36.5 percent support, not 45 percent as originally reported.

3. *Check the sample.*
   Is the sample drawn from the target population? Is it too small? Is the sample representative of the target population with respect to those feature known to affect the target property? Is it random? If not, how was it selected and why should we think that it is representative of the population with respect to the target property? Was the sample self-selected?

4. *Check the measuring instrument and method of contact.*
   a. What was the question? Is there reason to think it is loaded—that it invites a particular response?
   b. What was the method of contact—in-person interviews, telephone interviews, mail? Is there reason to think the method of contact could have skewed the responses?

5. *Check the margin of error/confidence level.*
   What is the reported margin of error? When assessing the significance of this poll's findings, note whether the difference reported in the poll falls within the reported margin of error. What happens when you follow the proposal that you double the reported margin of error? Or are the results significant whatever the probable range of the margin of error?

6. *Check the timing of the poll.*
   When was the polling done? Were there any events just prior to that time that might have caused responses untypical of long-term opinions or different from present or future opinions.

7. *Check the pollster and sponsor.*
   a. Who did the polling? Was it a reliable company or organization? Is there any reason to doubt pollster's expertise?
   b. Who sponsored the poll and released the results? Is there any reason to suspect that their interests might have influenced the results in some way or have influenced which results have been disclosed?

B. Assess the Reporting of the Poll

8. *Is the information adequate?*
   Is the report of the poll deficient in that information you need to assess the poll was not provided?

9. *Are any inferences made by the reporter warranted?*
   Did the report contain statements that, in the light of the information provided, are not justified? Did the report contain statements that depend for their credibility on evidence not provided? Did the headline express or imply a conclusion not warranted by the information provided?

C. Overall Assessment

10. *Summarize your assessment of the information.*
    a. Does the poll provide a reliable picture of the target population, so far as you can tell from what was reported? What specific limitations does the poll have, if any? In what ways should the pollster's statements be modified, if at all?
    b. Do the poll results really support the generalizations made and the conclusions drawn in the report?

7.7 SUMMARY

Polling is a special case of generalizing about what proportion of a large group possesses a certain target property, by examining a smaller subgroup taken from that larger group. The target property is some opinion or attitude, the smaller subgroup who are examined are called the sample, and the large group in which the pollster is interested is called the population. To be reliable, a poll must meet several conditions: the sample must be representative of the population, the questions must be valid (accurately measure the target property), the timing and method of contact must be appropriate, and the generalizations should be properly qualified (by citing margin of error and confidence level).

The best way to achieve a representative sample is to use a random method of selection—either simple random sampling (that is, a method in which every member of the population has an equal chance to be included) or, if there are different significant subgroups in the population, proportional stratified random sampling (each subgroup is represented proportionately, with random sampling performed within subgroups). A much less reliable method, which is nevertheless often used, is quota sampling (each significant group is represented proportionally, but no random sampling is performed). Highly unreliable sampling methods are sometimes used, for example, self-selected samples, which are extremely unlikely to yield samples representative of the population one is interested in.

There are several possible problems with polls, or with the reporting of polls, or both. Problems with polls include the following: the sample may be too small, not broad enough, not representative, not selected in a reliable way; the instrument can have loaded questions, have a distorting method of contact, or be administered too near in time to distorting events; the pollster may lack expertise. Problems with reporting include the following: the pollster or the sponsor may not be identified; the margin of error and confidence level may not be supplied; there may be insufficient information about the questions, the timing, the method of contact to permit any assessment. Problems with conclusions include the following: the pollster, the sponsor, or the report can make inferences based on the poll that are in fact not warranted by it. Perhaps the most common problem is supposing that differences which fall within the margin of error are significant.

7.8 EXERCISES

A. For each example assigned, do the following.
   (a) Identify (i) the target population, (ii) the target property, (iii) who constituted the sample, (iv) the method of contact, (v) the margin of error (sampling error) and degree of confidence, (vi) the timing of the poll relative events that might influence its outcome, (vii) the sponsor of the poll, (viii) the polling organization, (ix) data reported from the poll, and (x) inferences based on the polling data.
   (b) Determine whether any differences reported were too close to call. Support your contention.
   (c) Decide whether there is any reason to challenge the representativeness of the sample used. Support your judgment.

B. For each example assigned, use the guidelines to prepare a succinct critique of the reported poll results. Distinguish between problems with the polling and problems with the reporting of the poll. Also discriminate between major or significant problems, and less important ones.

**1. *Background*: Here is a fairly typical news report of the monthly Gallup poll of the fortunes of the three major political parties in Canada—the Liberals, the Conservatives (or Tories), and the New Democratic Party. (Gallup is a long-established commercial polling company.) It appeared in Canadian newspapers in February 1984.

Liberals cut Tories' lead in Gallup poll

Montreal (CP)—A Gallup poll published today indicates the federal Liberals have cut into the Progressive Conservatives' lead in voter support, but not as much as Liberal party polls made public last month had suggested.

The Gallup poll, conducted in early January, indicates the Conservatives have a 20-percentage-point lead over the Liberals, down from 23 percentage points in December.

Fifty-two per cent of decided respondents questioned in January supported the Tories, a drop of one percentage point from the previous month, while the Liberals gained two percentage points to 32 per cent.

The new Democratic Party had the support of 15 per cent, unchanged from December.

Gallup says its poll is accurate to within four percentage points either way 19 times out of 20, meaning the apparent changes may be illusory.

The margin of error means, statistically, that voter support for the Conservatives could have been as high as 56 per cent or as low as 48 per cent, while the Liberals could have had the support of as many as 36 per cent of voters or as little as 28 per cent.

Twenty-one per cent of the 1,046 respondents were undecided or refused to state a choice, down from 27 per cent in December.

---

2. *Background*: The following Reuters News Service report appeared in November 1987—at a time when the Soviet Union was involved in a war in Afghanistan and before it had announced or begun its withdrawal from that country.

Poll in Moscow shows majority favor pullout from Afghanistan

Reuter

PARIS—A Western-style opinion poll conducted in Moscow shows that the majority of Soviet citizens favor pulling troops out of Afghanistan and issuing visas to people who want to emigrate, the French magazine Le Point said yesterday.

The survey of 1,000 Moscow-area residents between 18 and 65 was conducted by the Soviet Institute of Sociological Studies and sponsored by Le Point, Radio France-Inter, the French television channel TFI and the French polling organization IPSOS.

It showed 53 per cent favored a "total withdrawal of Soviet troops from Afghanistan" against 27 per cent opposed.

The respondents also approved "Issuing exit visas to Soviet citizens and their families who wish to leave the USSR for good" by 73 per cent to 18 per cent.

The poll turned up majorities of between 79 and 83 per cent in favor of multiple candidates in local elections, self-employment, workers' selection of management and curbs on the sale of liquor.

Respondents were selected at random and interviewed by telephone Oct. 1-12, Le Point said.

The percentage of "won't say" answers varied between six and 31—with the high score coming when respondents were asked whether they approved of the "anticipated liberation of so-called dissidents from incarceration."

A resounding 85 per cent opposed abolition of the death penalty.

**3. *Background*: Here is an Associated Press report of a poll that was published in June 1987.

Date rapes acceptable, students tell U.S. survey

Associated Press

PROVIDENCE—Nearly one-quarter of boys and one-sixth of girls who responded to a U.S. survey on rape said it is acceptable for a man to force a woman to have sexual relations if he has spent money on her.

The survey was taken of 1,700 students in grades 6 to 9 who participated in the Rhode Island Rape Crisis Centre's assault awareness program at schools across the state.

"I didn't believe it," said Jacqueline Jackson Kikuchi, the centre staff member who conducted the poll.

Ms. Kikuchi presented the findings last week at the National Symposium on Child Victimization in Anaheim, Calif.

She said she was most surprised by the students' answers about whether it would be acceptable for a man to rape a woman if he had dated her for a long time or spent money on her.

"Basically, the kids were very much into blaming the victim of the sexual assault."

The survey also found that:
- 50 per cent of the students said a woman who walks alone at night and dresses seductively is asking to be raped;
- 51 per cent of the boys and 41 per cent of the girls said a man has the right to force a woman to kiss him if he has spent "a lot of money"— defined by 12-year-olds as $10 to $15—on her;
- 63 per cent of the boys and 57 per cent of the girls in grades 7 through 9 said it is acceptable for a man to force a woman to have sexual intercourse if they have been dating for more than six months;
- 87 per cent of the boys and 79 per cent of the girls said rape is acceptable if a couple is married.

Continued.

"So many of our kids have attitudes that sexual abuse is okay," Ms Kikuchi said.

She said the attitudes found in the survey could lead to date-rape and other forms of sexual assault.

Twenty per cent of the girls and 6 per cent of the boys in the survey said they had been sexually abused.

Ms Kikuchi conducted the survey from February to December, 1987, when she conducted workshops for students at public and private schools.

She said the workshops were successful in changing some attitudes. After taking part in them, less than 25 per cent of the students thought rape or forced kissing was appropriate in any situation.

4. *Background*: During the U.S. presidential election campaign of 1988, polls were taken regularly to try to detect shifts in voter preference. George Bush and Michael Dukakis, the Republican and Democratic candidates for president, held a televised debate shortly before this poll, which was reported in *The New York Times* on September 29, 1988.

Post-Debate Poll Sees No Change

Special to The New York Times

Washington, Sept. 28—Vice President Bush leads Michael S. Dukakis by 50 percent to 46 percent, according to the latest ABC News Poll.

The poll, conducted on Monday and Tuesday, produced a result that was identical to that of an ABC News/Washington Post Poll conducted from Sept. 14 through 19, before the nationally televised debate Sunday. Both telephone polls had the same methodology. The new poll involved interviews with 674 likely voters and had a margin of sampling error of plus or minus 5 percentage points.

"I think we can reach the conclusion that the debate was a big washout in terms of shifting voter opinions," said Jeff Alderman, director of polling for ABC News. "Ninety percent of the people seemed to stay with the candidate they favored before the debate."

The new poll showed Mr. Bush holding a narrow lead among independents, who make up about a third of the electorate.

Mr. Alderman said Mr. Bush was also having more success than Mr. Dukakis in taking his own party. Mr. Bush was getting 93 percent support from Republicans; Mr. Dukakis was getting 83 percent of the Democrats. Among Democrats who voted for President Reagan in 1984, Mr. Dukakis led by a ratio of about 5-to-4. This summer, Mr. Dukakis was winning among Reagan Democrats by a 3-to-1 ratio.

5. *Background*: This Associated Press report is reproduced in its entirety. It appeared in September 1988.

60% favor aid to family planning

Associated Press

WASHINGTON—A majority of U.S. citizens favor financial assistance for family-planning programs in rapidly growing nations, according to a new poll. Sixty per cent of adults polled for the Population Crisis Committee and the Planned Parenthood Federation of America said the United States should finance foreign family planning programs, regardless of whether abortion is legal in those nations. In recent years, the Agency for International Development has withdrawn support where abortion is a part of the programs.

6. *Background*: The Harris Poll is the trade name for a regular poll taken and distributed by the Harris organization, a large and well-established polling company based in the United States. This report appeared in August 30, 1988.

U.S. Faith in Key Institutions Has Plunged Since '66

Confidence in U.S. institutions has taken a nosedive since 1966. Back then, 73 percent of Americans said they had confidence in medicine, while just 40 percent do today. And while 41 percent said they had confidence in organized religion in 1966, just 17 percent feel the same way now, according to a survey by The Harris Poll.

Also, the percentage of Americans who have confidence in the military has plummeted from 61 percent in 1966 to 33 percent today; in major corporations, from 55 percent to 19 percent, and in major educational institutions, from 61 percent to 34.

7. *Background*: This report appeared on the first page of *The Detroit Free Press* on December 5, 1989. Berkley and Southfield are wealthy suburbs of Detroit. Kalamazoo is a small city in lower Michigan, about 100 miles from Detroit.

Women have 3 sex partners by 35, study finds

By Patricia Anstett
Free Press Medical Writer

By age 35, 81 percent of Michigan women have had at least three sex partners, and 14 percent have had 13 or more, according to data collected for a national survey.

The statistics are among the few available recently on how sexually active women are, according to health and federal government experts.

In a survey of 962 Michigan women by Richard Reid, a Southfield gynecologist and obstetrician, eight of 10 had at least three partners by age 35, and 6 percent had more than 25 partners.

The survey of women ages 18 to 35 in Detroit, Berkley, Southfield and Kalamazoo found that:
- 9 percent had had one sex partner, and
- 9.6 percent had two.
- Nearly half had three to seven partners.
- Nearly 19 percent had had eight to 12 partners.
- About 14 percent had 13 or more partners, including 4 percent who had 50 or more.

Sixteen was the median age for first inter-

Continued.

course, and 98 percent of the women had had intercourse before age 21. The survey is part of a study for the federal Centers for Disease Control to test the reliability of methods to detect a virus linked to cervical cancers. Reid did his survey in 1985, but the federal study has not been published.

8. *Background*: The following Associated Press story appeared in November 1990.

Many of Japan's salaried workers have mortal fears about their jobs

Associated Press

Tokyo—More than 40 percent of Japan's salaried employees surveyed said they fear they may work themselves to death, a study reported Wednesday.

The Fukoku Life Insurance Co. conducted the survey in October among 500 employees with more than 15 years at the same companies in metropolitan Tokyo.

Results indicated that the fabled workaholicism of Japanese white-collar employees takes its toll.

The poll revealed a strong fear of *karoshi*—death from overwork. Dr. Kiyoyasu Arikawa, who advises executives how to reduce their risk, said the number of *karoshi* grew from 10 in 1969 to about 150 in 1987.

The Labor Ministry received 777 applications for compensation because of sudden death at work, up from about 500 requests three years ago. Researchers believe many such deaths stem from working too hard.

Asked whether they feared death by overwork, 43 percent of the respondents said yes.

Fierce competition among employees as well as a strong sense of company responsibility lead many workers to stay well into the night and refuse to take all of their vacation time. Nearly two-thirds of respondents to the survey take less than 10 days of vacation a year.

To ease work-related fatigue, 85 percent of respondents said they "just want to sleep more."

9. *Background*: This story appeared in *The Windsor Star* on June 25, 1991.

Do they really have more fun?

BLONDES THINK they've got a leg up on the competition when it comes to hair color, according to a recent survey.

Most blondes think they're sexier and trendier than brunettes or redheads, according to a major attitudes survey conducted by Clairol in the United States.

The hair coloring manufacturer surveyed users of Ultress Gel Colorant to uncover some surprising myths and truths about the way women see themselves according to their hair color. The study revealed that blondes believe they've got the market cornered when it comes to popularity.

Here are some of the study's findings.

• Blondes think they're more popular with men. Ninety-one per cent believe they were especially well liked by men. Only 74 per cent of brunettes felt that way, says the study. Redheads came a distant third, with only 64 per cent feeling positive about their image in male eyes.

- Blondes don't have more fun. Of those surveyed by Clairol, 65 per cent said blondes don't enjoy themselves more.
- Blondes consider themselves tops when it comes to setting trends, according to the study. Fifty-four per cent of blondes said they were trendy while only 36 per cent of redheads felt that way.
- Brunettes and redheads are considered more sympathetic, says the study.
- Almost half of all blondes admit that they consider themselves naive. Forty-nine per cent express such feelings and 50 per cent of

other women agree. In contrast, only 25 per cent of brunettes rated themselves as naive and redheads classified themselves as the saviest group, with only 14 per cent admitting to feelings of naivete.

- Brunettes have more self-confidence than blondes, says the study. Seventy-five per cent of the brunettes surveyed said they saw themselves in a very positive light. Only 65 per cent of blondes felt that way. As for redheads, those surveyed topped other women in the self-esteem department with 80 per cent expressing strong feelings of self-confidence.

10. *Background*: This article appeared in *Time*, July 9, 1990.

The Tuned-Out Generation
A new survey reveals that young people are ignoring the news

Television and radio news floods the airwaves; major events from across the globe pop instantly onto home screens; computers and fax machines relay information in a flash. But anyone who thinks the media boom has created a nation of news junkies needs to readjust his antenna. A sobering new study titled *The Age of Indifference*, released last week by the Times Mirror Center for the People & the Press, reveals that young Americans are barely paying attention. The under-30 generation, it reports, "knows less, cares less and reads newspapers less" than any generation in the past five decades.

The sharp drop in newspaper readership is the survey's most dramatic, if least startling, revelation. Only 30% of Americans under 35 said they had "read a newspaper yesterday." That compares with 67% of young people who answered the question affirmatively in a 1965 Gallup poll. More surprisingly, TV has not filled the gap; only 41% of young people said they had watched a TV newscast the day before, down from 52% in 1965.

When it comes to major news events, young people are less interested and informed than their elders. Respondents between the ages of

18 and 29 were 20% less likely to say they had followed important news stories and 40% less likely to be able to identify a newsmaker like German Chancellor Helmut Kohl. Two exceptions: they showed high interest in sports and issues that affected them directly, such as abortion.

The generation gap has widened drastically in recent years. Surveys conducted in the 1940s, '50s and '60s showed that young people were just as interested as their elders in major stories like the McCarthy hearings and the Vietnam War. But since the mid-'70s, the under-30 group has been tuning out. The result is a generation that votes less and is less critical of government and business. They are thus an "easy target of opportunity for those seeking to manipulate public opinion," the study warns.

Some news executives attribute this youthful apathy to information overload and the explosion of media options. "We had one television in the house, and we had to watch the news when Daddy came home," recalls Steve Friedman, 43, executive producer of NBC's *Nightly News*: today's young people "have got their own TV and their own video systems." Friedman is

Continued

trying to make the NBC newscast "more relevant" to young viewers by stressing family issues and adding touches of irreverent humor. Louis Heldman, who is studying how to counteract declining readership for the Knight-Ridder newspaper chain, observes that people today, especially young working women, have less spare time for news. "Information needs to be delivered more efficiently," he says, "to people who are trying to get the kids dressed for school and who may spend most of their time with the paper on the seat beside them in the car stalled on the freeway."

The Times Mirror study notes that the young audience has "buoyed the popularity of the new, lighter media forms," such as *People* magazine and TV's *A Current Affair*. The survey may give news executives a further excuse to soften and glitz up their products to try to woo the young. But that means walking a tricky tightrope: in trying to make the news more appetizing, they risk turning it into something other than the news.

—By Richard Zoglin
Reported by Georgia Harbison/New York

NOTES

1. The *relative frequency* of males in the population of the United States is the number of males living in America divided by the number of all people living in the Unites States. It will be a decimal number between 0 and 1 (end points included). Strictly speaking, the *percentage* of U.S. residents who are male will be the relative frequency multiplied by 100. That's why percentages range from 0 to 100, while relative frequencies range from 0 to 1.
2. Quota sampling was used by the Gallup organization to estimate U.S. federal voting preferences until the late 1940s, when it was replaced by cluster sampling. See Chester H. McCall, Jr., *Sampling and Statistics: Handbook for Research* (Ames: Iowa State University Press, 1982), and George H. Gallup, *The Sophisticated Poll Watcher's Guide* (Princeton, NJ: Princeton University Press, 1972).
3. Stratified random sampling comes in two varieties. In proportional stratified sampling, the number of subjects in each stratum or group in the sample is proportional to the number in that group in the population. In nonproportional stratified random sampling, the proportions of subjects in the strata of the sample need not be proportional to those in the population; mathematical adjustment for the differences is made when figures are computed for the sample as a whole.
4. The major determinant of margin of error at a given confidence level is sample size. But it is also affected by two other factors. For populations under 1,000,000 (and especially those under 25,000), population size has some effect. But also the distribution of the target property in the population affects the margin of error; the margin of error decreases as the percentage possessing the target property approaches 100% or 0%, and it increases as the percentage approaches 50%.
5. Quoted from "Comments on an Approach to Teaching 'Critical Thinking'" by Alex Michalos, draft notes for the Conference on Teaching Informal Logic and Critical Thinking at Colleges and Universities, McMaster University, Hamilton, Ontario, May 6, 7, 8, 1988. p. 11.

Reasoning About Causes

8.1 INTRODUCTION

Causal reasoning—reasoning about cause and effect—figures prominently in everyone's daily thinking. When you want to know why something happened or happens, what you usually are after is what *caused* or *causes* it to happen. Why did your watch stop? Why is the bus late? Why is it so humid in Baltimore in the summer? Why am I so nervous when she speaks to me? Why can't you catch perch in this lake any more? What wakened the baby? What startled the dog? What ignited the fire? Why am I having so much trouble understanding sociology? Why do birds always go back to the same nesting areas each year? Why does paint peel? Why did the lights just go out? Clearly, the list could be endless, and all these questions ask about causes.

We have different kinds of reasons for wanting to know the causes of things. Often, it is so we can avoid or prevent or stop those things—if we don't like them—or so we can start or get or keep them—if we want them. Knowing causes is often necessary in order to get what we want. But sometimes we want to know causes simply because we are curious. We find it satisfying to understand them.

We reason about causes when we have either of two goals.

1. *To discover causes.* We reason in order to figure out what caused or causes what. From various sorts of evidence, we draw conclusions about causes.

2. *To apply causal knowledge.* We reason using our knowledge of causes as premisses, and from them infer other things, such as what action to take to obtain, retain, remove, or avoid something.

The present chapter is restricted to reasoning of the first sort—drawing conclusions about or discovering what caused or causes what.

Incidentally, we less often use the nouns 'cause' and 'effect' and the verb 'to cause' and their cognates (causal, causation)[1] than we do the many synonyms they have. For example,

- For 'cause' (noun): basis, origin, root, source, antecedent, motive, reason
- For 'effect' (noun): outcome, result, consequence, aftermath, impact
- For 'cause' (verb): lead to, generate, bring about, make happen, effect, precipitate, produce, incite, induce, make, prompt, provoke, originate, accomplish, create, beget, achieve, result in

In addition to these more or less generic terms, there are lots of more specific words that indicate causation. For example, to *light* a fire is to cause it to start up, and to *douse* a fire is to cause it to go out; to *startle* the dog is to cause it to be startled; to *waken* the baby is to cause it to wake up. Our vocabulary is chock full of terms indicating causation.

8.2 PARTICULAR AND GENERAL CAUSAL PROPOSITIONS

A statement is said to be about **particulars** if it is used to assert a proposition about a *unique* thing or event—a thing or event which existed or occurred (or does or will do so) at an identifiable place for an specific duration of time, and there is only one of them in the universe. Marilyn Monroe (a person), the moon landing module called "Eagle" used for the first trip to the moon (a thing), and the 1990 Persian Gulf War (an event) are all particulars in this sense. So are the cause of your computer's crash last Tuesday, the causes of the Civil War, or the cause of your friend's cheerful mood today.

We shall introduce the term **particular causal proposition** for any proposition about the causes or the effects of particular events or phenomena. Thus, "The 1990 Detroit plane crash was due to pilot error" is a particular causal proposition, as are "Poor organization and a misjudgment of the Red army's loyalty caused the attempted coup in the Soviet Union in August 1991 to fail" and "The effect of today's federal budget announcement on the stock market will be devastating."

A **general statement** asserts a proposition about a type or kind or class of things or events. General statements are used to make assertions about the properties shared by all the things or events of a given type or kind. They tell us that all, most, some, or none of the things of a certain sort are a certain way. They tell us that events of a certain kind always, usually, seldom, or never happen in a certain way, or for a certain reason, and so on. For example, "Spacecraft tend to be relatively light and enormously strong" or "Wars are never fought by the generation that starts them" are general statements.

We shall introduce the term, **general causal proposition** for any proposition about the causes or the effects of some *type* of thing or event. Thus,

(a) The reason why latex paints dry so quickly is that the water used to thin them evaporates quickly.

expresses a general causal proposition because it purports to give the cause of the general phenomenon of latex paint drying quickly. So do the following two sentences:

(b) Sexist stereotyping is a bigger contributor to violence against women than is poverty.
(c) Tornadoes are caused by violent convection resulting from intense heating of the ground by the sun, aided by opposing winds of greatly differing temperatures.[2]

Each of these statements expresses something about the causes of repeatable phenomena: (b) refers to the causes of violence against women, (c) to the causes of tornadoes.

To sum up, causal propositions are about the causes and the effects either of particular events (particular causal propositions) or of types or classes of events (general causal propositions). We are going to construe the notion of causal proposition quite broadly. To give the reasons or causes why something *did not* happen is to assert a causal proposition. Moreover, to say that one thing was *not* caused by another, or will not cause another, is to assert a causal proposition as well—a **negative causal proposition**. The knowledge of negative causal propositions can be important. A youth might need to know that masturbation is not harmful behavior (a true negative general causal proposition, since it says that masturbation does not cause harm); historians might want to know that Julius Caesar's death was not caused by any natural disease (a true negative particular causal proposition).

We can now state the topic of this chapter more precisely. It discusses the reasoning involved in drawing conclusions that are either particular causal propositions or general causal propositions. We shall describe reasoning strategies to use when drawing these two sorts of conclusion, and we begin with reasoning designed to conclude to particular causal propositions.

8.3 ESTABLISHING PARTICULAR CAUSAL PROPOSITIONS

A cultural historian might want to investigate the cause(s) of the Beatles' astounding success in selling records in the 1960s. Or the historian might be interested, instead, in the effects of the Beatles' success on popular music in the 1960s and 1970s. In the first case, the historian would be looking for an *explanation* of the Beatles' success, in the second case, for an *account of its results*. Either way, the historian is interested in the truth of particular causal propositions. Again, when someone wonders what the effects will be of something that has just happened (what effect taking that part-time job will have on your grades) or what effect an action being considered would have (for example, what the results would be if you took a year off school), the person is interested in the truth of particular causal propositions.

In this section, we are going to concentrate on finding causal explanations — looking for the causes — of particular events that have occurred.

The Causal Web

It never happens that there is one and only one event which is causally responsible for another. There are two reasons why this is so.

1. Causes always operate as a *conjunction* of factors which play a role in bringing about the effect.

Striking the match causes it to light — if the match is dry *and* there is sufficient oxygen to sustain combustion *and* there's not a wind that will blow cool the phosphorous before it ignites the wood. So we must say that what caused the match to ignite was that it was struck *and* it was dry *and* . . .

When all the causal factors are constant or normal except for one, and it's the addition of the latter's occurrence to the others that triggers them to function together to bring about the effect, then we often refer to that one variable as *the* cause. When there are two or more variables that play the triggering role, we speak of them as **joint causes**, again assuming the cooperation of the other causal factors (for example, we might say the lightning and the dryness of the grass jointly caused the grass fire).

2. The causes of any event are always part of a *causal chain* that extends over time.

Striking a match causes it to light because striking raises the temperature of the phosphorous and that initiates (that is, causes) a process of combustion in the match head. Moreover, something caused the match to be struck (perhaps your desire to light a campfire), and that is among the causes of the match igniting. (In general, if A is a cause of B and B is a cause of C, we can say that A is a cause of C.)

A cause that is close in time to the effect and triggers it is sometimes called a **proximate cause** of the effect; those that happened a considerable time before the effect, the **remote (distant) causes**.

When we look for causal explanations, we are looking for salient threads in a complicated **causal web**. What sort of threads interest us varies with the practical situation we find ourselves in. In many cases, we want to know about the causal factors that *we* might readily manipulate in order to control whether or not the effect occurs (for example, what will cause you to get to sleep the night before the test). In other cases, we are interested in the causal factors for which somebody might be blamed (for example, in investigating the causes of automobile accidents).[3]

There is one further complication. Sometimes, there are two or more distinct factors, any one of which by itself is sufficient to account for the effect. Why won't my car start? Well, the battery is dead, but also it's out of gas: take your pick. In cases like these, we speak of **independent** (as opposed to joint) **causes** of the effect.

Strategies

In this section, we discuss the steps you can take to draw reasonable conclusions from evidence about the causes of particular events. Before starting we should note that tracking down the cause of something is often a complicated and time-consuming task, so before embarking on it, you should consider whether it is really necessary to do so.

- Has someone else already figured out the explanation, and is it readily available? It might be more efficient to ask around or look it up than to undertake a causal inquiry yourself. For example, what will cut down food odors in your fridge? Ask somebody. (Our mom says: Leave an open box of baking soda in the fridge.)
- Can someone else figure out the cause better than you can? It might be smarter to consult someone else who knows more about the matter. (For example, why isn't your printer giving you near-letter-quality print? It might save a lot of time to consult a more knowledgeable friend instead of trying to figure it out from the manual.)
- Is it worth the time and effort to try to discover the cause? (For example, why doesn't this sealed flashlight work any more: Is the battery dead, the bulb burned out, or the switch broken? If you take it apart to find out you can't fix it anyway, and you can buy a new flashlight for a few dollars.)

Should you decide to look for an explanation on your own, there are four main steps to take.

1. *Get clear about what it is you are trying to explain and* **why** *you want an explanation of it.*

This step is a crucial preliminary to the next one, which is formulating hypotheses. You need to be clear about what you want to explain and why in order to know what *sort* of cause you are looking for, and hence to know what sort of hypotheses to consider. If you are searching for the reason why something does not work so that you can fix it, you probably will not be interested in the **remote causes** (for example, sloppy workmanship at the factory where it was produced), but rather the causal factors that you can presently do something about. On the other hand, if the purpose of your causal investigation is to help in a lawsuit against the manufacturer, you will be very interested in such remote causes as sloppy workmanship or faulty design.

Suppose you go to the fridge for a snack in the middle of the night and the fridge light doesn't go on when you open the door. That might mean that the refrigerator isn't working, which would be serious if you have 40 pounds of ribs in the freezer for a party on the weekend. But it's not serious so far as keeping the ribs refrigerated goes if it's due to the bulb being burned out or a failure in the switch mechanism. You want to know *something* about the cause, but all you really need to know right away is whether the cause of the light not going on will affect the cooling of the freezer.

2. *Formulate as many plausible hypotheses as you can about the causes of the event.*

Hypotheses are possible answers to the question you are interested in, answers worth exploring and testing in order determine which is true. Much of empirical science consists in the formulation and experimental testing of hypotheses. In our contexts, plausible hypotheses will be possible explanations which have some real likelihood of being true.

One frequent mistake in reasoning about causes is to fixate on the first answer or explanation that comes to mind. Another is to identify too few possible causes when using the method of elimination discussed shortly. So it's important to think of as many reasonable or plausible explanations as you can and to consider each as an hypothesis.

Your hypotheses will ordinarily come from two sources.

a. Your **background knowledge** about the factors that cause or contribute to things of the kind you are trying to explain can provide a list of hypotheses.

If you want to know why your car engine won't turn over, and you know a bit about cars, you will know the problem might be due to a dead battery or to a malfunctioning ignition system.

b. *Atypical or unusual events* coinciding with the effect can reasonably be suspected of playing a causal role and so suggest an hypothesis.

If your car won't start after you have just come through a car wash, but started readily before that, it is reasonable to suspect that passing through the car wash has something to do with the problem and you might hypothesize that water or moisture is causing the problem.

A misuse of the last-mentioned source of causal hypotheses can lead to (that is, cause!) a person to commit a common error or fallacy in causal reasoning. The mistake is to jump to the conclusion that an unusual or atypical event that preceded the effect in question *must* have been the cause of it. This error goes by the Latin name *post hoc, ergo propter hoc* ("after that, therefore because of that") or just "post hoc reasoning," for short. Although it is eminently reasonable to consider the hypothesis that what noticeably preceded the effect also contributed to it causally, it is premature to draw that conclusion without ruling out other plausible hypotheses.

In the case of the refrigerator light, a number of hypotheses that are relevant to your concern about keeping the ribs refrigerated should suggest themselves immediately:

H1. The bulb is burned out.
H2. There is a failure in the subsystem that supplies electricity to the light (the wiring, or the spring-loaded button in the door that acts as a switch and turns the light on when the door is opened).
H3. The refrigerator is not receiving any electrical power.
     (a) The refrigerator is not plugged in.
     (b) The fuse or circuit breaker is blown or tripped.
     (c) There is a power failure in the neighborhood; no electrical power is coming into the house.
H4. There is a "general failure" of the entire refrigeration system, of which the nonfunctioning light is just a symptom.

These hypotheses have two features worth noting.

First, they are formulated in a way that is geared to your concern. If the explanation is H1 or H2, you go back to bed confident that the ribs are safe. If the explanation is H3(a) or H3(b), you plug in the fridge, replace the fuse, or switch back the circuit breaker. If the explanation is H4, you might try to find someone else with a freezer where you can store the ribs. If the explanation is H3(c) all you can do is hope that the power utility restores power before any damage can be done.

Second, someone might overlook some of these possibilities, and if they did they would waste time or money. For instance, it is easy enough to overlook H3(a) and H3(b), call for service, have to wait, and then pay a service charge for getting the fridge plugged in or the fuse replaced—which you could have done quickly and easily yourself.

3. ***Decide on a Strategy for Testing or Evaluating the Hypotheses.***

There are two ways to test or evaluate the hypotheses. One is to look for evidence that would rule out or *falsify* one or more hypotheses; the other is to look for evidence that would *confirm or establish* one of the hypotheses.

To **falsify** an hypothesis, find some fact which rules it out. If the kitchen light is on, that falsifies or rules out the hypothesis that the nonfunctioning fridge light is due to a general hydro failure. However, if the kitchen light doesn't turn on, that would not by itself confirm a general power failure (perhaps the kitchen light bulb is burned out). So the state of the kitchen light can falsify, but cannot confirm, one of the hypotheses.

To **confirm** an hypothesis, find evidence which shows or tends to show that it is true or correct. If you can see that the plug is not in the socket, that confirms hypothesis H3(a). If no other light or appliance in the apartment goes on, and you look out the window and see that the surrounding buildings are completely dark and the street light on the corner is unlit, that tends to show that there is a general electrical utility failure, and so provides confirmation for H3(c)— though it does not conclusively prove H3(c), since that particular street lamp might be the only one that is not lit and by chance everyone's lights are turned off (what time of night is it?).

Often a combination of falsification and confirmation works best. First eliminate a couple of hypotheses and then proceed to look for confirming evidence for the remaining ones. Check the plug and the other lights in the house, even the circuit breaker on the service panel in the basement. If they are all okay, eliminate all of H3. Change the light bulb in the refrigerator; if the light stays off that eliminates H1. Now start looking for something that would confirm H2 or that would confirm H4. Examine the light switch button in the door. If it's stuck, that tends to confirm hypothesis H2, but you probably should unstick the button and see whether that makes any difference. Or, if it is worth the risk of losing what may be the last cold air in the fridge, you might leave the door open for a while and then close it, and see whether the motor then comes on; if it does not, that tends to confirm hypothesis H4 (assuming the thermostat is working).

In deciding on a strategy for testing, also consider the order in which you test. Sometimes there is a best order in which to proceed, though it does not always make much difference. There are three considerations in settling on order of testing:

a. Probability of the hypothesis

Other things being equal, it is better to test the more likely hypotheses first, especially when looking for confirming evidence. Check the spring-loaded button before you start worrying about a general failure of the refrigerator, if it is more likely that the button is stuck than that your refrigerator has failed.

b. Difficulty and length of the test procedure

In general, it is better to conduct the easier and quicker tests first. For example, check the refrigerator plug before you trek to the basement to look at the service panel.

c. Consequences of the test

Tests that involve risk or damage should always be performed as a last resort, if at all, for example, leaving the fridge door open for 10 minutes to see whether that makes the motor go on.

4. ***Test or evaluate the hypotheses.***

In devising ways to test hypotheses, keep the following three questions in mind.

a. *Did the event which your hypothesis says is the cause really occur?*

If you suspect a child is upset because his teacher yelled at him this afternoon, you need to know whether his teacher really did yell at him then. Look for evidence that the event occurred or evidence that it didn't occur. If you can establish that the child skipped school today, you rule out the teacher's yelling as an explanation. Another example: Did the plane crash because of an on-board explosion during flight? Professionals investigating air accidents face this kind of question regularly, and answer it by examining the physical evidence at the crash site. There are certain physical signs whose presence establishes, and whose absence rules out, the occurrence of an on-board explosion.

b. *Is the event which your hypothesis says is the cause sufficient to produce this sort of effect?*

Often you already know that it is sufficient and have formulated your hypothesis based on that knowledge. But sometimes a person will suggest a possible cause whose causal efficacy you aren't sure of. And sometimes some unusual event will have preceded the effect, and you want to consider the possibility it was a cause without knowing whether it could be. Your uncle had a heart attack right after drinking some homemade wine. Could the wine have caused the attack? You're nauseous after coming home from a dinner party. Could the food you ate at the party be the cause of your illness? In most such cases, you will have to turn to expert opinion to find the answers. But sometimes in such circumstances you can gather evidence yourself that tends to confirm or disconfirm the hypothesis. For example, you might inquire whether others who ate what you did at the party also became ill. If several did, that would tend to confirm the hypothesis that the food was the cause (though the cause might have been something you all drank or some other factor you all shared. Also, even if no one else became ill, the food might still be the cause; you might have an allergy to what was served that no one else at the party had).

    c. *Are there factors which are required for the hypothesized cause to have its effect and, if there are, were they present?*

Strychnine can cause death *if* the dosage is large enough. Was the dosage large enough? A single unextinguished cigarette can cause a forest fire *if* the woods are dry. Were they dry?

Some General Observations on Reasoning About Particular Causal Propositions

In reasoning about particular causal propositions, it's necessary to draw on background knowledge of the related general causal propositions. Unless you know what sorts of things cause other sorts of things in a given area, you will be limited in the plausible hypotheses you can formulate and you'll have trouble devising strategies for testing any hypotheses (moreover, you should be cautious about speculating).

When testing hypotheses, you are drawing inferences from evidence or data to conclusions about the truth or falsity of those hypotheses. Thus everything that holds for good inferences in general applies here: the evidence or data must be acceptable, and it must lend a significant degree of support to the conclusion.

Two mistakes are particularly tempting when trying to arrive at explanations. One is post hoc reasoning; the other is oversimplification—treating one of several causal factors as the only cause, or the main cause. For example, opponents of legislation controlling the ownership of handguns have argued that "guns don't kill people, people kill people." They are right that guns alone do not kill people. However, the need for people to point the gun and pull the trigger does not show that people are the only cause of the high incidence of fatalities due to gunshot wounds. If fewer guns were available, there would be fewer opportunities for people to use them. People are one causal factor in shooting fatalities, but they are not the only one—and human anger and fear reactions are probably less amenable to control than gun ownership is. Anyone who accepts the "Guns don't kill, people do" argument seems to us guilty of mistaking a single causal factor for the main cause.

Reasoning About Causal Consequences

We have been concentrating on finding explanations of particular events, which are situations in which we know that an event has occurred (or we want it to occur) and we want to discover its causes. Another kind of reasoning about particular causal propositions occurs when we try to predict the results of some actual or contemplated action or event. In those situations, one draws on background knowledge of the typical effects of certain *kinds* of event under various circumstances and tries to apply that background knowledge to the present circumstances. For example, if I know that one bottle of beer makes me tipsy when I am tired, and I know that I'm tired, I can be pretty sure I will get tipsy if I take that bottle of beer you are offering me. Such reasoning about results is, as we shall see, essential to deliberation or reasoning about what to do.

One type of mistake in reasoning about consequences is **causal slippery slope** reasoning. An example: "If lesbians and gays are allowed to be ministers of the church, the next thing you know they will be preaching homosexuality to children in Sunday School and sexually molesting them."

Causal slippery slope reasoning is a fallacious variation of what might be called "causal chain" reasoning. The general form of such reasoning is this. If we allow a particular step to be taken, that will set off a chain of events which will end up in some undesirable outcome; we do not want that outcome to occur; therefore we should not allow the first step. There is nothing wrong with such causal chain reasoning *provided that the causal propositions inherent in it (along with the value judgments) are warranted.* Such reasoning is legitimate in deliberating about public policy decisions, for instance. But the reasoning errs when an outcome that is at best only remotely possible, or merely the product of wild fantasies, is projected on the basis of inadequate grounds, or none at all. The first step is predicted to put us on a slippery slope, and it's claimed without (sufficient) evidence that we will be swept down that slippery slope, one thing leading inexorably to the next, until we reach the undesirable outcome. The conclusion inferred is that the first, fatal step onto that slope should not be taken. The mistaken form of such reasoning relies on a false or an insufficiently supported causal proposition.

The foregoing example illustrates this error. Whatever reasons there may be for opposing homosexual ministers in the church (and on that issue we do not here pass judgment), there is no evidence of even a correlation between being a homosexual and either proselytizing for homosexuality or sexually abusing children. The causal connection alleged is fanciful. In general, when you encounter this "causal projection" reasoning, a good policy is to examine the plausibility of its essential causal propositions.

"Free trade between Mexico and the United States will lead eventually to the economic and the political absorption of Mexico into the United States. So the free trade deal should be opposed by all who value an independent Mexico." That is a causal chain type of argument. Quite possibly the causal proposition *is* true, but we must see the evidence so we can check it out to make sure it is not a case of causal slippery slope reasoning.

8.4 REASONING ABOUT GENERAL CAUSAL PROPOSITIONS

It is the daily business of the working scientist to search for the general causal propositions needed to explain the causes of particular events. The specialized knowledge required usually puts such investigations out of our reach. Fortunately, many of the general causal propositions we need to know in order to deal with everyday situations have already been established and may be treated as reliable.

Nonetheless, it is useful to know a few things about the reasoning used to establish general causal propositions—in other words, of the reasoning methods of working scientists. However, be forewarned that, in spite of a few general similarities (which should not be underemphasized), there is not a single universal scientific method or structure of scientific reasoning.

People reason about general causal propositions for different purposes. Often the objective is to get the background information needed in order to intercede with particular causal factors. We want to be able to cure the people who have AIDS, we want to resuscitate our lakes and forests, we want to create an economy without debilitating recessions—and so we are led to do the research that we hope will yield true general causal propositions which can then guide our medical, environmental, and economic interventions. Another motivation is sheer intellectual curiosity, often combined with a belief that an increased understanding of the general causal relations in the world will find its own applications.

Causes and Correlations

The reasoning strategies used to uncover general causal connections rely on, among other things, the distinction between a causal relation and a **correlation**.

Two properties are said to be **correlated** just in case *the value of one property varies in a systematic way with the value of the other*. For example, among human beings height and weight are correlated: taller people tend to weigh more than shorter people (that is, variations in height are associated with variations in weight).

A correlation will be either positive or negative. A correlation is **positive** when *as the value of one property or variable increases (or decreases), so does the value of the other*. Variations occur in the same direction: both go up and both go down. The correlations between height and weight, smoking and lung cancer, smoking and heart disease, and years of formal education and lifetime earnings are all positive. A correlation is **negative** when, *as the value of either property or variable increases, the value of the other tends to decrease (and vice versa, as one decreases the other increases)*. Variations occur in opposite directions: as one goes up the other goes down, and conversely. For example, the correlation between smoking and appetite, alcohol ingestion and motor control, and between industrialization and family size in a society are all negative. In either a positive or a negative correlation there is a systematic covariance between the correlates.

The proposition that the values of two properties vary in a *systematic* way can be illustrated as follows. If you made an ordered list of individuals based on how they ranked on the first property—from highest to lowest, for example—and then made another ordered list of those individuals based on how they ranked on the second property, the order of the individuals on the two lists would be similar. In a perfect positive correlation, the order would be exactly the same; in a perfect negative correlation, the order would be the exactly the reverse. If you were to list an actual group of people from the tallest to the shortest, and also from the heaviest to the lightest, although the order on the two lists would not be exactly the same, it would be fairly similar; you would have found a high positive correlation, though not a perfect one.

Statisticians have devised a number of ways of measuring the degree to which two properties vary in a systematic way. Their numeric measures of degree of correlation are called *coefficients of correlation*. Coefficients of correlation are positive or negative decimal numbers ranging from + 1 (for perfect positive correlation) to − 1 (for perfect negative correlation). A coefficient of correlation of 0 means that there is no correlation, that there is no systematic relation between the two variables, that the two properties are perfectly independent of each other.

A correlation is not the same thing as a causal connection. The occurrence of a correlation *usually* indicates that *some* kind of causal connection exists between the correlates, though occasionally a correlation is just a coincidence.[4]

Scientists are interested in correlations that are not "coincidences," and so they look for correlations where the covariance is too great to be attributable to mere chance—in other words, correlations that are *statistically significant*. In the typical situation, scientists looking for a correlation select a sample from a general population. Using descriptive statistics, they calculate the degree of correlation among properties in the sample.[5] Next they ascertain whether the correlation in the sample indicates some causal connection. To do so they turn to probability theory and inferential statistics, and calculate the likelihood that the correlation in the sample is due to chance. If that likelihood is low, the correlation is said to be statistically significant.

Even where a correlation is statistically significant and so may be taken to indicate that a causal connection is operative, nothing follows about which of the variables is the cause of the other. Nor does it even follow that one of the correlates is the cause of the other, for their covariance may be due to the fact that some third factor is causing or influencing both correlates. Here's an example. There is a statistically significant positive correlation between the number of suits males own and the size of the houses in which they live. But clearly, owning a lot of suits doesn't *cause* a man to live in a big house, and living in a big house doesn't cause a man to buy a lot of suits. Still, the correlation does indicate the existence of some causal relationship involving the correlates. They are, we would hypothesize, both effects or consequences of wealth or a desire for the appearance of wealth.

The search for correlations, then, is an important part of the scientific enterprise, especially when the scientist is trying to uncover the causes of things. But finding a correlation is just a first step toward finding a causal connection.

By the way, not every connection between two things is a correlation. For example, there is a connection between the hockey games in which Wayne Gretzky plays with his sweater out of his pants on one side and those in which he scores one or more points. But this is not a correlation. Gretzky *always* leaves his sweater out on one side (why? we wonder), and he is such a good player that he scores or assists in nearly every game. There is no information about whether Gretzky's point production would drop if he tucked in his sweater because he never tucks it in. To establish a correlation, we would need to find that, systematically, Gretzky's scoring is higher with his sweater out and lower with his sweater in. Without such information there's no correlation, even though the two go together.

Once it has been established that there is a statistically significant correlation between two properties (in other words that their association is not likely to be due to chance), then there is more to investigate before being able to infer a general causal proposition. As we have seen, the causal connection can be either of two sorts: (1) one of the correlated properties causes the other (again, the correlation does not establish which is which), or (2) some third factor causes them both.

The next step in the methodology is to formulate **hypotheses** which would explain the correlational findings in a causal framework. The hypotheses are always formulated with possible methods of testing them in mind, since an untestable hypothesis cannot be confirmed or refuted. Last, much as with hypotheses explaining particulars, the tests are carried out, the findings recorded, and conclusions inferred.

Where we as laypersons are most likely to encounter scientific investigations into general causal propositions is in the reports of studies that appear on a regular basis in the media—in news reports, in special science sections or programs, or in popular science magazines such as *Scientific American*. Hence we turn, in the next chapter, to an examination of such studies and to some recommendations about how to make use of them. The brief discussion of the investigation of general causal propositions in this section will serve as background for that examination.

8.5 SUMMARY

We are continuously interested in causal explanations, whether in the mundane business of daily life, in the working world of planning and carrying out policies, or in the realm of pure scientific research. In our thinking about such matters, we reason in order to discover causes and we reason in order to act on the basis of our beliefs about causes. Our interest is directed at both particular causal propositions and at general causal propositions.

Given the complexity of the causal webs producing particular events, we need to focus the search on the kinds of causes that will matter to us, given our interests, for example, whether it is proximate or remote causes we are interested in, whether it is the design features or the human actions, and so on. Thus the first strategy in hunting for causes of particulars is to get clear about precisely what is to be explained, and why. Then formulate as many plausible causal hypotheses as you can, and settle on methods for testing the hypotheses—either to falsify or to confirm them. Finally, do the testing. In reasoning about the causes of particulars, caution is advisable about post hoc reasoning, causal over-simplification, and causal slippery slope projections.

We reason about general causal propositions both in order to apply that knowledge to particular cases but also out of general curiosity about how the world works. Much of the research to establish general causal propositions is, and must be, carried out by specialists. But having a general knowledge of their several and various methodologies helps in understanding the reports of the investigations that we do encounter. Common to all sciences is the distinction between correlations and causes, the former being systematic covariations among properties (positive or negative). Correlations are not themselves causes, but statistically significant correlations indicate the presence of a causal relationship. The mere existence of a correlation does not settle the question of which correlate is cause and which is effect, or whether both are the effects of some third factor which is their common cause. Investigations into general causal propositions proceed similarly to those into particular causal propositions, via the formulation and testing of hypotheses.

8.6 EXERCISES

Exercise 1

In each of the following passages, identify causal propositions asserted or quoted and classify them as (a) particular causal claims or (b) general causal claims. (Note: Some passages contain no causal claims at all.)

1. "The White House budget director admitted to Congress on Wednesday that an error made by the administration resulted in a $113 billion over-estimate in its five-year projection for tax revenues." (*The Windsor Star*, July 18, 1991.)

2. "Fewer people are drinking and driving and crashing." (*The Windsor Star*, July 18, 1991.)

3. "Until recently, researchers assumed that shyness was strictly an acquired habit. But the ground has shifted in recent decades. Many experts now

agree that the trait is at least partly hereditary." (*Newsweek*, Summer Edition, 1991.)

4. "Whatever else the allied victory over Iraq accomplished, it may have stopped Saddam Hussein in mid-course as he sought to develop an atomic bomb." (*Detroit Free Press*, July 19, 1991.)

5. "Pure oxygen neither speeds recovery from fatigue nor enhances athletic performance, a new study shows." (*The Globe and Mail*, July 22, 1989.)

6. "Putting on a sad face or a smile reproduces the feelings that the expressions represent, according to a new theory of how emotions are produced." (*The Globe and Mail*, July 22, 1989.)

7. "In [one] study, West German researchers were able to induce happy feelings by having people hold a small pen clenched in their teeth, imitating a smile. When the people held the pen in their protruding lips, imitating a pout, they felt unhappy." (*The Globe and Mail*, July 22, 1989.)

8. "Golf is just a complicated way to decide who buys the drinks." (Supposedly a Scottish saying.)

9. "The measures taken to reduce trade with South Africa by nine industrial nations . . . cut that country's export earnings by 7 per cent, according to [a] report prepared for an August meeting of Commonwealth foreign ministers." (*The Globe and Mail*, July 22, 1989.)

10. "It's a bright blue day, and the child is back at the National Institute of Health in Bethesda, Md., for another monthly infusion of genetically engineered blood cells. She has adenosine deaminase (ADA) deficiency, a rare inherited condition that makes her unable to manufacture ADA, an enzyme crucial to the immune system. Without ADA, she is as vulnerable to infection as a person with AIDS." (*The New York Times Magazine*, March 3, 1991.)

Exercise 2

For each of the following problems, (a) formulate as many testable hypotheses as you can think of to explain the cause of the particular event, and (b) indicate for each hypothesis the most practical way to confirm and/or refute it. If your background knowledge is limited for any particular problem, indicate what sort of thing you think you would need to know in order to be able to formulate hypotheses and describe tests for them.

1. Your iron won't heat when it is turned on and you want to be able to use it.

2. There are a lot of cockroaches in your house/apartment and you want to get rid of them permanently.

3. Your cat/dog just threw up on the living room carpet. You want to know what you should do for your pet.

4. Often when you write an exam you get physically upset (sweaty, nauseous, dizzy), and you want it to stop.

5. A close friend of yours is getting really drunk every weekend. This behavior is worrying you, and you wonder if there really is any problem and if you can do anything to help, if there is.

Exercise 3

For each of these examples, if a correlation is claimed, (a) identify the correlates, and (b) state whether it's a positive or negative correlation. (c) Identify any causal claim based on the alleged correlation.

**1. G. W. Comstock and K. B. Partridge found that the more frequently people attended church, the lower their incidence of fatal arteriosclerotic heart disease tended to be. ("Church Attendance and Health," *Journal of Chronic Disease*, Vol. 25, 1972; 665–672.)

**2. As the price of beef increases, the amount of chicken sold in supermarkets tends to increase, and conversely, as the price of beef decreases, the amount of chicken sold decreases. Evidently, the higher beef prices induce people to purchase meat that is more affordable. This also shows that generally people like beef better than chicken.

3. The taller a person is, the more the person tends to weigh; the shorter the person, the lower their weight tends to be.

4. The late Punch Imlach, former Toronto Maple Leaf hockey coach, always wore the same hat to Maple Leaf games. When asked for his reason, he claimed that whenever the Leafs won, he was wearing that hat.

5. Obtaining a university degree will get you more money. Statistics show that the more years of education a person has, the greater his or her annual income tends to be.

6. The lower women's salaries are, the greater the incidence of sexual harassment against them on the job.

7. Statistics show that the shorter a judo expert, the higher the incidence of tournament wins. Being built close to the ground evidently makes you more effective in judo.

8. As the number of miles on a car's odometer increases, the resale price tends to decrease.

9. Whenever I wash my car, it rains!

10. Changing careers is apparently not a very good idea. When you change careers, you start with no experience in your new line of work. And studies show that as a person's years of experience in a given line of work increase, his or her average annual salary tends to increase as well.

11. Countries with higher average personal income tend to have lower fertility rates than do countries with lower average personal incomes. A country's fertility rate is the number of births per year per thousand citizens. Apparently, being poor makes people want to have more children.

Exercise 4

For each passage, identify the principal causal claims made in it, and say whether each one is particular or general. Are any correlations offered in support of any of the causal claims? If so, what are they?

1. *Background*: The excerpt below is from the "Beauty" column of *The New York Times Magazine* by Linda Wells, "Leaders of the Pack" (August 28, 1988) about the packaging of women's cosmetics.

LEADERS OF THE PACK

Executives at Elizabeth Arden repackaged all its makeups in an effort to upgrade the company's image, as well as to attract a new, more affluent customer. Designers started with the lipstick tube, and went on to repackage the lip gloss and nail lacquer. The new cases are metal rather than plastic, with a fluted column and a wavy base. With the repackaging, and a reformulation of the lipstick, its price jumped from $8.50 to $11. Sales also increased by 40 percent, a leap executives attribute entirely to the packaging.

Despite the fact that women seem to want small, easily portable makeup, these cases are heavier and more decorative than the previous designs. "When a consumer picks up a lipstick case, she weighs it in her hand," says Marc Rosen, vice president of design and communications at Elizabeth Arden. "If it's very light, she assumes it's cheap and low quality. A heavier package implies quality. It feels substantial."

It's one thing for a lipstick or compact package to be flashy; these items are often pulled out in public. Because nail lacquer usually stays at home, its package is traditionally nondescript and functional. Still, when Elizabeth Arden switched to a decorative metal and glass nail polish bottle, sales of the products soared.

That women are embracing more elaborate packages shows a change in taste, one that has already affected clothing and home design. "There's a return to a period of time when people appreciated little luxuries," says Rosen. "They aren't looking for disposable things anymore." And now that architects and designers have rediscovered the vanity table, cosmetics and fragrances are being treated as attractive objects to be displayed, rather than stashed away in a medicine cabinet.

2. *Background*: The following excerpt is taken from the "Hers" column of *The New York Times Magazine* of Sunday, August 28, 1988, p. 77. The column, titled, "Appearance Anxiety," was written by Susan Jacoby. Jacoby was discussing the phenomenon of women rushing in large numbers to obtain a drug called Retin-A that was about to be approved by the American Food and Drug Administration for treatment of wrinkles caused by sun damage.

Appearance Anxiety

More than 25 years after the first hints of the women's movement surfaced in Betty Friedan's "The Feminine Mystique," we are spending more money and cutting into our flesh with greater frequency than ever in a battle against the inevitable imprint of time. When the feminist movement began, it was surely reasonable to believe that a reverse phenomenon might occur—that feminine "appearance anxiety" would diminish in some measure as women gained wider access to economic and job op-

portunities that provide a sounder basis for the future than wrinkle-free skin.

Ironically, the increased spending power of successful women is one of the underpinnings of the growing popularity of cosmetic surgery. I recently spent several months exploring the world of cosmetic surgery for a women's magazine and found that the typical patient is increasingly likely to be a working woman in her 30's or 40's.

So who gets hurt if a woman chooses to spend

her own money this way? The tab for breast enlargement—the single most common cosmetic operation—ranges from $1,800 to $4,000. More than 94,000 women paid the bill for this procedure in 1986 alone and more than 1.5 million living American women have undergone breast implant surgery. What's wrong, for starters, is that $1,800 to $4,000 is a nice contribution to a retirement savings account. Silicone gel makes a poor nest egg.

In the 80's, a clever psychological twist has been added to the selling of appearance anxiety. Such fears in women have traditionally been linked to low self-esteem, but today's hucksters insist it is *high* self-esteem that makes women rush to spend their money on potions and operations that may have nasty side effects. Modern women are said to be so self-confident that they no longer feel the need to apologize for pursuing beauty at any price. You've come a long way, baby.

I don't buy it. For my generation, the shortage of available men over age 35 provides a disturbing emotional subtext to the resurgence of appearance anxiety. To a greater or lesser degree, most of us are worried about finding a man or keeping the one we have.

The joke is—and it's a bad joke on us—that men are considerably more tolerant than women of departures from ideal standards of beauty. In any event, a man who wants a much younger woman will not be deterred by the erasure of crow's-feet. With or without wrinkles, a 40-year-old body is a 40-year-old body.

Instead of wasting money and energy in this futile quest, we need to cultivate the kind of unconditional self-acceptance embodied in the zestful marriage proposal that concludes Shakespeare's "Henry V":

"But, in faith, Kate, the elder I wax, the better I shall appear: my comfort is, that old age, that ill layer-up of beauty, can do no more spoil upon my face: thou hast me, if thou hast me, at the worst; and thou shalt wear me, if thou wear me, better and better . . . ."

And if no woman alive is quite that self-confident, she may still look in the mirror and recognize a dear, familiar friend.

3. *Background*: Recently, the use of irradiation to preserve food, which is very common in the United States, has come under attack from some who believe it may be a health hazard. The following passage is adapted from responses to those attacks.

It is ludicrous that so many anti-irradiation groups regularly disseminate misleading statements and negative suggestions about food irradiation.

Irradiation is a long-proved microbiologically and toxicologically safe food preservation process (and not an additive, as so many groups claim) that destroys decay-causing insects, bacteria, and other microorganisms.

Irradiation maintains the nutritional qualities of food without significant impairment, in comparison with conventional food preservation methods. In some cases, it may even enhance food quality.

Irradiation destroys foodborne pathogens such as salmonella. Irradiation can alleviate much hunger in Third World countries by reducing the degradation of millions of tons of foodstuffs caused by insect infestation and microbial changes— food storage losses range from 20 to 50% a year.

Most important, food irradiation offers a free choice. Nobody can or will force consumers to buy irradiated food. Each consumer has a free choice to select, for instance, tropical fruit possibly treated with chemicals, some of which may be carcinogenic or irradiated and properly labeled clean fruit.

4. *Background*: The following Associated Press story is a brief report of the British Association for the Advancement of Science annual meeting appeared in September 1988.

~~~~~~

Fibre Could Cause a 'High'

LONDON (AP)—A hefty helping of granola or whole-wheat bread could contain enough natural LSD to produce a mild high and the dragons of fairy tales really may have existed.

Welcome to the British Association for the Advancement of Science which concluded its annual meeting at Oxford University on the weekend.

While it still produces some of advanced research in Britain, its meetings are also a forum for more far-fetched concepts designed to stimulate debate.

For example, eating eight to 10 slices of whole-wheat bread or a large bowl of granola or bran flakes in one sitting may induce mild euphoria because of wheat's natural LSD content, said Dr. David Conning, director of the British Nutrition Foundation.

And David Unwin of the Palaeontological Institute in Moscow told the conference the dragons of fairy tales may have existed. He said they were flying dinosaurs with five-metre wingspans and dominated the skies 140 million years ago.

~~~~~~

Exercise 5

For each example given,
   (a) Identify the principal causal propositions asserted, and classify them as particular or general.
   (b) Identify any correlations offered in support of the causal claims made.
   (c) Summarize the evidence offered in support of causal claims.
   (d) Assess that evidence. Does it have any weaknesses? Does it adequately back up the causal proposition based on it? Explain your judgment.

**1. Here's an example of the importance of traditional values. When women abandon their traditional roles as wives and mothers and enter the work force, the result is divorce. There's lots of evidence to show that this is so. First of all, it is well known that the divorce rate has soared in this century as the percentage of married women who work outside the home has increased. Second, I'm personally acquainted with two different men who were happily married for more than 15 years until their wives took jobs outside the home; both these men were served with divorce papers a few years after their wives went to work. Finally, in a recent study, 75% of the divorced women surveyed had jobs while they were married.

2. *Background*: This item is taken from a speech by Vincent Stone, president of the Marijuana Education Society of British Columbia. It was reported in *The Silhouette* in November 1979.

   The growing gay population is largely due to cannabis (marijuana). Marijuana contains the female hormone estrogen, which is affecting male users.

3. *Background*: This United Press International item appeared in December 1990.

Toothpaste flavorings linked to asthma flare-up

United Press International

BOSTON—Asthma sufferers who find themselves wheezing and coughing might look to their toothpaste as a possible cause of their problems.

An artificial mint flavoring found in a brand of toothpaste made from an opaque paste apparently triggered breathing problems in a 21-year-old woman with a history of asthma, according to a letter from two doctors published Wednesday in The New England Journal of Medicine.

The woman had been using Crest Tartar Control Formula toothpaste, "but when she switched to a gel-based toothpaste her wheezing resolved dramatically," wrote Drs. Bruce Spurlock and Thomas Dailey of Kaiser Permanente Medical Center in Santa Clara, Calif.

The gel included a spice-blend flavoring, and the paste had spice-mint or wintergreen flavoring, the doctors found.

4. *Background*: This item appeared in the *Oakland Press* on April 16, 1974, under the title "A Good Way to Cure Colds." It was reprinted in the *Informal Logic Newsletter Examples Supplement* for 1979.

University of Michigan medical researchers have discovered that highly educated people with low incomes catch cold more than others, suggesting that susceptibility to colds might depend on one's frame of mind. Furthermore, more people come down with colds on Monday than any other day.

Well, practically everybody thinks he is not being paid as much as his education calls for; and it's on Monday morning when this feeling becomes most acute. So obviously, it's not a germ or virus that's causing all our colds but those cold-hearted people in the front office who never seem to realize how smart we are. A cure for cold? One way would be to give everybody a raise and tell them to take Monday off.

5. On November 14, 1989 *The Windsor Star* reported that "the recent births of two deformed babies have revived fears that something is seriously wrong with the drinking water" in Wallaceburg, Ontario.

The 22-year-old mother of a deformed girl born October 10 reported that during her pregnancy she experienced no illnesses and took great care to avoid consuming anything that might adversely affect her unborn child. Nine days after the birth of her daughter, a close friend gave birth to a deformed son. Two such births in a single month in a town of just 11,000 residents is very suspicious.

The drinking water for Wallaceburg is drawn from the St. Clair River. That river has been the site of frequent spills from several large chemical plants 40 km upstream in Sarnia. According to figures provided by the provincial Environment Ministry, since 1985 more than 350 spills have poured into the St. Clair. Some residents have pointed out that "even the water from the taps smells funny."

Environment Ministry officials insist that the quality of the water falls within established guidelines. However, there have been famous cases, such as Thalidomide, in which people were assured that chemicals were safe, only to discover that they produced birth deformities. It is only reasonable to conclude that these tragic birth deformities in Wallaceburg are a direct result of the chemical spills. Something must be done to stop these companies from threatening our unborn children!

6. *Background*: This excerpt appeared in *Harper's Magazine* in May 1991.

From "The Problem with Highlighters," by Lawrence A. Beyer, in the Summer 1990 issue of Academic Questions, *a quarterly journal published by Transaction Periodicals Consortium in New Brunswick, New Jersey. Beyer is a research scholar at Yale Law School.*

The use of highlighters—those marking pens that allow readers to emphasize passages in their books with transparent overlays of bright color—is significantly retarding the education of university students by distorting and cheapening the way many read.

. . . The most common use of highlighters is for simply marking, with a colorful coating over the words, the gist of a text that the student needs to read. While this might seem harmless, such highlighter use in fact encourages passive reading habits in young adults who very much need to learn to read actively, critically, and analytically.

At best, most students who use the high-lighter in this fashion are uncritically—almost unthinkingly—ingesting some of the authors' phraseology and gaining sketchy outlines of the texts. At worst, their "reading" consists merely of a skimming sensitivity to those conventional textual indicators that point out which passages are part of the skeletal gists of the texts ("In sum," "The main issue is," etc.). In accenting these passages, students are performing a typographical function that could be accomplished, with the same absence of understanding, by computers. . . .

. . . Students, already expert at the simplistic regurgitation of ideas, now have an instrument for applying a pretty coating of color that makes texts even easier to ingest without thoughtful chewing. Reading becomes a mindless swallowing of words that pass through such students without making any lasting impression.

7. *Background*: This story appeared in *USA Today* on July 19, 1991.

Caffeine withdrawal, a real grind for coffee lovers

By Tim Friend
USA TODAY

Abruptly stopping caffeine intake—even if you drink just two or three cups of coffee a day—can cause significant withdrawal symptoms within 48 hours, new research shows.

That means people who want to eliminate caffeine from their diets should taper off instead of quitting cold turkey, says Dr. Roland Griffiths, Johns Hopkins University School of Medicine, Baltimore.

Skipping the usual caffeine fix "appears to significantly affect daily activities," most often through the sudden onset of headaches and lethargy, says Griffiths, who reported his findings Tuesday at a National Academy of Sciences Committee on Problems of Drug Dependence.

About 51% of people in the USA over age 10 drink coffee regularly; many complain of jumpiness or trouble sleeping and some worry about conflicting reports of other health effects. While Griffiths says there is no compelling evidence to suggest everybody should stop, they should be aware caffeine is a potent drug.

Caffeine consumption in his study of 62 healthy daily caffeine users averaged 235 mg. and ranged from 28 mg. to 587 mg. One cup of strong coffee has about 100 mg. Average coffee consumption: two or three cups a day. Heavy consumption is usually defined as six or more cups a day.

course, and 98 percent of the women had had intercourse before age 21. The survey is part of a study for the federal Centers for Disease Control to test the reliability of methods to detect a virus linked to cervical cancers. Reid did his survey in 1985, but the federal study has not been published.

8. *Background*: This *New York Times* piece appeared in January of 1991.

IRS reports new evidence of cheating on taxes

By Tamar Lewin
New York Times

NEW YORK—The Internal Revenue Service has striking new evidence that large numbers of Americans have been cheating on their taxes, claiming deductions for children who do not exist and child-care credits for babysitters who were paid in cash they did not report to the IRS.

In 1989, the agency began requiring taxpayers who take the dependent-care credit to give the name, address, and Social Security number of the baby-sitter or day-care center that they paid.

The requirement was intended to force child-care providers to report their income. The year it went into effect, 2.6 million baby-sitters effectively vanished, since the number of taxpayers claiming the credit dropped by 30 percent.

"What probably happened, in most cases, is that people were paying their baby-sitters off the books, and their baby-sitters would not provide their Social Security number or go on the books, so the family had to choose between finding a new baby-sitter or giving up the tax credit," said John Szilagyi, an IRS researcher who is compiling the results of the new law.

Only 6.1 million taxpayers claimed a dependent-care credit in 1989, compared with 8.7 million in 1988.

The dependent-care credit can be claimed by any taxpayer who is paying someone to care for a dependent child or disabled adult so that the taxpayer can work. For those with two or more dependents, the credit can be as much as $1,440 a year, or 30 percent of up to $4,800 in child-care expenses.

Szilagyi estimated that the IRS collected an additional $1.2 billion from the 2.6 million families who stopped taking the dependent-care credit in 1989.

While the new law apparently led families to give up the tax credit, it also prompted many day-care providers to put their operations on the books for the first time.

According to Szilagyi, the number of child-care businesses reporting income to the IRS rose to 429,569 in 1989, from 261,372 in 1988, an increase of 64 percent.

Another change in the tax law has yielded blatant evidence of widespread cheating. Starting in 1987, the IRS required that taxpayers report the Social Security number of all dependents over the age of 5. And that year, 7 million American children disappeared from the nation's tax returns, representing a 9 percent drop in the 77 million dependents claimed on the previous year's returns and $2.9 billion more in yearly tax revenue.

The tax agency said about 20 percent of the vanished dependents were children who had been claimed as dependents by both parents after a divorce. Under the law, only one parent may claim the child as a deduction.

Most of the others probably never existed, Szilagyi said. And some families apparently became quite greedy in creating dependents.

About 66,000 taxpayers who claimed four or more dependents in 1986 claimed none in 1987, after the Social Security identification rule went

Continued

into effect. More than 11,000 families claimed seven or more dependents in 1986, but none in 1987.

Those returns are now under investigation, with more than 1,000 audits in which the 1986 dependents were disallowed, and back taxes and fines collected. According to Szilagyi, some cases in which there is evidence of fraud have also been referred to authorities for criminal investigation.

NOTES

1. People with mild dyslexia often get the words 'causal' and 'casual' mixed up. The first has to do with causes, the second is a synonym for 'relaxed' or 'informal.' Try to get them right, but don't worry about it too much.
2. *Columbia Encyclopedia*, 3rd. ed., Columbia University Press, New York, 1963, Tornado, p. 2151.
3. The concept of cause in Western thinking has been heavily influenced by the ancient Greek concept of cause. The word the Greeks used for cause was *aition*, a term that originally meant "the guilty party."
4. We have seen it claimed that some researcher was able to show that over a 20-year period the Dow Jones Industrial Average (an index of the selling price of stocks on the New York Stock Exchange) rose and fell in covariance with the fashionable height for hemlines of woman's skirts (D. Morris, *Manwatching: A Field Guide to Human Behavior*, Abrams, New York, 1977). We do not know whether that story is fiction or not, but if it is true, it is an example of a correlation that we would expect to be pure coincidence.
5. There are various ways of doing this, and most ways yield a coefficient of correlation.

9

Studies

9.1 INTRODUCTION

Our knowledge of general causal claims is not, for the most part, something we acquire on our own. Some of it is common knowledge which we have acquired from other people as a part of growing up (for example, that refrigerating foods retards spoilage and decay or that taking aspirin reduces or eliminates the pain of headaches).[1] Some of it we learned at school (for example, that reducing the pressure to which a volume of a gas or vapor is subjected will cause its temperature to be reduced by an amount proportional to the reduction in pressure). But our knowledge of such truths is both limited and defective. It is limited because there is an enormous amount of information about causal connections of which we are just ignorant, and it is defective because some of the things we may think we know are just wrong (for instance, that keeping sex education out of the schools helps prevent teenage sexual activity and therefore tends to reduce the number of teenage pregnancies) or highly controversial (for instance, that capital punishment discourages capital crimes). Our causal knowledge needs to be supplemented and corrected, and there is a continuing stream of research studies that holds out significant promise of meeting that need.

In today's "information age," numerous studies are widely publicized, and we are regularly invited to adopt new beliefs, or alter old ones, on the basis of reports of their findings. Often such studies will be described as "scientific," in order to lend them authority. How can you, as a layperson reading these reports, know whether or not to believe what they say? This chapter provides background information and guidelines to use when it comes to making up your mind about whether to accept the reported results of such studies.

Even when we consider only studies whose purpose is to prove, disprove, or clarify the existence of causal relations, we find a great variety of types of study, differing both with respect to subject-matter and with respect to methodology or the approach used to investigate that subject matter. In what follows, at the expense of some oversimplification, we will try to put some order into that variety.

At one level are the causal relations that hold in the realm of inanimate (non-living) nature. These are the sorts of causal relations that are studied in physics, astronomy, inorganic chemistry, and geology, to name some of the sciences which deal with inanimate nature. Studies in these sciences tend to be quite precise and exact, highly mathematicized and to a large extent laboratory based.

At another, somewhat more complicated, level are the causal relations within and between living organisms. The various ways of studying these range from the techniques of organic chemistry, through those of zoology and botany, to those of ecology and the study of animal behavior.

At a still more complicated level are the causal relations that play themselves out in human social interaction, which tend to be enormously difficult to identify. These are the traditional province of such sciences as psychology, sociology, and anthropology.

Of necessity, many of the investigatory techniques that are appropriate and fruitful in one domain are of limited use or inapplicable in another. Yet at a very general level, there are certain features which distinguish all studies worth taking seriously. Such studies base their conclusions on evidence, and that evidence is systematic rather than anecdotal (see the minithesaurus in Section 9.6 for this distinction). Respectable studies seeking to establish the truth or falsity of causal generalizations use trustworthy methods for establishing significant relationships and then select among plausible causal explanations or hypotheses on the basis of either correlational or experimental evidence.

9.2 Two Basic Types of Data Gathering

We want first to describe in more detail two of the most common strategies for systematic data gathering in causal studies: one associated with *experimental* research and the other with *correlational* research.

Experimental Research

In **experimental research**, two or more factors (or **variables**) are studied. One factor is manipulated or selected by the researcher and is called the **independent variable**; it is usually the factor suspected of being a cause. Experimental research investigates the relationships between such factors and others called **dependent variables**. The latter are those factors which are suspected to depend on—be caused by—the independent variables.

In an experiment or experimental study, the researcher actively intervenes and alters the factor called the independent variable. The researcher then observes the outcome of this manipulation on other factors (on what are called the dependent variables). Flipping a wall switch in a strange room several times and watching what then happens to the lights is performing such an experiment.

Experiments with Strict Laboratory Controls

The idea behind the strictly controlled experiment is ingeniously simple. You create a setup in which both the phenomenon whose cause or effect you are looking for, and also all the factors which are likely to play a causal role in that phenomenon, are *completely under your control*—or at least are held constant. Then you manipulate or alter one of these supposed causal factors, keeping all the others constant, and see what happens. For example, suppose you want to discover whether and to what degree reward affects subsequent behavior. You create a setup in which you can "control" for rewards. That is, you want to be able to compare two situations which are identical except that a reward is offered for certain behavior in one case and is absent in the other. Does the subsequent behavior differ in the two cases? If so, and if you have been able to *control* the setup so that the only difference between the two cases is the presence or absence of the reward, then you may conclude that the reward is a causal factor in any variations in behavior between the two situations. (By the way, since the reward might have been functioning in conjunction with other factors in the situation that you set up, you cannot conclude yet that reward alone has the effect you observed. You have to run the experiment varying those other factors as well. If doing so also correlates with changes in behavior, then you know that those other factors are also causal.)

Test Group/Control Group Experiments

In many real-life situations, especially with human subjects, it isn't possible to control or hold constant all of the factors that might be influencing the dependent variable. To deal with this problem, the researcher can use the following general strategy. A pool or sample of subjects is *randomly assigned to two or more different "treatment" groups*. One group, called the **test group** (or the experimental group), is subjected to the treatment or intervention whose effects you are interested in; the other group, called the **control group**, is subjected to a different treatment (which can be no treatment at all). Following the "treatment," the performance of the two groups in the activity that you hypothesized might be affected by it is then assessed, usually by comparing the mean or average value of some dependent variable for each group.

For example, the test group receives special tutoring in math and the control group does not; the average scores of each group on a subsequent math test are then compared. If the difference between the averages is large enough, you can attribute it to the different treatments the two groups received and conclude that the tutoring caused better performance on the test. Because subjects have been *randomly* assigned to the two groups, it is reasonable to assume that other factors which might affect the performance are operating equally on the two different groups. And the fact that the assignment is a random one makes it possible to use inferential statistics to determine whether the difference in math scores between the two groups is statistically significant.

This technique is very widely used in psychological and medical research. In medical research, a particular variant—the "double-blind" experiment (see Section 9.6)—has become the norm.[2]

Experiments are frequently used to test causal or explanatory hypotheses *indirectly*. For example, a psychologist trying to explain why people are good at solving one kind of problem and bad at solving another, might speculate that people tend to use for both kinds of problem certain problem-solving strategies which are effective for only one of them. There is no way to observe internal thought processes directly, and people are often unaware of, or mistaken about, how they do in fact go about solving problems, so their own reports cannot be relied upon. A common research method, then, is the following.

The researcher determines that if a subject is using the given strategy, it will take that subject longer to solve problem A than to solve problem B, whereas if a subject is using other known strategies, it won't take longer to come up with an answer to A than to come up with an answer to B.[3] So an experiment is designed in which subjects are given problems A and B to solve, and their "reaction times" are measured—that is to say, the time it takes them to come up with an answer. The experimental data about reaction times can then be used as an indirect test of hypotheses about how subjects are solving problems and why they succeed at certain kinds and fail at others.

Correlational Research

In experimental studies, an independent variable (the suspected causal factor) is actively manipulated or changed by the researcher. But it isn't always possible or ethical to engage in such manipulation. If we're interested in the effects of height on personality, we cannot affect or change the height of our subjects. If we're interested in the effects of terminal disease on personality, it would be unethical to cause such diseases in our subjects. In cases where experimental research is impossible, impractical, or unethical, scientists can turn to correlational research.

Correlational research differs from experimental research in that it does not involve *the attempt to manipulate or change* an independent variable. Rather, the investigator simply tries to discover the properties or features that the object (or subject) already has and to discover statistically significant relations among them.

Typically, correlational research uses some of the techniques and ideas of surveying and sampling. We encountered one specialized application of surveying or sampling techniques in Chapter 7, when we looked at opinion polls. In those applications, the aim was to find out what portion of a given population possessed a certain property (usually an opinion or attitude) by examining a sample drawn from that population. But surveying or sampling techniques also play a prominent role in the investigation of general causal relations. When used in the context of causal investigation, the point is not to find what proportion of the population possess a certain property, but rather to find which properties tend to "go together" or be associated in the population, or to find how the quantitative measurement of one property tends to vary with the quantitative measurement of another. In short, the researcher is looking for *correlations* in the sample that can be projected onto the population from which the sample is drawn.

Finding such correlations can play at least two distinct roles in the search for causes.

1. Even though correlates are not always related as cause and effect, causes and effects are virtually always correlates. Hence (a) finding that two properties or variables are *not* correlated tends to show that they *are not* related as cause and effect, and (b) finding that two properties or variables *are* correlated shows that they *might* be related as cause and effect. In short, finding or failing to find correlations can *rule out* causal hypotheses and can *suggest* causal hypotheses.
2. Finding or failing to find correlations through sampling techniques can supply crucial *indirect* evidence for and against causal hypotheses. Thus some people have hypothesized that estrogen (a female hormone) inhibits the formation of plaque in coronary arteries (a buildup of fatty substances inside the arteries that inhibits the flow of blood through them and is a prime contributor to heart attacks). *If* that is true, and since it is known that estrogen levels decline in menopausal women, there should be a lower incidence of heart attacks among premenopausal women than among men, and a higher incidence of heart attacks among menopausal women than among premenopausal women. As a matter of fact, there is a lower incidence of heart attacks among premenopausal women, and that correlational fact lends indirect support to the explanatory hypothesis.

The Three Phases of a Study

Whatever the type of subject matter, and whatever the method of data gathering, a causal study is going to have three principal phases or steps:

1. Choosing the subjects to examine and measure (and, where applicable, assigning them to treatment groups)
2. Performing observations, tests and measurements on those subjects
3. Drawing conclusions from those data

In the next three sections we examine each of these phases in turn.

9.3 CHOOSING THE SUBJECTS (OR OBJECTS) TO EXAMINE AND MEASURE

Studies which aim at establishing the truth of general causal propositions still need to be based on the observation and measurement of *particular* things. A researcher therefore needs to assemble or create a collection of particulars to be observed or measured. If it is the effect of hydrochloric acid on aluminum that is to be investigated, bottles of hydrochloric acid and pieces of aluminum have to be assembled; if the aim is to study the therapeutic effectiveness of psychoanalysis on claustrophobics by comparing a control group and a test group, individuals suffering from claustrophobia have to be selected for the control and test groups and psychoanalysis has to be administered to the members of the test group.[4]

Two questions have to be asked about the selection of subjects.

1. Is the *sample size* adequate?

Two considerations affect how big the sample has to be. (a) If there is very little individual variation, the sample doesn't have to be very big at all. The chemical properties of one piece of (relatively pure) aluminum are pretty much the same as that of every other (sizes and weights are not, but chemical properties are). There is no need, therefore, to experiment with many pieces of aluminum to get a good idea of what the effect of hydrochloric acid is on aluminum; it's just necessary to make sure the pieces being examined are (sufficiently) pure aluminum. The physiology of animals (including humans) varies from individual to individual quite a bit more than the chemistry of metals, but a lot less than the behavior and personality characteristics of humans. As studies move from chemical to physiological to psychological issues, the numbers needed for an adequate sample increase. (b) If inferential statistics are used to estimate the significance of the results (as they probably should be in most cases dealing with human subjects), then a sample big enough to give statistically significant results will be needed.

2. Is the sample *representative* of the population we are interested in?

Where there is individual variation, and a large sample is necessary, size alone is not enough. It is also important that the sample be representative of the population with respect to those features that are pertinent or relevant to the matter being studied. One way of trying to achieve representativeness is by truly random selection. In most studies, this is not attempted. Rather, the researcher attempts to assemble a sample with a composition that she or he knows or believes to be representative. For example, in a study of *human* behavior, one makes sure that the female-male split in the sample is close to 50-50.

9.4 EXAMINING AND MEASURING THE SUBJECTS

Once a sample is selected, it is necessary to determine for each member of the sample whether or to what degree it has the features the study is interested in. Suppose you are studying the effect of alcohol consumption during pregnancy on the mental capacity of children. Some way must be found to determine both the mental capacities of individual children and the extent to which their mothers consumed alcohol during pregnancy. A *technique* or *test* to measure each of those factors is needed. The techniques or tests used to ascertain or measure those features are generally called *instruments*. Sometimes the instrument is an actual physical instrument such as a thermometer or a spectroscope. Often it is not a physical instrument at all, but simply some kind of investigatory procedure, such as a questionnaire or an aptitude test.

In the example just given, one would probably use some sort of standard IQ test to measure the subjects' mental capacity and a questionnaire to ask the mothers about their drinking habits during pregnancy. But this raises questions about whether these "measuring techniques" really do tell us what we want to know about the individual subjects. (For example, will the mothers tell the truth about their drinking habits?)

When scientists—especially social scientists—evaluate such measuring or testing instruments, they assess their **reliability** and **validity**. These are technical terms, and they do *not* mean what you might expect them to mean.

Reliability

In its technical sense, the term 'reliability' is used to denote the *consistency* with which an instrument or person measures objects. Reliability is a matter of getting the same results with the same objects (whether or not the results are "correct"). An oven thermometer that records 100 degrees one day and 150 degrees another day for exactly the same oven temperature is not reliable in this sense. A teacher who rates an answer by one student as worth a "B" and a similar answer to another student as worth an "F" is not reliable in this sense. But, and here is where the technical terminology is counterintuitive, an oven thermometer which is always wrong *by the same amount* is reliable in this technical sense—as is a teacher who consistently undervalues students' work.[5]

Since a test can be reliable in this technical sense without giving accurate results, why worry about reliability? Because almost without exception, if the instrument is *not* reliable, then it is not giving correct results. Reliability is not enough to guarantee the accuracy of an instrument, but it is necessary.

Test and measurement specialists have ways of establishing the reliability of data-gathering instruments and tests. These are complex, and in any case not readily applied by us who are trying to assess the reported results of a study. But *we can ask* whether the instrument used in the study was checked for its reliability. A thorough research report would say so. And we can also speculate about possible impediments to reliability in any particular case.

Validity

An instrument is said to be **valid** when the results of its application are not only consistent, but also *correct*—when the information it yields is the information we are actually looking for. There are tests whose reliability has been clearly established, but whose validity is very much disputed—IQ tests have historically been a prime example.

Three different kinds of "validity" are distinguished.

(1) Does the measuring instrument measure what it is intended or claimed to measure? It is often difficult to do so. For example, a course evaluation questionnaire might be designed to assess whether the students found the course valuable, but might in fact measure whether they liked the instructor. In that case, a high score would indicate a popular instructor, but not necessarily a valuable course. Such a measurement would lack what is called **content validity**.

One of the objections made to IQ tests as they were once formulated was that the questions concerned subjects that were familiar to middle-class children but were outside the experience of poor children, so they were easier for the former than for the latter, and so they gave artificially higher IQ scores for white children (who tended to be middle class) than for black children (who tended to be poor). This objection (successfully) challenged the content validity of those tests and caused them to be changed.[6]

Understanding what content validity is permits you to ask whether a study's data-gathering methodology really did measure what it was supposed to be measuring. You might not be able to get an answer from the information made available, but just raising the question gives you a focus on the details of the study and on possible confusions.

(2) Does the measuring instrument yield results that enable us to predict how people will perform in the future or on other tests? Decisions about whom to hire, whom to admit to university or law school, etc., are often based on or heavily influenced by tests administered to applicants or candidates (SAT,

TOEFL, LSAT, GMAT or GRE in the case of applicants to university programs).[7] The scores obtained on such tests may or may not correlate highly with actual performance as measured later in some more or less formal way (such as scores on a post-probationary job assessment, or actual grades obtained, or successful completion of the program). A test which whose results correlated highly with such other measures would be said to have **predictive validity** or **external validity**. A measuring device has external validity if it measures the factor being studied just as well as does some other, independent, method.

The questions to be asked, then, are these: "Is there any reason to think that the data reported in the study might not correspond to some other, independent way of collecting that information?" and "Might the differences reported be due to the external invalidity of the measuring instrument used, instead of to actual differences among the subjects?"

(3) Usually what is being studied is not itself directly observable. For example, the health of a country's economy, or the job satisfaction of the workers in a plant, are not things we can find out by just looking and seeing (or listening and hearing), or by reading off some measuring device like a thermometer or a pressure gauge. Scientists often call such properties "theoretical constructs." Since we cannot measure theoretical constructs directly, we are forced to use indirect methods to assess them. For example, the health of a country's economy might be partially measured by its rate of inflation. The job satisfaction of workers in a plant might be partially measured by their absenteeism rate. But why should the inflation rate indicate an economy's health or the absenteeism rate indicate workers' satisfaction? These criteria make sense only in relation to theories about how economies and workers function. But are those theories themselves defensible? Questioning the acceptability of a theory on the basis of which a measurement is made is questioning what is called the **construct validity** of the measurement.

Unless you are familiar with the theory being used to generate the measurement of a theoretical construct, it will be difficult to raise specific challenges. However, you can decide whether a theoretical construct is what is being reported on. And you can also ask yourself whether you know of the existence of any theoretical disagreements about such constructs.

For example, without being able to state them, most of us know that there are socialist and capitalist economic theories, and even different versions of each. Thus we can at least raise the question for ourselves whether a particular analysis of the economy coming out of a conservative capitalist research group is using constructs that are generally agreed upon, or whether it is using constructs that economists from other schools would challenge.

A point worth stressing is that even where the instrument is known to be both reliable and valid, it matters very much *who* is using it. Unless the lab technicians, psychometrists (people trained to administer psychological tests), interviewers, and so on, are competent and impartial, their measurements and observations should not be trusted.

9.5 DRAWING CONCLUSIONS FROM THE DATA

There are three possible aspects or stages to drawing conclusions from the data. The first is determining whether the data reveal correlations among the factors or variables studied. The second is drawing inferences about causal relations that hold among those factors. From the discussion so far, you can see that these first two aspects or stages are very much related. A third aspect or stage is the extrapolation of the conclusions of stage 2 into a wider perspective.

1. Determining whether the data reveal correlations—statistically significant relationships—is usually a matter of tabulating the results and subjecting them to a suitable variety of statistical analyses. Some of these mathematical analyses have as their aim to reveal interesting patterns in the data. (This is the task, roughly, of descriptive statistics.) Other mathematical analyses have as their aim the determination of whether the patterns found are statistically significant, that is, whether it's likely that the pattern found among the data is due simply to chance. (This is the task, roughly, of inferential statistics.) These are not jobs for amateurs; even the best of scientific researchers consult with professional statisticians about the proper way to carry out these analyses on their data.

2. The second stage consists in the attempt to draw causal inferences from the statistically significant patterns in the data. Here, two things have to be done. One is to draw on one's background knowledge to suggest possible causal explanations of the correlations found—this is a matter of generating explanatory hypotheses. In experimental research, the experimental design will often have eliminated any explanation other than that one of the factors is causing the other. If 200 animals are assigned in equal numbers by a genuinely random method to a control group and a test group, if the members of the two groups are treated identically except that members of the test group are injected with a certain amount of chemical X, while members of the control group are injected with a similar quantity of ordinary water, and if at the end of a week all the members of the test group are dead while all the members of the control group are still alive, then it is safe to conclude that injection of that amount of chemical X causes death among this species. (Even here some caution is necessary: it must be possible to rule out the possibility that the needles used to inject the animals in the experimental group were contaminated!)

In correlational research the causal implications of the data will seldom be clear. There will be several causal hypotheses consistent with the correlational results. It then becomes necessary to look for further correlations, or for experimental results, that will rule out all plausible hypotheses but one. For example, we discover a significant correlation between smoking and lung cancer—that is, that the incidence of lung cancer is significantly higher among smokers than among nonsmokers. But why? One possible explanation is that smoking contributes to lung cancer. But there are other possible explanations as well. Perhaps people smoke because they are under pressure, and such pressure is the common cause of both smoking and cancer. Or perhaps smoking is fashionable among men but not among women, and it is the male genes which are the causal factor accounting for the higher incidence of cancer among smokers. Or perhaps it is city dwellers who tend to smoke, and it is urban pollution which is causing the higher incidence of lung cancer among smokers. Explanations like these need to be ruled out before we can say with much confidence that smoking is a causal factor in generating lung cancer. (As a matter of fact, such explanations have been ruled out by correlational evidence that female smokers, rural smokers, and unstressed smokers are at increased risk of contracting lung cancer as compared with female nonsmokers, rural nonsmokers, and unstressed nonsmokers.)

3. Often researchers extrapolate their conclusions beyond the narrow limits of their study. Suppose that from the undisputed fact that large doses of saccharine tend to cause cancer in laboratory animals, researchers conclude that the use of saccharine to sweeten coffee poses a threat to humans. They are extrapolating their results from animals to humans, and also extrapolating results using large doses to cases where small doses are used. How reasonable are such extrapolations? This is itself a technical matter, in some cases much debated among scientists. When such extrapolations are found in, or on the basis of, reports of studies, you should look to see whether the issue of their legitimacy has been addressed.

9.6 A MINITHESAURUS OF TERMS USED IN REPORTS OF STUDIES

Anecdotal versus Systematic Evidence

Any inference about a whole set or class of things should be based on evidence that is representative of that set or class. For example, inferences about males or females in general need to be grounded on evidence that can be expected to portray the properties generalized about as they are found in males or females everywhere. Since it is often impossible or impractical to study every member of a group, researchers have developed methods of data collection that stand a high chance of yielding evidence that is representative. Evidence gathered according to such methods—for example, by properly designed polling—is referred to as **systematic evidence**. The alternative is to rely on the evidence that is encountered haphazardly or related to the special circumstances of the investigator, and which is therefore not likely to be representative. For example, if someone draws an inference about males based on her or his male acquaintances, it is almost certain the evidence will not be typical. Such evidence is called *anecdotal*. **Anecdotal evidence** often consists of a single anecdote, but it can also be a large body of data. The teacher nearing retirement who generalizes about students based on the students he has taught is probably using anecdotal evidence, even though he might have encountered hundreds or even thousands

of students. For in all probability he has not gone over the list of students he
has taught in any systematic way.

Animal Studies

Researchers interested in the effects that certain drugs, chemicals, and so on
might have on humans often perform experiments on animals first, or instead.

Lately, this practice has come under criticism from a moral point of view
from people concerned with the suffering, and general welfare, of animals. But
even apart from those moral questions, there are methodological questions about
animal studies that are frequently in dispute.

These questions arise, for example, about the attempts to determine
whether substances are carcinogenic through experiments with, say, rats. One
such question concerns the extrapolation of findings about rats to humans.
Though experience has shown that many phenomena are transferable from one
species to the other, not all phenomena are.

A second source of controversy concerns the dosages used. In order to get
statistically meaningful results from a sample of manageable size, it is necessary
to subject the test animals to exposures of very high quantities of the substances
being tested. The assumption is that if large dosages have very noticeable effects,
smaller dosages will have real, though less noticeable, effects. There is debate
about the reasonableness of that assumption.

Double-Blind Studies

It has been discovered that human subjects who think they are receiving a certain
treatment, but in fact are not, will respond as if they actually were getting the
treatment. This is called the **placebo effect**. In order to control for this phenomenon, it is essential that subjects of experiments not know whether they
have been assigned to the experimental group or the control group. An experiment in which this information is withheld from the experimental subjects is
call a *blind experiment.*

It has also been discovered that researchers and their assistants may, when
they expect to observe a certain result, think that they do observe it, and record
having observed it, even when it does not occur. This is the phenomenon called
wishful thinking that we are all familiar with. In order to control for this bias
of the observer, experiments are often designed so that those who are observing
the phenomena do not know whether they are observing the experimental group
or the control group.

Studies in which both the subjects and the observers do not know who is
in the control group and who is in the experimental group are called **double-
blind studies**. Any study in which the placebo effect and wishful thinking could
possibly affect the outcomes should be designed as a double-blind study, and if
it is not, serious doubt should be raised about the acceptability of its findings.

Findings, Data, Conclusions

These terms are not used consistently, but it is important to distinguish between the data or evidence that the study uncovered and any inferences based on that data. The *data* are the observations or statistical summaries of the observations. The *conclusions* are inferences based on the data—usually the inferences which constitute answers to the questions which originally motivated the study. The word *findings* sometimes refers to the data and sometimes to conclusions the author(s) have drawn from the data. You have to check the context to see how it is being used in a given report.

Replication

A **replication** of an experiment or experimental study is a repetition of the study by different researchers using different subjects which obtains the same results. If a study can be replicated, that lends strong support to its conclusions; if attempts to replicate it fail, that casts doubt on the original study and its conclusions. Sometimes the scientific community suspends judgment unless and until results can be replicated. Examples include the 1989 experiments that allegedly demonstrated that cold fusion is possible, and the 1991 study that suggested physiological differences between the brains of homosexual and heterosexual men.

Longitudinal Study

A **longitudinal study** entails a series of observations of a group of subjects over an extended period of time, often for many years, even decades. There have been a number of longitudinal studies done on groups of physicians. They were started when the subjects were medical students (and thus presumably willing to cooperate in a long-term study). The subjects' health was then checked on a regular basis. Correlations for the group as a whole emerged over time. For example, many more smokers than nonsmokers had heart disease. Such studies, especially of groups that are quite homogeneous (such as doctors, who tend to live similar life-styles) can reveal suggestive correlations for closer examination.

Participant Observer Study

As the name suggests, a **participant observer study** is one in which the researcher takes part in the activity that he or she is studying and observes it from the vantage point of a participant. An advantage of such studies is that they can help the researcher to "get the feel of" the experience or activity under study. Often such experience is crucial to an understanding of the phenomenon, and sometimes it is difficult to study the subjects in any other way. Police have been studied using participant observer studies, for example, with researchers spending extended periods accompanying police officers during their work and leisure activities. A disadvantage of participant observer studies is that the researcher can identify too closely with the subjects and lose the detachment needed to analyze their behavior in an illuminating way.

"Scientific" Study

Science, for good reason, is held in high repute. Accordingly, to call a study *scientific* is to praise it. Those who have conducted studies, and especially those who are anxious to gain acceptance for their conclusions, are often eager to call their studies "scientific." There is, however, no very precise, generally accepted or universally followed criterion for when a study is or is not scientific, so one should not be impressed by the fact that a particular study is labeled "scientific."

The term 'scientific study' should probably be used only to denote either (1) an experimental study or (2) a correlational study using true random sampling and sophisticated statistical analysis of data.

9.7 A Checklist for Evaluating Reports of Studies

A report of a study normally presents the conclusions of the study and information about how those conclusion were arrived at. A report of a study in a scientific or professional journal, prepared by those who conducted the study, virtually always contains a complete account of the research design, a careful statement of the findings, summaries of the data and of the reasoning that led from the data to the conclusions, and comments on the limitations of the methodology and the qualifications that need to be attached to the conclusion.

By contrast, a report of a study in the media or a textbook is at least secondhand. The reporter often has no firsthand acquaintance with the study itself, no scientific training, and not even any superficial exposure to the nature of causal explanations and of studies of the sort provided by this book.[8] Consequently, reports of studies in the mass media can at times be defective sources of information from which to draw justified inferences. Either they may not supply enough information about the study to permit an informed judgment of its reliability, or they may draw inferences of their own that go beyond the study's conclusions and that are not warranted by the study's findings. Or both. Assessing a report of a study, therefore, requires distinguishing between what can be gleaned about the study itself and what is added (or left out) by the report of the study.

A. *Assessing the study*
  1. *What sort of study is it?*
     a. Is it concerned with inanimate objects and their effects, with biological or physiological matters, or with human behavior, attitudes, and character traits?
     b. Is the study based (i) on a strictly controlled laboratory experiment, (ii) on an experiment with control and test groups, (iii) on a nonexperimental analysis of correlational data, or (iv) on none of these.
     c. Is this a pilot or preliminary study, or does it purport to establish firm conclusions about causal relations?
  2. *Identity of the researcher(s).*
     Do they have credentials for designing, carrying out, and generalizing from this study? Do they have a personal stake in the study's confirming or disconfirming one particular hypothesis rather than any of the others?
  3. *Assess the data and how they were collected.*
     a. Is the sample size adequate or reasonable, as far as you can tell?
     b. What "instruments," tests, and/or observational techniques were used? Are they known to be reliable and valid, as far as you can tell?
  4. *Try to assess the study's findings.*
     a. What relations were found among factors or variables studied? Are reasons given for thinking those relations are significant?
     b. How do the researchers get from those relations to the main causal conclusions? Does background knowledge guarantee that the factors are related as cause and effect? If not, were other explanatory hypotheses considered and eliminated? If so, which ones and how? Were any plausible explanatory hypotheses overlooked, as far as you can tell?
  5. *Identify and assess the conclusions.*
     What inferences or extrapolations were drawn, either by the researchers or by the reporter, from the findings? Do they seem reasonable?
B. *Assessing the report*
  1. *Is the report sufficiently informative?*
     a. Does it leave out key details needed to determine whether some particular possible problem with the study exists.
     b. Does the report supply only the conclusions drawn by the author(s) of the study, but no account of the study itself?
     c. Can answers to the 5 questions listed above be found in or inferred from the report?
  2. Does *the report seem to be faithful to the study?*
     For instance, when the report does not quote from the study, but paraphrases its findings or its conclusions, is there any reason to suspect the fidelity of the report? Does the reporter (or the headline writer!) state conclusions that go beyond either the data or the conclusions directly attributed to the study's author(s)?

C. *Overall assessment*

In light of the adequacy of the report and of the study, what attitude should you take toward the conclusions of the study? Here are some of the answers you might give to that question:

    i. Not enough information is given in the report to make a decision about the conclusions.

    ii. The study is very seriously flawed; its conclusions should be discounted

    iii. Though the study lends some support to its conclusions, a decision should await further investigation (for example, replication or additional evidence of some other kind that would rule out certain other hypotheses).

    iv. The study warrants tentative acceptance of its conclusions.

    v. The study seems to firmly establish its conclusions.

Where several conclusions are reported, your verdict might well vary from one conclusion to another.

9.8 SUMMARY

The purpose of this chapter is to provide background information and guidelines to enable you to assess many of the reports of studies you will encounter. A general distinction can be made between experimental studies, whether laboratory controlled or test/control group experiments, and studies using survey or other sampling techniques.

Any study can be divided into three phases. The first is the selection of subjects to examine or measure. Here the size and representativeness of samples are important. The second phase is performing observations, tests, and measurements on the subjects. The measuring instruments used must be "reliable" and "valid" (in the case of validity, internal, external, and construct validity are all concerns). The third phase is drawing conclusions from the findings or data. Typically, any of three kinds of conclusion might be inferred: significant correlations, causal relations, and extrapolations beyond the data.

The chapter ends with two sets of tools. A minithesaurus briefly defines some terms often encountered in reports and discussions of studies. A checklist for evaluating reports of studies suggests questions to ask both about the study itself and about the report.

9.9 EXERCISES

Instructions. For each example assigned, use the checklist on pages 187–188 to prepare a succinct critique of the reported study.

(a) Describe the type of study conducted [see item (i) in the checklist] and identify the principal causal claims (if any) made by those who conducted the study or those who are reporting the study.

(b) Distinguish between problems with the study and problems with the reporting of the study. Also discriminate between major or significant problems and less important ones.

**1. The following Associated Press report appeared in August 1989.

Drug dulls urge to tear hair out, study says

FDA HAS NOT GIVEN FULL APPROVAL FOR USE

BOSTON—(AP)—An experimental drug can help women conquer an overwhelming urge to tear out their hair, a disorder that affects millions of Americans, leaving some bald, researchers say.

Victims of this condition, called trichotillomania, cannot stop themselves from plucking out their eyebrows and eyelashes as well as the hair on their head.

A new medicine known as clomipramine can help people reduce their hair pulling and sometimes stop it entirely according to a report in today's New England Journal of Medicine.

The drug "allows them to say no," said Dr. Susan Swedo. "They still have the urge, but their ability to resist is increased."

Swedo estimated that 2 million to 4 million Americans, almost all of them women, have trichotillomania.

Swedo, a researcher at the National Institute of Mental Health, tested clomipramine on 13 women. Three stopped pulling their hair, while the rest had at least a 50 percent reduction in the severity of their symptoms.

Clomipramine has been shown in other studies to be effective in helping people with obsessive-compulsive disorder, which causes people to irrationally do something over and over, such as wash their hands. The medicine has not yet been approved by the U.S. Food and Drug Administration for routine use. However, doctors can obtain it for treating severe cases.

A newly approved drug called fluoxetine, or Prozac, also appears to be effective against obsessive-compulsive disorder and hair pulling, although it has not been as extensively tested as clomipramine.

The next three examples contain newspaper reports of studies on the effects of video display terminals (VDTs), the display screens used with computers.

2. This newspaper report appeared in *The Globe and Mail* on September 13, 1989. VDTs are the video display terminals used with computers. Britain's Inland Revenue department is the equivalent of the IRS—the department of the government that processes tax returns. Tax records in both countries are entered into computer programs, requiring many employees to work in front of video display terminals for extended periods of time.

Study links use of VDTs to menstrual problems

By Jane Coutts
The Globe and Mail

Women who work with video display terminals report more menstrual problems than women in similar jobs who do not work on computers, a study of British government workers shows.

The difference may be related to the greater stress that computer operators experience on the job, according to Rosalind Bramwell, an occupational psychologist from the University of Manchester Institute of Science and Technology.

Her study of almost 4,000 female employees of Britain's Inland Revenue department showed that all the workers, whether or not they used display terminals, listed the same major causes of stress. These included balancing personal demands and work, work overload and depression. Ms Bramwell said in an interview yesterday.

The study used a standard index to measure stress in the women, whose ages ranged from 16 to 35. It showed that display unit workers suffer free-floating anxiety, depression and physical symptoms of anxiety at levels substantially higher than those of co-workers who did not use terminals, although their jobs were otherwise essentially the same.

As a result, women who work on computers seem to suffer more from menstrual problems, including complete cessation of periods, painful or tender breasts, irritability, moodiness, cramps and weight gain or bloating before or during menstruation, she said.

Ms Bramwell noted that display unit workers also report a significantly higher use of cigarettes and alcohol, which she said might be used to alleviate stress.

Ms Bramwell said the effects of stress are difficult to measure "but apparently it is affecting their health because their menstrual distress symptoms are very real."

"It has probably mostly got to do with the fact that having video display units in offices has increased the expected work factor and decreased things like social contact and worsened office conditions," she said.

3. Here is a *Canadian Press* report that appeared in September 1989. It is reproduced in its entirety.

VDTs harmless, study says

Montreal (CP)—The partial results of a major study by the University of Toronto and Ontario Hydro suggests that magnetic fields emitted by video display terminals do not cause miscarriages and stillbirths, a conference was told Tuesday.

The potential hazard of VDTs to pregnant users has been hotly debated for a decade.

The study was conducted on 600 female mice.

4. This next *Canadian Press* report appeared in November 1989. Again, VDTs are the video display terminals used with computers. We think it might be about the study referred to in the previous report; do you agree?

Pregnant mice reveal no effects from VDTs

Toronto (CP)—Working at video display terminals during pregnancy shouldn't be harmful—to mice, anyway.

A study sponsored by Ontario Hydro and International Business Machines exposed 600 pregnant mice to three levels of magnetic fields similar to those that come from office computer terminals.

The study followed controversial reports of high rates of stillbirths and deformed babies among women who worked at VDTs while pregnant.

After one year, doctors from the University of North Carolina, Health and Welfare Canada and Rocke University in New York found no significant statistical differences between the mice and a control group that had not been exposed.

Dr. Michael Wiley of the University of Toronto department of anatomy said the study, released today, does not prove that video display terminals are safe for pregnant women.

"I don't think any biologist would want to jump from an animal model to a human situation," said Wiley, who headed the study for the federal government.

But he said the experiment will be helpful to scientists in continuing research.

5. This Associated Press story appeared in April 1990.

Study links stress to health problems

Chicago (AP)—Job stress can lead to high blood pressure and cause potentially dangerous physical changes in the heart, says a study of male workers.

The findings are based on a study of 215 men ages 30 to 60 at seven work sites in New York City, including a stock-brokerage firm, private hospital and garbage collection facility, researchers wrote in the Journal of the American Medical Association.

Job strain resulted when workers felt they faced high psychological demands without having much control over day-to-day decisions, said Dr. Peter Schnall, the lead researcher at Cornell University Medical College in New York.

Twenty-one per cent of the subjects suffered job strain, and faced about a three times greater risk of having high blood pressure than those who did not experience job strain, said Carl Pieper, a Cornell statistician.

All men ages 30 to 40 years old with high-stress jobs had a "clinically significant" thickening of the heart's left ventricle, or chamber, a condition that often precedes coronary disease and heart attacks, Pieper said in a telephone interview Tuesday.

Their heart muscles were an average of 20 grams bigger than those without job stress, a "substantial" difference but still within normal range, Schnall said by telephone Tuesday.

The men studied had all worked in the same job for at least three years, none was more than

Continued

20 per cent overweight and none had suffered heart disease before the study began in 1986. Eighty-one per cent were white, the remaining were mostly blacks.

The authors concluded that job strain was "significantly related" to high blood pressure and increased heart mass after adjusting for factors such as age, alcohol intake and smoking.

"We're not showing that job strain is causing heart disease," Schnall said. "What we're showing is that job strain is causing a change in muscle mass" that could lead to disease.

The study, based on data gathered through 1989, is continuing for another five years to determine if the changes are permanent or progressive, he said.

6.   This story appeared in the *Detroit Free Press* on April 17, 1991.

Fetal alcohol syndrome causes lifetime of problems

By Patricia Anstett
Free Press Medical Writer

Children with fetal alcohol syndrome face a lifetime of serious mental problems and physical shortcomings, according to the first published long-term study of the disorder.

Five to 12 years after a childhood diagnosis with the disorder, teenagers and adults had an average IQ of 68, Dr. David Smith, senior author of the study in today's Journal of the American Medical Association, said in a telephone interview Tuesday. Most couldn't function beyond fourth-grade levels, and many had problems with math.

Average IQ is about 100 to 110.

Victims are shorter, skinnier, have small heads, short attention spans, learning disabilities and behavior problems, such as lying and promiscuity, Smith said, because of what alcohol does to the brains and developing organs of fetuses.

Most can't hold jobs and most live in foster and group homes. The best they can hope for is "to be supervised closely," Smith said. The study surveyed 61 people ages 12–40; 74 per cent were American Indians; 21 percent were white, and 5 percent were black.

Fetal alcohol syndrome, a cluster of problems caused by the mother's chronic drinking in pregnancy, is the leading cause of mental re-tardation, surpassing Down's syndrome, the study says, citing a 1987 report by Dr. Robert Sokol and Ernest Abel, with the Fetal Alcohol Research Center in Detroit.

Nationally, one or two babies of every 1,000 newborns have fetal alcohol syndrome, Smith said.

It causes spontaneous abortions, stillbirths, prematurity, mental retardation and brain, facial, heart and kidney problems in babies.

Researchers are trying to determine whether risk of fetal alcohol syndrome is greater among certain racial groups.

Black babies may be more at risk than white infants, though no one knows why, according to research from the Detroit center, a federally funded program that is part of the Wayne State University School of Medicine.

Certain American Indian tribes also may have higher rates of the disorder. But Dr. Jon Aase, another author of the study in the Journal of the American Medical Association, said many people wrongly assume the syndrome is rampant in all American Indian tribes because of "the myth of the drunken Indian."

Southwest tribes with a "strong sense of social integration" frown on drinking and have low rates of the disorder, said Aase.

7. The following is a Canadian Press story that appeared in March 1991.

Rising suicides blamed on men's inability to cope

Ottawa (CP)—The rate of suicides among Canadian men has jumped dramatically over the past 20 years, rising by nearly 42 per cent, a federal study released Tuesday revealed.

But the rate of suicides among Canadian women remained nearly constant, said the Statistics Canada report.

The report simply states the data. But the director of a Calgary-based international clearing house on suicide information says men have fewer resources than women when they reach the end of their rope.

"They don't have the close relationships and the close friends," said Gerry Harrington, director of the Suicide Information and Education Centre. "And they don't have the ability to talk and to open up and ask for help.

"We're seeing the macho-man image who can't ask for help and can't solve their own problems. So, rather than look for another solution they take the only one that they can think of."

The increase in the rate of suicides among Canadian men follows an international trend. The World Health Organization has reported suicide rates among both men and women have been on the rise since 1950.

The Statistic Canada report compares suicide rates for native-born Canadians with rates of first-generation immigrants to Canada, according to sex and age, for the period from 1969 to 1987.

The report shows the suicide rate among Canadian-born men was consistently higher than for first-generation immigrant men, until the age of 64. Among women, immigrants had higher suicide rates than native-born Canadians.

But suicide rates among women didn't begin to compare with the suicide rates of men, which were three times higher.

The rate for men rose to 22.1 for each 100,000 men in 1987 from 15.6 per 100,000 in 1967. The rate among women remained stable throughout the period at 6.2 suicides per 100,000 women.

Harrington said he suspects a portion of the increase in male suicides can be attributed to better reporting.

But that doesn't account for the entire increase, or the fact that three times as many men commit suicide as women.

Men are more dependent on their spouses than women, Harrington said, and have more problems coping with the loss of a spouse.

Also, Harrington said, men are more likely than women to succeed at killing themselves. Statistics Canada says 3,510 Canadians killed themselves in 1988, or five per cent of all deaths that year.

8. The following is a newspaper account of a scientific report presented at the 1989 annual meeting of the American Heart Association.

Changed lifestyle repairs arteries

New Orleans—For the first time, scientists said, they have found that a radical change in lifestyle can dramatically reverse the hardening of arteries that leads to heart attacks.

By going on a strict regimen of moderate aerobic exercise, stress reduction training, group support meetings and a fat-free vegetarian diet, four women and 14 men were able to reverse their severe heart disease, researchers at the annual meeting of the American Heart Association said Monday.

The University of California, San Francisco study, headed by Dr. Larry Scherwitz, followed 41 patients for more than a year. Twenty-two underwent the strict lifestyle changes, while 19 followed standard medical recommendations to reduce their overall weights and decrease fat consumption. Neither of the groups used drugs during the study.

The process of hardening of the arteries continued among the group on standard therapy, and their condition steadily worsened.

The number of clogged artery sites per patient increased and the size of those clogs expanded.

In contrast, nearly all people in the university regimen improved markedly, and, Scherwitz said in an interview, "the degree of improvement directly correlated with how closely they adhered to the program."

Those who cheated on their diets or avoided the exercise had little or no improvement.

The most striking finding, Scherwitz said, was that serum cholesterol levels did not closely correlate to the rate of improvement.

Stress, decreased fat intake and exercise were the key factors.

"Diet alone will never do it," Scherwitz said. "Cholesterol is not a mechanism (of heart disease) by itself."

The changes observed in blood vessels were dramatic, and photos of the test results drew large crowds at the presentation here.

Although the university regimen is stricter than the famed anti-cholesterol Pritikin diet, Scherwitz had little difficulty getting most of the participants to stick with the program.

"We get a range of responses from them," he said. "Some act like martyrs saying, 'I still miss my cheesecake,' and it goes all the way to zealots who say nobody should live any other way."

Overall, however, the dramatic improvements in their health reinforced the participant's commitment to the university program.

"After all," said Scherwitz, "within a week all chest pain goes away. It's not hard to convince somebody when pain disappears."

9. The following excerpt is from M. Gabriel Khan, *Heart Attacks, Hypertension and Heart Drugs* (Toronto: McLelland and Stewart-Bantam Ltd., 1986), pp. 15–16.

In 1964, the Lipid Research Clinics Program reported the results of a successful trial that they conducted in the United States over a period of ten years at a cost of $150 million. The trial showed that a reduction in blood cholesterol resulted in a small but significant reduction in fatal and nonfatal heart attacks.

The study was randomized, and scrupulously conducted in many centers in the United States and in two centers in Canada. More than

480,000 men aged thirty-five to fifty-nine were screened to find subjects who had a cholesterol level greater than 265 milligrams per 100 milliliters of blood (mg/dL) but were otherwise healthy and, in particular, had no evidence of heart disease or hypertension. The 3,806 men found suitable for the trial were asked to follow a cholesterol-lowering diet. A random half of the men were given a drug to lower cholesterol (cholestyramine, 24 g daily); the other random half were given an identical-looking but non-medicinal preparation (placebo). The drug caused an 8 percent lowering of the blood cholesterol.

After follow-up for an average of 7.4 years, there were 187 fatal or nonfatal heart attacks in the controls and 155 in the drug treated group. Unfortunately, cholestyramine is a powder that is mixed with fruit juice and is unpleasant to taste. Patients do not comply with taking it two or three times daily, and it is not surprising that the reduction in cholesterol was 8 percent rather than an expected 25 percent. Nevertheless, the study shows that lowering of cholesterol by a special drug reduces the occurrence of heart attack. Thus a reduction of blood cholesterol by diet should have a similar good effect.

10. This *Los Angeles Times* report appeared in December 1989.

Hair growth sparked by drug, study says

By Los Angeles Times

A drug that blocks the action of testosterone on scalp cells shows promise at reversing baldness that starts on the top of a man's head, a dermatologist at the University of California, Los Angeles, reported Monday.

The drug, Cyoctol, was expected to be tested by Bristol-Myers Squibb Co. to treat acne and baldness—and a derivative is being investigated as an anti-wrinkling drug.

At a presentation to the American Academy of Dermatology in San Francisco, Dr. Richard Strick described a small study in which balding men who used a solution of Cyoctol had 12 per cent more hair on a test patch of scalp than they had had a year earlier. Men who had not been treated lost nine per cent of their hair in a patch the same size.

And unlike steroid preparations, Cyoctol appears to have no side effects.

Animal studies have shown Cyoctol to have no systemic effects at many hundreds of times the 0.5 per cent concentration used in the study, Strick said. Human studies have shown concentrations of 15 per cent do not even cause skin irritation, he said.

The only drug approved for use in the United States against male pattern baldness is minoxidil, or Rogaine, a non-steroid that is used at a 2 per cent concentration. Strick suggests using a combination of Cyoctol and Rogaine could produce results even more dramatic than in his study.

11. This *New York Times* report appeared in December 1990.

Study of alcoholics finds no evidence of gene defect

By Gina Kolata
New York Times

Federal researchers have been unable to confirm a widely publicized study that linked a gene to a predisposition to alcoholism.

The finding published today does not necessarily challenge the idea that genetic predisposition is a significant risk factor for alcoholism, but the researchers said it suggests that more work will be needed to identify any gene or genes that may be at fault.

In April, researchers at two universities reported that defects in a gene involved in the transmission of messages between brain cells strongly predisposed people to become alcoholics.

But in a study being published in the Journal of the American Medical Association, a group of federal investigators report that they could not find such an association with the gene.

Dr. David Goldman, the principal investigator and chief of the section on genetic studies at the National Institute of Alcohol Abuse and Alcoholism, and his colleagues said they looked for the gene in 40 alcoholics and a control group of 127 people who were not alcoholics.

But one of the scientists who made the observation reported in April, Dr. Kenneth Blum of the University of Texas Health Sciences Center in San Antonio said the discrepancy might be due to differences in the people studied.

Blum and a fellow researcher, Dr. Ernest Noble of the University of California in Los Angeles, studied people who were such intransigent alcoholics that they died of the disease.

Goldman studied a group that included less severe alcoholics.

"They are such different populations that you can't compare the studies," Blum said.

Goldman agreed that he studied less severely affected alcoholics.

The Blum and Noble study gained wide attention. The investigators examined the brains of 35 people who died of alcoholism and compared them to the brains of 35 people who were not alcoholics. They found that the alcoholics had a variant of a gene that could determine the way the brain responds to such things as pleasure-seeking behavior.

The gene was a blueprint for a dopamine receptor, a protein that protrudes from brain cells and latches onto dopamine, a chemical that transmits nerve impulses. Researchers previously had gleaned hints that dopamine plays a role in behavior such as alcoholism.

But Goldman said other researchers were highly skeptical that alcoholism could be explained so simply.

"Among the scientific community, there was a great deal of skepticism," said Goldman.

He said his group chose to try to replicate the previous study not because they were suspicious of it but because scientists need to see multiple proofs of a finding before they fully accept it.

"Very few of us accept a finding before we see it replicated by several groups," he said.

NOTES

1. Although *how* cold a particular food has to be kept in order to retard its spoilage significantly, and for exactly how long it is safe to keep a given food refrigerated, are things we need to turn to more specialized sources to learn.

2. When subjects are randomly assigned to treatment groups, we have what social scientists call a "true experiment." There are also "quasi-experimental designs" in which there are control

and test groups, but in which subjects are not *randomly* assigned to the two groups. Such quasi-experiments are thought to lend some support to causal hypotheses but a significantly weaker degree of support.

3. Social scientists usually call the people they study "subjects"—they are the people who have been the subjects of the study or the experiment. We will follow that convention.

4. There is a controversy about what should be done, in an experiment like this, to the members of the control group. Some think they should get no treatment at all. Others think they should receive an alternative form of treatment (or pseudotreatment)—compare the use of placebos on the control group in medical experiments.

5. There is a useful subdivision of reliability into two kinds: (1) test-retest reliability and (2) interjudge reliability. Many psychological tests which are test-retest reliable are not interjudge reliable. That is to say, psychologist A gets consistent results using the test (he gets the same results whenever he retests a subject), and psychologist B also gets consistent results using that instrument. But their results do not tally with each other: the two get different results when they test the same subject.

6. There continues to be considerable debate about the validity of the standard IQ tests when used on certain populations.

7. SAT is short for "Scholastic Aptitude Test," TOEFL for "Test of English as a Foreign Language," LSAT for "Law School Admission Test," GMAT for "Graduate Management Admission Test," and GRE for "Graduate Record Examination."

8. Recall the cautions about citations and reportage discussed in Chapter 3.

10

Evaluation

Evaluating something is determining or estimating its value—its merit or its worth. When we decide whether an object is good or bad, or how good it is, or whether it is better or worse than something else, we are evaluating it.[1]

Evaluation is not the same thing as deliberation—deciding or reasoning about what to do (see Chapter 11). To be sure, much of the evaluation we engage in or are interested in has a direct bearing on our decisions about what to do. The evaluation of products has a direct bearing on our purchasing decisions; the evaluation of employees has a direct bearing on decisions about hiring, promotion, and firing, and evaluations of political candidates have a bearing on voting decisions. Moreover, reasoning about what to do is itself a special case of evaluation, since it involves a decision about which of the alternative actions open to us is *best*.[2] But there can be evaluations which are made quite independently of any decisions about what to do. An historian might judge John F. Kennedy's performance as a senator, or a film critic might assess Garbo's acting in her movies, with no intention that the evaluation should have a bearing on decisions anyone is ever likely to make.

We devote this chapter to evaluation, before discussing deliberation in Chapter 11, for three reasons. First, evaluation can occur independently of deciding actions or policies; second, such deliberation usually presupposes evaluation; and third, evaluation is a large topic in its own right.

10.1 VARIETIES OF EVALUATION

There is an almost endless variety of kinds of things that can be evaluated, and the problems, techniques, and prospects of evaluation vary considerably from one to another. Just to indicate how wide the variety is, here is a small sample.

1. Consumer products (as in *Consumer Reports, Car and Driver, PC Magazine,* and so on)
2. Student performance (assigning grades for essays, tests, courses)
3. Teacher performance
4. Applicants for jobs, or for entrance to educational programs (used as a basis for deciding whom to hire or to admit)
5. Personnel (evaluations and ratings of employees, often used to determine raises, promotions, etc.)
6. Educational programs (How good is the education offered in your local primary schools? How good is the program in chemistry at the University of Alabama?)
7. Social service programs (For example, how well is your local child welfare service doing its various jobs? Is it, for instance, adequately protecting children who are at risk of physical or sexual abuse?)
8. Entertainment: movies, tapes and CDs, videos, books, plays, concerts, exhibitions, performances, games (as found in reviews of all of these)

In some of these cases, there are standard, recognized ways of going about the task of evaluation. For certain kinds of product evaluation (for example, stereo receivers), there is a recognized series of physical tests a product is put through, and its evaluation is largely a matter of how it measures up on these tests. Evaluation of student performance is usually via the grading of tests, labs, essays, assignments, and exams; on the whole, there is a relatively small number of types of widely used tests and assignments and a relatively small number of approaches generally followed in grading them. There is, to be sure, some latitude in the emphases selected by different evaluators, and sometimes more than a little variation in the way individual evaluators grade particular performances, but to a surprisingly high degree, different evaluators tend to agree in their assessments of individual student performances. At the other extreme, techniques and approaches for evaluating movies, or record albums, are much more fluid, indeterminate, and subject to personal preferences, and as a result the variation in the assessments by different evaluators (reviewers) is considerable.

Somewhere in between lies the evaluation of such things as educational or social service programs. There are people who work as professional evaluators of such things, and there is a burgeoning literature discussing which methods are best. Although disagreement exists about the preferred techniques of evaluation in these areas, there is an emerging consensus about which techniques are reliable and valid, and about the major strengths and weaknesses of different methods of evaluation.

Professional evaluation can also be classified by its general approach. Here are four examples of general approaches: **Objectives-based evaluation** attempts to evaluate programs or products, for instance, in light of their intended or stated purposes. **Goal-free evaluation** stresses the needs of the populations impacted by the thing being evaluated, and downplays the importance of the aims of product and program creators. The **systems approach** attempts to evaluate objects and programs with reference to their roles in larger systems. **Responsive evaluation** tries to avoid any predetermined evaluation design and to evolve evaluation strategies in response to what is unearthed in the process of evaluation itself.

Evaluation can also be classified as either global **(holistic)** or analytic. **Global evaluation** or grading allocates a single grade or evaluation to the overall character or performance of what is being evaluated. **Analytic evaluation** bases its verdicts on the evaluation of a variety of components or a variety of dimensions, or both.[3]

10.2 ELEMENTS OF EVALUATION

Although the problems and techniques vary considerably from one object and type of evaluation to another, several steps must be taken in almost any attempt at evaluation.

1. *Decide on the **possible verdicts**. Settle on the language or categories your final overall evaluation will use.*

By a *verdict* we mean the final evaluative judgment at which you are aiming in your evaluation. Are you judging merit (intrinsic value) or worth (value to a consumer or an institution)? Are you interested in ranking, scoring, or grading the things you are evaluating (see Section 10.3)? If you are grading, what are the grade categories that you will use? (By the way, usually there is no basis for distinguishing more than two or three grade categories, and no need for fine-grained distinctions anyway.)

2. *Identify or select **criteria**. Decide the dimensions on which the final evaluation will depend.*

You must decide which features are important and need to be taken account of in the evaluation. For example, you might decide that in evaluating teachers account should be taken of (a) how well they understand the material they teach, (b) how clearly they explain it, (c) how good they are at making it interesting, and (d) how fairly and perceptively they grade student work. The dimensions to be used in evaluating movies, to give another example, might be acting, plot, cinematography, special effects, and sound track. We shall use the term **criteria** as the name for such dimensions of evaluation, following one convention. ('Criteria' is the plural form of the word; the singular form is **'criterion'**.)

3. ***Establish standards.*** *Decide on the norms to be used to determine the extent to which each criterion is met.*

First, you have to decide on some way of measuring or testing for the criterion.[4] Second, you must decide what outcomes, scores, or information will qualify the object as acceptable, good, excellent, and so on. For example, what will count as excellent, good, mediocre, or poor in assessing the following: grasp of the material, explanations of it to students, sustaining of student interest, and fairness and validity of grading? We reserve the term *standards* to refer to these levels or measures used to rate or grade how well any given criterion is met.[5]

The standards for meeting a given criterion or receiving a given grade or rating can be laid out in at least three different ways.

a. Where the extent to which an object satisfies a criterion is measured by a numeric score on a test, the standard can consist in a *cutting score*. For example, determining that a mark of 90 or above merits a grade of "A" sets the cutting score for an "A" at 90. Or again, determining that a stereo receiver with less than 0.5% total harmonic distortion at a certain wattage is "good" in that respect sets that numeric value as a cutting score for a rating of good.

b. Sometimes an object satisfies a criterion or earns a particular grade if it possesses a certain *feature* or *cluster of features*—if it fits a certain description. Thus a lawyer can be considered qualified if she has a degree from an accredited law school and has passed the bar exam in the state where she practices.

c. Sometimes standards are set by reference to *models* or *exemplars*. One can draw up a model or example of an essay that deserves an "A" and of an essay that deserves a "B," and use such exemplars as reference points in assigning grades to essays handed in by students. As a matter of fact, evaluators trained to grade essays using exemplars as guides can achieve an amazingly high degree of interjudge reliability. The use of exemplars is an effective way of setting standards to be used in global evaluation or grading.

4. *Gather and interpret **factual information** and apply the standards or norms to it.*

If, for example, you decide to use surveys of student opinion to determine how interesting a teacher makes his or her subject, someone must administer the questionnaire, tally the results, and assess them in light of the standards.

5. *Try integrate the findings into a coherent **overall evaluation**.*

Continuing the example, imagine a teacher whose grasp of the material is only adequate, who is superb at explaining concepts but weak in getting details across, impressive in sustaining interest but arbitrary and unpredictable in giving grades. Someone has to decide how to determine the overall rating to assign such a teacher.

10.3 CRITERIA AND STANDARDS

Let us give an example of how criteria and standards interact with factual information in making evaluations. We arrive at evaluations by drawing conclusions from grounds consisting of factual information plus values or value assumptions. The values are embodied in the criteria or indicators and the standards that we apply to the factual information in drawing conclusions about the value of particular things.

Suppose you decide that freedom from harmonic distortion is one important criterion to use to judge stereo receivers and that harmonic distortion of less than 0.05% at 40 watts is excellent (given available technology). And suppose you know for a fact that receiver X's harmonic distortion is 0.03% at 40 watts. You can then conclude that receiver X is excellent in one important respect. Knowing which features stereo receiver should have (freedom from harmonic distortion, sensitivity, electrical safety, channel separation in stereo mode, and so on) is knowing the *criteria* for evaluating stereo receivers. Knowing when and to what degree a criterion is satisfied, requires **standards** for applying those criteria—knowing how much harmonic distortion counts as good, how much as excellent, how much as unacceptable. And deciding how good any product is on a given criterion requires *factual information* about that product.

Grading, Ranking, and Scoring

In assigning an "A-" or a "C+" to a student's performance, a teacher is grading it. In deciding to stamp a side of beef Prime or Choice, a meat inspector is grading it. In giving Chez Pizza two stars out of five, a restaurant critic is grading it. Here is a definition of **grading** (or rating):

> Allocating individuals to an ordered (usually small) set of named categories, the order corresponding to merit, for example, A–F for "letter grading."[6]

Grading is different from **ranking**, as when you say that Elizabeth was the best in the class, with Ralph coming next, Elise after her, and John at the bottom. It could be a four-student class, with John getting a "B+." Here is a definition of ranking:

Placing individuals in an order, usually of merit, on the basis of their relative performance on (typically) a test or measurement or observation. Full ranking does not allow ties, that is, two or more individuals with the same rank ("equal third"), partial ranking does. . . .[7]

In one respect, full ranking is more informative than grading, since in a full ranking it is always known whether one individual is better or worse than another, whereas no differentiation is made between two individuals with the same grade, even though one may be better than the other. But in two other respects, ranking is much less informative than grading:

1. The fact that something or someone ranks first does not by itself imply that it or he or she is any good at all—one may simply be dealing with the best of a very bad lot. Grading, on the other hand, gives some idea of *how good* something is.
2. The fact that one individual is ranked above another does not mean that the first is better than the second to any important degree; indeed, the difference between the best and the worst of a given lot is sometimes insignificant. With grading, on the other hand, something of the significance of the difference between two objects is known when their grades are compared.

Scoring is assigning numbers on some kind of scale to the things being evaluated, especially to their performance. Performances in competitive diving, ice skating, and gymnastics are evaluated by scoring. For scoring to be meaningful for evaluation purposes, each point on the scale must have equal value, that is, the difference in value between a 5 and a 7 must be comparable to the difference between an 8 and a 10.[8] Such "point constancy" is often difficult to achieve, so it is wise to be at least a little bit skeptical about accepting scores at face value. For example, consider movie reviewers who score on a scale from 1 to 10: they might see little difference between awarding a 7 instead of a 6, but a big difference between awarding a 10 instead of a 9.

Scores need to be interpreted in two respects:

1. What size of difference in scores is meaningful or significant?

For example, *Consumer Reports* will often assign scores to products and advise readers to ignore a difference of less than 6 points as not very important. On many grading schemes you get a "B" in a course whether your average is 84% or 80%.

2. What score qualifies as excellent, what qualifies as good, and so on, in the particular scoring convention in question?

This is the problem of going from *raw scores* to grades. Suppose you get only 40% of the questions on a multiple-choice test right. Is that poor? Does it warrant a failing grade? It depends how hard the test was and what could reasonably be expected of a student who had mastered the subject-matter.[9] Somebody needs to decide, on some basis, what that score means.

In short, evaluators cannot avoid the issue of grading. And that means evaluators require *standards*[10] enabling them to determine when the object being evaluated qualifies for a given grade.

Where Criteria and Standards Come From

How do we know, or find out, what the criteria of good teaching are? Or the criteria for judging jobs? Or rock albums? And how do we know, or find out, or decide, the standards by which performances are to be measured?

There is a variety of different ways criteria and standards can be learned, arrived at and validated. In many cases there are already recognized criteria and standards we can look up or consult. Publicly available and legally enforced criteria and standards exist for the grading of fresh and processed meat, fruits, and vegetables. Medical care is supposed to meet standards required by the medical profession of its members, standards which sometimes come into play in the courts. Indeed, most professional associations have explicit standards of conduct for their members, defining at least minimal levels of acceptable performance.

But how were such criteria and standards arrived at in the first place? If we come to have doubts about their validity or adequacy, how can we test or assess those standards? And what can be done in the thousands of cases in which standards do not yet exist?

Here are three sorts of ways that criteria and the standards which measure their achievement get discovered and get validated.

1. According to function

Many of the things, programs, and performances to be evaluated occur in contexts in which they have a certain *function*. Indeed, knowing what they are for is often knowing what they are. Hammers are tools for driving nails; schools are places for learning (that is, acquiring knowledge); physicians are people whose job is to restore and maintain health and to reduce or eliminate injury, disease, and pain; a stereo receiver is a device for reproducing (together with loudspeakers) recorded or transmitted sound.

In each case, an analysis of its functions will begin to suggest the features that the thing in question ideally should have. In general, it should have the properties that will enable it to perform its function(s) well, and these properties or features will then be the criteria for evaluating things of that kind. For example, since the function of a stereo receiver is to help to reproduce the sounds of a live performance, a receiver should have the properties that enable it to produce sounds as much like the original performance as possible. An empirical or scientific analysis will unearth the features that affect the "faithfulness" of a receiver's sound reproduction—features such as degree of total harmonic distortion, which is a highly technical phenomenon known significantly to affect fidelity of reproduction. Hence low harmonic distortion is one criterion of a good stereo receiver.

What about standards? That's a matter of determining what an acceptable level of such a feature is. In the case of the level of harmonic distortion in a stereo receiver, it's partly decided by discovering what is achievable at reasonable cost (measured in such terms as money, time, and convenience). What it was reasonable to accept as good sound reproduction in the 1950s would be considered unacceptable today. The point is that starting from a thing's function, logical and scientific analysis can settle many questions about criteria and standards.

2. According to needs

Objects, activities, and programs affect people who come in contact with them, for good or for ill. One basis for judging such effects is their relation to the **needs** of the people affected. An effect that satisfies or fulfills a need is good, one that "frustrates" a need is bad. These considerations can be independent of, or in addition to, the question of whether the object satisfies the functions or goals it was created to satisfy. Thus an educational program that contributes to meeting children's needs for self-esteem is better, other things being equal, than one that does not. A factory that interferes with people's need for clean air to breath is, other things being equal, worse than one that generates little or no air pollution. A means of transportation that breaks down after very little use is, other things being equal, a poor vehicle.

It should be emphasized that the determination of people's needs depends in large part on things that are established in objective, scientific ways.[11]

3. According to wants or desires

People have **wants** or desires. To want something is to be favorably disposed to having or experiencing it. Other things being equal, it is good that people's wants are satisfied, provided this does not interfere with their needs, or the needs and desires of others. The satisfaction of such desires is another source of criteria and standards. Since people generally desire physical comfort, for instance, the comfort of its ride is a criterion for evaluating cars, the comfort of its beds is a criterion for evaluating a hotel, and so on.

Global Evaluation

Global evaluation is the allocation of a single grade or evaluation to the overall character or performance of what is being evaluated. Some people deem global evaluation or grading to be subjective, and dismiss it for that reason. We think that would be a mistake. Such evaluations can be insightful and, when made by people with experience and training, very reliable. However, when evaluating globally, there is a risk of falling prey to its potential deficiencies. For instance, global evaluation can be compromised by the *idiosyncrasies* of the evaluator (a teacher has a prejudice against the use of contractions, for example, writing "it is" as "it's"). *Extraneous factors* can infiltrate the evaluator's judgment (one teacher is easily swayed by ingratiating students; another thinks all athletes are stupid). And the *ambiguity of values* can result in inconsistency (a teacher thinks of a "good argument" now as one that will persuade people, now as one that contains no logical errors).

These risks noted, a number of things can be done to minimize them when evaluating globally. Here are five.

1. *Use models or paradigms, and have the evaluator judge on the basis of how close the object comes to the models.* This is a way of coping with the ambiguity of values. It is a way of keeping all the evaluators on the same track, even where it is not possible to formulate clear-cut standards. For example, show the evaluators several model essays, or model answers to a question, and ask them to refer to the models when making up their minds about the student essays they are grading.

2. *Use a panel of evaluators, not just one.* This will tend to reduce the effect of idiosyncrasies. If there is a consensus among the evaluators (for example, four out of five agree the object is substandard), that will give credence to the evaluation. If it is a standoff (three say the object is substandard, two say it is good), no firm judgment seems warranted.

3. *Use only evaluators who are experienced with the objects being evaluated or who have been specially trained for the evaluation task at hand.* Inexperienced evaluators have no idea what to look for or expect, so their judgments run a high risk of being heavily influenced by extraneous factors and by their own idiosyncrasies.

4. *Wherever possible, have evaluations done "blind."* An evaluator who is ignorant of extraneous factors cannot be influenced by them. If the teacher does not know whose essay this is, a prejudice against athletes cannot affect the grade, nor can the student's past performance. For example, it is well documented that evaluators are unduly influenced by what they know of the past performances of a person being evaluated. Their expectations affect their judgment. This is one form of the "halo effect." When scholarly journals have articles evaluated for publication, it is a widespread practice to withhold the name of the author from the evaluator for just this reason. (The practice is called "blind refereeing.")

5. *Ask or require the evaluators to use checklists.* For example, ask the evaluators to give ratings for organization, clarity of expression, and cogency of argument and only then rate the essay as a whole. Or ask evaluators of speakers to rate them for how realistic they sound and how pleasant they sound before giving them an overall rating. Checklists tend to reduce the influence of idiosyncrasies and extraneous factors by focusing the attention of evaluators on the sorts of things that matter.

When global evaluators use these techniques, their evaluations become much more reliable. That is to say, the chance that a second round of evaluation will come to the same conclusion as the first round is much higher when these techniques are used than when they are not.

10.4 OVERALL EVALUATION

In typical cases of evaluation, the overall evaluation of the object is based on more than one criterion. For example, the evaluation of a frozen food product might recognize four criteria: nutritional value (determined by the application of recognized nutritional standards to chemical analyses of the product), flavor (blind-graded globally by a panel who like that kind of food, be it German, Indonesian, Greek, or whatever), ease of preparation (measured by such factors as the number of steps and time required), and impurities (for example, the amount of insect parts, rodent hair and feces, or animal bone, determined by microscopic examination of randomly chosen samples of the product).[12] To arrive at an overall evaluation of the product, it is necessary to combine the evaluations based on each criterion. How can that be done?

Overriding Factors: Essential or Minimum Criteria

In some cases an unacceptable rating on one criterion is all it takes to rate the object as unacceptable. A food product that tastes so bad that people gag on it is unacceptable, no matter how nutritional and easy to prepare it may be. Or a canoe that is so tippy it is dangerous to use is unacceptable, no matter how lightweight, maintenance free, and inexpensive it may be.

Weight and Sum

It is rare for there to be one overriding factor that by itself settles the overall evaluation. That leaves the problem of finding a way to combine the various subevaluations into an overall evaluation.

A traditional way to do this is by a process called **weight and sum**. The object is first graded (using a numerical scale, say, 1 to 5) on each value dimension or criterion. Next, numbers are assigned to the criteria themselves to reflect their relative importance or weight. Then, each criterion grade is multiplied by the weight assigned to that criterion. Finally, the results of the multiplications are added up (or summed).

For example, Uncle Ho's Freeze-Dried Noodle Soup might be rated as follows:

	Weight	Grade*		Grade × Weight
Nutritional value	.4	Poor	1	0.40
Flavor	.4	Excellent	5	2.00
Ease of preparation	.1	Very good	4	0.40
Purity	.1	Satisfactory	2	0.20
		Sum of grades times weight		3.00

*Grades: Excellent = 5, Very good = 4, Good = 3, Satisfactory = 2, Poor = 1.

One commentator says of this method:

> Although this method is a very convenient process, sometimes approximately correct and nearly always clarifying, there are many traps in it, ... The most intransigent problem arises from the fact that no selection of standard scales for rating weights and performances can avoid errors, because the number of criteria are not pre-assignable. . . . So, either a large number of trivia will swamp crucial factors (to a degree you did not intend), or, they will have inadequate total influence, depending on how many factors there are.[13]

The method is a crude and approximate way of taking into account estimates both of the relative importance of criteria and of how well something does on each criterion. Because it is crude and approximate, it should in most cases only be used as a rough guide. It is a way of generating hypotheses about overall value; those hypotheses then need to be scrutinized more carefully by going back to the facts and making both commonsense and impressionistic judgments.

For example, Uncle Ho's Noodle Soup score results from our giving flavor a weight equal to nutritional value and giving the two together 80% of the weight assigned. Seeing the resulting score ("good") might make us want to rethink the weights we assigned. We might hesitate about recommending a food product which rates only poor in nutritional value as "good." With only a slight change in weighting, Uncle Ho's Noodle Soup drops from a "good" to closer to a "satisfactory" rating, as the following chart shows.

	Weight	Grade		Grade × Weight
Nutritional value	.5	Poor	1	0.5
Flavor	.3	Excellent	5	1.5
Ease of preparation	.1	Very good	4	0.40
Impurities	.1	Satisfactory	2	0.20
		Sum of grades times weight		2.60

An overall evaluation is maximally informative when the rating is accompanied by a list of the main strengths and weaknesses of the thing being evaluated. Thus one might say about Uncle Ho's Noodle Soup, "It is a satisfactory product which scores high on flavor but is weak in nutritional value." That is a more useful evaluative report than one that just says, "Uncle Ho's soup passes because its overall score is in the 'satisfactory' range."

Indeed, sometimes because of complexities, it won't be possible or sensible to offer a single overall grade or rank to the objects being evaluated. In such cases, you will have to be satisfied with just a summary account of strengths and weaknesses. In our experience, the evaluation of candidates for college teaching jobs is such a case.

10.5 USING EVALUATIONS

To use an evaluation intelligently, it is essential to keep in mind the strengths and weaknesses of the object being evaluated as well as the overall verdict.

There are at least two reasons for doing so:

1. A product or service that is best overall might not be the best or right one for you. The strengths that make it excel might be only moderately important for someone in your circumstances, while its weaknesses might make it unacceptable to you. For example, a passenger car that is superior in almost every way but can seat only four passengers is a poor choice for a family of five.
2. Often (though by no means always) the very best products or services cost much more than the others to buy or use. When making choices regarding them, it is important to know how and why they excel, so that you can decide whether or not the differences between them and less costly alternatives are important to you.

10.6 SUMMARY

Evaluating something is determining its value or merit. We evaluate an amazing variety of kinds of things. For some, settled standards and methods exist, for others they do not. Typically, evaluating something entails settling on the criteria to use, deciding the standards to use for each criterion, getting information about the thing being evaluated to find out how well it satisfies the standards for each criterion, and deciding on an overall, all things considered assessment of the thing.

Evaluations can be given in various ways, for instance by grading, ranking, or scoring. Grading tends to be more informative than ranking, since it gives an idea of how good a thing is (either along one criterion or in general), whereas ranking just gives the comparative position. Scoring has potential drawbacks in that point constancy is essential but difficult to achieve and the significance of scores always needs to be interpreted.

Criteria can be based on the use or function to which the thing being evaluated is put, or on the needs of some person or group, on the desires of some person or group, or on some combination of the three, depending on the purpose of the evaluation.

Sometimes global evaluation, with no explicit appeal to identified criteria components or dimensions of evaluation, is most appropriate or efficient. While it can be purely personal and idiosyncratic—which is inappropriate in some contexts—using a panel of experienced evaluators judging "blind" against ideal models and utilizing checklists can often secure remarkable agreement among different evaluators.

Overall evaluation is tricky, since it involves comparing different scores on different criteria. An evaluation might be quickly decided because an object fails to meet an essential criterion. Otherwise, the method of weight and sum can be used to give at least a provisional evaluation. Also, the overall verdict aside, particular strengths and weaknesses are almost always relevant to the decisions one makes on the basis of evaluations.

10.7 EXERCISES

**Exercise 1

Look at examples of things to be evaluated. Describe the examples in enough detail to reveal the practical motivation of the evaluation (for example, if you decide to evaluate universities, then suppose you are a high school student deciding which universities to apply to for a good undergraduate education), and include some background information about the objects to be evaluated. For each example,
  (a) Is there a small number of criteria that are the most important ones on which the evaluation should be based? What are they? Explain your recommendation.
  (b) For each criterion or dimension you have identified, explain what kind of standards you would use and how you would go about setting them up.
  (c) How would you weight those criteria? Explain and defend your weighting.

Exercise 2

Look at a series of examples of reports of evaluations. For each example,
  (a) What additional information would you want provided in this evaluation?
  (b) On the basis of the evaluation offered, which would you choose? Explain and defend your choice.

Exercise 3

Obtain an example of an evaluation of a piece of computer hardware or software from *PC Magazine* and an evaluation of the same item from another computer publication. Which do you think has more informative and reliable evaluations? Defend your judgment by reference to the criteria, standards, and data presented in the evaluations.

Exercise 4

Obtain an example of an evaluation of an automobile from *Car and Driver* and an evaluation of the same automobile from another publication. Which do you think provided the more informative and reliable evaluation? Defend your judgment by reference to the criteria, standards, and data presented in the evaluations.

NOTES

1. In the language of the field of evaluation, the words "merit" and "worth" refer to slightly different things. According to that terminology, we judge the *merit* of an object when we judge its internal or intrinsic value; we judge the *worth* of an object when we judge it value to a consumer or an institution.

2. Deliberation also involves evaluating the *results* of proposed actions and alternatives.

3. See Michael Scriven, *Evaluation Thesaurus*, 4th ed. Newbury Park, CA: Sage, 1991), entries for Global (p. 177) and Analytic (pp. 54–55).

4. Sometimes you will measure *indicators* of a criterion variable rather than directly measure the criterion variable itself (for example, a golfer's judgment that lessons from the club pro have improved her game). Such a (secondary) indicator is some feature or variable that is empirically connected with the criterion variable. Scriven, ibid., entry for Indicator, pp. 193–94.

5. The terms 'criteria' and 'standards' are not always used the way we stipulate here. Sometimes people use 'criteria' ambiguously, failing to distinguish between the dimensions of evaluation and the degree to which each dimension is satisfied. Some use 'standards' to refer to what we call 'criteria.' To avoid being confused you will need to look behind the terminology to discover which of these two kinds of norms of evaluation is being referred to.

6. Scriven, *Evaluation Thesaurus*, p. 183.

7. Scriven, ibid., p. 299.

8. Scriven, ibid., entry on Scoring, pp. 323–334.

9. The class average or mean does *not* settle the question of what a score of 40% correct answers is worth. If the majority of those in the class did not study for the test, or have no aptitude for the subject matter, then a class mean of 40% could be compatible with 40% being worth an "F". Or, if the class contains an unusually large number of bright, overqualified over-achievers, a class mean of 70% could be compatible with 40% being worth a "D". Establishing what are called "statistical norms," (means and other averages) does not solve the problem of establishing "evaluative norms," that is to say, the standards appropriate for intelligent evaluation.

10. Here is Michael Scriven's definition of a standard: "The performance level associated with a particular rating or grade on a given criterion or dimension of achievements. For example, 80 percent success may be the standard for passing the written portion (dimension) of the driver's license test. A cutting score defines a standard, but standards can be given in non-quantitative grade contexts, for example, by requiring a B average in graduate school, or by providing exemplars, as in global grading of composition samples." see Scriven, *Evaluation Thesaurus*, p. 335.

11. Needs are not the same as wants or desires. A need may be defined as ". . . anything essential for a satisfactory mode of existence or level of performance" Scriven, ibid., entry for Needs Assessment, p. 342). Wants or desires, on the other hand, can be both nonessential and unrelated to, or even incompatible with, "a satisfactory mode of existence or level of performance."

There is room for argument about the details of a satisfactory or acceptable level of existence or performance. But two things restrict the scope for intersubjective disagreement here. (1) There are plenty of things that are obviously and uncontroversially components of a satisfactory level of existence, for example, freedom from disabling disease or constant pain, regular contact with other people, sanity, enough knowledge and clear-headedness to be able to do useful work, freedom from uninvited bodily assaults. (2) It is an objective, decidable matter what is and is not necessary for a mode or level of existence so described.

Also telling against the subjectivity of needs is that we often have needs that we know nothing about; for example, a need for a vitamin we have never heard of (recall the early European explorers of North America who died of scurvy—a vitamin deficiency—which they could easily have prevented, had they known about it, by adopting the diets of the aboriginal inhabitants).

12. Such impurities are found in almost all samples of grains, for example, and are acquired during periods of storage.

13. Scriven, *Evaluation Thesaurus*, entry for Weight and Sum (or Weighted Additive), p. 380.

Deliberation

To deliberate is to reason about what to do. We deliberate when we reason about whether to buy a stereo or about which one to buy. When two partners try to figure out whether their company should expand into new product lines, they are deliberating. When a congressional committee discusses modifications that might be made to a bill before the House, it is deliberating. We deliberate individually and jointly with others; we deliberate about individual, group, or corporate decisions, and we deliberate about particular actions and about policies governing classes of future actions.

To be sure, we perform most of our actions without any protracted **deliberation**. Frequently we act from habit (for example, having a cup of coffee in the morning when we get up). Sometimes it is "obvious" what is to be done, that is to say, we can infer effortlessly what action is called for (for example, rolling up the car's windows when it starts to rain). But at other times we must, or should, stop and think about what to do. We might be *forced* to, as happens when we are not sure what to do next. Or it might be that, although we think we know what to do, it would be prudent to deliberate before making a final decision. In particular, we should deliberate when a lot hangs on our decision (for example, making a career move, investing a large amount of money, or marrying) or when, even though the stakes are moderate, the decision concerns matters with which we are not completely familiar.

We are not advising deliberation about every decision. A life without spontaneity and impulsiveness is sad, even deprived. But getting pregnant while single just on a whim or taking off on a cross-country drive the week before final exams in your graduating year for no reason are decisions that may well harm yourself and others, and that stand to diminish your chances for a happy life. Somewhere a balance must be struck.

11.1 DECISIONS AND VALUES

When we deliberate, or reason about what to do, our reasoning has to take *values* into account: deliberation requires value judgments. There are two reasons why this is so.

1. To a large extent, we choose our actions in light of the *results* or effects we expect them to have, and we prefer one action to another because we think that, on the whole, it will have the *better* results of the two. This means that in reasoning about a proposed action, we must (a) determine or estimate what its results will be and (b) *evaluate* those results. We must bring to our decision making some idea of what is good and bad, or better and worse, in the way of results.

2. Sometimes our decisions about what to do are influenced by ethical, moral or legal considerations.[1] We might be inclined to reject an option because it requires transgressing our personal or professional code of conduct or because it involves lying or theft. In such cases, we have to decide two things: (a) whether some moral or legal requirement really does apply to the case at hand (for example, is it really unethical to tell a white lie—a minor lie to avoid some harm to yourself or to another), and (b) whether to honor that requirement even if we decide it does apply.[2]

"Other Things Being Equal"

In reasoning about what to do, we draw on value assumptions to the effect that things of certain *kinds* are good or bad, better or worse, or right or wrong. For example, most people assume that having enough wealth to satisfy their needs is a good thing, that being rejected by someone they love is a bad thing, that cars with high fuel economy are better than cars with low fuel economy, and that killing innocent human beings is wrong. We all have lots of such assumptions that guide us on a daily basis in deciding what to do.

Nevertheless, almost always such assumptions are reasonable only if they are qualified, that is, only if they are assumed to hold "other things being equal." Cars with good fuel economy are better than those without, *other things being equal*. And other things are often not equal. A car with medium gas consumption that is extremely safe in a collision may well be a better car for you than an highly fuel-efficient death trap. Or suppose you ask someone you love to marry you and they turn you down; rejection is a bad thing *other things being equal.* But this rejection might be a blessing in disguise if (unbeknownst to you) the person is self-destructive or violence-prone.

Even the most fundamental moral principles seem to admit of exceptions and therefore to hold only if other things are equal. For example, consider the following principle, formulated so as to admit of no exceptions:

(a) Taking the life of an innocent human person is always and without exception wrong.

Now think about the following case, which actually occurred in Philadelphia a few years ago. A woman gave birth to Siamese twins, joined at the midsection and sharing just one heart, liver and set of kidneys. The medical prognosis was that joined together they would not survive more than a few months, but if they were separated and one of the two were given all the vital organs (thus killing the donor twin), then the recipient twin would survive and have a good chance for a normal life. The parents, who were Jewish, consulted a Council of Rabbis; the doctor, who was Roman Catholic, consulted his bishop. Application was also made in a court of law, to ascertain that a charge of murder would not be laid should the doctors proceed with the operation. Opinion was unanimous that there was no moral or legal wrong in proceeding to give the vital organs to one baby, thus killing the other one. If you agree with this judgment (as we do), then you must allow that assumption (a) needs to be changed to something like:

(b) Taking the life of an innocent human person is seriously wrong *unless* there is some overriding reason to do so.

That is to say, even the moral requirement not to kill an innocent human being holds only "other things being equal."[3]

11.2 REASONS "ALL THINGS CONSIDERED"

When we find reasons for saying that something is good (or bad) or that some action ought (or ought not) to be undertaken, those reasons *might* be outweighed or overridden by stronger reasons—even when, as we have just seen, our premiss is a fundamental moral principle.

In order to mark the distinction between the cases where we think our reasons are or may be outweighed by stronger reasons, and the cases where we think no such reasons have been overlooked, we shall use the phrases **prima facie reasons** and **reasons all things considered**.[4] The following example illustrates the distinction.

Suppose you want to be a cardiovascular surgeon, and you are offered a four-year residency in heart surgery at a hospital in Boston that is reputed to be one of the top teaching hospitals in the country. Let's say it is clear you cannot get better training anywhere in the world. You thus have an extremely strong prima facie reason to accept the offer. At the same time, your spouse has just been admitted to the Texas bar, has an excellent job offer in Houston, and wants to start practicing law, and, moreover, cannot practice law in Massachusetts without a year's delay to prepare for and take the bar examination there. If you accept the Boston offer, either your spouse's career will be postponed or delayed, or you will have to carry on a long-distance marriage for four years. So you have a strong prima facie reason to decline the Boston offer. Clearly, you will need to decide what the best thing for you to do is, all things considered.[5]

In cases like this, a certain "value" or "good" pushes us in one direction (for example, the value of some of the best medical training available, plus access to excellent job offers later), but in the existing circumstances that value conflicts with some other value or good (for example, the values of your spouse's career taking off, and of living together with your spouse). In face of such conflicts between prima facie reasons, it is in the nature of the case that one value *has* to override or take precedence over the other when all things are considered— when one of the two options, or any other option, is chosen.

There is a lot of anecdotal evidence suggesting that once people find reasons in favor of a course of action, they tend to stop deliberating, and fail to consider even the possibility of contrary reasons. But thorough reasoning about what to do is always going to involve *weighing pros and cons*—balancing the reasons for and the reasons against a proposed action in order to see which are stronger all things considered. Before we can discuss what is involved in the weighing of pros and cons, there is another preliminary matter to be dealt with—the fact that decisions are always made in the face of alternatives.

11.3 ALTERNATIVES

Deliberating about what to do always involves choices among *options* or *alternatives*. Otherwise there would be nothing to choose between, and no point to deliberating. Two consequences for how to go about deliberating follow from this fact.

1. In weighing pros and cons, it is necessary to consider the pros and cons of two or more alternatives.

In considering whether to take the offer of a residency in Boston you need to consider *both* the pros and cons of accepting the offer *and also* the pros and cons of the other alternatives open to you (for example, taking a residency in Houston).

2. Deliberation is impaired if important alternatives are overlooked. Instead of either moving to Boston or going to Houston, perhaps you can set up an arrangement that will permit you to divide your training between Boston and Houston.

In actual practice, the nature of the alternatives varies according to the type of decision problem one is facing. In most situations calling for deliberation, the question about alternatives will arise in one of the following ways:

a. There are two or more things you definitely want to do, but they conflict, so you can do only one of them. Your question then is, which one of those specific things are you to do? For example, a rock concert for which you have tickets, your cousin's wedding, and the opening performance of a play you want to see all fall on the same night. Which one should you attend? We can call this sort of case a **dilemma**.

b. There is a specific goal or objective you are committed to achieving (a specific result you want to bring about), but there are different ways to achieve it (to get that result), and they may seem incompatible. Your question is, then, What is the best way to achieve or advance that goal or result? Deciding on a career path is a case in point. Let's say you want interesting work, good income, and job security. What is the best way for you to try to obtain these objectives? We can call this sort of case *deciding on the means to an end*.

c. You are requested, invited, advised, commanded, or tempted to do some one particular thing, but you always have the option of declining, disobeying, or resisting. Your question is, then, Shall I or shall I not do that particular thing? For example, you are asked to become president of a club to which you belong, your friend wants to move in with you, you have an offer of a new job if you quit your present one. We can call this sort of case a **yes/no decision**.

When faced with a dilemma, the alternatives are already spelled out. The dilemma was created in the first place by your knowledge of the alternatives (combined with your belief that they are incompatible), so there is little worry about overlooking one of them. However, it is always possible that, caught up in your quandary, you overlook some *additional* alternative(s). And the given alternatives may turn out not to be incompatible.

In decisions about the best means to an end, at least two alternatives will have presented themselves. But there might be additional ways of achieving the end, which you have overlooked, and which you ought to consider. Moreover, the given "alternatives" may not in fact be incompatible. Additional alternatives that should be considered are ones which (a) are more than just a shade different from those you are already considering, (b) are practical or feasible, and (c) promise a mix of pros and cons comparable to or better than the alternatives you are already considering.

Faced with a yes/no decision, the alternatives appear to be just the two: *yes* and *no*—perform the action or don't. The alternative of *not* performing the action will usually have certain negatives and positives clearly associated with it. If you don't accept the presidency of the club, then you avoid the unpleasant parts of the job, but you lose out on whatever experience and prestige are associated with it.

But notice also that the "no" alternative opens up, or at least leaves available, the possibility of choosing from a range of other options. If you say "no," you can do or choose other things instead. If you turn down the club presidency, for example, you will have extra time and energy that you can devote to any number of other things: increase your study time *or* go on a trip you were thinking of taking *or* go out for the track team *or* . . . , and so on.

Furthermore, it can turn out that what initially appeared to be a yes/no decision is not so clear cut, and in fact an "in between" possibility is available. You might serve as vice president of the club instead of president, for example. Although such an option is, strictly speaking, another option opened up by the "no" decision, it is not, like the others mentioned, a completely different kind of activity from that offered by a "yes" decision. Thorough deliberation, then, requires considering the benefits represented by the opportunities gained by a "no" decision. One way to do so is to take into account the most significant or valuable opportunity thereby gained.[6]

11.4 PROS AND CONS

It may give a clear and concrete idea of what pros and cons are if we list some of the major kinds.

Results or Consequences

Like any other events, actions have effects: their results or consequences. The effects of any action are innumerable. It would be impossible to take account of every effect on the world of your having soup for lunch tomorrow: there are too many of them, and most of them are (and will remain) unknown to any investigator. Yet *some* of the consequences of a proposed action have to be taken into account when one reasons about whether to perform it. Which ones? The ones that (1) you have good reason to think will or might occur *and* (2) are desirable or undesirable in some significant degree.

People usually act in order to achieve certain results. Those are the intended results of the action. But actions always have consequences over and above their intended results, and some of those unsought results may be significantly desirable or undesirable. Desirable consequences that are certain or likely are pro considerations; undesirable consequences that are certain or likely are con considerations. It makes no difference to its bearing for or against an action whether a result is intended or unintended.

Costs: Resources, Time, and Energy Consumed

Just about anything we do has costs of some sort. It will take time (which could be put to other uses), it will consume energy, and it will likely use up material resources (money, wear and tear on equipment or tools, paper, fertilizer, and so on). But some actions involve greater costs than others. High cost is a con consideration; low cost is a pro consideration.

Efficiency

In deciding on a means to achieve an end, an important consideration is usually the relative efficiency of the alternatives. Efficiency is a matter of the amount of output you obtain as a function of cost, normally including time and effort. Of two ways equally likely to achieve an objective, the one that takes less effort, money, time, risks, or known disadvantages, is the more efficient.[7]

Lost Opportunities

The opportunities and chances that must be give up in order to engage in a certain action are relevant to any decision concerning it. That few or only minor opportunities need to be given up is a pro consideration; that many or major opportunities need to be given up is a con consideration. We mentioned opportunity cost when discussing yes/no decisions, earlier.

Risks and Potential Benefits

When an undesirable consequence is not certain, but remains a probable or possible result, it is a **risk** of the action. When a desirable consequence is not certain, but is a probable or possible result, it is a **potential benefit** of the action. Clearly, risks are cons and potential benefits are pros. The significance of risks and potential benefits depends both on (1) how likely or probable they are and also on (2) how desirable (or undesirable) they are. A consequence which is minimally undesirable and not very likely is usually not worth taking into consideration. But a great evil (for example, a nuclear power plant disaster) is worth taking into consideration even if its likelihood is very small.

Ethical or Moral Considerations

When ethical or moral considerations apply, they can function either as pros or as cons. That an action would violate someone's rights is a strong con consideration. That it would fulfil an obligation is a weighty pro consideration. Ethical and moral considerations can be more or less weighty. Lying about something unimportant is a less serious wrong than is lying about something important, and both are much less grievous wrongs than murder. As we have seen, even fundamental moral principles only have prima facie application, and can, in principle, be overridden. Normally, though, what justifies overriding one ethical or moral consideration is another, weightier ethical or moral consideration.

Some people hold that moral considerations can never justifiably be overridden by nonmoral ones. Others contend that if the nonmoral benefits are very great and the moral wrong done is a small one, then doing the wrong to get the benefit is justified. We cannot discuss this controversy here, but you will yourself face choices in which you will have to take one side or the other. Suffice it to say that moral considerations carry great weight, and often are **disqualifiers** that rule out, or rule in, a particular option—regardless of other costs, benefits, or alternatives.

11.5 Weighing Pros and Cons

Sometimes weighing the pros and cons of a proposed action is easy. One alternative promises great benefits at little cost, and all the other alternatives offer only minor benefits at comparably greater cost. Other decisions will not be so simple or clear. Each alternative can have many pros and cons, and it can be hard to compare the pros and cons of one to those of another. For example, most people find choosing a career or profession an enormously difficult decision. It requires weighing large numbers of pros and cons: potentially high salaries against job security, the excitement of the new and different against the comfort of the familiar, what interests them now compared to what might interest them in the future, the likely effects of different sorts of careers on the family life they want, the work load of various different sorts of jobs; the risks of failure, of unemployment, of damage to their health; and so on. How are such complicated considerations to be balanced out?

There are no easy solutions for the difficult cases. Besides suggesting a thorough review of the alternatives and their consequences, and an attempt to evaluate them fairly systematically, we can offer only two pieces of special advice.

1. Watch for 'disqualifiers'—the decisive objections that straightaway rule out an alternative. For example, if an alternative entails serious risk to someone's life or health, or requires you to engage in criminal activity, that by itself normally should put it right out of the running. Looking for dis-

qualifiers has two advantages: (a) it can simplify your task by reducing the number of alternatives to be examined, and (b) it can save you from some bad decisions.

2. Where you are faced with more than two alternatives, start by comparing them two at a time. That way you might readily be able to rank them clearly and rule some out automatically. Suppose you have discerned three alternatives, A, B, and C. If you discover that you clearly value A more highly than B, and you also value C more highly than B, then you can rule out B and focus on which of A and C you value more highly.

There exist mechanical methods of decision making that have been devised for certain limited ranges of problems, involving the mathematical notion of probability and a quantified notion of "utility"—relative value or preference. Such methods are often fruitful when applied to problems they were designed for: situations with clear-cut alternatives, unproblematic evaluations or rankings, and values that are not misrepresented by quantification. In our opinion, however, the methods are artificial and potentially misleading when applied where these conditions are not present. We won't discuss them further here. For those who are interested, they will be found under the headings of "decision theory" or "game theory," especially in economic literature.

11.6 APPRAISING DELIBERATION

In deliberating we evaluate alternative courses of action. It's advisable, in the process, to evaluate our own deliberation, since it is so easy to overlook pertinent factors. You can check your deliberative reasoning in much the same way you can assess any reasoning, but we advise examining two features in particular with special care.

1. In assessing your premisses—the grounds and assumptions of your inferences—check in particular to ensure that your factual assumptions are sound.

A common cause of bad decisions is *miscalculating the results of various alternatives*. We can make mistaken causal judgments (for example, we think being really nice to someone will make them like us). We underestimate how long something will take (for example, chores or errands almost always take longer than we expect because we fail to allow time for unforeseen delays: traffic, lineups, slow service, and so on). It is common to underestimate how much something will cost (for example, in budgeting for vacations we tend to forget about "incidental" expenses such as tips and entrance fees). And we tend to overestimate or underestimate the risks we are taking because we make unreasonable assumptions about how probable they are or how harmful they would be (for example, we worry more about how much a new set of tires will cost than about the dangers of continuing to drive on the bald ones now on the car and the costs of an accident should one occur).

2. Check to ensure you have not overlooked important alternatives or important pros or cons for one or more of the alternatives.

Too often we make important decisions on just one or two features of two alternatives, when we could have and should have considered many more features and perhaps should have taken into consideration one or two other alternatives. (For example, we rent a house because we like the way it looks from the street and it is more conveniently located than the one other house we looked at. But we neglect to ask to see the heating bills, or to find out how hot the top floor is in the summer, or to check out the neighbors, and so on. And we overestimate the risk of someone else renting this house or the inconvenience of taking the time to look at a few more houses.)

11.7 SUMMARY

Deliberating is reasoning about what to do. Values are relevant to deliberation, because we act on the basis of our evaluation of the consequences, and in light of moral considerations. Most of the values we apply hold provisionally or "other things being equal," since it is always in principle possible for them to be overridden by others in particular circumstances. Correspondingly, we distinguish between prima facie reasons for doing something (which give us an "other things being equal decision") and judgments "all things considered." In deliberation, we are after a judgment that takes into account all the prima facie reasons and balances them appropriately, resulting in a sound decision "all things considered."

Deliberation entails choosing between alternatives. Alternatives occur in different ways depending on the situation: having to resolve a dilemma, having to decide the best means to an end, having to make a yes/no decision. We want to make sure there are no other options in a dilemma, to make sure all the possible means to the end have been considered, and to check out the opportunity cost in the case of yes/no decisions.

The pros and cons of each alternative need to be assessed. This is done by considering a variety of factors, not all of which are present with each kind of deliberation. They include costs of various kinds, efficiency, opportunity cost, risks and potential benefits, and the ethics involved. When the pros and cons of each alternative have been spelled out, a final all-things-considered judgment must be made. There is generally no mechanical way to do this. Keep in mind disqualifiers, and remember that ranking pairs can help.

A decision resulting from deliberation is a conclusion about what to do that is inferred from the facts and their evaluation. Particularly if it is important to make the right decision, it pays to check over one's deliberation. When doing so, it is key to ensure that the grounds relied on are in fact the case. Have *all* the important alternatives and all their important pros and cons been considered?

11.8 EXERCISES

Instructions for 1–8

The following passages contain reasoning about what to do. For each passage, do the following:
- (a) Identify the main conclusion.
- (b) State how good you think the reasoning is. Support your judgment. In doing so, be sure to
    - (i) Identify the alternatives mentioned and say if any significant alternatives were overlooked (supporting your claim either way).
    - (ii) For each alternative, call attention to the pros and cons mentioned and say if any pros or cons that should have been considered were overlooked (supporting your claim either way).
    - (iii) Note any assumptions or other premises which you think are unreasonable, explaining why you think so.

**1. If you are a college student living at home, it is probably a good idea to try to earn or borrow the money and buy a car. The bus service from most residential areas is slow and inconvenient, whereas by car you can get to the campus in under 20 minutes from almost anywhere in the city. A reliable secondhand car can cost in the thousands, it's true. Still, you have it during the summer months as well as during the school year, and it helps you get to work quickly if you have a part-time job.

2. Many students believe you should take as many easy courses as you can, in which you can get a high grade without much effort. But the truth of the matter is, you should take nothing but the hardest, most demanding courses you can find. If you do, then you will develop your skills and abilities to their maximum, and so you will be well prepared for many of the challenges you will encounter in your life after university. If you take nothing but easy courses, while you will no doubt have time for a pleasant social life, you will not develop your capacities and you will also probably find yourself bored.

3. Universities and colleges should adopt a policy of permanently expelling anyone caught plagiarizing on an essay. It's true that the first few students caught would suffer a great hardship. But once it is known that the schools are serious about imposing such a heavy penalty, plagiarism would stop almost immediately. That would be good for everybody, since it would enhance the schools' reputations. To continue the present policies, which at many schools do not define a fixed penalty for plagiarism, is unfair to students, since they are not sure what to expect if they are caught.

4. The following is based on a letter written in response to a newspaper editorial which had advocated increased efforts by the U.S. government against the influx of drugs.

Prohibition did not end alcoholism, nor did its repeal increase alcoholism. Dire predictions of the proliferation of drunks lying besotted in our streets did not come true with repeal. However, repeal did end most of the problems such as gang wars, murder, deaths from poisoned alcohol, and police corruption. In addition, cities and states reaped substantial tax revenues, and so did the federal government.

The same arguments against repeal were made during the alcohol prohibition years. More and more money and law enforcement tactics were used then with the same result. Now we are going far from our borders and getting involved in Panama, Colombia, Bolivia, and Mexico.

The conclusion is obvious: we should decriminalize or legalize drugs. It worked with liquor and will work with drugs as well. Throwing more money at the drug problem or sending our armed forces to other countries to destroy their crops and overthrow their governments is no solution to our drug problem. Despite expanded enforcement activities over the last 20 years, our prisons, police, and courts are overburdened with drug offenders.

A new approach should be taken, and some form of decriminalization or legalization seems to be the remedy.

5. The following reasoning addresses the problem of access to expensive medical procedures.

Medicare should not pay the cost of coronary bypass operations for anyone who is more than 65 years old.

First, each one of these operations costs tens of thousands of dollars. Since close to half the population is eventually affected by coronary artery disease, providing such operations for every old person with that disease will involve costs that are astronomical and that may eventually bankrupt the health care system.

Second, many of the older people who would receive such operations will live only a short time even if the operation is successful. It is true that even a few extra weeks of life are a precious thing. But the money spent on these old people could be better spent on other things—such as finding a cure for cancer or for AIDS— that would lengthen the lives of younger persons by much more considerable amounts.

Finally, making such operations available to everybody contributes to the false and irrational hope that we can cheat the grim reaper and live forever.

6. *Background*: In Peter Hellman's "Stealing Cars Is a Growth Industry," a veteran, very professional car thief who lives in New Jersey reasons as follows. You may not know that giving a stolen car "paper" means making counterfeit registration documents for it.

What I do is good for everybody. First of all, I create work. I hire men to deliver the cars, work on the numbers, paint them, give them paper, maybe drive them out of state, find customers. That's good for the economy. Then I'm helping working people to get what they could never afford otherwise. A fellow wants a Cadillac but he can't afford it; his wife wants it but she knows he can't afford it. So I get this fellow a nice car at a price he can afford; maybe I save him as much as $2,000. Now he's happy. But so is the guy who lost his car. He gets a nice new Cadillac from the insurance company—without the dents and scratches we had to take out. The Cadillac company—they're happy because they sell another Cadillac.

The only people who don't do so good is the insurance company. But they're so big that nobody cares *personally*. They got a budget for this sort of thing anyway. So here I am, a guy without an education, sending both my kids to college, giving my family a good home, making other people happy. Who am I really hurting?

7. The following is excerpted from a piece that appeared in the June 1991 issue of *Scientific American*. The full piece was entitled "Nuclear Power in Space" and was authored by Steven Aftergood, David W. Hafemeister, Oleg F. Prilutsky, Joel R. Primack, and Stanislav N. Rodionov.

Nuclear Power in Space

by Steven Aftergood, David W. Hafemeister, Oleg F. Prilutsky, Joel R. Primack, and Stanislav N. Rodionov

Space nuclear power is a double-edged sword. Although it has played a constructive role in the exploration of space and could continue to do so, it has been burdened by an extensive history of accidents and failures, both Soviet and American. Numerous nuclear-powered spacecraft have released radioactive materials. Spent reactors now in Earth orbit exacerbate the threat posed by orbital debris. And radiation from orbiting reactors has interfered with the operation of other satellites.

In addition, nuclear power in space has in general been a source of international tension because of its role in Soviet and American military space programs. As a result, organizations of both Soviet and American scientists (of which we are members) have proposed banning the use of nuclear power in Earth orbit. Such a ban would reduce the risks associated with nuclear power in space, while permitting its use in those deep-space missions for which nuclear power is essential.

. . . [Most of the article.] . . .

In view of the various dangers they present, we favor an international agreement to ban nuclear reactors and RTGs from Earth orbit. This readily verifiable measure would eliminate many environmental hazards, enhance international stability and help to protect the space environment; it would also preserve the possibility of using nuclear power for scientific and exploratory missions in deep space.

Since space nuclear reactors possess a variety of distinguishing characteristics, an international agreement to prohibit them in orbit could be verified with confidence. In the first place, space reactors necessarily radiate large amounts of waste heat. They therefore give off a strong infrared signal that can be easily detected. Soviet *RORSATs* have been observed with a satellite-watching telescope at the Air Force Maui Optical Station on Mount Haleakala. An operating SP-100 reactor would be readily detectable at geosynchronous orbit or even beyond.

Operating reactors also emit strong gamma and neutron radiation signals that are easy to spot. Indeed, the type of gamma-ray interference that has disrupted scientific missions is uniquely produced by orbiting reactors and is a highly reliable, though unwelcome, sign of their presence.

It is true that a nation planning to "break out" of an arms-control treaty could conceivably place reactors in orbit without activating them, thus making the violation much more difficult to detect. But until large reactors have been thoroughly tested in space, they are unlikely to be covertly deployed.

Nuclear power has greatly enhanced space exploration. But it has also demonstrated the potential to produce significant environmental damage. Even if it is wisely controlled, nuclear power in space is likely to remain a challenging and costly technology.

8. This editorial appeared in *USA Today* on June 26, 1991, with the title "States Should Keep Out of Sports Betting."

"States should keep out of sports betting"

In previous editorials USA TODAY has opposed states' spending large sums on lottery promotions; it has also opposed a national lottery that would compete with the states.

Sports gambling is another bad bet for states—

• Because it encourages gambling, particularly among our youth.

• Because it can lead to crime; one study showed 10% of teen-agers committed crimes to support their habit.

• Because money doesn't always go where it is intended; in Oregon, for the first two years, much of the revenue went into the general fund instead of college sports.

• Because the odds are poor; the odds of winning Lotto America, for example, are 13 million to 1.

• And because it preys upon the poor.

Gambling is especially bad for sports because it would raise concerns about the fixing of games. Fans would root for their bets rather than for their home teams.

States see gambling as a way to fill their coffers, but too many people see it as a way to fullfill their dreams.

Look across the USA, and you'll see the broken lives and unfullfilled dreams of those who took the risk—and lost.

Art Schlichter's promising National Football League career was cut short when he was suspended for gambling.

Chet Forte was at the pinnacle of the TV industry at ABC Sports until sports gambling destroyed his life.

Pete Rose was headed for baseball's Hall of Fame.

Compulsive gamblers have doubled in the last decade to 8 million—a million of them teenagers.

Gambling is already reaching the saturation point. States should not be using sports to try to make a big score.

NOTES

1. Some people use the words "ethical" and "moral" interchangeably. Others use the word "morality" to refer to those norms of conduct required of everyone for society's well-being, norms whose violation harms others, and restrict the use of "ethics" to refer to professional, and more rarely, personal, codes of conduct. On either usage, ethics and morality are distinct from law, the state-enforced rules of conduct. Still there is much overlap among codes of conduct, moral norms, and law.

2. Most people would agree that *some* moral or legal requirements are *sometimes* overridden by other considerations. For instance, if events have made it enormously inconvenient to keep a minor promise, many would allow that the promise may be broken; many have no objection to illegal jay-walking to save time. There is considerable disagreement, however, about which requirements may be overridden, and about what is a sufficient reason for overridding them (for example, when is it okay to renege on a promise to your mother that is important to her?).

3. Some writers and speakers still use the Latin phrase for "other things being equal," *ceteris paribus*, (one pronunciation of which is "kay/turiss par/ibus").

4. The phrase *prima facie* (one pronounciation of which is "pree/ma fay/shie") means literally "on first look" and is borrowed from its use in the law. In legal parlance, to make a "prima

facie case" for something is to present enough evidence to establish it *provided* no contrary evidence is brought to light. If I can show that none of Lee's relatives and friends has seen or heard from him for seven years, that constitutes in law a prima facie case that Lee is dead, and it creates a legal presumption that he is dead. But certain contrary evidence can refute that presumption, for example, a document with Lee's signature on it that is only three years old. Thus a prima facie case can always in principle be overridden. (Notice that the contrary evidence does not prove Lee is alive today; what it does is refute the presumption that he is dead.)

5. We have made the choice seem harder than it would be in real life. There is world-class training in heart surgery available in Houston, and you might well be accepted there if you apply. But you still would have to decide whether to accept the Boston offer.

6. Those who have studied economics may recognize that we are talking here about something like an opportunity cost. "Opportunity cost is what one gives up by selecting one option or engaging in a particular activity; either it is the value of the most valuable forsaken alternative, or it may specify the whole array of alternatives." See Michael Scriven, *Evaluation Thesaurus*, 4th ed. (Newbury Park, CA: Sage, 1991), entry for Opportunity Cost, p. 249.

7. Speed is not always a virtue. That a meal takes only 15 minutes at McDonald's does not make eating at McDonald's better than eating at a restaurant where a meal takes two hours—even in respect of length of meal. In many human activities, speed is considered a defect.

APPENDIX A
Some Elementary Formal Logic

Formal logic includes the study of the sorts of relations between propositions that were discussed in the chapter on logical relations—compatibility, consistency, entailment. It approaches those relations in a highly abstract way, showing that if certain *patterns* hold between sentences, then the propositions expressed by those sentences are compatible or incompatible, or that one entails the other, and so on. In a course in formal logic you would learn about a variety of such patterns, and you would master a set of techniques for proving that certain patterns guarantee (or do not guarantee) the existence of various logical relations.

Formal logic doesn't deal with inferences as such, but it sometimes has application to inferences. For in studying or considering a particular inference, you may want to know whether the propositions which play the roles of premises and conclusion in that inference do or do not stand in various logical relations. In particular, you may want to know whether the premises entail the conclusion. Formal logic can sometimes help you to answer that question.

In this appendix, we will not attempt to offer you more than a whiff of formal logic. We will say nothing at all about techniques or methods for proving things about these patterns, and we will expose you to at most a couple of common patterns. Still, it can be worthwhile to get a glimpse of formal logic, for two reasons: to help you see clearly what "logically necessary" inferences are like and to help you begin to develop a sense for what is called logical form.

A.1 FOUR ELEMENTARY "PATTERNS OF INFERENCE"

When the premises of an inference entail its conclusion, the inference is said to be *valid*. ('Valid' is used by logicians in a technical sense and is defined as follows: a valid inference is one whose conclusion *must* be true *if* all its premises are true.)

When inferences are spelled out in words, frequently (but not always) interesting patterns occur in the sentences used to express the premises and conclusion of the inference. The "interesting" patterns are the ones whose presence guarantees that the premisses taken together entail the conclusion. We will call such patterns *valid patterns of inference.*

There are four valid patterns of inference we think it particularly worthwhile to know.

Modus Ponens

Here are some examples of brief, if silly, inferences:

- If he left today, he will arrive by Thursday. He did leave today. Therefore, he'll arrive by Thursday.

- If she has been warned about the danger, then she'll be careful. But she has been warned, so she will be careful.

- If you like coffee, you'll love Folger's. You like coffee. Therefore, you'll love Folger's.

- He won't get the job. And if he won't get the job, he'll go bankrupt. So he'll go bankrupt.

There are three things to notice about these inferences. First, in each there is an inference drawn, something is concluded: that he'll arrive by Thursday, that she will be careful, that you'll love Folger's, that he'll go bankrupt. Second, the premisses lead to the conclusion and lead to it inexorably: if those propositions are true, the conclusion proposition absolutely has to be true. A relation of entailment holds between the premisses and the conclusion. And, finally, the four examples are instances of a common pattern. We might capture the pattern as follows:

- If _____ ,..............
- And/but _____ .

- Therefore, ...

The idea is, of course, that sentences go in the blanks and that the sentence in the first blank is repeated in the third and the sentence in the second blank is repeated in the fourth. Since it is not easy to see the difference between the two sorts of blanks (and since sometimes patterns need more than two sorts of blanks), it has become customary to use letters to stand for the sentences in the blanks.

- If p, q.
- But p.
- Therefore, q.

In fact, the more usual way of representing the pattern is as follows:

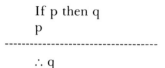

> If p then q
> p
> -----------------------------------
> ∴ q

There are exactly three assertions made in any instance of this pattern. In the first example, "If he left today, then he'll arrive by Thursday" is the first. Although it is compounded of two propositions which *could* be asserted separately, what is asserted is a conditional proposition of the sort you were introduced to in Chapter 5. "He left today" is the second assertion, and "He'll arrive by Thursday" is the third.

Among logicians, this pattern is known by its Latin name *modus ponens* (literally, the "method" *modus* of "putting" *ponens*).

If the premisses in any inference with a modus ponens pattern are true, the conclusion must be true. (Test this claim for yourself.) In other words, any inference with this pattern is *valid*. By extension, it is said that the pattern is valid: modus ponens is a valid inference pattern.

Modus Tollens

A second pattern resembles modus ponens, in that it has two premisses, the first of which is an "if . . . then . . . ," or conditional, proposition. Here are some examples.

- If she really loved you, she would have agreed to marry you. She wouldn't agree to marry you. So she didn't really love you.

- If the world is created by God, it would be a happy place. But it's clearly not a happy place. Therefore, it wasn't created by God.

The pattern in these inferences is

> If p then q
> It's not the case that q
> ---
> ∴ It's not the case that p

Logicians refer to this pattern by its Latin name *modus tollens* (literally, "the method of taking away," *tollens*).

Like modus ponens, modus tollens is valid; if the premisses of a modus tollens inference are true, its conclusion *must* be true.

It is worth noting that a conditional proposition can be expressed in a many different ways—among others:

- If it's Thursday, then we're in Rome.

- If it's Thursday, we're in Rome.

- We're in Rome if it's Thursday.

- On the condition it's Thursday, then we're in Rome.

Any form or words that's equivalent to "If p, then q" can function as the first premiss in a *modus ponens* or a *modus tollens* pattern of reasoning.

Disjunctive Syllogism

A third pattern is found in the following examples.

- Either she'll buy my Porsche or she'll buy a Mercedes. But she won't buy a Mercedes. Hence she'll buy my Porsche.

- He's either a scoundrel or a fool. He's not a fool. Therefore, he must be a scoundrel.

The pattern in these examples is

Either p or q
It's not the case that p

∴ q

Recall (from Chapter 5) that logicians call either/or propositions (like the first premiss in these inferences) *disjunctive propositions*. They call an inference from two premisses to a conclusion a *syllogism*. Hence they have adopted the term *disjunctive syllogism* as a technical name for this pattern of inference.

Disjunctive syllogism is a valid pattern of inference—as in the case of our example. If the premisses are true, then the conclusion cannot be false.

Hypothetical Syllogism

A fourth pattern is found in these examples.

- If I sell my car, I'll have 1200 dollars. If I have 1200 dollars, I'll be able to go to Florida in February. Hence if I sell my car, I'll be able to go to Florida in February.

- If you don't pay me what you owe me, I'll expose you as a fraud. If I expose you as a fraud, you'll lose your job. Hence if you don't pay me what you owe me, you'll lose your job.

The pattern in these examples is

If p then q
If q then r

∴ If p then r

The pattern is called *hypothetical syllogism*: syllogism because it has two premisses, hypothetical because its premisses and its conclusion are conditional propositions, and "hypothetical propositions" is another name for conditional propositions.

This pattern of inference is also valid; that is, it never leads from true premisses to a false conclusion.

A.2 THREE ERRORS IN REASONING

We would like to call your attention to three errors or mistakes that sometimes occur when people try to make inferences in these patterns. The first two involve falling into patterns that superficially resemble modus ponens and modus tollens, but which are not valid inference patterns. The third involves a common mistake made when drawing an inference in the pattern of disjunctive syllogism.

Affirming the Consequent

Occasionally, people will reason as in the following example.

- If cigarette smoking is harmless, then many people who smoke will live to an advanced age. But it's a well-known fact that many heavy smokers live to be very old. Therefore, cigarette smoking must be harmless.

The pattern here is superficially like modus ponens, but is importantly different. The pattern of inference in the example is

If p then q
q

∴ p

Genuine modus ponens is

> If p then q
> p
> ------------------------------------
> ∴ q

Here is a way of describing what has happened. Recall (from Chapter 5) that the first part of a conditional proposition—the "if" part—is called the *antecedent*, and the second part—the "then" part—is called the *consequent*. In a genuine modus ponens, the second premiss asserts the antecedent (the "if" part of the first premiss), and the conclusion of the argument is the consequent (the "then" part of the first premiss). In the "bogus" modus ponens, the second premiss asserts or *affirms the consequent* (the "then" part of the first premiss) and attempts to conclude that the antecedent is true.

Is the difference between genuine modus ponens and affirming the consequent important? Judge for yourself: where a modus ponens has true premisses, it *always* has a true conclusion; but when you affirm the consequent, you frequently go from true premisses to false conclusion.

What makes affirming the consequent fallacious can be explained as follows. The consequent of a conditional proposition is compatible with the antecedent, but—lacking any additional information to the contrary—it is often equally compatible with the denial of the antecedent. Consider the conditional propositions:

- If it has just rained, the ground will be wet.
- If Larry's first record sells a million copies, he'll become rich.

The ground will be wet if it has just rained, but it also could be wet without rain, for instance, if the sprinkler has been on or floodwaters have just receded. Larry will become rich if his first record sells a million copies, but he might become rich even if it doesn't—his first record might be a flop and his second record might sell a million copies, or he might just win a big lottery or make a fortune in real estate.

So the fact that the consequent of a conditional proposition is true does not guarantee that the antecedent is true. That is why the *affirming the consequent* inference pattern is not valid: sometimes it leads from true premisses to a false conclusion.

Denying the Antecedent

Still another inference pattern which is not valid is illustrated in the following example:

If Gertrude does all the assignments in her logic course, she will get a "B" or better. But she failed to do all the assignments. So she won't be getting a "B" or better.

The pattern here is superficially like modus tollens: the second premiss denies one of the parts of the conditional proposition asserted in the first premiss. But there is an important difference. In modus tollens the consequent is denied, while here the antecedent is denied. Genuine modus tollens is

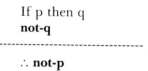

> If p then q
> **not-q**
> ------------------------------------
> ∴ **not-p**

The pattern of inference in our example is:

> If p then q
> **not-p**
> ------------------------------------
> ∴ **not-q**

What happens in this pattern is that the second premiss says that the antecedent (p) is false, and concludes that the consequent (q) is also false. That is why the pattern is called *denying the antecedent.*

The pattern of denying the antecedent is not valid—it sometimes leads from true premisses to a false conclusion. The first premiss says that doing all the assignments guarantees a "B" or better for Gertrude. But it doesn't say anything about what will happen if she fails to do all the assignments. It leaves open the possibility that she might skip all the assignments and then bribe her logic instructor or that she's brilliant and that a quick read of the textbook is all she needs to master the material.

Incomplete Disjunction

Think about the following piece of reasoning, which might occur in the context of American politics.

- The political candidate who just spoke on the radio must be either a Democrat or a Republican. But she just blasted the Democrats. So she must be a Republican.

Embedded in that reasoning is a disjunctive syllogism.

(a) Either the speaker is a Republican or else she's a Democrat
(b) She's not Democrat.

Therefore,

(c) She's a Republican.

That inference, like all disjunctive syllogisms, is valid in the sense we defined earlier in this appendix: it is impossible that it have true premises, and a false conclusion. But it may well have false premises; and in the event that it does, the validity of the inference will *not* guarantee the truth of the conclusion. Now when people reason in the pattern of disjunctive syllogism, they not infrequently begin from a false disjunctive ('either/or') proposition, because they forget about other alternatives. The person reasoning in the preceeding example *may* have good reason to think that the speaker was either a Republican or a Democrat; in that case, his reasoning is faultless. But he may have forgotten that there are other parties in United States; he may have *overlooked* the possibility that the speaker belongs to the Libertarian party or to some other party.

If someone overlooks a relevant possibility when using disjunctive syllogism, they are guilty of a mistake called *incomplete disjunction*. It is also called *false dilemma*. The mistake is a common one, easily made: you ought to watch out for it—in your own inferences and in those of others. When you encounter a disjunctive syllogism, stop and ask yourself, Is the disjunction complete? Are there relevant[1] alternatives being left out of consideration?

A.3 OTHER PATTERNS OF INFERENCE

Please understand that the patterns of inference described in this appendix do *not* by any means exhaust all the patterns of inference that are available for good reasoning.

The patterns we have discussed all come from just one branch of formal logic, and there are a host of important patterns from other branches of formal logic.[2] For example, here is an inference exhibiting a pattern that would be dealt with by a different branch of formal logic.[3]

- All students complain of too much work. Some Floridians are students. Therefore, some Floridians complain of too much work.

The pattern a logician would see in this is as follows:

All A is B
Some C is A

∴ Some C is B

Don't worry about remembering the details of this example. We mention it simply to illustrate the point that there are valid patterns of inference quite different from the ones we described earlier.

In addition to the patterns studied by formal logic—patterns of *valid* inference in which the truth of the premisses guarantees the truth of the conclusion—there are very common types of reasoning in which premisses support a conclusion without guaranteeing its truth. Here are a couple of examples:

- Almost all adults living in Wyoming are fluent in English. Jean lives in western Wyoming, so Jean is probably fluent in English.

- All the swans that have ever been seen have been white, so probably there are no black swans.

In these examples, the premisses support the conclusion but don't *guarantee* its truth; it is possible (but unlikely) that the premisses are true and the conclusion false. These aren't the sort of valid patterns of inference which formal logic studies,[4] but they exemplify very important patterns of reasoning in everyday life and in science.

A.4 A BIT OF PRACTICAL ADVICE

Don't expect that you will find these patterns of inference, or these errors in reasoning, in the majority of inferences or arguments that you come across. When should you look for them? And how will you find them? The keys and clues are the words "If . . . then . . ." and "Either . . . or . . .". When you encounter conditionals or disjunctions in the context of an inference or an argument, check to see if the rest of the context fits one of these patterns. If you find modus ponens, modus tollens, or hypothetical or disjunctive syllogism, you know you have encountered a valid pattern of inference—that *if* the premisses are true, the conclusion must be true as well. If you find affirming the consequent or denying the antecedent, you know that you have found an error in reasoning. Finally, if you find disjunctive syllogism, think about whether the disjunction is complete.

A.5 EXERCISES

Exercise 1

For each of the following patterns of inference, make up an example of an inference which fits the pattern.
  1. Modus ponens
  2. Modus tollens
  3. Disjunctive syllogism
  4. Hypothetical syllogism
  5. Affirming the consequent
  6. Denying the antecedent

Exercise 2

Each of the following passages contains an inference. For each passage, do the following:
  (a) Identify the premises and the conclusion of the inference.
  (b) Determine whether the inference exhibits one of the patterns described in this appendix.
  (c) Determine whether the inference contains one of the errors described in this appendix. If so, identify the error and explain why you think it is committed.

  1. If withholding information is just the same as lying, then it's wrong too. But they are the same. So withholding information is wrong.

  2. If you eat too much pasta, you'll become gross and ugly. Hence if you eat too much pasta, no one will love you, since if you become gross and ugly no one will love you.

  3. If capital punishment—killing those who have killed—really did deter further killing, then it would be an acceptable solution to a real social problem. But it doesn't have any measurable deterrent effect. It follows that capital punishment isn't an acceptable solution.

  4. Either communism will take over the entire world as Marx predicted it would, or else it will disappear completely from the face of the earth. Since the communists will never be able to dominate every part of the globe, it's only a matter of time before communism fades entirely from view.

  5. Most Canadians hate beer and most Canadians like hockey. Hence some people who hate beer like hockey.

  6. Where in the devil did I leave my car keys? Let me see. They've got to be either in the hall (because I had them when I came in the front door, I remember that) or in the kitchen (because that's the next place I went and after that I don't remember having them). I can't see them anywhere in the hall, so they must be in the kitchen.

  7. If that cute guy in Psych. 115 liked me, he'd have sat beside me again yesterday, but he was sitting with his buddies way up at the back of the lecture hall, so I guess he doesn't like me.

  8. If Pinto and Blair weren't sexists, they wouldn't use examples that stereotype female students as just interested in men, but they do, so they are.

  9. You *have* heard of Shoeless Joe Jackson? Oh, so you must have read W. P. Kinsella's novel, *The Iowa Baseball Confederacy*, because if you read that book you've heard of Shoeless Joe Jackson.

  10. We should believe in ghosts. If we can't prove the non-existence of ghosts, then we should believe in their existence. And there's no way to really prove that ghosts don't exist.

  11. In *The Brothers Karamazov*, Ivan overcame his doubts about the existence of God when he became convinced that if there is no God, then everything is permitted. But it is false, he thought, that everything is permitted; it's evident that some things are wrong, forbidden. So there must be a God.

12. Either my friends will all stand by me if I get into trouble or they'll all dump me. I know they won't all stand by me, so I guess they'll all dump me.

13. If the United States does not do something about acid rain, Canadian lakes will continue to die. As a result, there's little hope for Canadian lakes.

14. Everyone knows what's morally right and wrong. But many people perform actions which are morally wrong. Since what people do knowingly they do voluntarily, it follows that people want to perform morally wrong actions.

15. Very few Americans play lacrosse. So chances are you won't find a lacrosse player in any of your classes.

16. If Vanna White is secretly married to Elvis, then Elvis is still alive. And if Elvis is still alive, then the prayers of millions have been answered. So if Vanna White is secretly married to Elvis, then the prayers of millions have been answered.

17. If Larry pays you back on time what he owes you, then he's an honest man. But I know he won't pay you back on time. So he isn't an honest man.

NOTES

1. One way to make sure that our disjunctions are complete is to exhaust the logically possible alternatives. But in many, many cases there are logically possible alternative that simply are not relevant—that are simply too unlikely to be worth considering. It is logically possible that my local congressional representative is a member of the Nazi party, but normally that is so unlikely that it need not be accounted for.

2. Our instances are from what is called propositional logic, which is the most elementary part of formal logic.

3. The example belongs to what is called predicate logic (and more specifically, first-order predicate calculus). It belongs to that part of predicate logic that Aristotle explored when he first developed the theory of the syllogism.

4. In this century there have been a number of attempts to develop a formal logic for inferences like these. None of those attempts has been completely successful yet.

Ambiguity, Equivocation, Vagueness and Value-Laden Language

In trying to understand what you read and hear, you will encounter words and expressions which can raise problems because of their *meaning*. It's important to be able to diagnose such problems and to know what, if anything, to do when they occur.

B.1 AMBIGUITY

Examine the following two sentences.

(a) We know that the carpenter went to Chicago with most of his tools, but we don't know whether he took a plane.

(b) To prevent it from getting stuck, the carpenter shaved a sixteenth of an inch off the door with a plane.

It isn't clear what the *first* sentence means, because it isn't clear whether 'plane' in that sentence refers to an airplane or to a tool for smoothing and shaping wood surfaces. In the *second* sentence, there isn't a problem. The meaning there is clear. Why the difference? The first sentence makes perfectly good sense on either interpretation of 'plane,' while the second sentence stretches credulity if 'plane' is taken to refer to an airplane.

We say that the occurrence of 'plane' in the first sentence is *ambiguous* but that it's occurrence in the second sentence is not. Notice what makes 'plane' ambiguous is not merely the fact that the English word 'plane' has more than one meaning. Most common words in English have more than one meaning, but occurrences of them aren't usually ambiguous. The ambiguity occurs because in the context of (a) we cannot tell which meaning to assign.

Ambiguity can occur even when there aren't two different dictionary meanings at stake, as in the following examples.

(c) I asked Martha to ask her sister, but she didn't respond to my request.

(d) They are playing cards.

In (c), the 'she' is ambiguous because it isn't clear whether it refers to Martha or to her sister. In (d), the sentence as a whole is ambiguous between "Those things are cards used to play card games with" and "What those people are doing is playing a card game."[1]

Ambiguity occurs when we can't tell from the context which of two or more possible meanings or references is the intended one.

What can you do when you encounter ambiguity? When speakers or writers are present, you can ask them what they mean. With most written material, that's not possible. All you can do is search the context more carefully for clues; if you don't find any you won't be in a position to know what the speaker or writer intended to say. In such cases, be careful not to jump to conclusions.

B.2 EQUIVOCATION

Ambiguity occurs when a word or expression has two or more possible meanings and the context doesn't enable us to settle on one of those meanings as the intended one; the upshot of ambiguity is that the intended meaning is *unclear*. A related but importantly different phenomenon is *equivocation*. Equivocation occurs when a speaker or writer tries to shift the meaning of a word or phrase in an objectionable way.

For example, Mel asks Taya whether she's ever been to Greece, and she answers, "I've been to Athens many times." Later, it comes out that she's in fact never been to Athens, Greece, and she tries to exonerate herself by saying that she was referring to Athens, Ohio, where she use to live. This kind of objectionable playing with words is equivocation: the context of her original utterance (answering a question about being to Greece) requires that by "Athens" she should mean Athens, Greece. But she tries to justify uttering what she did by claiming that in saying "Athens" she intended to refer to some other place.[2]

More misleading cases of equivocation occur when a speaker uses a word or phrase two or more times, shifting its meaning from one occurrence to the next when the context requires it have the same meaning in both occurrences. Consider the reasoning advanced in the following passage.

> Defenders of civil disobedience hold that conscience is the ultimate guide about whether to obey the law, but they are clearly wrong. Law has to be the ultimate guide, because without law there could be no conscience: law is what conscience appeals to.

The first reference to "law" in this passage is to the *laws of the state* (sometimes called "civil law"); people who advocate *civil* disobedience advocate breaking the laws passed by Congress or by state legislatures. But the second and third oc-currences of "law" refer to *the fundamental principles of morality* (sometimes called "the moral law"), for that is the kind of law that conscience is supposed to appeal to. Moreover in *this* passage (but not always), there's something objectionable about the shift in meaning. The argument against civil disobedience relies on the shift, and the shift is illegitimate since the conclusion follows from the premiss in this case only if the word "law" means the same in both the premisses and the conclusion. Because of the shift, the argument invites an unwarranted in-ference.

Sometimes a shift in meaning occurs that's not objectionable; then there isn't equivocation, as in Pascal's famous saying:

The heart has reasons which reason doesn't know.

In its first occurrence, the word 'reason' means ground, basis, or motive; in its second, it means the faculty of reasoning. But there's no equivocation here, since the context doesn't require that the second occurrence carry the same meaning as the first.

Equivocation occurs when (1) a speaker uses a word or phrase which has two or more meanings, (2) the context requires that it be used with one of those meanings, and (3) the speaker treats it as having some other of its meanings.

Shifts of meaning may or may not be conscious and deliberate. Pascal undoubtedly was aware he was using 'reason' in two different senses, but the objector to civil disobedience, we suspect, may not have realized that a shift of meaning took place in his argument and rendered him guilty of equivocation. If he wasn't, then he was as much a victim of his equivocation as anyone who might have thought the inference in his argument to be a good one.

When ambiguity occurs, in the context you *cannot* determine which of two (or more) possible meanings to attribute to a word or phrase. When equivocation occurs, in the context you *can* attribute the two particular meanings exploited in each of the two uses, but the speaker or writer's inference trades on the listener or reader not noticing the switch. Clearly, reasoning which relies on equivocation is bad reasoning.

B.3 VAGUENESS

What's said or written can be lacking in clarity even when it contains no ambiguity. One of the important ways this happens is through *vagueness*. Vagueness isn't necessarily a problem: sometimes its opposite, precision, is impossible or un-desirable. An expression is too vague if it's insufficiently precise or definite for the purposes at hand.

Think of expressions as occurring in statements that are answers to ques-tions. One can sometimes give a correct answer to a question but, in doing so, withhold the information the person asking the question was looking for.

(a) Where did you go? Out. What did you do? Nothing important.

(b) How old are you? Over 21.

Example (a) exemplifies vagueness—twice—and possibly undesirable vagueness from the questioner's point of view (though perhaps not from the answerer's). Example (b) is vague too, but whether unhelpfully so will depend on the context. If, for example, the question is put by a bartender in order to learn whether someone is of legal drinking age, the answer supplies the needed information. If, on the other hand, the question is put by a physician in course of taking a medical history, the answer doesn't supply the information the physician wants and needs.

Whether a statement (or expression) is objectionably vague does not depend, then, simply on what the statement says (or what the expression means). It also depends on the context in which the statement is made or the expression it used. More specifically, *a statement or expression is objectionably vague in relation to a given audience on a given occasion, if it isn't precise enough to tell that audience what it wants to know on that occasion.*

Sometimes people want to know things which they don't have a clear right to know and which it might be better for them not to know (at least for now). Where that's so, vagueness is not a fault and may indeed be a virtue. Diplomatic language is often studiously and appropriately vague.

Species of Vagueness

We can usefully subclassify instances of vagueness into two different kinds.

(1) In the first sort of case, a term or expression is too *general* to supply the information required or wanted for the purposes at hand. This situation calls for something *more specific* than what's actually said, and the result is objectionable vagueness. Suppose any of the following is uttered in situations in which more specificity is needed:

- "Where did you go?" "Out."

- "Where is North Dakota?" "West of the Mississippi."

- "How old are you?" "Over 21."

- "How long should I make the piece of lumber I'm cutting for you?" "A couple of feet."

This sort of vagueness is corrected by substituting a *more specific* word or expression for the vague one: "To the market," "On the Canadian border, between Minnesota and Montana," "28," "Two feet six inches long."

(2) The second sort of case arises because many words and concepts depend for their applicability on *likeness to a paradigm.* Consider the word 'jazz' as the

name for a kind of music. Jazz originally referred to what was played by certain Afro-American musicians in New Orleans at the beginning of the twentith century (what's now called Dixieland jazz), but it's now used to refer to a much wider spectrum of music (from Dizzy Gillespie to Miles Davis to Wynton Marsalis to Dave Brubeck). There is no *definition* of the word "jazz" that would help in settling the question of whether a given piece of music is jazz or not. How then do we decide whether something is jazz? We call a piece jazz if it's sufficiently similar to the clear-cut or paradigm cases of jazz. But *how* similar is sufficiently similar? And similar in which respects? (Is the length of the piece a relevant consideration? Is how loud it's played relevant? Is it essential to jazz that it be improvised?) There is no straightforward answer to these questions, and when it comes to deciding whether a new piece of music is jazz, there are no simple rules or tests or definitions we can apply. Interestingly, there's widespread (but not total) agreement about most cases, even in the absence of anything like a definition. But there's always a penumbra of cases about which it's not possible to achieve a consensus because of this kind of "looseness" in the concept.

Now notice that the "looseness" in the concept of jazz *usually* doesn't cause problems or create objectionable vagueness in what we say or think. If you ask me what kind of music I like, or what kind of music Herbie Hancock played when he was young, the answer "jazz" is a perfectly good and perfectly definite answer; it would be quite inappropriate to call such answers too vague. But there are contexts in which the "looseness" in the concept will render it too imprecise for the purposes at hand. Suppose we're drawing up rules for a competition for musical composition, and we're snobs who want to exclude what we think is "low-brow" music. To say that "jazz compositions" won't be eligible for the prize—and leave it at that—is probably not precise or definite enough for the purpose of spelling out eligibility requirements; the result would be problem-causing vagueness in the rules.

This sort of conceptual "looseness" can give rise to unclarity, and muddy thinking, in many different contexts. Some examples are "democratic," "socialistic," and "religious," and "freedom." Such vagueness can often (but not always) be avoided by *stipulating* what is to count as, for example, democratic or socialistic or religious or jazz. You say, "For my purposes I will mean by 'freedom' the following: . . ." and then you state how you will be using the word. Your readers or listeners can then understand you, without becoming confused by other possible meanings.

B.4 VALUE-LADEN LANGUAGE

Meaning and Value

What is known about the manifold ways in which meaning is expressed and communicated through language cannot be reviewed here. But we want to draw your attention to some ways language can be used to convey value judgments, and point out some ways claims can be affected by them.

Consider the following lists of words.

LIST 1

- good, better, best
- bad[3], worse, worst
- poor, fair
- right, wrong
- should, ought, must

The words in this list are explicit value words, which are used to appraise or evaluate things, persons, or actions. They carry virtually no "descriptive content." For example, if all you are told about a movie is that it is good, you know next to nothing about the features that supposedly make it good or the ways in which it is good.

LIST 2

- murder, murderer, to murder
- cheating, cheater, to cheat
- theft, thief, to steal
- scoundrel

The words in List 2 all have descriptive content, but their meaning includes an evaluative component as well. Consider 'murder.' Murder is the killing of one human by another, but it is not only that. It is such killing which is wrong—which is morally unjustified. The latter judgment is essential; if the killing is regarded as morally justified, then it is not called murder—which is how many regard killing in self-defense or the killing by a soldier of an enemy soldier in battle. In similar ways, evaluations form part of the meanings of the other words on the list—and a great many others like them.

Here is a quick run-through. Cheating is taking unfair advantage, and it is wrong to be unfair. Theft is the wrongful appropriation of property which rightfully belongs to another, and so is by definition wrong. A scoundrel is a disreputable person, who takes advantage of others by acting in improper and unfair ways.

Now consider two more sets of words.

LIST 3

- democracy, democratic
- human
- totalitarian
- terrorist

LIST 4

- feminist
- humanism
- liberal

The words on these two lists have something in common, and they are also different in at least one respect. What they have in common is that, although their *meaning* (what they denote) is value neutral, their *normal use* (their connotations) at this time in our society conveys an accompanying value judgment. For instance, "democracy" denotes a particular class of political systems or procedures. These systems or procedures are widely regarded as highly desirable today (although as recently as the nineteenth century that was not so), so to label a political system democratic is to imply praise. A terrorist is someone who uses the method of random killing (or specific threats of it) as a means of advancing political goals. Such a political method is almost universally condemned, so to call someone a terrorist is to condemn him or her.

The only difference between the two lists in respect to this property of conveying an evaluation is that the words in List 3 convey almost universally the same evaluations, positive or negative, whereas the values associated with the words in List 4 vary markedly from group to group. 'Feminist' is a word of praise in some circles, but a word of condemnation in others. Humanism is held in high regard by members of the Humanist Society, but despised by many fundamentalist Christians. In the American presidential election of 1988, George Bush accused Michael Dukakis of being a liberal, thereby appealing to the antagonism associated with that label in some circles. But Dukakis (at least toward the end of the campaign) proclaimed that he was indeed a liberal, thus appealing to the approval associated with the label in other circles.

Misusing Value-Laden Terminology

Value judgments are among the most important kind of judgments we make, and the use of value-laden terminology is an indispensable tool in our reasoning and communicating about ourselves and our world. Judicious use of such terminology is essential to clear and critical thinking.

We want to call your attention to a couple of common abuses of such terminology.

Question-Begging Epithets

To beg the question is to assume without proof something that needs to be proved, demonstrated, or defended. An epithet is a word or phrase used to characterize something, typically carrying an evaluative connotation. A question-begging epithet is a word or phrase that

1. has an evaluative meaning or connotation
2. is used in a situation which requires that the evaluation it carries be defended
3. is used with no defense of that evaluation

The reason such evaluations need to be defended in such contexts is usually that the people whom the author is addressing include just those who doubt or challenge the evaluations implied by the use of the words or phrases. For example, in a debate about abortion—where there is disagreement about whether abortion is always or ever wrong—it is sometimes argued that abortion is wrong because it is murder. The claim that abortion is murder may or may not be true, but it is a claim that is controversial precisely in arguments about abortion. So the claim that abortion is "murder"—that is, that it's *wrongful* killing—needs to be defended in the context of such debates. To establish that abortion is murder, you would *first* have to establish that it is wrong—which is just the question at issue in the first place. In such contexts, therefore, if you claimed that abortion is murder without first having shown it is wrong, you would be guilty of using a question-begging epithet.

Vituperative Obfuscation

When used carefully and responsibly, value-laden language contributes to clear and critical thinking. But strongly charged value-laden language—especially negative language used in personal attacks—sometimes makes careful consideration of important issues difficult and occasionally even well nigh impossible.

Suppose Adams has presented a carefully reasoned case for increased government funding of day care centers, and Wong opens his response to her remarks by saying, "I'm tired of listening to these man-hating, hairy-legged feminists whining and spouting their radical socialist ideas . . .". The chances are slim that the conversation or debate which follows will address the issues in a way that clarifies or illuminates them. When value-laden language is used in a way that discourages reasoned argument and rational consideration of issues, we will call it *vituperative obfuscation*. Vituperation is violent denunciation or condemnation. To obfuscate is to confuse or bewilder, or to make obscure. Vituperative obfuscation is all too common on the op-ed pages of North American newspapers, not only in letters to the editor but also in "commentary" pieces done by well-known syndicated columnists.

B.5 SUMMARY

In this appendix we have presented some of the ways language use, or misuse, can cause confusion, misunderstanding, or faulty reasoning.

The richness and economy of language results in words having to do multiple duty, usually carrying more than one meaning and often several.

Ambiguity, equivocation, and vagueness are often confused. Ambiguity occurs when we can't tell from the context which of two or more possible meanings or references is the intended one. We gave examples of several different kinds of ambiguity. Equivocation is an objectionable shift in a word's meaning. It sometimes just causes confusion, but when used in an inference or argument, it can produce or invite bad reasoning. Vagueness is a lack of precision in the use of a word or expression. Often not a problem, and sometimes even beneficial, it is objectionable in contexts in which there is a desire or need for greater precision. A special case of vagueness occurs with concepts which get their meanings from paradigm cases or exemplars, and which accordingly can have vague boundaries. In some situations it is possible to avoid the problems which can accompany vagueness by stipulating the way a term is to be understood.

Language is often used to convey value judgments and assumptions. Although some words seem to have purely descriptive connotations, any word can acquire value connotations too. Some terms are almost purely evaluational, used to express attitudes rather than to refer to things or properties. Sometimes a word will have opposite value connotations for different people or groups. Confusion can be caused by simple inattention to these complexities of language use. We also mentioned two special cases: the use of question-begging epithets (the use of words with the very value judgment that needs to be argued for built in) and the use of vituperative obfuscation (name calling that blocks rational discussion).

The subject of confusions due to language deserves a book all to itself, so we make no claim to completeness in these comments.

Notes

1. Sentence (a) is an example of *lexical* ambiguity, sentence (c) of ambiguity of *reference*, and sentence (d) of *syntactic* ambiguity. Lexical ambiguity occurs when it's not clear which of two or more meanings from the dictionary (or "lexicon") is the meaning intended in a piece of discourse.
2. There are towns called Athens in Alabama, Arkansas, Georgia, Illinois, Indiana, Louisiana, Maine, Michigan, New York, Ohio, Pennsylvania, Tennessee, Texas, West Virginia, and Wisconsin.
3. Normally, the word 'bad' is used as the opposite of the word 'good.' However, it has acquired a use in slang with directly opposite value implications to the ordinary connotation of the word. Thus, to call a person "bad" is to praise him or her.

APPENDIX C
Unfamiliar Words and Unfamiliar Meanings

Obviously, you have to understand discourse before you can critically analyze any reasoning contained in it. To understand it, among other things you have to be able to cope with new words or strange uses of old ones. In this appendix, we address two questions related to that task. First, how do you find out what an unfamiliar word or expression means? And, second, how do you spot and find out unfamiliar meanings attached to familiar terms?

C.1 UNFAMILIAR TERMS

If in Doubt, Ask

When you encounter a term whose meaning you don't know at all, ask someone to explain what it means and (this is important) to give you some examples of its correct use. They don't have to be able to give a definition, contrary to what is widely believed. For one thing, that's usually extremely difficult to do. (Check for yourself: try giving a definition of a word whose meaning you know perfectly well, say, 'chair,' 'cat,' 'idea,' or 'color'.) For another, a definition can be as hard to understand as the word itself. What you need to know, in any case, is how to use the term. Examples of its correct use, particularly examples of its use in paradigm cases, as well as some terms and examples that normally contrast with it, are the best route to understanding how to use a term.

Let us illustrate by explaining what we mean by 'paradigm case.' We'll give first a rough explanation, and then some examples. A paradigm case is a clear, model, typical, exemplary case of something and is to be contrasted with a "borderline case." Suppose someone comes to North American not knowing what a "skyscraper" is. You could best explain the word's meaning by referring to paradigm cases of skyscrapers—the tall office buildings in Manhattan, downtown Chicago, or indeed downtown in almost any large city in North America. There is no specific minimum number of floors a building has to have to qualify as a skyscraper. A 40-floor office tower is a skyscraper, a 3-story professional building in a mall isn't a skyscraper, and a 10- or 15-floor building found downtown in a small city is a borderline case.

When no one who knows the meaning of an unfamiliar term is available, or no one who seems to know its meaning in just the usage that concerns you, then turn to a dictionary. That seems obvious, and the end of the matter, but a dictionary is a tool that can be misused or used inefficiently.

How to Use a Dictionary

Some Information About Dictionaries

It helps to know how dictionaries are compiled. Words exist because people use them. That is why obsolete words are available only through the records of old books or dictionaries. New words—like 'vaporware' (computer software that is announced by a manufacturer, but is never actually produced) or 'nerd'—and new senses of existing words—like 'crash' in the sentence, "My computer crashed"—are established by being picked up and spread through contemporary discourse. Dictionaries are collections of definitions which (are supposed to) accurately summarize the essential features of the ways words that have some currency in a language are used.

Good dictionaries are more complete and up to date than poor ones. They include more words and more of the variations in uses of given words. (But be wary of word counts in dictionary advertisements; some dictionaries count each entry as a separate word, others don't, so the advertised word counts aren't generally a reliable basis for comparison.) Good dictionaries also include obsolete words and meanings. And they include extra useful features, such as pronunciation guides; etymologies; the spelling of participles and plurals; synonyms and antonyms; and drawings, diagrams, and photographs. Since it's rare for two words to mean exactly the same thing (languages don't waste words), a dictionary that gives no more than supposed synonyms of each word misses the bull's-eye. Better is a brief description of the meaning of each word, and better yet is such a description accompanied by a sentence or phrase illustrating its use.

Many words have more than one distinct *sense*, and the same configuration of letters can denote more than one *word*. What is the basis of these distinctions?

Distinctions between words are based on differences in their origins. The "bank" of a river, the "bank" in which you keep money, and the "bank" of seats in an amphitheater are three distinct words because each has a different source—each developed from a different original word. The first comes from an early Scandinavian word meaning hill or elevation, the second from an old German word meaning table or counter, and the third from an old English word meaning bench. A good dictionary will list the meanings of all the instances of different words with the same spelling and cite the different origins of the words. (We got our information about the word "bank" from *The Random House Dictionary of English Language*, unabridged edition.)

The groupings of the *different senses of a single word* are based on historical connections. Thus the "bank" you hope to break at Monte Carlo and the "bank" which charges too much for customer services are different uses or senses of the same word; both trace back to the word that referred originally to a money-changer's table.

How to Look Up a Word

Suppose you are reading something and you come across a word whose meaning you don't know (or that you aren't sure of). So you turn to your good dictionary and look it up. Suppose you find 4 listings for the one spelling and, under each listing, anywhere from one to 11 numbered meanings. Which one is your word, and which is its sense or meaning? How do you tell?

There is no automatic way to tell which meaning is the one being used in the text you are reading. Deciding is a bit like solving a puzzle or a Whodunit. Look for the obvious clues first. Is your word a noun or a verb, an adjective or an adverb? Are you reading in a specialized or technical context? If so, look for a note in the dictionary that might indicate such a sense. (Many dictionaries use abbreviations for various technical areas, and these will be listed at the front, for example, "chem." for "chemistry.")

If no special clues help, you will have to read over all the senses of all the words with the same spelling, and try out the different senses in the context in which your word appears. The question is, Which meaning is consistent with that context and makes the most sense there? Resist the temptation to stop after finding one sense that seems to fit; there may be another that fits better. What you are doing is formulating an hypothesis about which meaning is intended, and then checking it, by seeing what meaning a particular sense of a word gives to the sentence in which it occurs, and by judging how consistent that meaning is with what is said before and after that sentence.

What a Dictionary Won't Do

1. *A dictionary won't explain stipulated meanings*. When a writer *stipulates* the sense she gives to a particular word, she is in effect imposing her own meaning on that word and is telling her readers to understand it in that sense in the domain to which she assigns it. As long as the writer sticks to the stipulated meaning, and also does not try to apply it outside its assigned domain, there should be no serious problem, although the special sense may take some getting used to. The way to find out the meaning of such a word is to find where the writer defines it—not to look it up in a dictionary. Check the book's index, or look at the table of contents to see where it might first have been introduced.

2. *A dictionary won't settle moral or value disputes*. Suppose someone wants to argue that abortion is perfectly moral, and the person tries to do that by pointing out what the word 'abortion' means. He points out that the per-

tinent definition in one dictionary is, "the expulsion of a human fetus within the first 12 weeks of pregnancy," and notes that the dictionary says nothing about this act being immoral. He is quite right about what the dictionary says. But a dictionary is not a source of authority about what actions are right and wrong, or what things are good and bad. All a good dictionary does is *report* how *words* are used.

3. *A dictionary won't tell you the essential nature of something.* What is love? If you look up the word 'love' in a dictionary, what you will learn is how the word is used. If it is a good dictionary, it will list a variety of senses—different ways the word is used—and it might list some of the historical senses—ways the word was once used, but is no longer. Those different uses or meanings of the word may well serve as clues or hints that can help in an attempt to determine what love is. However, usually questions like, "What is love?" are asked by people who already know what the *word* means. They can use it correctly in sentences and can understand sentences in which it appears. What they want to understand better is the phenomenon or relationship or attitude that the word denotes. Here, a dictionary will not supply the answer. That is not its function. And turning to a dictionary for the answers to such questions shows a misunderstanding of its purpose. A dictionary just describes how words are used.

A similar point can be made about any attempt to use the dictionary to resolve deep questions about the nature of such things as freedom, democracy, justice, goodness, history, art, humanity, or any other such phenomenon, ideal, or concept.

If these questions cannot be answered by a dictionary, how can they be answered? There is no simple or easy way. The field or discipline called philosophy is one of the routes that have been followed, and its study is in part the study of various ways people have tried over history to answer such questions in systematic ways.

C.2 Unfamiliar Senses of Familiar Terms

When you see a word you've never encountered before, you at least know that much. For example, you probably don't know the verb 'to rive,' (which means, "to tear or rend apart") or the word *Entfremdung* (which is a German word that is often translated as "alienation"). If you came across these words you would realize that you needed to find out what they mean. But how are we to recognize that we need to check out language which seems perfectly familiar, yet which happens to have, in the context, a different meaning from its ordinary or familiar one? How are we to spot unfamiliar senses of familiar terms? It's a problem on a par with the difficulty of knowing when not to trust an honest face.

To start, it helps to distinguish two somewhat different kinds of situations in which there is an unfamiliar sense of a familiar term. In one, the term has a special sense which is used deliberately to try to mislead us. In the other, the term just has a sense unfamiliar to us in that particular context—for example, a technical sense—and we happen to be unfamiliar with that special usage. We will deal with each type of situation in turn.

The Use of an Unusual Special Sense to Invite Unwarranted Inferences

The Case of Advertising

The clearest and most striking example of the sort of confusing language we are talking about is found in advertising. The laws governing advertising prohibit outright lying. But they do permit a rather specialized terminology, which it pays to know. For example consider the following list. "New" means new, right? "Improved" means better than before, right? "Best" means better than all the others, right? Wrong! Not in advertising. Here is a short thesaurus of terms that have a different use in advertising than they have ordinarily.

"Best" = None is better

But all the competitive brands may be just as good. So in advertising if a brand is called the best on the market, that is *not* claiming that none of the other brands is as good. It is in effect claiming that none of the other brands has been proven to be better. It follows that each one of several brands of the same product may call itself the "best" one, and they all might be of equal quality.

"Better" = Superior . . . (But to what? In what way? No comment!)

This one is tricky. If a product is just claimed to be "better," with no comparison mentioned, nothing has to be proved—but then the claim is empty. The advertisers trust you to fill in some specific comparison. They say, "Puffs are better," and you think, "They are claiming that Puffs are better than other cereals." But they don't say that, and neither do they even imply it—according to the strange laws and regulations governing advertising. So it doesn't have to be true, and it probably isn't true.

Also, "better" used without any completion does not specify any respect in which the product might be better. So if, when you hear "Puffs are better," you reason, "Oh, so Puffs are better tasting than other cereals" or "I guess that means Puffs are more nutritious than other cereals," then *you* are the one who inferred those claims. The advertiser never made them, and never implied them—again, not so far as the laws and regulations governing advertising are concerned.

"Better" = Demonstrably superior in some identifiable respect (if, but only if, some competitor is mentioned by name).

If a product is advertised as "better" *and* a competitive product is mentioned (for example, "Colgate is better than Crest"), then the advertiser has to be able to prove that its product is indeed superior to the other one in some respect that is mentioned. In the latter case, "better" is a *stronger* claim than "best"—the complete reversal of the ordinary meanings of these terms!—for such use implies that the product can be demonstrated to be superior to the named competitor, at least in the respect that is mentioned. (By the way, that may well be a minor and unessential respect.)

"Full" as in "pays full coverage" = Pays for what it says it will

When a hospitalization insurance ad says its policy has "full" coverage, it would be natural to assume that the policy will pay all the costs entailed in being hospitalized (such as room and meals, drugs, and tests). What it actually says is that the policy will pay what the policy states it will pay—which may be a good deal less than all such costs.[1] Read such a policy as saying, "We will pay for only what we state in writing we will cover, and no more."

"Improved" = Changed, different from before

If the advertiser claims that a change makes the product better than it was before in some respect—however minor or unessential—then it is allowed to advertise the product as "improved." Hence, the detergent can simply have different-colored soap pellets than before, that the advertiser can claim some consumers like better than the old ones, but be no better at getting out those famous stubborn stains, and still be called "improved."

"New" = Not nationally advertised for more than six months

A product can be advertised as new if it has been on the market for years; it just can't have been nationally advertised for more than six months. Moreover, a product can be advertised as "new" without being better than it used to be in any respect.

"Noncancelable" = noncancelable for a while

Some insurance policies are advertised as noncancelable, which suggests the insurance company cannot cancel the policy. That seems a desirable feature, since as one gets older, the chances of ill-health (not to mention death) increase, and one wants particularly to be covered by one's insurance policy in one's later years. But in the insurance industry, "noncancelable" is used as a technical term, and it means that, providing the insured pays premiums regularly, a so-called noncancelable policy cannot be canceled by the company before the insured reaches the age of 50. But it can be canceled thereafter by the insurance company. (If one buys a "noncancelable" policy when one is 44 years of age or older, it cannot be canceled by the company for five years, but after that five-year period the insurer can unilaterally cancel the policy.) Similarly, a "guaranteed renewable" policy must be renewed by the insuring company—if rates are paid—but only up to age 50, or for five years if purchased when the insured is over age 44. Thereafter, the insurer can refuse to renew the policy.[2]

"Pure" and "natural" = pure and . . .

One hundred percent pure juice is pure juice, with no sugar or water fillers. But 100 percent natural juice means nothing; the juice can include water, sugar, or other sweeteners.

"Replace" = replace a portion

When an insurance company advertises that it will "replace your income" in case of an accident that puts you off work, read the fine print. The policy will almost certainly *not* replace your full salary; instead, it will pay you a portion of your salary.[3]

Caveat Emptor—"Let the Buyer Beware"

The examples just discussed suggest that, at least in situations in which there are potentially conflicting interests, there is a temptation to use language deceptively. A market relationship, between buyers (who tend to want to get as much as possible for as little as possible) and sellers (who tend to want to give as little as possible for as much as possible), is a classic case of such a conflict. In a perfectly free market, where there are no constraints, it is the sole responsibility of purchasers to make sure that they get what they pay for, and that what they buy really is or does what is claimed for it. In our economy, which is not a perfectly free market, there is some legislation designed to protect consumers. However, you should not rely on it. It does not cover all cases, and its protection is limited in the cases that it does cover.

One piece of general advice, then, is to be particularly cautious about accepting advertising claims and about accepting without careful checking the promises of those selling you goods and services. In the marketplace, *caveat emptor*.

We don't suggest blanket skepticism; that would be overreacting. Plenty of ads are straightforward and accurate; contract language is generally honest and increasingly uses plain English. And we think most merchants and people selling services are genuinely honest and helpful. But an attitude of healthy questioning still seems justified, since otherwise you cannot identify the exceptions until it's too late.

The Use of Terms With Technical Meanings
in Specialized Contexts One Might Not Know

Not all unfamiliar uses of familiar terms are intended to deceive us. A term just may have a new-to-you sense in a particular context, and you happen to be unfamiliar with that specialized usage. Checking the various uses or meanings listed for that word in a dictionary may solve the problem. But sometimes the use is a technical one, and the following advice may help in that case.

Marketing Terminology

One group of such terms are the classifying and grading terms used in trades, in marketing, and in specialized activities. Here is a list of some examples.

We remember an ad for a sofa bed which stated the sofa's cover was, "Crafted from a select top grain leather . . . ." Did you know that "top grain" leather is a particular type of leather—the outside of the skin? "Top grain" does not refer to the quality of the leather (as in "top quality"), but to the type.

In Canada, canned fruits and vegetables are graded as "Canada Fancy," "Canada Choice" and "C Grade", indicating classes of grading standards, from highest to lowest (see the discussion in Chapter 10 of standards and grading). So a tin of pears marked "Canada Choice" is not the best quality you can buy (which is why it is cheaper than the tin marked "Canada Fancy").

Canadian maple syrup is classified, in descending order of quality, as "Canada No. 1 Extra Light," "Canada No. 1 Light," "Canada No. 1 Medium," "Canada No. 2 Amber," and "Canada No. 3 Dark." So "No. 3" is in fact the fifth and poorest grade of maple syrup, and "Canada No. 1 Light" is the second best—not the best, as one might have thought.

Lumber that is graded as "clear" can still have knots in it: however, the percentage and size of knots is limited by that grading. Even an inch may not be an inch. If you are making a bookcase and you buy a piece of lumber sold as 1″ x 8″, you will find if you measure it that it is in fact ¾″ x 7½″. You haven't been cheated: lumber is sold according to its "rough-sawn" size, before it is planed smooth (the initial sawing of logs into boards leaves the wood rough and splintery; drying causes shrinkage). If you buy "dressed" lumber, you don't buy wood with clothes on: you buy such planed lumber.

We could multiply examples. The general rule of thumb is to check the meaning of all such classifying and grading terms. But how, practically, is that to be done? The salesperson or manager should be able to explain, or at least refer you to agencies which can. If they cannot, they do not know their merchandise. You would be well advised to be skeptical of claims that they make about it, therefore. Or you can ask someone who has experience with the product. The library, or a source of government publications, are other places to look for the explanations.

Scientific and Academic Terms

Be on the watch for unfamiliar uses of familiar terms in academic or scientific discourse, such as textbooks or reports of research. Theorists find it useful to assign technical meanings to some of the words they use, in order to make distinctions that are useful for theoretical precision, or to give an exact and measurable sense to a concept, or to name hitherto undiscovered phenomena. Sometimes they make up words (such as "erg" or "neuron" or "superego"), but equally often they borrow a word from regular English and assign their specialized definition to that word for its use in a particular context. A description of the specialized way a word is being used is called a "stipulated definition."

The title of a recent book in philosophy is *The Intentional Stance*, but it is not a book about taking a position "on purpose" or "intentionally." 'Intentional' has a specialized meaning in philosophy. (It means, roughly, representing or referring to some object; for example, belief is considered to be an intentional state because having a belief involves representing to yourself the objects which the belief is about.) In a psychology text, "conditioning" does not refer to one's state of physical fitness, as it does in ordinary English; it has a technical meaning (it means, roughly, training to respond automatically in a particular way to a given stimulus). When physiologists speak of the "motor" functions of the brain, they aren't claiming that brains have motors in them: "motor" has a technical sense in physiology (it means, roughly, having to do with those movements of the body that are under our conscious control).

The situation can get more complicated. When sociologists write about social classes, for example, they are *not* using exactly the same vague concept we use when we refer to "upper-class," "middle-class," and "lower-class" people. A sociologist will try to give a fairly precise meaning to her use of the term 'class,' usually a meaning that will permit clear identification of class members. But in addition, different schools of sociology mean *different* things by 'class.' There isn't one uniform technical sense of 'social class' in the discipline of sociology. Some define class in terms of wealth (and even wealth can be measured in different ways); others, in terms of occupation; others, in terms of economic power. There are similar contending definitions of 'rhetoric' in the disciplines of speech, literature and communications, and 'civilization' in the discipline of history, for example.

A large part of what is entailed by learning an academic discipline or a science consists of learning its specialized vocabularies and how exactly to use them.

Rule of thumb: When, in a specialized context, you find that you cannot make sense of what you read or hear, even though only what seem to be ordinary words are in use, you may be in the presence of a specialized technical use of a term. Try to pinpoint the puzzling terms, and check for a stipulated definition or look for a technical sense in a good dictionary.

C.3 SUMMARY

The appendix makes some suggestions for finding out what words mean. Unfamiliar words can be most conveniently explained by those who know their meanings, and most clearly explained by examples of their use. A paradigm case example is exemplary or particularly clear or typical example of a word's use or reference.

The best dictionaries distinguish many meanings of words and give examples of their uses. Check all the entries when looking up a new word. Form hypotheses about the most likely use of the word in question; then check by seeing if the surrounding text is consistent with them. All a dictionary can do is report how people actually use words.

Unfamiliar uses of familiar words can be checked against a dictionary, but sometimes specialized or technical senses of terms are used and a dictionary won't help. Advertising is a word game of its own, where many often-used terms do not have their normal meanings. The best rule of thumb is, "buyer beware." Marketing, product grading, and scientific texts are places were technical uses are standard.

NOTES

1. Burton Leiser, "Deceptive Practices in Advertising," in Tom L. Beauchamp and Norman E. Bowie, eds., *Ethical Theory and Business* (Englewood Cliffs, NJ: Prentice Hall, 1979), p. 475.
2. Ibid.
3. Ibid., p. 474.

Diagramming the Structure of Reasoning

Sometimes an author's reasoning seems complicated and hard to sort out. That happens, for instance, when the reasoning seems to involve inference chains and parallel inferences—and especially when it involves both. In such cases, it may help you discern the structure of the reasoning if you represent that structure in a diagram. This appendix outlines a simple approach to diagramming the structure of reasoning.

The idea behind diagramming is to create a spatial representation of the inference relationships among the propositions in someone's reasoning. We have found that some people have more trouble mastering and using a diagramming method than figuring out the structure of complex reasoning in some other way. However, most people find such spatial representations clarifying.

There are several methods of diagramming in the literature. We will illustrate the one we recommend here, using an example drawn from in Chapter 4:

E1 It makes sense to take challenging courses at university because they prepare you better for later life than do easy ones. For instance, from a challenging course you can acquire much more new knowledge than from an easy course, and that's added preparation for later life.

Step 1: Identify each proposition that has been asserted and mark role indicator words, conjunctions, and assertion qualifiers.

We find it most helpful to go through the text putting brackets around each assertion and giving each a number (to be able to refer to it in the diagram). Keep in mind the discussion of the assertion of disjunctions, conjunctions, and conditionals in Chapter 5. Where a conjunctive proposition is asserted, treat each conjunct as a distinct assertion, and give it its own number. But remember that the disjuncts which make up a disjunctive proposition, and the antecedent and consequent of a conditional proposition, are *not* asserted; so give a number to the whole disjunction or the whole conditional proposition—and not to their constituent parts.

What will help you to distinguish between distinct propositions are the role indicator words, conjunctions (such as "and" and "but" when they're used to join sentences), and any assertion qualifiers the author uses, so mark these at the same time. Remember, however, that role indicator words and assertion qualifiers are not part of the propositions asserted. We'll underline them; some prefer to circle them or put a wavy line under them.

Usually a couple of passes through the text are needed, and you'll likely revise your initial judgments, so use a pencil so you can erase. (That's why using highlighters is a mistake.)

Here is our final markup of E1:

> [It makes sense to take challenging courses at university](1) <u>because</u> [they prepare you better for later life than do easy ones](2). <u>For instance,</u> [from a challenging course you can acquire much more new knowledge than from an easy course](3), <u>and</u> [that's added preparation for later life](4).

It's usual for a text to contain incomplete sentences and to contain pronouns and demonstratives with unclear referents. Identifying precisely what propositions are asserted may, therefore, require interpretation on your part. Also, getting the right number for each proposition can be a problem in a much-marked-up text. For these reasons, many people find it worth the trouble to write out each proposition separately, turning it into a clear, grammatically complete sentence, replacing any pronouns and demonstratives with their referents, and replacing unclear expressions with clearer synonymous expressions. There is a risk that such rewriting will alter the meaning of the original, and it's vital that a rephrased sentence express exactly the same proposition as the one it replaces; otherwise you have a different inference. So be conservative, and careful, when you change any wording. Here is how we would restate the propositions in E1:

1. It makes sense to take challenging courses at university.
2. Challenging courses prepare you better for later life than do easy ones.
3. You can acquire much more new knowledge from a challenging course than from an easy course.
4. The extra new knowledge gained from a challenging course is added preparation for later life.

When diagramming the inferences in a text, you may find it easier to keep track of the propositions and their numbers if you have a written-out numbered list of the propositions like the one just given.

Step 2: Identify and diagram each inference.

Make a diagram of each separate inference by joining the numbers of the propositions that are the premisses and the conclusion with an arrow, the arrowhead pointing to the conclusion.

When you do this, there are two things you have to get clear about. First, you have to see which propositions *directly* support which others (see the discussion of inference chains and premiss support in Chapter 4). Second, if several propositions directly support one and the same proposition, you have to decide whether to treat them all as belonging to the same group or whether to split them up into separate groups (see the discussion of parallel inferences in Chapter 4).

We put a box around each group of premisses, but some people prefer circles and still others prefer lines underneath or above them. We put the conclusion at the top and the premisses underneath, but many prefer to put the conclusion at the bottom and the premisses above it. There's no "right" way; use the method you find most natural (or that your instructor requires), so long as each arrowhead points at exactly one number, and each group of premisses is clearly separated from the others.

Start with the inferences you notice right away. Then go over the text to see if there are any you missed. The order in which you diagram them does not matter at all.

Applying this technique to E1, we first noticed the role indicator word "because" linking the propositions numbered (1) and (2). We inferred that the author is inferring (1) from (2). That inference is diagrammed as follows:

We then notice a second inference in E1 suggested by two features of the text. First, the phrase, "for instance" joins (2) and (3), indicating that (3) is meant to support (2). Second, the conjunction "and" between (3) and (4) suggests that it is the conjunction of (3) and (4) which in fact is intended as support for (2). We concluded that the author meant to infer (2) from (3) and (4). That inference is diagrammed as follows:

Step 3: Make a full diagram showing all the inferences in the reasoning. In doing so, link up any inference chains or parallel inferences.

As our two diagrams reveal, in E1 (2) is playing two roles. It is the premiss of the inference which has (1) as its conclusion, and it is the conclusion of the inference which has (3) and (4) as its premisses. So in fact the reasoning in E1 has the structure of a chain of two inferences, and that structure can be diagrammed as follows.

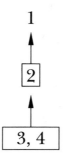

Full Diagram of E1

The main conclusion of E1 is (1), and it is supported directly by (2), and indirectly by the premiss support for (2) consisting of (3) and (4).

Here's another example—a more complicated version of one of the examples from Chapter 4.

E2   Morelli is the best qualified woman who has applied for the job, and since we are trying to correct the male-weighted gender imbalance in our staff, we should try to hire her for that reason alone. She's the best qualified woman because her training is equal to that of any other woman, and she's had more years of work experience than any other woman applicant. But besides the fact that she's the best qualified woman, she is the only candidate who has actually had extensive job experience with mainframe computers, and we can't afford to hire someone without hands-on experience of that sort. So for this reason as well we should offer the job to her.

We'll illustrate the three steps of our diagramming method by applying them to E2.

Step 1

[Morelli is the best qualified woman who has applied for the job](1), and since [we are trying to correct the male-weighted gender imbalance in our staff](2), [we should try to hire her](3). [She's the best qualified woman](1) because [her training is equal to that of any other woman](4), and [she's had more years of work experience than any other woman applicant](5). But besides the fact that [she's the best qualified woman](1), [she is the only candidate who has actually had extensive job experience with mainframe computers](6), and [we can't afford to hire someone without hands-on experience of that sort](7). So for this reason as well [we should offer the job to her](3).

Notice that proposition (1) is found in the text three times, expressed in slightly different ways, and proposition (3) occurs twice. Here is how we would list the propositions in E2:

1. Morelli is the best qualified woman who has applied for the job.
2. We are trying to correct the male-weighted gender imbalance in our staff.
3. We should try to hire Morelli.
4. Morelli's training is equal to that of any other female applicant.
5. Morelli has had more years of work experience than any other female applicant.
6. Morelli is the only applicant who has actually had extensive job experience with mainframe computers.
7. We can't afford to hire someone without hands-on experience with mainframe computers.

Step 2

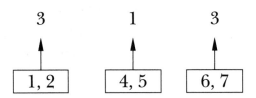

Partial Diagram of E2

Step 3

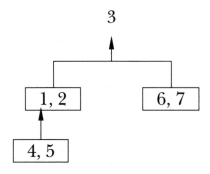

Full Diagram of E2

APPENDIX E
Model Answers

E.1 THE PURPOSE OF THESE MODEL ANSWERS

The model answers in this appendix are offered as examples to show what good answers to questions like those in the exercises look like. We call them "model answers" rather than "correct answers," since most of the questions in the exercises can be answered correctly, and equally well, in more than one way.

You will note that in most of the model answers in this appendix *reasons* are given for the judgments made. The reasons are not just window dressing; they are the very heart of the answers. If you cannot give reasons for an answer, you do not understand it well and your answer is worth little or nothing. Also, it is possible to give the right answer or a good answer for the wrong reasons, which is also a case of a lack of understanding. Your instructor cannot tell the difference between an answer based on correct understanding and one based on a misunderstanding, or a lucky guess, unless the reasons for the answer accompany it. A principal goal of these answers is to show you how to develop and set out reasons for the kinds of judgments you are asked to make and defend.

We strongly suggest you attempt to answer a question by yourself before you read the model answer to it. (You will only discover what you understand and what you don't, and where you have difficulties, by trying the exercises on your own.) Then compare your answer with the model answer you find here. If your judgments differ from ours, try to decide whether the reasons you've developed outweigh the reasons we offer for our judgments. (Our answers are open to improvement, and even correction. If you think we are mistaken, or have overlooked something, try to explain how we have gone wrong.) Also, note especially those occasions on which we have included points which your answer omits, and try to figure out why we think a good answer should include those points.

E.2 MODEL ANSWERS FOR CHAPTERS 1–11

Chapter 1

Exercise 1, passage 1

(a) Soviet divers recovered two flight recorders from the South Korean jumbo jet 50 days after it was downed.

Indirectly quoted (paraphrased) in the passage. In the opening paragraph, this proposition is attributed to "South Korea's semiofficial news agency." This is an example of indirect quotation or paraphrase.

(b) Soviet divers uncovered evidence that KAL flight 007 was on a spy mission.

Neither asserted, quoted nor implied in the passage. Though the Soviets claim the plane was on a spy mission, no one in the article claims (or implies) that the divers discovered evidence of this.

(c) KAL flight 007 strayed into Soviet airspace.

This is explicitly asserted in paragraph 5 of the article. Note that here the reporter is supplying background information and not just quoting what the news agency said.

(d) The Soviet Union has only recently announced that it found the flight recorders shortly after the plan went down.

This is neither asserted nor quoted in the passage, nor is it implied by the author of the passage or by anyone quoted in the passage. There is no mention of a recent Soviet government announcement. If anything, information in the article suggests that this proposition is false.

Exercise 2, passage 1

The headline is not justified by the content of the article—it exaggerates the claim made by the "experts" quoted in the passages. In the opening paragraph, experts are paraphrased saying that untidiness is a "sign" of happiness, but not that it's a *sure* sign. But even that paraphrase is a bit suspicious. If you read further, you learn that Dr. Daoud actually said that people who are *very strictly organized* "are not sure of themselves" and that Dr. West said that *overly tidy people* are trying to give themselves "a feeling of control over life." Untidy people, by contrast, are claimed to "have their lives well-organized in their heads." That just doesn't add up to what the headline suggests—that being untidy guarantees that you're happy. The fact that you lack that faults of an overly tidy person doesn't guarantee that you're happy.

Chapter 2

Exercise 1, passage 3

(a) The proposition asserted, "women ought not to feel guilty about taking the time for their own needs and interests," is attributed by the article's author, Eleanor Jungkind, to Toronto psychologist, Dr. Judith Milstein Katz. She is classed by Jungkind as a "mental health expert."

(c) (i) We are told that Ms. Katz is a "Dr." and that she is a psychologist. It is reasonable to infer that her credentials consist of at least a Ph.D. in psychology. (Background information used: a "Dr." who is a *psychiatrist* must be a medical doctor; someone identified as a *psychologist* who is a "Dr." will usually be a Ph.D. in psychology.) No other credentials are mentioned in the excerpt. (ii) We are not told anything about Dr. Katz's special expertise beyond that it belongs within "mental health"—which covers a lot of psychology. (iii) The proposition is about when women ought not to feel guilty, and as such is a recommendation about what attitude to take, and it's related to a recommendation for action, namely, that women should take some time off for themselves. That makes it a tricky case. On the one hand, psychologists have no special authority to tell us how to feel or what to do with our lives. On the other hand, they can be in a position to know what the consequences of various patterns of conduct are likely to be. By pointing out the benefits of certain behavior patterns, and the problems that come from not engaging in them, psychologists can both remain within their area of expertise and also be offering well-grounded advice. So the proposition attributed to Dr. Katz is advice about what to do, but it is based on her expert knowledge about the benefits of taking time for oneself and the harm of failing to do so. (iv) On the basis of the information supplied in the excerpt, we have no way of knowing whether Dr. Katz has herself directly investigated the consequences of taking time for oneself (and of not doing so), or is relying on reports by those who have, or is talking off the top of her head. It may not be unreasonable to assume Katz has at least checked the literature, but that involves taking Jungkind to be a reliable source (someone who wouldn't quote a source who does not have credentials on the topic quoted), which may involve taking *Chatelaine* itself to be a reliable magazine (one that checks its articles, or use material only from reliable writers). (v) One can reasonably have some hesitation about simply accepting Dr. Katz's word here, since her area of expertise hasn't been pinned down and since the matter concerns how one ought to live one's life—which is something that, ultimately, we all have to decide for ourselves and can't simply take directions from an expert on. Nevertheless, Dr. Katz's opinion probably shouldn't be dismissed out of hand, either; since she presumably has some expertise in the broad area of "mental health," a reasonable person would, at the very least, consider it a very real possibility that what she says is correct.

Exercise 2, passage 4

(1) We are invited to accept a number of propositions about Panamanian General Noriega in this newspaper report—all on the basis of the testimony of *an unidentified former U.S. government official*. We are told that *Noriega supervised the killing of a Rev. Gallegos and was on board the helicopter from which Gallegos was allegedly thrown to his death*. We are asked to believe that *the United States knew about Noriega's participation in Gallegos's death on the basis of its monitoring of Panamanian military communications at the time*. And we are asked to believe that *the Nixon administration did not seek to punish Noriega or the head of Panama's military, General Herrera, because of larger interests than human rights violations at stake in Panama at the time*.

(2) There are serious difficulties in accepting the unnamed official as a reliable source.

Opportunity: It is extremely unlikely that a U.S. government official would be aboard a helicopter in from which Gallegos was murdered and with Noriega aboard: firsthand observation can be ruled out. Then this official had to either hear the telephone intercepts (live or tapes) or learn of them from some other source, such as documents or some other person. We do not know what sort of access the unnamed official had at the time (if any) or recently to the information attributed to him or her. Nor can we determine whether he or she had the opportunity to know firsthand or to interpret the U.S. government's policy motives. We do not know whether the official is or was senior or junior, and we do not know how long or in what branch(es) of the U.S. government this person has been an official. We do not even know *when* this individual was an official.

Ability: While ability might not seem a factor in this case, there are a couple of respects in which it enters the picture. The language of Panama is Spanish, so the official (or his or her sources) had to understand Spanish. Also, telephone conversations are often cryptic to an outsider, with much left unsaid, and many references indirect or vague. It's quite possible that the allegations against Noriega are based on interpretations of telephone transcripts, not on intercepts of explicit reports. Hence a detailed knowledge of the Panamanian military and perhaps much else about Panamanian society at the time could be a requisite for making a correct interpretation of telephone transcripts. We do not know whether the unnamed U.S. government official, or his or her sources if any, had this knowledge. Finally, the long time lag (17 years since the events referred to) raises the problem of the accuracy of memory over that period.

Dependability: Third, we have no way to judge the anonymous official's dependability. We can wonder about it. For example, why is the report coming out only in 1988, 17 years after the alleged events? In 1988, the U.S. government was engaged in a campaign to try to remove Noriega from power in Panama; were the official's claims part of a government-organized campaign to discredit Noriega with the American people and so get their support for some sort of U.S. government action against him? We cannot know, but that possibility cannot be discounted. The problem here is not that we know the official did not have the opportunity or the ability, or is not dependable. We just do not know whether he or she has or is. We do not disbelieve the official: we must remain agnostic.

Some additional comments about Rohter's report: You were not expected in this assignment to bring up the points which follow, since you were not asked to assess the reliability of the reporter who wrote the story. However, you should know that the points that follow would be relevant to a thorough analysis of credibility of the claims quoted in the story.

We are not in a position to determine that the unnamed U.S. government official is reliable. Should we, however, assume that Rohter (and *The Times*) would not have published this piece unless *they* had ascertained that the unnamed source is reliable?

Not knowing Rohter personally, and knowing nothing about his reputation for reliability as a journalist, we cannot make any direct judgments about his opportunity, ability or dependability. We can, however, draw some inferences on the basis of what is generally the case about journalism. Reporters are encouraged to get "scoops"—exclusive and dramatic accounts of events—and news media are motivated by their competitive position to print or show such reports.

The unnamed official's accusations against Noriega are dramatic, since Noriega was at the time both the de facto leader of Panama and had recently been in the news as allegedly involved in drug smuggling into the United States. It seems reasonable to conclude that it is *possible* that Rohter wrote this story, and *The New York Times* Services carried it, because of its dramatic impact even though Rohter was not in a position to assess his source's reliability. Hence, we conclude, there is a reason to be hesitant about assuming that the reporter or newspaper has in fact established the source's reliability.

Chapter 3

Exercise 2, passage 1

This news story is written in such a way as to leave a strong impression of dereliction or wrongdoing on the part of the hospital which "turned away" this mother and "forced" her to fly, without her husband, to another city to give birth to triplets. This is the aspect of the story that is emphasized in the *lead*. The most conspicuous fault of the story lies in the fact that the *impression of wrongdoing simply isn't justified* by the "hard facts" presented in the story, since there is nothing in the hard facts to show that staff and equipment should have been available in Toronto or that some other form of transportation should have been used to get the mother to Kingston. Suggestions of fault are explicit in the quotes attributed to the mother and the father and implicit in the *language* of the report itself: "turned away," "forced," "ironic," "If things weren't bad enough," . . ..

The "slant" in the story seems to be a result of a number of things. First, insufficient *background* is provided for you to understand why these events transpired. No attempt is made to unearth the *reasons* for the insufficient staff and equipment at Toronto East General, for the unavailability of another suitable Toronto hospital or for the lack of room for the husband on the Learjet. You can guess that the fact that it was a holiday (New Year's Day) had *something* to do with it—but what exactly you don't really know.

Second, the *sources* are woefully limited or skewed; *all* the concrete information comes from the woman and her husband. The only other person quoted is the parliamentary secretary, and he offers basically a "no comment for now" statement.

Third, in this case the skewed sources result in a *lack of balance*. The couple are apparently at odds with medical authorities about the appropriateness of the service they got. We are given their point of view but the point of view of the medical authorities isn't presented.

Finally, the story is presented so as to stress the *drama* or dramatic elements. The focus is on the trials and tribulations of the two individuals—presented as "up against the system," as it were ("nobody should be put through this"). The facts that the *doctor* found another hospital and the *government* apparently provided a plane for transportation do not get any emphasis. The dramatic elements here are questionable. The hard facts presented don't warrant the conclusion that the couple has been wronged, and the story seems to rely on skewed sources and an unbalanced presentation.

Notice, too, that dramatic elements seem to be responsible for the fact that this story is considered newsworthy—indeed, sufficiently so as to appear on page 1. It might perhaps have been made newsworthy in more serious ways, if some legitimate link could have been made between this event and alleged shortages in beds, staff, and equipment in Ontario hospitals. But no attempt seems to have been made to develop the story along those lines.

Chapter 4

Exercise 4, passage 1

The conclusion is: *We have our priorities sadly wrong.*

Note. The clause "This does not make sense" expresses one of the premisses; it is not part of the conclusion. The words "it shows that" are role indicator words which introduce the conclusion.

Exercise 5, passage 2

Conclusion: Modern prisons are an abysmal failure.

Premisses:
• They don't rehabilitate anyone.
• They don't so much punish as provide free room and board.
• By bringing criminals together, prisons allow them to swap information and refine their crafts.

Exercise 6, passage 1

In this example there is premiss support; that is, there are premisses that support the main premisses.

Main conclusion: A person without money can have no self-esteem.

Main premisses (that is, premisses directly supporting the main conclusion):

1. No one without power can preserve his self-esteem.*
2. A person without money is a person without power.

Notice that premiss 1 is marked with an asterisk; that is because it is supported by the following, which is premiss support: "Self-worth depends on an ability to exert some control over oneself and one's surroundings, and this ability is nothing else than power."

Chapter 5

Exercise 2, assertions 1–3

1. The proposition asserted is a *disjunction*. Its two disjuncts are (a) *professional sports stars are vastly overpaid* and (b) *I'm a monkey's uncle.*

2. The proposition asserted is a *conditional proposition*. Its antecedent is: *the power goes off*. Its consequent is: *the data stored in the computer's random access memory are lost*.

3. The proposition asserted is not a compound proposition (that is, it's not a conjunction, a disjunction, or a conditional).

Exercise 3, passage 1

The following propositions are asserted in the passage:

1. If you are in Section 01, you have 60 minutes to complete the test.
2. If you are in Section 03, you have only 45 minutes to finish.
3. Students in Section 02 will write next week.
4. If you are enrolled in Section 02, you should not be reading these instructions.

(Notice that two sentences in the passage are not used to make *assertions* at all. One is a command: "Do not begin the test until told to do so or communicate with any other student during the test." The other is an expression of goodwill: "Good luck.")

Exercise 5

(a) In North America, pop singer Madonna is more popular than jazz singer Ella Fitzgerald.

(b) Ella Fitzgerald is not the most popular singer in North America.

Logical relations: (a) entails (b). Also, (a) is consistent with (b).

Brief explanation: To be the *most* popular means that no one else is more popular. So if Madonna is more popular than Fitzgerald, then necessarily Fitzgerald is not the most popular.

(c) Ella Fitzgerald is not as popular as she used to be in North America.

Logical relation: (a) and (c) are consistent.

Brief explanation: (a) doesn't entail (c): Madonna could be more popular because *her* popularity increased while Fitzgerald's remained the same. (c) doesn't entail (a): Fitzgerald's popularity could decrease but not fall below Madonna's. But even though neither entails the other, they could still both be true, so they are consistent.

(d) North Americans as a group prefer jazz singer Ella Fitzgerald to pop singer Madonna.

Logical relation: (a) is incompatible with (d).

Brief explanation: Being more popular than another singer involves being preferred to that other singer. So it is impossible that Fitzgerald is preferred to Madonna at the same time that Madonna is more popular than Fitzgerald. Accordingly, the two propositions are incompatible.

(e) In North America, jazz singer Ella Fitzgerald isn't as popular as pop singer Madonna.

Logical relation: (a) and (e) are equivalent. Also, (a) entails (e) and (e) entails (a). Also, (a) and (e) are consistent.

Brief explanation: For one thing not to be as popular as another is the same thing as the other being more popular than it. So (a) and (e) really say the same thing, and each entails the other.

(f) In North America, pop singer Madonna is more popular than Whitney Houston and Whitney Houston is more popular than jazz singer Ella Fitzgerald.

Logical relation: (f) entails (a). Also, (a) and (f) are consistent.

Brief explanation: In general, if X's popularity is greater than Y's and Y's is greater than Z's, then X's popularity has to be greater than Z's. So it is impossible for (f) to be true while (a) is false.

Exercise 6, passage 1

Three interesting assertions are mentioned in the example. They are
  (a) The musical numbers in Lee's recent movie *School Daze* are beyond the range of Lee's technical abilities.
  (b) Black people don't have the technical know-how to be film makers.
  (c) Black people do have the technical know-how to be filmmakers.

Maslin has asserted (a); Lee attributes (b) to Maslin; and Lee defends (c).

Of these three, only the pair consisting of (b) and (c) are incompatible. Are they exhaustive alternatives? It depends how you interpret them. If you take (b) to mean that *no* blacks have such know-how and interpret (c) to mean that *some* blacks do have it, then they are exhaustive alternatives.

It's important to notice that (a) and (c) are *not* incompatible. That is to say, the assertion Maslin actually *made* is quite consistent with the view that Lee defends. It's quite possible that the musical numbers in *School Daze* exceeded one black man's technical abilities *and* that some (or even all) black people have the technical know-how to be film makers.

Chapter 6

Exercise 1, passage 1

Main conclusion: North American voters have grown tired of politicians' rhetoric. [The word "Obviously" is omitted because it is an assertion qualifier.]

Main Premises: 1. In the last federal election, 25% of Canadians failed to vote for the country's highest office.

2. In the United States only half of the registered voters bothered to turn out to elect the arguably most powerful man on earth.

Possible Situation: Suppose that in Canada a 75% voter turnout (which is what premiss 1 reports) is average or above average. Suppose that in the United States voter turnout in recent elections has been low whenever the results were a foregone conclusion and that widely reported polls showed Bush with a big lead over Dukakis going into the 1988 presidential election. This possibility is consistent with the premises being true and the conclusion false, since on it the percentage of those voting has nothing to do with changed attitudes toward politician's rhetoric.

How likely is possible situation in which the premisses are true and the conclusion false? Those familiar with the political scene in Canada and the United States will judge it highly probable. [We think that if you check data on voter turnout over the past two or three elections and look up media reports of poll results in the United States prior to the last election, you will agree with that assessment of its probability.]

Because there is an alternative possibility which is fairly likely, *the inferential link* between these premisses and the conclusion is quite *weak*.

Exercise 2, passage 23

Main conclusion: The judge committed the murder. ["Must have" is an assertion qualifier.]

    Main Premisses: 1. Either the butler committed the murder or the judge committed the murder.

                2. The butler did not commit the murder.

Premiss support: Supporting main premiss 2, the butler was passionately in love with the victim.

Degree of support the main premisses give the main conclusion: There is no conceivable situation in which the main premisses are true and the conclusion is false. In any possible situation in which the conclusion is false, the murder would be committed either by the butler or by some third party. But premiss 2 is incompatible with the butler being the murderer. And premiss 1 is incompatible with some third party being the murderer. So there can't be an alternative possibility here.

Hence the main premisses together *entail* the main conclusion and therefore provide *maximum* strength support for it.

Premiss support: Here is a possible situation in which the premisses are true and the conclusion is false.

> The butler was not only passionately in love with the victim, but also (like many lovers) extremely possessive and jealous of him or her. The victim rejected the butler (perhaps in favor of the judge), and in a fit of rage, the butler killed him or her.

This possibility is consistent with the butler being passionately in love with the victim, yet also being his or her murderer.

Can such a possible situation be judged highly improbable? We think not, since many lovers are jealous and lovers are frequently rejected by those they love. Moreover, lots of similar probable alternative possibilities can be imagined in this case.

Hence the premiss support for main premiss 2 is *weak*.

Chapter 7

Exercise 1

(a) The most striking problem with the report of the poll is the claim that the Liberals have cut the Tory lead—a claim featured in the headline and repeated in the first paragraph. However, if you compare the percentages of decided voters in the two polls (December and January), then the Liberals have made a gain of just 3%. But this change is within the margin of error of the poll (plus or minus 4%), so the difference is not significant and the headline's claim is not justified.

A second, less important problem is that the newspaper has not included information that would allow us to judge how representative the sample is.

(b) It is not possible to judge the poll itself in any significant way because of lack of information, particularly about how and where the polling was done and what were the questions asked. (By the way, the sample size—1,046— is *not* too small; if the sample is properly drawn, and is properly representative, a sample that size will yield results within the margin of error given in the report. Also, it is *not* a fault that the poll was taken well in advance of any election; the purpose of such polls is not to predict the winner of the next election, but rather to measure fluctuations in voter support in the period between elections.)

Exercise 3

(a) The reporting of the poll. There is are several important things that are missing in the report of the poll.
(i) Things definitely left out of the report.

We aren't told how the respondents were selected. Did *all* grade 6-9 students in certain schools participate, or only some? Were all schools in the district included, or only some? If only some students and / or only some schools, who did the selecting? Chances are that the respondents were all those enrolled in Ms. Kikuchi's classes, but what determined who got into and who didn't get into those classes? Were the students self-selected? We need answers to these questions to try to determine whether the sample is representative.

We aren't told how the poll was taken. Were students interviewed individually, or did they fill out a questionnaire? Or was some other method used? This is especially important to know, since we're trying to find out the attitudes of *children* on a rather sensitive topic.

We aren't given the wording of the questions. This is a very serious omission in this case, since (1) the quoted results are *very* surprising (Kikuchi says that at first she didn't believe them) and (2) it's easy to imagine how badly worded questions might seriously skew the results on an issue like this, either because the words used might have very different meanings to different respondents or because the questions were leading questions.

We are told who conducted the survey, but know nothing about her except that she's a staff member of the Rhode Island Rape Crisis Center. Does she have training or expertise in constructing valid survey instruments (i.e., questions that will give us the information we want about respondents' attitudes)? Does she have the training and expertise necessary to select a sample appropriately?

We're told nothing of the timing of the poll, although it is not clear how any specific prior event might produce untypical responses.

(ii) Things missing from the news report, perhaps because they don't exist.

It's not explicitly stated what the target population is. The person who conducted the poll seems to want to draw some general inferences from it; she says, "So many of our kids have attitudes that sexual abuse is okay." But the report just doesn't make clear what the target population for the poll is supposed to be. It's quite possible that those who conducted this survey were not clear about this themselves.

There's no mention of margin of error and confidence level. Again, it's quite possible that those who conducted the poll made no attempt to calculate margin of error, and so on.

(iii) The headline of the report ("Date rapes acceptable, students tell U.S. survey") isn't justified by what's in the report. The headline implies that students in general think date rapes are acceptable, whereas the report says only that one quarter of the boys and one-sixth of the girls in grades 7 to 9 thought forced sexual relations acceptable, and then only under specified conditions.

(b) Because of what's missing from the report of the poll, it isn't possible to make any firm judgment. But there are reasons to be deeply suspicious.

When a survey is done by a professional polling organization, the pollster's basic competence can be assumed. But, otherwise, one needs evidence that those doing a survey know what they are doing. In the present case, there's no evidence that the person constructing and conducting the poll has any expertise in survey research. Hence there's no reason to be confident in the validity of the questions. Similarly, there's no evidence that any thought was given to issues of what the target population is, how to select a sample appropriately, what the margin of error is, and so on. That is to say, there's no evidence that the survey was conducted in a responsible or professional manner.

Chapter 8

Exercise 3, passages 1 and 2

1. A correlation is claimed to exist between the following correlates:

- frequency of church attendance
- incidence of fatal arteriosclerotic heart disease

The correlation is *negative*. No causal relationship is claimed.

2. A correlation is claimed to exist between the following correlates:

- price of beef
- amount of chicken sold in supermarkets

The correlation is *positive*. The second sentence claims there is a causal relationship between higher beef prices and the purchase of less expensive meats (note the word "induce"). The third sentence contains neither a correlation nor a causal claim.

Exercise 5, passage 1

1. Principal causal claim: *When women abandon their traditional roles as wives and mothers and enter the work force, the result is divorce.* This is a *general* causal claim.
2. A correlation is offered in support of that causal claim.
   (a) The correlates are
       (i) divorce rate
       (ii) percentage of married women working outside the home
   (b) The correlation is *positive.*
3. Three pieces of evidence are offered in support of the principal causal claim.
   (a) A positive correlation between the percentage of working wives and the divorce rate.
   (b) Anecdotes about two friends whose wives divorced them after starting to work.
   (c) The results of a study in which 75% of divorced women had worked while married.
4. The weaknesses in the evidence are glaring. It definitely does *not* provide anything like adequate support for the causal claim. Let us review each piece of evidence in turn.
   (a) The correlation cited is quite relevant and is a good beginning: if that correlation did not obtain, it would be strong evidence *against* the causal claim. But the correlation *by itself* is not sufficient to establish the causal claim. What needs to be shown is that the best explanation of the correlation is the assumption that wives' working tends to cause divorce. There are other possible explanations of the correlation that need to be considered and ruled out. For example, over the period of time cited, the average age at which people marry changed, the average number of children in families declined, the percentage of the population living in cities dramatically increased, and societal attitudes toward divorce became much more liberal. Any one of these changes *might* (from a commonsense point of view) affect the divorce rate, and taking all of them together you *might* be able to explain the change in the rate without supposing that wives' working tends to cause divorce. In short, the correlation cited does not by itself establish the causal claim, and no attempt is made to show that the correlation is symptomatic of a causal connection.
   (b) The second piece of evidence is next to worthless. It can be viewed as an instance of (or two instances of) *post hoc reasoning*, of supposing that because one thing happened *after* another it was caused by that other. No evidence has been offered to show or even suggest a *causal* relation between the two events in the stories. (Perhaps these wives went out and got jobs just because they had already made up their minds to divorce. Or perhaps there was no *causal* connection between the events, but only a coincidence; perhaps both wives discovered their husbands involved with other women and divorced them for *that* reason, and so on.)

(c) The last piece of evidence is an attempt to suggest a correlation, but an attempt that just doesn't work. The fact that 75% of divorced women had worked while married has no significance unless it can be shown that the percentage of still married women who work is different, indeed, is less. The sort of mistake that's made here is discussed in the text, on page 162.

Chapter 9

Exercise 1

(a) With respect to its subject-matter, this study is on the borderline between those concerned with biological or physiological matters and those concerned with human behavior and attitudes. It deals with the effect of a certain medication (clomipramine) on the ability of those suffering from trichotillomania to control their "urge" to pull out their hair. The study is *not* based an experiment with test and control groups, on a careful analysis of covariance or on a laboratory experiment (there is no suggestion of the kind of attempt to control for all relevant variables that is essential to a laboratory experiment).

The principal causal claim is that clomipramine increases the ability of those suffering from trichotillomania to control their "urge" to pull out their hair.

(The report mentions other studies of clomipramine, but does not name them or describe them in any detail.)

(b) *The report of the study.* The report quotes the conclusions of the study in the words of the person who conducted the study and should be accurate in that regard. It tells us the number of subjects and reports the findings on which the conclusion was based (three stopped pulling their hair altogether, the rest experienced a 50% reduction in the "severity of the symptoms"). However, the report is *very* skimpy on the details of the study. It tells us nothing about the conditions under which the medication was administered (in a hospital setting? on an outpatient basis?), how many times the subjects were administered the medication or the time period over which the study extended, who observed or estimated the amount of reduction in the "severity of the symptoms" (or what exactly that phrase means), whether there was any attempt to control for the placebo effect and what observational techniques were used.

The newspaper report tells us that the study was reported in the *New England Journal of Medicine* (a reputable medical journal) and that the research was conducted by Dr. Susan Swedo who is a "researcher" at the National Institute of Mental Health. We aren't told what Swedo's area of expertise is (or even what sort of doctor she is), though it's probably reasonable to conclude from her connection that she is competent to conduct this sort of research. (The methodology used might give one second thoughts, however.)

The study itself. The methodology of this study, as reported by the

Associated Press, is *highly* suspect. First, the sample size seems quite small, especially since the dependent variable being studied is a behavioral one. Where psychological factors come into play, as they do in what's being studied here, individual differences become quite important, and it is risky to try to generalize from a sample as small as this. Second, and more important, any convincing study of the effectiveness of a medication should involve a test group and a control group, which this study quite obviously did not. Use of a test group and control group would make it possible to administer a placebo to the control group and also make it possible to conduct a double-blind experiment. Only the use of such techniques can rule out possibilities that (a) it is the *belief* that they are receiving medication, rather than the medication itself, which is producing improvement and (b) what the observers "see" is not influenced by their expectation to see improvement.

Against the background of other studies which show clomipramine to be effective in helping people with obsessive-compulsive disorders, this study probably makes it reasonable to suspect that it is helpful to those suffering from trichotillomania. However, given the serious methodical flaws in the study, one ought to be *very* cautious concerning that conclusion.

Chapter 10

Exercise 1

To give you an idea of the sort of answer we expect, we indicate what we think a discussion of criteria and standards for a briefcase would look like.

(a) *Criteria.* Among the criteria one might use in evaluating a briefcase are *cost, appearance, capacity, durability, security, inside features,* and *carrying ease.* You might have thought of others. Which three of these are most important will depend on your particular needs and wants, which may be different from those of others people. Capacity will be important to almost everyone, since a briefcase that won't hold everything you need to keep in it has limited usefulness. If you are on a tight budget, cost will be important. Some might need to be able to lock confidential papers in their briefcase; others may have no such need. Some may have particular contents, such as a calculator, various pens and pencils, business cards, or a schedule book, for which it would be enormously convenient to have special pockets or holders inside the briefcase. For some, their job might require the appearance of prosperity conveyed by expensive leather and brass fittings; others may need only the most utilitarian of cases. You might want to have a briefcase that will look good with a variety of business outfits, in all seasons. Some might want a briefcase that can take rough treatment (for example, be checked on an airplane); others might not need such durability. And so on. In your answer you should have presupposed some position that would give eminence to some of these over others.

(b) *Standards.* In most cases, a case will fail, pass, or considerably exceed the minimum requirements of a criterion, so the grades of "Inadequate," "Satisfactory," and "Excellent" seem appropriate. In general, the fewer the grades, the better, both to make comparisons easier and also to force the evaluator to make up his or her mind. What it takes to achieve these grades will vary with each criterion and with the wants and needs of the person buying the case.

Appearance: Here impressionist or holistic evaluation should probably be used, but what would count as satisfactory would depend on use; a business-person who needed to impress clients would demand more than a student who needs only basic carrying power.

Capacity: What counts as "inadequate," and so on, will depend on the amount of stuff you will be needing to keep in your briefcase. Here again there might be disqualifiers. For instance, perhaps normally you won't have much to carry in your briefcase besides your lunch, but once a month you will want to be able to carry several thick reports or catalogues in it. This need might rule out any case that cannot accommodate that bulk. Probably some minimally acceptable interior depth should be specified.

Durability: There might be several ways to meet the standards here. Are the hinges flimsy or sturdy? Are the fasteners flimsy or durable? Is the external material durable? Soft calfskin can tear; heavy vinyl might last a lifetime. How well can the material withstand being dropped, scratched, spilled on, and squeezed?

Security: Locks will be ranked according such features as their sturdiness, their security (the ease of picking or forcing them), their convenience (that is, of needing to carry a key remember a combination).

Inside features: Do the features meet your needs, are they better than nothing, are they not better than nothing, or are none present? A list of essential inside features could constitute the standard for being satisfactory.

Carrying ease: Some cases might be light, have a convenient strap, or have a big enough handle; others might be heavy or bulky or have too small a handle to hold when you have gloves on; and so on. Impressionistic judgments would be appropriate here.

Cost: It will be necessary to look at briefcases to see how cost is associated with features. You might find there is a low-cost range, a medium-cost range, and a high-cost range. Possibly for you high cost will be a disqualifier: you might have to say that anything over a given amount, perhaps $100, is too expensive for your budget.

(c) *Weighting*. In defending the weights you assigned to the "most impor-tant" criteria you chose, you should appeal to assumptions about the relative importance of your needs and your wants as they affect the choice of a briefcase. One person's weighting may thus be quite different from another's.

Chapter 11

Exercise 1

(a) The *conclusion* of the inference is: If you are a college student living at home, it is a good idea to try to earn or borrow the money and buy a car. Notice that we have omitted "probably," which is an assertion qualifier, but have included "if you are . . . at home," which is part of the conclusion drawn.

(b) The reasoning here is *weak*. The reasoner considers just two of many alternatives, overlooking a couple of significant ones; the treatment of the pros and cons for the alternatives that are considered is too brief.

    (i) Only two alternatives are considered. Those alternatives are

        (1) buy a car

        (2) use the bus to get to and from school every day.

Among the significant alternatives left out of consideration are:

        (3) make arrangements to ride with someone else

        (4) use a bicycle (except in very bad weather, when you could take the bus)

        (5) buy a motorbike

        (6) try to find cheap accommodations within walking distance of school

The omission of (5) and (6) is not that serious, since they probably would not be significant alternatives for very many people (you would rule out 6 pretty quickly if you were living at home for free). But the omission of (3) and (4) is a genuine fault in this reasoning. Indeed, (3) is an alternative that ought to be explored by anyone who doesn't already have a car and who needs transportation to and from school.

    (ii) The consideration of the pros and cons of the alternatives considered—(1) and (2)—is superficial.

        Alternative (1). The reasoner mentions three pros and one con for this alternative. The three pros are

- by car you can get to the campus in under 20 minutes from almost anywhere in the city
- you will have the car during the summer months as well as during the school year
- a car would help you get to work quickly if you have a part-time job

The one con mentioned is the high initial cost of a car (it "can cost in the thousands").

There are actually a few additional pros that might have been added: a car will be available late at night after bus service stops, a car can enhance your social life during the school year, it can prove an important tool if you have field work assignments, and so on.

More significant are the many quite important cons that are left out of consideration. Among the significant cons that come readily to mind are

- the cost of gasoline and routine maintenance
- the cost of insurance, which can be very high
- the potential cost of unanticipated repairs
- the problem of finding acceptable parking on or near the campus
- the potential hassle from "friends" who want rides, and so on.

The result of these omissions is that some of the serious negatives occasioned by owning a car just aren't considered.

Alternative (2). The reasoner mentions no pros and just one con for this alternative.

The con mentioned is that bus service from most residential areas is slow and inconvenient. There are other cons as well: most buses don't run 24 hours a day; at peak periods, riding crowded buses can be very unpleasant; female riders are not infrequently subjected to sexual harassment; and so on.

There are pros to riding the bus that aren't considered:

- No capital outlay is required; this is a pro compared not only with buying a car, but with acquiring a bicycle or a motorbike.
- The "operating costs" (for example, the weekly outlay for bus fare) is modest.
- The bus protects you from rain and from cold (as compared with walking or riding a bicycle or a motorbike).

   (iii) There is not a problem here with questionable assumptions. The factual assumptions all seem to be reasonable ones.

Overall, the most serious flaws in the reasoning here are (a) the failure to consider any but two means for achieving the objective of getting to school and (b) the failure to consider many of the important cons or negatives in acquiring a car to achieve that objective.

Glossary

This glossary contains most of the specialized and technical terms used in the book. The boldface terms within an entry have independent glossary entries of their own. The chapter references at the end of each entry refer to the chapter in which the term is introduced and in some cases to other chapters in which it figures prominently.

Ability.   One of the three dimensions or components of a source's credibility: having the *skill* or *competence* needed to find out the truth, given the opportunity the source has had. (Ch. 2)

Acceptability.   The criterion for evaluating the premisses of inferences: a premiss is **acceptable** if it is reasonable to believe. Among the main ways a proposition becomes acceptable are (1) it is accepted on the say-so of a credible source, and (2) it is the conclusion of a previously drawn good inference. (Ch. 6)

All things considered.   A judgment or decision made with all things considered is based on a thorough assessment and balancing of reasons pro and con. (Ch. 11)

Analytic evaluation.   Evaluation which bases its verdict on the evaluation of a variety of components or dimensions of what is being evaluated. (Ch. 10)

Anecdotal evidence.   Evidence gathered in a nonsystematic or haphazard way, especially evidence drawn from one person's experience or from a single experience. (Ch. 9)

Antecedent.   In logic: denotes the proposition expressing the condition in a **conditional proposition**. The proposition following "if" or its equivalent. (Ch. 5)

Argument.   (1) An extended disagreement or dispute. (2) A set of reasons alleged or believed to support a proposition or presented to others to convince them to accept a proposition. (Ch. 4)

Assert.   (Verb) To put forward a proposition as true—in language, by means of the speech act of asserting. **Assertion**. (1) (process) A speech act or other act of putting a proposition forward as one that is true. (2) (product) A proposition which has been advanced or put forward as true. (Ch. 1)

Assertion qualifier.   A term used to indicate the character or degree of a belief attitude. Can be an adverbial phrase (example: "probably"); a "that" clause qualifier (example: "it may be"); a parenthetical phrase (example: " . . . , I'm quite sure, . . . "); a modification to the main verb (example: "she might forgive him"). (Ch. 4)

Assumption.   A belief, held consciously or unconsciously, which serves as a premiss in one's reasoning. Sometimes used to denote a belief alleged to be open to question or challenge. (Ch. 4)

Attribution. One attributes a proposition to someone either (1) by quoting that person as having asserted the proposition or (2) by ascribing a belief in the proposition to that person. (Ch. 1)

Background. In news reporting: historical, technical or any other information which places recent events into the particular context necessary to understand them. A requirement of **topical completeness**. (Ch. 3) **Background knowledge**. In causal investigations: the knowledge about how things work which enables you to formulate **causal hypotheses**. (Ch. 9)

Balance. In a news report of a dispute between two or more parties: a complete and fair presentation of the viewpoints of each party and of its reactions to the viewpoints of the others. A requirement of **topical completeness**. (Ch. 3)

Beg the question. Make an **inference** from a set of **premisses** which include or assume the **conclusion** inferred. A **question-begging premiss** is a premiss in such an inference; a **question-begging inference** is such an inference. (Ch. 5)

Bias (noun; the adjective is "biased"). (1) A point of view or a perspective. (2) A special interest which causes deliberate distortion or misrepresentation. (Ch. 3)

Belief attitude. Also **belief-like attitude**. Any one from a spectrum of cognitive attitudes which may be taken toward a proposition, ranging from disbelieving it, at one extreme, to being completely convinced it is true, at the other. (Ch. 4)

Blind evaluation. The evaluation of something without knowledge of any incidental features (such as who made or wrote it, or who is associated with it) which might bias the evaluation if known to the evaluator(s). (Ch. 10) See also **double-blind studies**.

Causal chain reasoning. See **Slippery slope**.

Causal web. The multiplicity of events, ranging over time and space, which in combination produce any given thing or event. It is against the background of the causal web that different particular causal variables are selected for emphasis. (Ch. 8)

Citation. The acknowledgment of a source of information. (Ch. 2)

Clip. In news coverage: a very brief audio or video segment of someone talking, in answer to a question or a segment of an interview or a speech. Often as short as 5 seconds, rarely longer than 30 seconds. (Ch. 3)

Cluster sampling. In polling: a method of selecting a **sample** from a large **population**. First one randomly selects subgroups from the population (e.g., a manageable number of voting districts) and then one randomly selected individuals from the chosen subgroups (e.g., individual voters from the selected voting districts). As with **simple random samples** and **stratified random samples**, one can use probability theory to calculate **margin of error** and **confidence levels**.

Compound proposition. A proposition formed by joining two or more other propositions. (See **Disjunction, Conjunction, Conditional**.) (Ch. 5)

Conclusion. In logic and in reasoning: a **proposition inferred** from other propositions. In argumentation: a proposition asserted on the basis of support by one or more other propositions. (Ch. 4)

Conditional. A **conditional proposition**. A compound proposition typically formed by joining two propositions by preceding one by "if" and the other by "then" (or their equivalents). (See **Antecedent** and **Consequent**.) (Ch. 5)

Confidence level. In polling: the probability that the relative frequency of the target property in the sample is within a given **margin of error** of its relative frequency in the population. (Ch. 7)

Confirm. To confirm a causal hypothesis is to find evidence which shows or tends to show that it is true or correct. (Ch. 8)

Conjunct. Any of the conjoined component propositions in a **conjunction**. (Ch. 1) **Conjunction**. A compound proposition in which two or more propositions are joined by "and" or its equivalent. Also called a **conjunctive proposition**. (Ch. 5)

Consequent. In logic: denotes the alleged consequence of a condition in a **conditional proposition**. The proposition in a conditional proposition which follows "then" (or its equivalent). (Ch 5)

Consistency, consistent. See **Logically consistent**.

Contradiction, contradictories. See **Exhaustive alternatives**.

Correlation, also called **covariance.** Two properties are correlated when the value of one varies systematically with the value of the other. It's a **positive correlation** if the values move in the same direction (both up or both down); it's a **negative correlation** if the values move in opposite directions. **Correlational research**, unlike **experimental research**, does not attempt to manipulate independent variables, but seeks statistically significant correlations between two or more properties or variables (such as smoking and lung cancer). (Chs. 8, 9)

Credentials. Public tokens of the recognition of a person's **expertise** by other **experts**. (Ch. 2)

Credibility. Of **testimony**: the degree to which it should be relied on or believed. Of a **source**: the degree to which its testimony should be relied on or believed; a function of the source's **opportunity, ability**, and **dependability**. (Ch. 2)

Criterion (pl. criteria) of evaluation. A dimension or factor in terms of which something is evaluated. (Ch. 10)

Deliberation. Reasoning about what to do. (Chs. 1, 11)

Dependability. One of the three dimensions or components of a source's **credibility**: it consists in being *responsible* (observing or investigating in a careful and unbiased fashion) and *trustworthy* (reporting findings accurately and honestly). (Ch. 2)

Dilemma. A situation in which one must choose only one from two or more desirable options. (Ch. 11)

Direct quotation. A report of the exact words used by a speaker or writer. In writing, indicated by quotation marks. (Ch. 1)

Disjunct. Any component proposition of a **disjunction**. **Disjunction**. A compound proposition formed by joining two or more propositions by "or" or its equivalent; also called a **disjunctive proposition**. (Ch. 5)

Disqualifier. In evaluation: an unacceptable rating on a criterion that alone is grounds for rejecting the thing being evaluated regardless of how well it rates on other factors or criteria. (Ch. 11)

Double-blind study. A study in which neither the experimental subjects nor the researchers know which individuals are in the control group and which are in the experimental group. (Ch. 9)

Entail. In logic: a set of one or more propositions entails a proposition when if the first is true the second must be true. **Entailment**. A logical relation between a set containing one or more propositions such that one is **entailed** by the other(s): if they are true, it must be true. (Chs. 5, 6)

Equivalence, equivalent. See **Logically equivalent**.

Ethics. Values and principles reflecting people's needs, wants and beliefs about what makes life worthwhile. Often used interchangeably with **morals**, or **morality**. **Professional ethics** are codes of conduct governing the professional behavior of the members of a professional group. (Ch. 11)

Evaluation. The determination or estimation of something's worth or merit: deciding whether it is good or bad, or how good it is, or whether it is better or worse than something else. (Ch. 10)

Evidence. Something that furnishes proof of or a reason to believe a proposition. The word is usually used to refer to the sorts of grounds that are based ultimately on observations. (Ch. 4)

Exhaustive alternatives. Two propositions are exhaustive alternatives when one of them must be true and only one of them can be true. The technical name for this logical relation is contradiction, and the two propositions are said to be contradictories. (Ch. 5)

Experiment, experimental research. A study in which the researcher actively intervenes and alters the **independent variable**(s), observing the effect on the **dependent variable**(s). An **experiment with laboratory controls** is one in which all the probable causal factors are controlled or constant, so that it's possible to isolate or "control" the manipulation of independent variables. **Test group/control group** experiments involve creating two or more similar groups, giving them different treatments, and observing any subsequent differences—the treatment given the test group usually being hypothesized to cause specified results. In a "true experiment," subjects are randomly assigned to the different treatment groups; in a "quasi-experiment" the two groups are created or selected in some other way. (Ch. 9)

Expert. A person with **expertise** in some body of knowledge, area of experience, or type of skill. **Expertise.** Extensive, specialized knowledge or skill. (Ch. 2)

Express. (Verb) To state or put into words or some other form of communication; it is important to remember that a proposition can be expressed without being **asserted**. (Ch. 1)

Falsify. To falsify a proposition or hypothesis is to find some fact which rules it out, proves it is not true. (Ch. 8)

General statement. A statement that asserts a proposition about a type or kind or class of things or events. A general statement tells us that all, most, some or none of the things of a certain sort have a certain property, or that events of a certain kind always, usually, seldom, or never happen in a certain way, or for a certain reason, and so on.

General causal proposition. A proposition about the causes or effects of some type of thing or event. (Ch. 8)

Global evaluation. A single grade or evaluation to the overall character of the thing or performance being evaluated. (Ch. 10)

Goal-free evaluation. Evaluation based on the needs of the population served by a product or program, not the aims of the product or program creators. (Ch. 10)

Grading. Allocating individuals to an ordered (usually small) set of named categories, the order corresponding to merit. (Ch. 10)

Ground. In reasoning: the basis on which one infers a proposition, a premiss. In argumentation: the evidence or support adduced for the proposition being defended. (Ch. 4)

Headline. The title, printed in larger type at the top of a newspaper article. (Ch. 3)

Holistic evaluation. The evaluation of something without explicit reference to criteria. Also called **global evaluation**. (Ch. 10)

Hypothesis, or causal hypothesis. A possible answer to the question of what caused what, formulated when investigating causes. (Ch. 8)

Imply. (a) What is implied *by a proposition* is what a reasonable person may conclude just on the assumption that the proposition asserted is *true*. (b) What is implied *by a person* is what that person intends people to conclude from what she or he says or from the fact that she or he says it. (Ch. 1)

Incompatibility. See **Logically incompatible**.

Incompleteness. See **Systematic incompleteness** and **Topical incompleteness**.

Independent causes. Two or more factors causing a thing or event, each of which is sufficient by itself—against the background of the causal web—to produce the effect. (Ch. 8)

Independent premisses. A subgroup of premisses which provide support for a conclusion without the help of any other premisses. **Independent inferences.** Two or more inferences to a conclusion which have **independent premisses**. See also **parallel inferences**. (Chs. 4, 5, 6)

Indirect quotation.   A report of what was said by someone that does not repeat the exact words used but only **paraphrases** them. (Ch. 1)

Inferring.   The act of drawing a **conclusion** (that is, arriving at a belief or other attitude) on the basis of information or opinions already in one's possession. **Inference.** (1) An act of inferring. (2) A proposition inferred. **Inference chain.** A series of inferences, in which each conclusion (except the last one) also functions as a premiss in a subsequent inference. (Ch. 4)

Innuendo.   Hinting at or suggesting an unfavorable judgment by a communication that refrains from explicitly affirming or denying it, but that thereby, in the context, implies it. (Ch. 1)

Irony.   A figure of speech in which the author's intended meaning is the opposite of what is expressed by the words used. (Ch. 1)

Joint causes.   Two or more factors that play the triggering role in causing a thing or event by acting together. (Ch. 8)

Lead, lead paragraph(s).   The first few paragraphs in a newspaper story. Typically, they present the angle or point of view or "story line" which is going to be taken on the event(s) reported. (Ch. 3)

Leading questions.   In polling: questions used in the **measuring instrument** which might influence the respondent to give one particular answer instead of his or her own opinion. (Ch. 7)

Logical relations.   Relations which hold between propositions irrespective of the roles they happen to play in inferences or arguments. They are functions of the implications of the truth of one proposition for the truth of another (or others). See **Entailment, Logical equivalence, Logical incompatibility, Logical consistency,** and **Exhaustive alternatives.** (Ch. 5)

Logically consistent.   Two propositions are logically consistent when it is possible that both of them are true. **Logical consistency** is the name of this logical relation. (Ch. 5)

Logically equivalent.   Two propositions are logically equivalent when if either one is true, so must be the other one. **Logical equivalence** is the name of this logical relation. (Ch. 5)

Logically incompatible.   Two propositions are logically incompatible when they cannot both be true. **Logical incompatibility** is the name of this logical relation. In traditional logical vocabulary, two propositions which are logically incompatible but which are not exhaustive alternatives (see earlier entry) are called *contraries*. (Ch. 5)

Longitudinal study.   A **correlational study** of a single group of subjects over an extended period of time, usually years. (Ch. 9)

Main conclusion.   In reasoning and logic: the final **conclusion** in a chain of inferences (see also **inference chain**). In argumentation: the thesis or point of view at issue in an argument. (Ch. 4)

Main premiss.   Any one of the set of **premisses** from which a **main conclusion** is directly inferred (without intermediate premisses). Also, any one of the premisses offered as immediate support for the conclusion of an argument. (Ch. 4)

Margin of error.   In polling: the amount, expressed in a ± percentage, by which the **relative frequency** of a **target property** in a **sample** may different from the relative frequency of that target property in the population. A margin of error is always for a given **confidence level**—which is the probability that the sample frequency has the stated margin of error. (Ch. 7)

Mass communications media.   The physical and institutional means whereby information is communicated to large numbers of people. They include broadcasting networks, newspaper chains, mass circulation magazines and newspapers, wire services, radio transmission, microwave and satellite transmission. The **news media**, print and electronic, fall within this category. (Ch. 3)

Means-end decision. The choice among alternative ways or means of reaching or achieving a given goal or objective. (Ch. 11)

Measuring instrument. In polling: the procedure or test employed to determine whether an individual in the **sample** actually possesses the **target property**. Examples would be the set of questions asked in an interview, or psychological or medical tests administered to individuals in the sample. (Ch. 7)

Media. See **Mass communications media** and **News media**. (Ch. 3)

Method of contact. In polling: the way the pollster applies the **measuring instrument** to the **sample** (for example, a questionnaire administered by telephone). (Ch. 7)

Morals, morality. An individual's and society's general norms governing interpersonal interactions with a view to ensuring the social relationships necessary for a good or satisfying life for members of the society. Often used interchangeably with **ethics**. (Ch. 11)

Need (noun). Anything essential for a satisfactory mode of existence or level of performance. **Need** (verb). To need something is to require it in order to meet a satisfactory mode of existence or level of performance. (Ch. 10)

News media. Sources of information about current events, including newspapers, news magazines, current affairs magazines, radio news and current affairs programs, television news, and current affairs programs. (Ch. 3)

News story. A report of an event which appears in the news media. (Ch. 3)

Non sequitur. A proposed or alleged **inference** in which the **strength** of the support for the conclusion supplied by the **premises** is zero. (Ch. 6)

Objectives-based evaluation. Evaluation of a product or program in light of its intended or stated goals or purposes. (Ch. 10)

Observation report. The report of a thing or event witnessed firsthand by the source. (Ch. 2)

Opportunity. One of the three dimensions or components of a source's credibility: the source's chance to observe, research, or otherwise come to know the truth of a proposition which he or she asserts. (Ch. 2)

Opportunity cost. What one gives up when one selects one option rather than another, usually the most valuable alternative given up. (Ch. 11)

Overall evaluation. The **evaluation** of a thing on the basis of all the **criteria** which apply to it taken together and somehow summed up. See **Weight and sum**. (Ch. 10)

Paradigm. An exemplary instance of something. Paradigms are used in evaluation, and in identifying the meanings of words. (Ch. 10, Appendix C)

Parallel inferences. Two or more **independent inferences** with the same conclusion. (Ch. 4)

Paraphrase. (Verb) To restate a text using different words from the original but expressing exactly the same ideas or propositions. (Noun) A text so produced. (Ch. 1)

Participant observer study. A study in which the researcher participates with subjects in an activity, either or both of which are under study, using data based on observations made while doing so. (Ch. 9)

Particulars. Unique events or things. **Particular causal proposition**. A proposition about the causes or effects of particular events or phenomena. (Ch. 8)

Perceptual acuity. Degree of power and sensitivity of an observer's senses of touch, taste, hearing, sight, and smell. (Ch. 2)

Placebo effect. In studies: a response among subjects caused by the belief that they are receiving experimental treatment, which can ruin the study's **validity**. An aim of **double-blind studies** is to correct for the placebo effect. (Ch. 9)

Plausibility. A proposition is plausible if it has some real likelihood of being true, given what is already known and believed. (Ch. 2)

Population.   In polling: the group under study by surveying a **sample** of it. The generalizations about the **target property** derived from the survey are intended to be about the population. (Ch. 7)

Potential benefits.   The probable or possible desirable results of an alternative. The degree of potential benefit is the degree of probability times the degree of desirability. Its opposite is **risk**. (Ch. 11)

Premiss.   In logic and reasoning: a proposition from which another (the **conclusion**) is **inferred**. In argumentation: a proposition asserted in support of another. (Ch. 1)

Premiss support.   Grounds from which any premiss is inferred. Also, support for any premiss in an argument. (Ch. 4)

Prima facie.   Prima facie reasons justify a decision or judgment in the absence of reasons to the contrary. They create a presumption in favor of the decision or judgment. (Ch. 11)

Proposition.   The "content" of an assertion, or any belief, doubt, or other cognitive attitude. What it is that is asserted, or believed, doubted, feared, hoped for, and so on. (Ch. 1)

Proximate cause.   A cause that is close in time to the effect. (Ch. 8)

Quotation.   See **Direct quotation** and **Indirect quotation**. (Ch. 1)

Quota sampling.   In polling: a method of selecting a **sample** from a heterogeneous **population** in which the **target property** is known not to be distributed evenly, but be present with different **relative frequencies** in different subgroups. A quota is set for each subgroup according to its percentage of the population and then filled in a *nonrandom* way. (Ch. 7)

Random.   In polling: a sampling method is random if and only if every member of the population has an equal chance of being chosen when that method is used. (Ch. 7)

Ranking.   In evaluation: placing individuals in an order, usually of merit, on the basis of their relative performance or assessment on (typically) a test or measurement or observation. (Ch. 10)

Reasons.   (1) Evidence or grounds for believing a proposition. (2) Explanation of an event or occurrence. (Chs. 4, 11)

Relative frequency (of a **target property**).   In polling: the proportion of the **sample** or the **population** that has the target property, expressed as a decimal number between 0 and 1. The relative frequency is turned into a percentage by multiplying it by 100. (Ch. 7)

Reliable, reliability.   Of a method of evaluation: one which measures consistently, in whatever circumstances it is used. (Ch. 10) Of a measuring technique in scientific studies: one which gets *consistent* results, whether accurate or not. (Ch. 9)

Remote cause.   A cause that is distant in time to the effect. (Ch. 8)

Replication.   The repetition of a study by different researchers, using different subjects and obtaining the same results as the original study did. (Ch. 9)

Responsive evaluation.   Evaluation responsive to findings unearthed during the evaluation, and not restricted to a predetermined evaluation design. (Ch. 10)

Rhetorical question.   A sentence that has the grammatical form of a question, but in the context is used to make a statement rather than to ask a genuine question.

Risk.   A risk is a probable or possible undesirable result of a choice or option. The opposite of a risk is a **potential benefit**. (Ch. 11)

Role indicator term.   A word or expression used to indicate the role an **assertion** is intended to play in the surrounding discursive **text**. It might indicate order (example: first, second), contrast (examples: however, but), and inference role (examples: therefore, because). (Ch. 4)

Sarcasm.   A form of **irony** in which something or someone is belittled through a biting remark. (Ch. 1)

Sample.   In polling: the subgroup of the **population** that is actually surveyed or questioned. See also **simple random sample**. (Ch. 7)

Scoring.   Assigning numbers on some kind of scale to the things being evaluated, especially to their performance. (Ch. 10)

Self-selected sample.   In polling: a **sample** comprised of whichever members of the **population** choose to express their opinions to the pollster. (Example: the sample compiled by a phone-in or write-in poll.) (Ch. 7)

Sentence.   The basic linguistic unit of communication. Declarative sentences are normally used to assert, interrogative to question, imperative to command or request, and so on. (Ch. 1)

Simple random sample.   In polling: a **sample** to which every member of the **population** has an equal probability of being selected, and for which selection is made directly from the population at large. There are other, more complicated kinds of random sampling methods—**cluster sampling** and **stratified random sampling**. (Ch. 7)

Slippery slope.   We use the phrase "slippery slope reasoning" to refer to a fallacious variation of **causal chain** reasoning. Causal chain reasoning is of the following pattern: if an initial step is taken that will set of an irreversible chain of events which will result ultimately in an extremely undesirable outcome, so that first step should not be taken. Such reasoning can be perfectly all right, but when the causal claims are dubious and unsupported, the fallacy of slippery slope is committed. (Ch. 8)

Sources.   People who supply information. In news: a reporter's sources of the information found in the report, such as documents, principals or witnesses, press releases, other journalists. (Ch. 3)

Sponsor.   In polling: the person or organization that hires the polling company to do the survey. (Ch. 7)

Standard of evaluation.   A measure showing the degree to which an indicator or criterion of evaluation has been met. (Ch. 10)

Story.   See **News story**.

Story line.   The dramatic outline of a news report, especially in television news, usually starting with a problem, building to a crisis followed by catharsis or solution, and ending with denouement or moral lesson. See also **Lead**. (Ch. 3)

Stratified random sample.   In polling: a sample constructed by **random sampling** of each of the strata or subgroups of the **population**. In many circumstances, a more efficient type of sampling than **simple random sampling**. (Ch. 7)

Strength.   Of an **inference** or premiss-conclusion link: the amount of support the **premisses** provide for the **conclusion**. Roughly, the strength of inference link corresponds to the degree of belief in the conclusion that would be justified if all the premisses were known for certain to be true. (Chs. 5, 6)

Support.   In logic or argumentation: a premiss or set of premisses supports a conclusion if and only if knowing the premisses to be true would make the conclusion more reasonable to believe than it otherwise would be. Support can vary in strength. (Chs. 5, 6)

Supposition.   A proposition assumed hypothetically to be true for the purpose of considering what inferences may be made on the basis of that assumption. (Ch. 4)

Symbolism.   In news reports: the use of buildings, objects, animals, places, and so on to symbolize abstract and emotional meanings such as power, loyalty, authority, and trust. (Ch. 3)

Systematic evidence.   In scientific studies: evidence gathered in a methodical way so as to make it likely that the totality of data gathered is representative of the broader populations about which the researcher wants to make generalizations. Systematic evidence contrasts with **anecdotal evidence**. (Ch. 9)

Systematic incompleteness. In news reporting: the systematic omission of whole categories of information which are necessary for acquiring an adequate understanding of our world. (Ch. 3)

Systems evaluation. Evaluation of objects or programs in light of their roles in larger systems. (Ch. 10)

Target property. In polling: the property in whose relative frequency in the **population** the researcher is interested. (Ch. 7)

Testimony. Information supplied by another or others. (Ch. 2)

Text. A fragment of discourse—of speech or writing—under examination. A text can be a phrase, a passage or an entire book.

Topical incompleteness. The omission of details a news follower needs in order adequately to understand a particular event. (Ch. 3)

Track record. A person's (usually an expert's) record of successes and failures in a given type of activity. (Ch. 2)

Unstated assumption. A premiss of an inference or an argument which is needed to get to the conclusion, but which is left unexpressed (and which reasoners may even not be consciously aware they are using). (Ch. 6)

Valid, validity. In polling, scientific studies and evaluation: a measurement is said to be **valid** or have **content validity** when the **measuring instrument** gives just the information, measures just the property, it is supposed to (example: a test of reading ability and reading ability). A test whose results correlate highly with other measures is said to have **predictive** or **external validity** (example: LSAT score and law school graduation). A theoretical construct used to measure properties not directly observable is said to have **construct validity** when it is defensible as a measure of that property (example: absenteeism as a test of job satisfaction). (Chs. 7, 9, 10) In logic: an inference is said to be **valid** when the premisses **entail** the conclusion. (Chs. 4, 7)

Variable. A factor whose relationships to other factors are studied. In experimental studies, an **independent variable** is manipulated by the experimenter, and the results on **dependent variables** is observed. In correlational studies, statistically significant correlations between two or more variables are sought. (Ch. 9)

Visuals. The film, video, and photographs making up the visual component of a television news report. (Ch. 3)

Want (verb). To want something is to be favorably disposed to having or experiencing it. **Want** (noun). Something that is wanted. (Ch. 10)

Weight and sum. A method of overall **evaluation** which consists of assigning numerical scores and weights to all the **criteria**, multiplying each score by the weight of that criterion and summing those products. (Ch. 10)

Wishful thinking. In scientific studies: the phenomenon of the experimenters thinking they are observing, and recording, the results they hope to observe, when those results are not present. An aim of **double-blind studies** is to remove the effect of wishful thinking. (Ch. 9)

Yes/no decision. A decision whether or not to do some particular thing; such a decision requires a "yes" or "no" answer. (Ch. 11)

ACKNOWLEDGEMENTS

"Blast kills 7 on Belfast army bus" on p. 12; "Krushchev's remarks 'absurd' say sons of executed Rosenbergs" on pp. 38–39; "Lovebirds Rock Jailhouse" on pp. 61–62; "'Nearly wild' kids found in filthy bus" on pp. 62–63; "Date rapes acceptable, students tell U.S. survey" on pp. 143–44; "60% favor aid to family planning" on pp. 144–45; "Many of Japan's salaried workers have mortal fears about their jobs" on p. 146; "Fibre could cause a high" on p. 168; "Drug dulls urge to tear hair out, study says" on p. 189; "Study links stress to health problems" on pp. 191–92. Copyright © 1985, 1987, 1988, 1989, 1990, 1991 by the Associated Press, Reprinted by permission.

"Postal strike 'won't happen' on p. 14; "Ads target smokers only, court told" on pp. 31–32; "Caught with prostitute, politician quits" on p. 35; "Triplets' birth has mom flying" on p. 60; "Liberals cut Tories' lead on Gallup poll" on p. 142; "VDTs harmless, study says" on p. 190; "Pregnant mice reveal no effects from VDTs" on p. 191; "Rising suicides blamed on men's inability to cope" on p. 193. Copyright © 1983, 1988, 1989, 1990, 1991 by Canadian Press (Press News Ltd.). Reprinted by permission.

"The benefits of solitude" on p. 33; "Do you need surgery?" on p. 38. Copyright © 1988, 1999 by *Chatelaine,* Reprinted by permission.

"Billy wasn't driver" on p. 37; "Women have 3 sex partners by 35, study finds" on pp. 145–46; "Fetal alcohol syndrome causes lifetime of problems" on p. 192. Copyright © 1989, 1990, 1991 by *Detroit Free Press.* Reprinted by permission.

Excerpt on pp. 194–195 from *Heart Attacks, Hypertension and Heart Drugs* (Toronto: McLelland and Stewart, 1986). Copyright © 1986 by Dr. M. Gabriel Khan. Reprinted by permission.

"The Problem with Highlighters" on p. 179. Copyright © 1991 by Harper's. Reprinted by permission.

"Bush says he'll work to settle Cyprus issues" on p. 61; "Illicit drug sales top $40 billion" on p. 65. Copyright © 1991 by Knight-Ridder Tribune News, Reprinted by permission.

"Hair growth sparked by drug, study says" on p. 195. Copyright © 1989 by the Los Angeles Times Service. Reprinted by permission.

"Being Messy is a Sure Sign of Happiness" on p. 13; "Our Health Has Never Been Better, But We're Worried Sick About It" on p. 14; "Why Gals Go for Baby-Faced Stars Like Michael J. Fox & Tom Cruise" on pp. 33–34; "U.S. Faith in Key Institutions has Plunged Since '66" on p. 145. Reprinted by Permission. Copyright © 1991 NATIONAL ENQUIRER INC.

"Mugging Suspect Dies in Custody in the Bronx, and Witnesses Say Officers Beat Him" on pp. 40–41; "Timing is Everything" on p. 36; "Noriega linked to killing of Panamanian priest" on pp. 36–37; "Post-Debate Poll Sees No Change" on p. 144; "IRS reports new evidence of cheating on taxes" on pp. 171–72; "Leaders of the Pack" on p. 166, "Study of alcoholics finds no evidence of gene defect" on p. 196, Copyright © 1988/89/90/91 by the New York Times Company, Reprinted by permission.

"A good way to cure colds" on p. 169. Copyright © 1979 by the Oakland Press. Reprinted by permission.

Ad for Powerbar on p. 32. From *Runner's World.* Copyright © by Powerfood Inc. Reprinted with permission.

"Soviets found KAL recorders, report says" on p. 11; "Poll in Moscow shows majority favor pullout from Afghanistan" on p. 143. Copyright © 1987, 1991 by Reuters. Reprinted with permission.

Excerpt from "Appearance Anxiety" on pp. 166–67. Copyright © 1988 by Susan Jacoby. Reprinted by permission.

Index